THE CRUSADER KINGDOM
OF VALENCIA

VOLUME ONE

THE CRUSADER KINGDOM OF

VALENCIA

RECONSTRUCTION ON
A THIRTEENTH-CENTURY
FRONTIER

Robert Ignatius Burns, S.J.

VOLUME ONE

HARVARD UNIVERSITY PRESS

CAMBRIDGE, MASSACHUSETTS

1967

Distributed in Great Britain by Oxford University Press, London

Publication of this book has been aided by grants
from the Ford Foundation and the Guggenheim Foundation

Library of Congress Catalog Card Number 67–10902

Printed in Great Britain

"By God who dwells on high, and with His help . . . I mean to establish a bishopric in the lands of Valencia" . . . God, how happy was all Christendom, that the lands of Valencia had a lord bishop!

Song of the Cid
(canto ii)

PREFACE

The medieval frontier is a topic coming into prominence today. "Few periods can be better understood in the light of a frontier concept than Western Europe between 800 and 1500," as Archibald Lewis remarks in his essay on the closing of the medieval frontier. Indeed, until "the mid-thirteenth century, Western Europe followed an almost classical frontier development."[1] There was a frontier of conquest, a frontier of exploration, an urban frontier, an internal frontier of vast forest and wasteland, a frontier of overseas colonial penetration and exploitation, and moving frontiers like that of eastern Germany. One of the more striking segments of this whole situation was the moving frontier of the Hispanic states.

Here, it would seem, is the prime analogue of the medieval frontier, a classic example of the frontier. Here, "of all the frontiers of medieval Europe," is "the one which most resembles those later developed in the New World." It is no accident that the recent Second International Congress of Historians of the United States and Mexico—historians concerned with New World history—devoted a fourth of their published *Proceedings* to a consideration of the medieval Spanish frontier. Sánchez Albornoz goes so far as to call it "the key to the history of Spain."[2]

But this frontier or *Reconquista* should be viewed rather as a series of frontiers. Each varied, from stages of peaceful assimilation or internal development, through bold raids and minor excursions, and through mass episodes which convulsed the whole peninsula, to a process of piecemeal conquest by land and by sea. It varied also from generation to generation, as the quality and tone of the inimical Moslem and Christian communities varied.

It was a society remarkably different from its previous form which threw itself against the Moslem world in the second quarter of the thirteenth century—a society technologically advanced, intellectually sophisticated, and fired with an aggressive and expansionist optimism. It was the dynamic world of communes and guilds, of Roman law and scholasticism, of universities, of bureaucratic efficiency and monarchical institutions, of nascent nationalism, of vernacular literatures, of "modern" warfare and financial techniques, and of Gothic art. This world had its ecclesiastical counterpart in the centralizing papacy, the councils and synods, the Mendicant movement, the university-trained cleric, the inquisition, and the perfected

vii

corporative mechanisms of all kinds, from cathedral chapters to hospitals. It was a world now sharply differentiated from Islam, its rival and fellow-inheritor of the Hellenistic past. It had a consciousness of its separate identity which went beyond the religious element involved.

When it conquered now it would inevitably impose its own forms; as far as it was able, it would Westernize. Where native forms remained they must either be absorbed into this alien system or survive as a merely tolerated, coexisting irrelevance. The Christian world would effect this transformation deliberately, thoroughly, one would almost say brutally, and yet with an innocent naturalness. There was a kind of tolerance nevertheless, and a respect for much of the Moslem structure. As an episode in the history of Western colonialism the process, with the psychology behind it, is instructive. To study it, however, requires a descent to the particular. One must take a specific conquest, preferably neither too small nor too large, where all the background and converging factors may be brought to bear. The Valencian crusade and settlement is such a conquest, almost a laboratory model for observing the medieval colonial process in a particular context.

With the collapse of the Moslem kingdom of Valencia the defensive frontier on Christendom's right flank advanced suddenly to the extreme south of Spain.[3] In the fallen kingdom, a hostile culture whose strength and tenacity equaled that of the conqueror stood in possession. The clash between the two, the uneasy footing of partial compromises, the purposeful supplanting of the old by the institutions of the new: here is the drama of the reconstruction of Valencia. Each step in the techniques and processes by which the frontier was assimilated, organized, and disciplined within a generation makes an absorbing subject for study.

The usual elements of frontier history appear: the sudden supply of free land; the reluctance of settlers to come to or remain in the lonely, alien environment; the hostility, and the successful rising of the native population; the mechanics of setting up civil administration and law courts, of establishing a garrison, of drafting an apt constitution, and of bringing to the area religion and education. There were problems of parceling the lands, chartering settlements, and coping with consequent lawsuits or claim jumping; problems of land reclamation and law enforcement; and the great problem of welding peoples with divers origins, customs, and tongues into one new people. The native population remained as a formidable majority; it was even to persist, as an unassimilable Morisco bloc, as late as the sixteenth century. Yet, from the start it was made to assume the defensive, to be more and more recessive and passive, to watch the environment in which it stood become Europeanized.

A primary element in this clash between cultures was the planting of ecclesiastical institutions—taking that word in its broadest sense—providing the framework for the church in the thirteenth century. On the one hand, diocesan and other mechanisms were transported to the frontier and established; on the other, the colonial power, quite consciously though not cynically, expected socio-political changes to result automatically from its complicity in this act of piety. In a unitary society, the establishing of an ecclesiastical order helped shape a kingdom.[4]

The time span indicated in the title of this book is symbolic rather than rigid. It is meant to encompass the first generation of settlement in the kingdom of Valencia. Where information exists before 1280, it will be preferred. But one must remember that even 1295 is only fifty years after the fall of Játiva. Nolasco came south to ransom slaves in Moslem Valencia in the thirties, and his companion of that trip was still available to give evidence in 1291. A young knight of, say, twenty-two years at the siege of Valencia city in 1238 would be in his early sixties in 1280. A similar younger man at Játiva's surrender in 1244 would be in his fifties by 1280. Two reigns are therefore particularly involved: the long rule of the crusader King James I the Conqueror to 1276, and that of his son Peter III the Great (I of Valencia, II of Catalonia, III of Aragon) to 1285. Peter's early documents are especially important because he had a role in Valencian affairs during his father's lifetime.

To do justice to the subject in hand, I must resolutely turn aside from allied problems. Research in the latter will affect one's viewpoint or approach; but the respective findings, together with their bibliographies and arguments, must be reserved for future volumes. The poignant story of relations between Christian and Moslem, of intolerance and of tentative efforts toward assimilation, especially must wait its turn—though I have published some preliminary studies.[5] The same must be said of civil and economic reconstruction, of land division and exploitation, and of the flow and rate of Christian settlement—all of which form a background to this book.

To avoid the chronological confusion attendant upon a specialized topical approach to any large subject, a date chart has been appended for occasional consultation.

Some special methodological problems require a note. Not all admit of a satisfactory solution. An ever-present problem is chronology. The nativity calendar, beginning on Christmas of each year, was not uncommon; the land grants of the Valencian *Repartimiento* are usually so dated. The Aragonese—using that term in its geographically restricted sense—liked the Spanish era; this began on January 1, but required adjustment by subtracting thirty-eight years. The incarnational calendar was favored in ecclesiastical documents in these regions; in Valencia it was established by law (until 1358) for other documents as well. This was not the Pisan style (predating by nine months, from an assumed conception on March 25), but rather the Florentine style (illogically postdated by three months, for ease of reckoning). Thus, the nativity and incarnational calendars coincide in Valencia from March 25 to December 24, but differ by a full year from December 25 to March 25. The eighth kalends of March 1262 may be February 22 of 1262 or of 1263. Context or intuition may aid one's decision. Many important dates in this book have been carefully worked out; some, where no issue seems involved, were simply taken over from catalogue dates. Happily, it has often not been necessary to come to a decision and to date a grant so precisely; a slight ambiguity has therefore been left in certain citations.

The choice of names is another problem. To leave Christian names in the original Catalan—Jaume, Ferran, Bernat, Pere, Arnau, and so on—would be intolerably quaint. To put them into modern dress makes these people less remote though perhaps a shade too contemporary. There is no excuse for translating them into Spanish. Often enough too it is difficult to transpose some Latin form into a reasonably exact equivalent in either Catalan or English. As far as possible, Christian names in this book have been anglicized, even to the use of relatively obscure equivalents. Surnames of a geographical nature are similarly translated where possible, though the reader will understand that "John of Montpellier," for example, did not necessarily originate in that city.

Other surnames are translated from the Latin, or selected from alternative forms, according to common sense rather than strict logic. Some surnames exist in consecrated English forms (Penyafort, Lull); others belong to well-known families with spellings in Spanish or Catalan already familiar in history; others are geographical, and so follow the Spanish-geography rule of this book. Where a less distracting Hispanic form is preferred to the Catalan, the knowledgeable reader can easily translate—Alagón to Alagó, Lavania to Lavània, Nuño Sancho to Nunyo Sanç, Pérez to Pèreç, and so on. On balance, more surnames have been Castilianized than rendered into the historically more accurate Catalan forms, medieval or modern. For the allied problem of citing Catalan or Castilian names for authors, in their formal or informal constructions, see the bibliographical essay.

Ambiguous or very difficult names have occasionally been allowed to stand; notes sometimes elucidate these. Feminine forms for masculine names—Bernarda, Guillelma—were written thus in the thirteenth century but spoken like their male equivalents. Other names and titles can be carried over into English without too much damage; *infante* is prince, San Victorián monastery is St. Victorian; but one boggles at transposing something as established as San Juan de la Peña. Surviving town, river, and similar geographical names are usually expressed in their modern Spanish forms, rather than Catalan, because most maps liable to be consulted by the reader give them thus. But the medieval forms Murviedro and Guadalaviar River have been preferred over the modern (and Roman) forms Sagunto and Turia River. Readers who are unsatisfied with one or other choice may be the happier for knowing that the author shares their distress. Where confusion arises, use of the index may help settle it.

The reader should also understand that a "castle" in thirteenth-century Valencia might represent anything from a walled settlement, or a rough fort or tower, to a formidable stronghold. The "town" allied to it might be a fair sprinkling of rural population, or a small commune together with its surrounding jurisdiction. A "village" (*alquería*) may be a fragment of some former country estate, or a scattered agricultural community, or a hamlet. Each town or castle or city had an attached *terminus*; this is properly an administrative division, sometimes with a natural basis; the meaning varied from immediate environs, to small fief, to extensive jurisdiction. Thus, though Corbera had its *terminus*, it was in turn enclosed within the *terminus* of Alcira. Approximations such as "countryside" have been used to express this. The words "Moor" and "Saracen" have been retained as synonyms, following the usage of our documents. "Baron" is any important vassal. "Sir" translates the Catalan *En*. "Huerta" is adopted bodily as an English word, designating an irrigated and very fertile plain. Similar makeshifts or adjustments are explained from time to time in notes.

Once named, the subject or place needs to be identified. I tried to bring to this perilous task the proper mixture of caution and boldness. *Celsonensis* finally emerges as Solsona, *Spelunca* as Espluges, and so on. Benijuart is in the manuscripts also as Benisuai, Benixuayp, and Benisuat; Alfeche as Fleix; Cheste as Gestalcam and Miralcam; Onteniente as Untiye; Daimuz as Atheymus; Guadasequies as Cequa. The variants are many and ingenious. One may find Bechor and Coracha[r] in one manuscript, Bochor and Teoraxia in its copy. And manuscripts can be dim, their shorthand symbols confusing, the damage from time or damp serious.

The best of my predecessors have been similarly tormented. Sanchís Sivera was led to introduce a "tal Galaubia" into Valencia (as did Huici independently and Miret y Sans and Tourtoulon); Galaubia proves upon investigation to be only Guillem Olabia. Martínez Ferrando founded a town called Sobirans. Bofarull transmogrified the Friars Minor into a settler named Michael Mores. Ramón de María converted the Christian Ferdinand of St. Martin into Ferdinand Sarracenus. Chabás fell into an old trap, interpreting as proper to Valencia an elaborate and important document belonging to Valence in France. Teixidor transposed LX to XL, thus misdating an important document by twenty years. With all his lexicons and nomenclators, the paleographer must sometimes proceed half by intuition; and he will occasionally be surprised into simple errors.

The unit of land measurement in Valencia was usually a fanecate—831 square meters today. Six of these made a cafiz, and six of the latter made a jovate or yoke. But these measures varied with the varied productivity of the specific section of land. Besides, the king could alter them in a given region or contract for purposes of equity; there are documents for example where he specifies six cafizes to a yoke, and elsewhere eight, or ten, or twelve. These measures are repeated in this book under their general names, adopted as English words.

There are similarly ambiguous, or even generic, terms for the kinds of money used. The most common term in this book is solidus, left in that form rather than translated as shilling. It was a ghost-money used in accounting; it comprised 12 pennies, and it varied in value from region to region in the realms of King James. Unless otherwise designated, the solidi of Valencia are meant; by a decree of 1246 this was equal to one and a third of the Montpellier solidus. The gold Josephine mazmodin (in origin a Moroccan money) was equal to 4 Valencian solidi, the gold Alphonsine mazmodin (in origin a Castilian money) to 6, the silver mark to 38, the silver besant to over 3, the gold morabatin (in origin a money of the Almoravids) to about $8\frac{1}{2}$.

Some idea of the real value of the solidus and its allied monies may be conjectured from the rare items available which indicate living expenses. The crusade-tax lists lead one to believe that a rector might have lived well, and probably hired a vicar, on 300 Valencian solidi or less a year (1280). Expenses for collecting this tax included 12 pence for transporting the money and for paper, 35 solidi for the secretary who had kept accounts for six months, and 20 solidi for the notary who organized and drew up the final accounts. A single knight's revenue in Aragon has been reckoned at 500 solidi—about 373 solidi when transposed to Valencian money; there were normally 800 of these in the king's gift.

Soldevila has collected some Valencian prices from the accounts of King James's son Peter. Thirty-eight pounds of cheese seem to have cost close to 10 solidi, six pairs of shoes (for a wealthy person) 7 solidi, scaffolding 6 solidi, a fine tunic 24 solidi, a mule 425 solidi. Prices varied from place to place, of course, and the common man would not purchase quality goods as did our prince. Commoners attending Prince Peter were hired on at daily salaries ranging from less than four pence up to about double that sum; knights might hold offices paying three or four solidi per diem.

Minor procedural problems have arisen, to be adjusted by common sense as well as can be. For example, a mendicant and a military Order have been removed from their proper chapters because it was felt that, on balance, they belonged where they now are. Again, there is both a rural and an urban Valencia, with the extant documents favoring the latter (and especially Valencia city); this necessarily focuses interest in a somewhat distorted pattern. A methodological assumption today is that the signature to a document assures the presence of the one named; I follow this, though uneasily and without conviction. Analogy may sometimes clarify, or at least put into perspective, the functioning of some Valencian institution; these may best be drawn from the other realms of King James or from Languedoc; Castilian or English examples are cited at some risk. But the imposing resources for English ecclesiastical history, elaborated in such fine detail, tempt the author to cite parallel English situations. These as well as Castilian, Belgian, and other examples are taken at random, and have been limited rather than multiplied.

Finally, it is interesting to note that the word "frontier" (*fronteria, frontaria*) was actually applied to Valencia during this period. Primarily meaning a property frontage or border, the word also designated an area serving as a battlefront. Quite commonly it was used to describe the moving frontier line, or danger zone of war, against the Moslems. People sentenced in the Albigensian troubles of Languedoc were sent to do battle on the Valencian "frontier"; a contemporary poet tells of a hero who led his troops from Roussillon "a la frontera" of Valencia; a court record speaks of evidence gathered from soldiers returning from the Valencian crusade—"de fronteria"; and the *Gesta comitum barcinonensium* has King James I conquer all the cities, "et complete tota Sarracenorum fronteria dicti regni." Papal documents will long continue to refer to the uneasy southern regions of the Valencia kingdom (in 1317, for example) as "fronteria regni Valentiae."

This book has taken a decade to piece together. It has involved three trips to Europe with a total residence there of five years. Throughout the years my debt of gratitude for help received has mounted considerably. The staffs at libraries and archives have been unfailingly courteous and generous with their time. Numbers of scholars have, in colloquy or correspondence, offered suggestions and encouragement. At each of the Spanish cathedrals I had the patient help of the archivists, knowledgeable priests like Antonio Durán Gudiol at Huesca, Peregrín Lloréns y Raga at Segorbe, Juan Francisco Rivera at Toledo, Manuel García Sancho at Tortosa, Salvador Pallarés Ciscar at Valencia, and Eduard Junyent at Vich. So many archivists, librarians, and historians gave of their time and experience to help the project forward that thanking them raises a dilemma. A mechanical litany of names reduces all the kinds of assistance to an unfair uniformity; a selection unfairly denies the help of those omitted; and yet a detailed essay imposes upon the reader.

Perhaps all obligations may be met by this general acknowledgment plus a few very special acknowledgments: Professor Sidney Painter of The Johns Hopkins University, and Canon Elías Olmos y Canalda, archivist of the Valencia cathedral (both recently deceased); Reverend Miguel Batllori, S.J., of the Institutum Historicum at Rome, and Canon Demetrio Mansilla y Reoyo of the Instituto Español de Estudios Eclesiásticos at Rome; Doctor F. Udina Martorell with his staff at the Archivo de la Corona de Aragón; finally, the John Simon Guggenheim Memorial Foundation both for the award of a Guggenheim Fellowship to complete the work for publication and later for a publication subsidy.

ROBERT IGNATIUS BURNS, S.J.

UNIVERSITY OF SAN FRANCISCO

Valencia
1964

CONTENTS

VOLUME ONE

Illustrations

FACING TITLE PAGE
    Seal of Valencia Commune, 1312

FOLLOWING PAGE 12:
    Thirteenth-century mural depicting the royal army of Aragon
    Soldiers with lances
    Crossbowmen of the royal army
    Knights with banners
    (All photographs reproduce parts of a mural in the Salón del Tinell, Palacio
        Real Mayor, Barcelona. Foto Mas.)

FOLLOWING PAGE 76:
    The Kingdom of Valencia (map by Mercator, 1512–1594)
    Valencia, showing medieval city within inner walls (by Tosca, probably from
        his 1704 map)
    The Benifasá "countryside" surrounding the monastery (1795 map)
    Archdiocese of Valencia and bordering dioceses, 1761

Maps (drawn by Samuel H. Bryant)

Spain, showing relative size and position of the Kingdom of Valencia *page* xx
Realms of Aragon   *page 6*
Suburbs of Valencia   *page 16*

CONTENTS

THE CRUSADER KINGDOM
OF VALENCIA

VOLUME ONE

FRANCE

GALICIA

PORTUGAL

LEÓN

CASTILE

NAVARRE

ARAGON
Zaragoza

CATALONIA

Barcelona

Morella
Teruel
Tortosa
Vinaroz
Villafamés
Burriana (1233)
Segorbe
Chiva
Turís
Murviedro
VALENCIA
Valencia
Játiva (1244)
Denia
Villena
Alcoy
Alicante
Elche

(1231)

(1229)

BALEARIC IS.

(1235)

MURCIA
Murcia

Lisbon

Cordova
(1236)

Jaén
(1246)

Seville
(1248)

Cádiz
(1265)

Spain
Relative size and position of the Kingdom of Valencia

Kingdom of Valencia

Conquered by James I, but only incorporated by James II

++++++ Moslem frontier at accession of James I and Ferdinand III

(DATE) Dates of conquests (James I in Valencia and the Balearic Islands)

A Scale of 200 Miles
0   50   100   200

Sam¹ H. Bryant

I

THE CHURCH AND THE
VALENCIAN FRONTIER

Valencia the Great[1] had fallen. Its Moslem defenders, under letter of truce, had fled into the south. Two miles away at the port of Valencia only the fleets of Aragon broke the blue monotony of the Mediterranean. The city itself lay empty, its mosques and shops deserted, its minarets desolate against the autumn sky. High above its battlements, upon the massive tower of the main city gate, the banner of Aragon flew, crimson bars against a sheet of gold. This was a day to be remembered in history—Saturday, the feast of St. Denis, October 9, 1238.

On the green plains outside, multitudes of jubilant Christians surrounded the conquered city. From their camps a colorful procession was being marshaled. Details in the royal memoirs and elsewhere help reconstruct the scene: mitered bishops and archbishops, and clerics in cloth-of-gold; ladies and courtiers and great barons with their panoplied households; troops of men-at-arms, militia from the towns, sailors, crowds of merchants and hangers-on; ranks of caparisoned chivalry, an unnumbered host of crusading volunteers from many lands; and the king and queen of Aragon themselves. All the pageantry of the age of chivalry glittered here. Above the bright trappings, the gaudy shields and glinting steel, sounded the murmur of the mob and the trumpets of victory. The magnificence would have held a solemn air too, a kind of awe. For this was a religious occasion. As the great assemblage in ordered array moved toward the city walls, the chant of the *Te Deum* rose into the morning air. The procession advanced to the gate of Bab-el-Schachard, passed under its grim tower entrance, and wound its way into the maze of narrow streets. James of Aragon (1213–1276) could at last write that he was king "from the Rhone to Valencia."[2]

The exploit rang through Christendom. While Islam "wept over this immense evil,"[3] imaginations in the West were stirred. Gregory IX dispatched a long, ecstatic message of triumph to the provinces of Aix, Auch, Arles, Narbonne, Genoa, and Tarragona.[4] From Milan, Piacenza, Bologna, and Faenza came an invitation to lead northern Italy against the Holy Roman Emperor Frederick II, offering to pay James's way and to become his vassals.[5] The troubadours of Languedoc heard the news about Valencia, and lamented in verse that such power had been diverted from their own land into the south.[6] In remote England, Matthew Paris enthusiastically recorded how "with his allies, the splendid and indefatigable warrior the lord king of Aragon had so ravaged the great city of Valencia by bloody war, and so closely invested it, as to force its surrender."[7] Louis IX of France would send a thorn from Christ's crown of thorns "as a sign of special affection" for Valencia.[8]

In 1245, shortly after the fall of Játiva, keystone in the southern defenses of the Valencian kingdom, Pope Innocent IV already saw in King James a champion for the recovery of Palestine.[9] Later, when the conquest had extended as far south as Murcia (1266), the emperor of Byzantium and the khan of the Mongols were to send ambassadors with an offer of alliance and crusade in the Holy Land.[10] It was at this time that King James sent presents of Moslems as slaves to the pope, the cardinals, Emperor Frederick II, and King Louis IX, as well as female slaves to the queen of France and other ladies.[11] And, in a document relative to the troubles between the Hohenstaufen Manfred and the papacy, in 1262, King James could rightly refer to his "fame" in Christendom as a crusader.[12] Locked in an unending and not always successful struggle with the world of Islam, the West had "exulted with a deep joy"—so Pope Innocent IV reported to King James in 1245— "when the kingdom of Valencia was torn from the grasp of the Saracens."[13]

⋈ THE CRUSADE

The conquest of Valencia had been a project King James had dreamed upon since childhood. If only he could subjugate the Moslem kingdom of Valencia, he could well say that he was "the best king in the world and the one who has done the most."[14] Nor was this only a young cavalier's dream. It was an inherited policy, a factor constant in the plans of the crown of Aragon. Many an expedition had been launched in that direction by James's predecessors, "who had fought hard to win it but were not able."[15] The brilliant exploits of the Cid, who had seized the southern part of the region and held it for a decade, were now a century old but vividly remembered.

Valencia was a kingdom worth having. In size it compared fairly well with either Aragon or Catalonia, the two major states of King James's realm. Its civilization was as ancient, its agricultural and commercial potential greater. Its most important city, Valencia, was a wonder in itself. A Moslem contemporary describing Moorish Spain devotes ten pages to Valencia city, and twice praises it as one of the greatest capitals of the country.[16] Essentially the kingdom of Valencia consisted of a ribbon of fertile coastline, hemmed in along its length by forbidding highlands and mountains. All down this pleasant coast lay a succession of lovely plains—some large and some small —irrigated, prosperous, and strongly defended. Somewhat below the city of Valencia, the shoreline thrust out to form a huge triangle of land. Here the kingdom spread at its widest, and here it erupted into a chaotic tumble of imposing sierras. Beyond this terrible bastion, the former pattern of plain and highland resumed, but now one was entering the region called Murcia.

Towns and hamlets covered the Valencian littoral and were scattered into the interior, even in the uninviting mountainous regions. The desolate escarpment at his back directed the Valencian toward the sea, to commerce and to continual contact with other Mediterranean peoples. It was a land of bustling little ports, luxuriant farmlands, well-traveled roads, and proud walled cities like Burriana or Peñíscola in the north, Játiva or Alcira in the south, and Cullera or Murviedro in the center. As a Christian land, the kingdom of Valencia was to be dominated, in law and in practical life, by the city of Valencia. It is not inappropriate, therefore, to refer to this city as the capital of the kingdom of Valencia.

The Moslems, whose graceful minarets adorned the land, represented an ancient civilization and a traditional enemy. It was their misfortune at this moment of history to be torn by violent civil wars. The catastrophic defeat at Las Navas de Tolosa in the center of the Spanish peninsula had splintered the unity of Moslem Spain into semi-independent entities. Decades of intrigue and bloody strife had subsequently racked these places, and North Africa as well. Even that section which the Christians called the "kingdom" of Valencia was plunged into civil war. The hour had struck for a new Cid to ride.[17]

It was upon this isolated and faction-ridden kingdom that James the Conqueror, ruler of the confederated Aragonese and Catalonian peoples, descended in 1233. His warrior father, the hero of Las Navas, had fallen at Muret in southern France fighting the Albigensian crusaders. With his death and with the advance of the Franks into Languedoc the ambition of the Catalans to dominate their linguistic brothers, the peoples of Languedoc and Provence, had grown dim. Instead, King James was to turn the military energies of his people toward the south and east, inaugurating that Mediterranean expansion which was to carry the standard of Aragon into Italy and Greece. His early conquest of the Balearic Islands struck a heavy blow at Moslem power in the western Mediterranean and won him fame. Majorca fell in 1229, Minorca in 1231, Ibiza in 1235. But his greatest renown was to come from his conquest of Valencia and from his energetic reorganization of that area as a Christian kingdom.

The crusade against Valencia was no easy undertaking. Even in its disordered state and even with one faction of its civil war aiding the Christians, Valencia bristled with castles and was far too strong to be taken by assault. King James had only an erratic force to employ—feudal levies who would disappear when their brief term of service ended, a small corps of faithful enthusiasts, an always unpredictable quantity of crusade volunteers, and the town militias. The crown was chronically embarrassed for supplies, and often preoccupied with domestic or baronial turmoil and with problems in Navarre or southern France. For almost fifteen years James would intermittently chip away at Valencian defenses, leading campaign after campaign, raid after raid. In the end, victory would be due as much to his combination of skillful maneuvering and negotiation as it was to brute force. Two major sieges, at Burriana and Valencia, ended with the mass expulsion of Moslems at those cities. Almost everywhere else the Moors managed to surrender on excellent terms, keeping intact their society, political structure, and way of life.

The story of the crusade may briefly be unfolded in a series of critical dates. In 1225 James made an abortive attack on Peñíscola. In 1229 he signed a pact with the Moslem king or governor of Valencia, Sa'īd, for a cooperative reconquest of his rebellious land. From 1232 to 1235 most of the modern province of Castellón was overrun. In 1232 Morella fell; in 1233 Burriana, Peñíscola, Chivert, and Cervera; in 1235 Pulpis, Castellón, Borriol, Alcalatén, Villafamés, and Almazora. The crusaders now dug in at Puig, a hill just north of Valencia (1236). From 1236 to 1238 a second great advance carried the Christians down to the Júcar River. In 1237 a major battle was won at Puig. The capital itself, held in a strangling siege, surrendered in 1238. From 1239 to 1245 the southern part of the kingdom was conquered. Cullera fell in 1240, Alcira in 1242, Játiva in 1244, Biar in 1245. Basically the line of the Almizra treaty with Castile contained further conquest or repopulation by the crown of Aragon. Below that line the Christian reconquest displayed a different political and social structure, a different pattern of repopulation, even a different mixture of peoples. From 1296, James II of Aragon would begin his bid to absorb the area, but this lies over our present horizon.[18]

Far off to the west, meanwhile, a similar surge forward had been in progress. The whole front of the Reconquest was advancing in hard-fought triumph. Here the Castilians, who were pursuing their own conquest of the demoralized Moslem states of Andalusia, kept a jealous eye on James of Aragon, lest he overstep the areas of crusade agreed upon by the two nations in the treaties of Tudilén (1151), Cazorla (1179), and Almizra (1244). St. Ferdinand entered Cordova in 1236, Jaén in 1246, and Seville in 1248.

Along the Valencian coastline, especially in the mountainous hinterland, several Moslem revolts erupted. These amounted to serious attempts at a war of reconquest. Al-Yazraŷī's outbreak came in 1248 and 1258, on the heels of the Christian victory. Another came in 1263 against the Castilians in Murcia; James in neighborly fashion put it down (1265–1266). A final and fearful revolution broke at the end of King James's life (1275–1277). This last revolt was subdued by the king's son and successor, King Peter, who was soon to be a major figure in Europe in the War of the Sicilian Vespers (from 1282).

A policy of conquest by surrender had facilitated the winning of Valencia;

but its potential dangers for the Christian state were obvious. An added tension in the new land was the mutual antagonism of Aragonese and Catalans. Aragon proper, the heavily feudal upland region which had given its name and royal title to the confederation, differed from Catalonia in language, temperament, interests, and tradition.[19] Each enjoyed its separate parliament, laws, and social structure. The Catalans, a commercial people related to those of Languedoc and Provence, had gained much from their Balearic crusade. The Aragonese had looked to the Valencian conquest as a compensating field of opportunity and expansion for themselves. Yet it was the Catalan peoples who would supply the bulk of the settlers, especially along the coast, and who were to be the active element in the reorganization.

King James cleverly established this new province as a kingdom apart, a balance between the two older entities, with its own coin of the realm, Romanized law code, liberal privileges, administration, and strong communes. This not only limited the Aragonese, but at the same time favored the ruling royal power over the baronial. As the distribution of estates, houses, and lands went forward, especially in the cleared areas at Burriana and Valencia, these and other tensions traveled south in the baggage of the settlers.

The success or failure of the new kingdom would owe much to the personality of the king of Aragon. When the city of Valencia surrendered, James the Conqueror was a bearded giant of a man, some thirty years of age, with a taste for letters and for war. The high ideals of chivalry entertained by "this holy king"[20] were marred in practice by an impulsive streak of tyranny and by an inveterate inclination to adultery and fornication. His talents as a ruler were considerable—as an administrator, as a legislator, as a planner, as a strategist, as a warrior, as a leader of men. On this man's shoulders now fell the task of converting the Moslem province into a Christian kingdom. He would associate his sons in the government; Peter especially was his alter ego in Valencia from about 1260, and was to succeed him as king of the several realms in 1276.[21]

The kingdom of Valencia contained almost 24,000 square kilometers. Of these, about 11,000 fall today within the modern province of Valencia; 6,600 into its northern neighbor, Castellón; and 6,000 into the southern province of Alicante—the province of Valencia roughly equaling the other two. King James I could write of almost fifty Moslem "castles" in this kingdom—and he is referring only to strongholds or forts which commanded respect from the professional warrior. Three hundred years later (1635), the Dutch geographer William Blaeu would describe this realm as: "about sixty leagues long, and seventeen wide at its widest point. It contains within its circuit four cities, sixty towns surrounded by walls, and a thousand villages. It is watered by thirty-five rivers, large and small, among which five are principal . . . It holds about 100,000 families." The section of Valencia

F R A N C E

NAVARRE

Jaca

Perpignan

ROUSSILLON

Urgel

OLD CASTILE

Huesca

C A T A L O N I A

Vich

Gerona

Zaragoza R. EBRO

Lérida

Barcelona

A R A G O N

Tarragona

Tortosa

B A L E A R I C   I S L A N D S

Albarracín

Morella

Teruel

Peñiscola

R. MIJARES

Castellón

Palma

R. GUADALAVIAR

Segorbe

Burriana

MAJORCA

R. JÚCAR

Valencia

N E W

IBIZA

CASTILE

Játiva

Biar

(Southern boundary
of James I)

Alicante

Orihuela

MURCIA

Realms of Aragon

(*After Delisle, 1789*)

GRANADA

A Scale of 100 Miles

0   25   50   75   100

Sam'l. Bryant

falling within the diocese of Valencia he calls "the heart and main section of the realm."[22]

It is not easy to reconstruct the pattern of Christian settlement, nor to measure its pace. Yet it is relevant, as in episodes like tithe-support or the placing of parishes. Though the immigration came down in a steady trickle, there were several notable surges. These altered the map of settlement strikingly; they also dictated the direction of diocesan growth and affected relations with the subject Moslems. The earliest experiments in mass repopulation came in the north, at the beginning of the crusade: the Morella town and countryside in the mountains and the evacuated city of Burriana near the sea (1232–1233). Smaller settlements here were sporadically attempted; but the northern half of King James's conquest now and later stayed relatively inactive. One school of historians argues that the area remained almost solidly Moslem; another school marshals evidence to suggest that it was almost vacated by Moslems and relatively empty as well of Christians.

The second surge of immigration followed the collapse of the city of Valencia. This was the main area of repopulation in the kingdom. Christians took over the great city and much of the immediate countryside. From 1238 to 1244 a Christian enclave of multiple small holdings grew. A lesser scattering of settlers moved out to leaven the Moslem masses who dominated from the Guadalaviar to the Júcar. Above the capital city, Murviedro enjoyed a small repopulation of its own; but this region north to the Mijares tended to remain Moslem. Below the Júcar immigration perforce waited upon the success of the crusade and was at first feeble. Settlement elsewhere had apparently run its course.

The Moslem insurrection in 1248 proved a turning point. As a result of this there was some expulsion of the native population, with another surge of immigrants. They came in irregular waves during the next twenty years; a general adjustment of titles in 1270 marks the end of this movement. The new lands below the Júcar particularly benefited. Towns like Alcira and Játiva received their colonies of Christians. Soon the mountains had little clutches of newcomers. A final stage of repopulation may be traced in the next decade, marked by the crisis of the second Moslem insurrection in 1275 and by the interest in settlement shown by the new king, Peter the Great. This last movement was brought to an untimely end by the reorientation of energies during the long War of the Sicilian Vespers. During all this time, what would be the total number of incoming Christians compared with the number of resident Moslems? Again it is difficult to attempt an answer. An assessment of Moslem population must await a solution of the controversy over the nature and scope of the several expulsions. An assessment of Christian numbers will be attempted in a later chapter on the parishes.

The social, legal, and economic frameworks of the new kingdom all are relevant to the study of her developing church. But they involve so much research and discussion that space forbids elaboration; much of this background will be made apparent as the story unfolds. During the period of the first generation after the conquest, Valencia was still a Moslem land, peopled by Moslems, with a colonial overgrid of Christians. Christian strength principally centered in the coastal cities. These cities were, or were rapidly evolving into, quasi-republican entities typical of the western Mediterranean. They were forward-looking, trade-centered, bourgeois, with an emerging social stratification within their merchant society. The rural society, on the other hand, tended to reflect an older feudalism. Here were the small castles and the village settlements, with the network of personal services and interlacing personal homages. Here too was the dead weight of Moslem dominance on the landscape, sometimes with hardly a token Christian presence.

A highly progressive, lawyer's law had been contrived by the king for his conquest—the *Furs*. This was contemned by the feudal powers, above all by the lords from Aragon proper. They schemed and resisted until they won exception for many of their holdings—largely in the upper half or third of the new kingdom. Their ambition was to see their own law predominant in the Valencian kingdom. The Catalans, though the new law was in many ways more sympathetic to their traditions, also wanted to retain their own local laws, at least as codes of private law.

King James himself was the most important single landlord in the new kingdom. He held a vast number of estates and many important castles; from these he arranged a steady series of infeudations and grants, each usually of small extent. The towns and church were bound to him by gratitude and self-interest. His personal presence in the towns of Valencia was frequent throughout his life, and forceful. His lieutenants, including his son and heir, and his officials and bailiffs represented him in local administrative details.

All these elements were juxtaposed on a strip of territory narrow enough to insure close contact and some friction. And they rested lightly in the interstices of a solid Moslem society. To James and his people Valencia was to represent a borderland or frontier. It was a land of opportunity, of a chance to rise rapidly in status or in wealth, of liberal privileges granted to induce settlement, of fewer taxes or feudal impositions, of a stronger crown and therefore more hope of order, of a heterogeneous population broken in their several molds and ready to form a new society.

Vacant land was here for all, and Moslem-operated estates for the well-to-do, beyond the capacity of this generation to expand into and exploit. Irrigation works and clearings would keep the supply of land increasing. The frontier was ready to act as a safety valve against overcrowding; it served the ambitious, the restricted, the inventive, the acute, the restless, the younger son, the rural rebel, the entrepreneur. Ports and cities offered an unlimited horizon of commercial possibilities. Rapidly expanding markets, employment and prosperity, fertile huertas, new townships, a fluid and urban-centered society which promised to overbalance the feudal elements and which sharpened the social struggle then under way, an increase of the use of parliamentary forms, a buoyancy, a sense of new beginnings, an impatience with older forms and abuses—all these factors may be discerned in the composition of this frontier. A new environment would hold new habits and fresh viewpoints. A distinct "section," a regional entity with a certain unity, psychology, and traditions proper to itself, would evolve in the Aragonese realms.[23]

ᖇᖇ THE CHURCH ON THE FRONTIER

The kingdom of Valencia was conquered. The presence of an army several thousands strong, and the standard of Aragon on the main tower of the capital, proclaimed as much. But minarets were ubiquitous in the land. League upon league of potentially rebel country stretched north from here to the settled Christian border. The overwhelming mass of the population remained Moslem, a people outmaneuvered rather than defeated, in possession of their arms, of many castles, of a military organization, and in contact with Africa.

The problems to be solved were formidable. A Christian people must be planted. Their culture must assert itself against this alien milieu, stamping it with a new personality; yet the number of Christians would be pitifully few for more than a generation. Much of the Moslem framework would have to be retained—their divisions of the land; their custom-law for water distribution; their labor force; and their mosques, whether kept for native use or pressed into service as churches. Above all, there was the presence of "all the barbarian nations"[24]—the entire Moslem communities, with their schools and worship and law courts and governing councils, with the muezzin chanting over the plains and valleys the praises of Allah.

Had this been modern times, the two cultures might have been able to mix, each enriching the other. But medieval cultures were intrinsically religious, with a stubborn exclusiveness. The civil and the social were inextricably confused into the ecclesiastical. One culture must dominate, one must be subordinate.[25] In a military sense this would not be too hard. The land could be garrisoned, the loyalty of key natives purchased, and rebellions met swiftly with the sword. In a social sense it would not have been difficult either, had there been masses of Christian population to send into the south. It was one of James's bitterest complaints that the people refused to come. Even in the last years of his life, the king was to complain to the folk of Barcelona that only thirty thousand households had been settled in the kingdom of Valencia, though he estimated that a hundred thousand were necessary to guarantee its security.[26] More than in any other part of Spain, this was to remain the overriding problem of the conquerors. In an age of expansion and cheap land, King James had expanded too fast and too far.

Yet the land did change. Within half a century it was, though a frontier, a Christian frontier, consolidated, confident. The dissident majority lay dormant and contained, their culture no longer dominant but regressive. This change comprises many stories, from land distribution to the privileges lavished to attract commerce. In some of these elements of change the church was of direct, immediate importance. One recalls the crusade money which financed the expedition; the bishops and Orders of chivalry who marshaled their troops to win and then to hold the new realm; the castles managed by bishops and clerics and religious houses; the Cistercian wool-growing protected by the crown; the tracts of land brought under cultivation or managed with experienced skill by Templars or Hospitallers; and the clergy who furnished so many officials, from the land distributors or the royal judges to the ambassadors and the chancellor of the realm. In a society which had not yet developed independently many important institutions—schools, hospitals, poor relief, proper taxation—the church had either to substitute for or to foster these. And, in an age which felt its religion deeply, she had an indirect role in almost every department of life. It is not without significance that the king both restricted the energetic church in Valencia and showered it with land and privileges. For it was at once a potential rival and a chief bulwark of the crown.[27]

Thus, clerics in Valencia could not hold public office, plead in court as lawyers,[28] or draw wills or any public paper.[29] The drift of land into clerical hands was opposed; no cleric could inherit, or buy, or receive as legacy or gift any Valencian immovable property from anyone, whether knight or citizen or another cleric. James was "aware that quite obviously a loss to our patrimony is the ultimate outcome, when our subjects transfer estates . . . to religious groups."[30] Clerics in the new kingdom had to bear their share of expense and labor in the maintenance and building of roads, bridges, walls, and irrigation canals.[31] Their vassals had to pay full taxes and appear before the civil courts.[32] Yet James's archives are filled with generous grants to the Valencian church, legacies approved, vast purchases authorized, and exemptions and privileges of great variety conferred; it was this, as much as crusading, which won him fairly heady praise from popes like Gregory IX and Alexander IV. One hears it commonly stated today—and the computation dates from medieval times—that the king founded two thousand churches,[33] the bulk of them, of course, on the newly opened frontier.

The king of Aragon was, as his contemporaries called him, a "fortunate" man: James the Well Served.[34] Lying within reach of his energetic arms was a set of institutions—a set of tested patterns of action, often under the supervision of corporate bodies of men—which perfectly fitted many of his requirements. This complex of ecclesiastical institutions and customs, together with the church and clerics and laymen who directed its activities, comprised an important element among the forces at work in his frontier kingdom. The church functioned directly in a frontier capacity as secular lord, as entrepreneur, as garrison, as purveyor of almost all the public assistance or social security available in those times. In many other ways, some of them very indirect, the church reveals itself in Valencia as a frontier institution, reshaping its environment while at the same time painfully assembling and expanding itself.[35]

In theory, a king might have provided for his frontier just by establishing a body of clergy. The conquered area could have been treated as a mission, and a more formal organization provided later. In thirteenth-century Valencia, however, a diocese was erected immediately. There was a complex of reasons for such action. The prestige of a prince increased with the multiplication of dioceses. His control of the region was more secure in that he forestalled any organizational activity by alien ecclesiastics like the primate of Toledo. A fully organized church provided a border area with an institutional framework more stable and resilient than any the crown could hope to erect for some time. Such an organization, once engaged with its environment and marshaling the energies of its people, could do more than anything else to impose the patterns of Christendom on the new region.

In 1247, at about the time of the Valencian ecclesiastical establishment, Pope Innocent IV set down the principal reason why a bishopric had been conceded, in 1172, to a beleaguered and unimportant salient of mountain territory just west of Valencia: "in this way not only were the consolations of religion provided for the faithful, but the assaults of the pagans could more easily be met."[36] In short, a diocese provided cohesion, direction, and moral force to a motley minority, in a way no other institution of that time could quite equal. To give depth and dimension to a new diocese, it was set wherever possible in a traditional center, where long ago Visigothic and Roman bishoprics had proudly stood for centuries. As each ancient see was liberated, it was formally restored, except when some practical or political consideration interfered to alter the pattern.

The ecclesiastical division of the kingdom of Valencia is somewhat awkward. The northerly and poorer part—most of the present province of Castellón—had been early detached in order to render more robust the well-established but financially ailing diocese of Tortosa. There were solid reasons for this. A diocese conterminous with the great kingdom of Valencia would have been unnaturally large and, in its organizational period, clumsy to handle. Tortosa, on the other hand, needed room for expansion and had already been promised such space in Valencia. Finally, King James badly needed for his arduous undertaking the financial and military help of this neighbor of Valencia. The augmentation to the older diocese was considerable, the major part of the Tortosa see being now within the new realm, so that it seemed only fair to give its bishop an equal vote with the bishop of Valencia in the parliament of the kingdom of Valencia. The dispositions and processes of the Tortosa diocese will be analogous to those of Valencia, but always as possessing the substantial advantage of a *point d'appui* in the homeland. The small diocese of Segorbe was something of a curiosity and can barely be said to have existed at this time except as an episode peripheral to the story of Valencia.

Emphasis will fall more heavily upon the diocese of Valencia, which held not only the bulk of the kingdom but also the heartland and the more purely frontier area. Its series of bishops, finances, and emerging diocesan mechanisms will serve as models for our investigation in detail. The relative poverty of documentation for the Valencian segment of the Tortosan diocese encourages this emphasis. Wherever it seems useful diocesan borders will be crossed, or ignored.[37]

⋙ THE CRUSADE SPIRIT

The Valencian crusaders walked with God. They held the remarkable conviction that their work, even in its details, was divinely approved. St. George appeared "with a great army of celestial levies" to lead the crusaders at the critical battle of Puig.[38] A painting of the Virgin miraculously came to light there. Mass linens, hurriedly put aside before a battle in the south, spontaneously tinted with the Blood of Christ.[39] Such incidents effected a religious exaltation; conversely, a religious exaltation had produced these incidents, for their extraordinary characteristics do not survive close examination. Shrines would keep their influence bright, however, and legend spread their fame.

When James coined a new money for Valencia, his avowed motive was precisely to change the pagan atmosphere to a Christian one: "to reform" the new realm "for the better," "according to the Christian manner of life," so as to suppress "the contemptible ways of the infidel."[40] This concept recurs in other documents. At times an almost lyrical note breaks from a staid official message. The announcement by Gregory IX of the capture of Valencia called for universal joy now that the lost sheep was found, the drachma recovered, oppression lifted, and the people of God returned from Pharoah's slavery; even the hard of heart must rise and rejoice.[41] A number of James's documents during the period of reconstruction speak of the blood he shed, when wounded while wresting this land from paganism to Christianity.

The clearest examples of this spirit may be found in the years of actual crusade, first against Majorca and then against Valencia. The archdeacon

Thirteenth-century mural depicting the royal army of Aragon

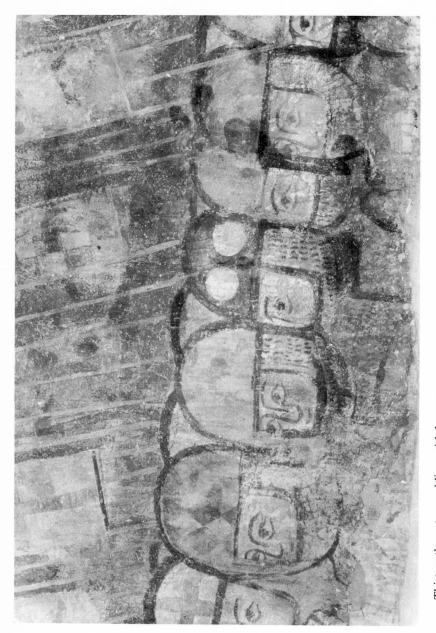

Thirteenth-century soldiers with lances

Crossbowmen of the royal army

Knights with banners

of Barcelona tells the king: "Sir! The noble matter which thou hast begun hath come to thee from God, and all that which is of God must be good and must come to some good end." No less directly the metropolitan of his realms assures James, on the eve of crusading: "your merit and your expansion are works of God"; the war "honors God and the whole heavenly court." His colleague the warrior bishop of Barcelona compares James to Christ transfigured on the Mount: "you are a son of Our Lord when you intend to hunt down the enemies of the faith and the cross."

The bishop later preaches to the army that he who dies in battle "will have paradise and glory eternal forever." James himself persuades the baron Entenza to remain at the perilous outpost of Puig near Valencia by offering him rewards on earth, if he survived, or paradise in the likely event of his death; he could not choose badly.[42]

The barons, too, see the crusade as God's will, which "none can deflect or stop." James will bluntly warn God in a moment of danger: "not only I will lose by this, for You will lose more. . . . And so, true God and powerful, You can guard me from this danger and see that my will is fulfilled, which is to serve You." When a knight asks to represent the crusading army before the walls of Valencia in single combat with the Moor champion, "I said to him that I marveled much how a man who was such a sinner as he, and of so bad a life, could request the joust." The king warns that: "I would be disgraced by him." Sure enough, out of favor with God, the knight is knocked off his horse![43]

When Valencia falls and the king sees his standard being run up on the battlements: "I dismounted from my horse and turned towards the east [Jerusalem], and wept with my eyes, and kissed the ground, on account of the favor which God had done for me." He does the same at the taking of Villena: "I dismounted from my horse and thanked our lord God for the favor He had done me; and I knelt down weeping and kissing the ground." After the victory of Puig, just before the investment of Valencia: "I took myself to the cathedral, before Jesus of Nazareth, and caused a *Te Deum* to be sung by the bishop and the canons." He is not surprised when he hears that a knight in white armor had led the van into the breach at Majorca. We should believe "that it was St. George." Who else, indeed?[44]

Other scenes sustain the same theme: the viscount of Béarn, leader of the left flank at the final charge into Majorca city, who first, "kneeling and weeping, received his Creator, the tears falling down his face." Or the saintly Dominican theologian Michael of Fabra who, between hearing confessions, urged on the tunnelling of the mines. Or the ranks of the army swearing on the Gospels not to turn back, not to stop unless fatally wounded, not to help the fallen. Then the usual Mass at dawn, the religious harangue by the king, and Moncada's men moving to the attack with "great joy and on fire with the love of God, resolved to die for Him if haply need should be."[45]

2—1

This spirit would not stop James and his knights (nor could they have thought of any reason why it should) from so directing their catapults at the siege of Cullera in the kingdom of Valencia, that when a stone missed the castle it would fall short near a place "which was completely filled with women, children, and cattle." The appeal of religion could miscarry on occasion too, when self-interest was not a concomitant, as when James at a parliament in Zaragoza introduced a Franciscan who had learned from an angel that God chose James to defend Spain. "Visions," the nobles judiciously replied, "were good," but they would have to think it over.[46]

James can confuse scripture with Ovid (and misquote the poet) and himself with Providence. "It will be as God will wish," some refractory nobles once told James stiffly; to which he snapped, "God wants just what I am telling you."[47] He very much needed the chaplain whom he kept on hand during campaigns, "lest I was forgetting any sins."[48] He cut out the tongue of the good bishop of Gerona, and habitually lapsed into long-term adulteries even as an old man. King James was piqued that the pope should bombard the welkin with dispraise of these genial failings.[49] All this is characteristic of his time, when men were stirred by a tangle of violent passions and splendid aspirations so that their actions tragic or triumphant often carried with them, like a court jester, a measure of absurdity.

But, when James writes, in a letter to Peter Nolasco, that "I will not raise the siege of Majorca until the Virgin's praise be sung in it, to that have I sworn," and when he makes a formal vow "to God and this altar which is in honor of His mother," never to return north of Tortosa until he has conquered the city of Valencia, and when he keeps a precampaign "vigil at the church of the Holy Cross of Barcelona in the company of all the knights and of many others with many candles and tapers and a great burning of lights" all through the night, the spirit is recognizably the same as that found in a more formal and diffused shape throughout the documents.[50]

That spirit is revealed in a number of incidents during the reconstruction of Valencia. It is in this spirit that James writes to the Dominicans of Valencia (1239), representing the military action as the first phase of a process, of which the assiduous promotion of religious institutions is to be the continuation.[51] It is in the same spirit that he lauds the immigrants coming to settle the Burriana area, as people "who daily strive to exalt the Christian name."[52] It is in this "fervent" spirit that he promotes education in Valencia.[53] In this spirit Pope Gregory IX had offered indulgences in 1230 to volunteers who might come and settle in any of the lands which King James should conquer—including therefore Valencia, on which the king had already made one attempt.[54] In this spirit in 1233 Gregory spoke of the land of Majorca as having been "converted to the Catholic faith" by the conquest; he offered special indulgences to those who would populate it for its defense and its cleansing.[55] It was not enough for a Christian king and his people to have reconquered Moslem territory; the area must subsequently "be restored and assimilated to Christian worship" by them.[56]

The custodian of this naïve but powerful spirit was the church of Valencia. Perhaps this subtle, pervading office was her most important contribution to the reorganization of the realm.

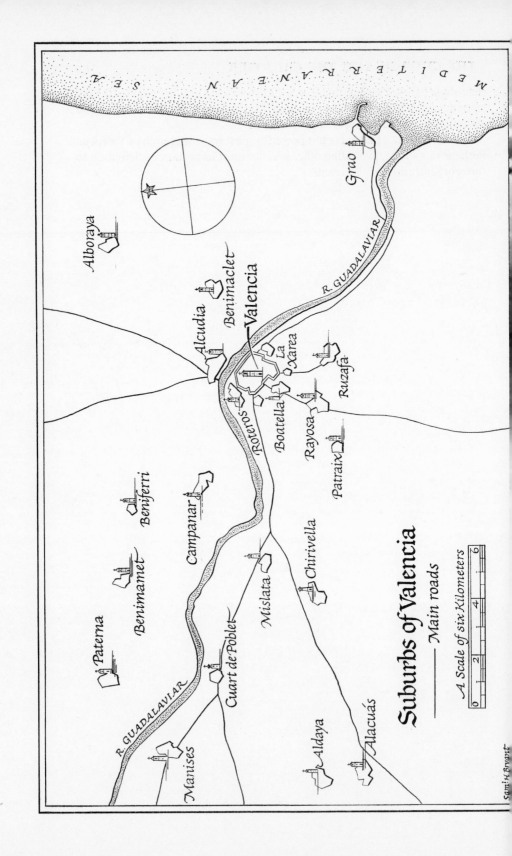

MEDITERRANEAN SEA

Grao

R. GUADALAVIAR

Alboraya

Alcudia

Benimaclet

Valencia

La Xarea

Ruzafa

Roteros

Boatella

Rayosa

Patraix

Beniferri

Campanar

Chirivella

Paterna

Benimamet

Mislata

Cuart de Poblet

Manises

Aldaya

Alacuás

R. GUADALAVIAR

Suburbs of Valencia

——— Main roads

A Scale of six Kilometers

0   2   4   6

Sam'l H. Bryant

I I

CATHEDRAL, BISHOP,
AND CHAPTER

Evaluation of the elements involved in reconstructing a rawly conquered kingdom and in molding it into startlingly different cultural shapes should begin with the cathedral. As the parish was the cell of the ecclesiastical body, the bishop in his cathedral was its heart and its head. The Valencian cathedral had to be the model and mother of the lesser churches. Her liturgical customs set the pattern throughout the diocese; her synods promulgated general laws; her bishop was the source of jurisdiction and the wielder of corrective powers. In the newly conquered land it was the bishop's responsibility to plant the parishes effectively, fighting the while to preserve their revenues and the powers proper to his see.

⋈ THE CATHEDRAL, HUB OF THE DIOCESE

The bishop must foster education, examine teachers, force upon law-breakers the Peace and Truce of God, put down clerical abuses, erect a professional legal system, arbitrate quarrels without number, wage disturbingly expensive lawsuits over diocesan rights, dedicate churches, confirm, make records, cope with a great flow of correspondence, slyly expand the limits of his diocese when claim and opportunity coincided, persuade a reluctant people to pay tithes, and rebuke impiety. The list is well-nigh inexhaustible, even if all mention of military, political, and seignorial activities is omitted. In fact, the contemporary Catalan canonist Raymond of Penyafort, after a brave effort to survey even the major spiritual tasks of a bishop in his day, abandons the list as involving "many other duties which it would be difficult to enumerate, because his is the pre-eminent government in all things [spiritual]."[1]

Episcopal courts tried the civil or criminal cases involving tonsured clerics (a sizable percentage of the population), and much that involved crusaders, orphans, widows, pilgrims, and students. These courts could also claim jurisdiction over the general populace for cases concerning tithes; for offenses done in holy places; for litigation involving an oath—an extensive field in medieval society; and for adultery, heresy, usury, and the like. In Valencia, the bishop was the equal of the greatest magnates. In Catalan lands generally, far more than in Castile or Portugal, the local bishop had long been a power in urban and secular affairs.[2] The bishop of Valencia was also the most important ecclesiastical figure in the *corts* or parliament of the kingdom of Valencia, along with the bishops of Segorbe and Tortosa, the masters of the Temple and Hospital, and the abbots of Benifasá and Valldigna.[3] And as a social force in Valencia the bishop had no peer except the king.

In the early days of the Valencian diocese, there would be fatiguing verbal skirmishes with king, nobles, and townsmen; determined conflicts to repel the bishops nibbling at his borderlands; intramural tussles with chapter and archdeacon; occasional legal-diplomatic sallies to Rome; and a fine battle royal with the primate of Toledo. The religious Orders particularly roused all that was bellicose in a Valencian bishop. To the conservative churchman the whole ecclesiastical order seemed to be turned upside down by the un-precedented spread and influence of the Mendicants and other activist re-ligious Orders. The status of exemption from episcopal control in much of their activity was provoking, as was their remarkable success as preachers, teachers, and confessors. The jurisdictional and financial aspects of this success became the focus of myriad local squabbles, culminating in a bitter "polémica universal" throughout Europe during this period.[4]

Taken all in all, the Valencian bishop was to have a lively time of it facing up to his many opponents. The list of episcopal battles is long and the trend of the fighting sometimes obscure. Enough material survives to assure us that, unless the man were pugnacious by nature, a Valencian bishop's lot was vexatious enough. Considering all this and throwing onto the balance the properly spiritual obligations and even those exacting civil duties im-posed by the king (two of the bishops concerned were royal chancellors), it is surprising that progress in the diocese was not more halting.

What the parish did in a local way to impose new shapes and meaning on its environment, the cathedral achieved in a larger and more comprehensive form. There was a preoccupation, perhaps not unconnected with the pre-scriptions of the Old Testament, to have an imposing and richly fashioned central cathedral. Here the splendors of the liturgy could be offered con-tinually to God, by a properly numerous gathering of distinguished clerics. Over Europe at this time some fifty cathedrals or equivalently large churches were being raised including Beauvais, Westminster Abbey, Strasbourg, and Cologne. In Valencia as elsewhere contemporary custom dictated many of the details. In these the new diocese was anxious not to appear inferior to her elders; a dash of rivalry spiced her efforts.

"The church of Our Lady St. Mary" was for some time the adapted cen-tral mosque, to which all the Moslems of Valencia city had been obliged to come on Fridays.[5] Its altars and furnishings now offered an odd contrast to the Koranic texts sculptured upon its chaste walls. This mosque-as-church would probably have covered the area presently filled by the cathedral sanctuary and apse, with the flanking chapels and sacristy; most of the choir may have stood on part of the court of ablutions. A bull of Gregory IX, on October 9, 1239, elevated this converted mosque to the status of a cathedral.[6] But it could hardly answer as symbol and center for a diocese so uncomfortably immersed in a sea of Moslems. Something more imposing, more aggressively Christian, was required.

It must also be comfortably large, since it was to be the scene of many an elaborate public function. In civil life the cathedral would house the occasional meeting of the Valencian parliament,[7] the annual inauguration to civic office,[8] and the royal solemnities when James proclaimed in Valencia the expulsion of the Moslems.[9] Its great bell sounded out in times of crisis; this alerted the citizens when fire broke out, and brought them running with weapons in hand when police action was required.[10]

To stage the spiritual and secular solemnities the Valencians planned a Romanesque cathedral. They saw the first stone laid on June 22, 1262.[11] Elements of the Gothic style were incorporated and very soon took over the dominant role. But Bishop Andrew, the well-traveled Dominican who inaugurated the work, failed to choose a French architect. Here, then, since Aragonese Gothic was not so advanced as Castilian, there would be no Burgos or León or Toledo cathedral, all of which were under construction. On the other hand, there would be no regression of Gothic influence in face of an upsurging Mudejar art, as happened in the contemporary Castilian conquest. In art, the spirit of the north persisted tenaciously.[12]

The forward portion of the church went up first, the nave continuing later as finances allowed; by the early fourteenth century the whole structure had assumed the same extension it has today. The floor plan is a Latin cross with very short nave. The principal nave stands out boldly, the collateral ones being narrow; small chapels cluster all around the semicircular apse or head of this cross. The low vault and wide arcades, among other elements, recall Italian churches like Santa Maria Novella at Florence.

A troop of wandering craftsmen, under "the master of the works of the cathedral," had taken up the job. Nicholas of Autun later became the second master, chosen by bishop and chapter in 1303 to direct construction, pictures, and all details at a life-contract guaranteeing board plus two and one-half solidi a day. To keep the circuit around the cathedral uncluttered—probably as much for dignity of appearance as for church processions—King James as early as 1249 had forbidden the encircling houses to build any portico, arcade, porch, overhang, connecting bridge, "or any kind of closure."[13]

Of the first building operations, one strikingly beautiful Romanesque doorway still remains. It seems to be the work of Lérida craftsmen, and provides evidence for those who see a special relation between the cathedrals (and the peoples) of Lérida and frontier Valencia. A companion portal surviving from the thirteenth century is the Gothic, exquisitely carved Door of the Apostles, begun by Bishop Jazpert about 1276; this served for the bishop's processional entrance just as a previous door here had served for the mosque entry.[14] In those early days the ground plan was much less ambitious; the whole building was on high ground, boasted a meandering cemetery hard by, and enjoyed rather more space around it.

In 1334 daring new plans were to incorporate the construction already achieved; a new cornerstone went down, and the cathedral began to expand to its modern proportions. The Gothic lines of later portions are visible today, since a good part of the plaster-cum-gilt, rococo interior masking it was mercifully knocked away during the last civil war. The dark interior, much larger than Bishop Andrew had planned, fails to convey any feeling of spaciousness or aspiration; still, seen for itself, as a huge edifice regular and ample, it is an achievement.

Even while the cathedral had been located in the mosque, a special privilege was sought and won from Pope Alexander IV (1257) allowing forty days' indulgence to those who, at the four great festivities of the Virgin, should visit the "church of Valencia established in honor of Blessed Mary the Virgin."[15]

Some fifteen benefices or chantries were secured for the cathedral during the organizational era of the diocese. A year after the conquest Peter Melet instituted one of the first, named in honor of St. Vincent (1240). King James followed with the benefice of St. James (1245). Others soon came from: James Sanz (1247), the cathedral precentor (1250), the archdeacon Martin of Entenza (two in 1252), the canon Bertrand of Teruel (1256), the canon William of Arenys (1267), the dean James Sarroca (1270), Berengar of Ciutadella (1272), the canon Vincent of St. Vincent (1272), the canon Nicholas of Hungary (1274), the canon Peter Pérez of Tarragona (1279), Raymond of Cardona (1281), and so on. The invocations for these varied: Vincent, James, Holy Spirit, Anthony, Matthew, Augustine, Margaret, Crown of Thorns, Lucy, Blaise, Benedict, Mary Magdalene, and Luke. The donor and his heirs retained the patronage.[16]

The formula for endowment followed that of a sale. It involved a perpetual patronage with right of presentation—or perhaps one may think of it as a benefice with right to propose a vicar:

> We [bishop and chapter] sell to you, William of Arenys canon of Valencia, the fruits of one prebend, which shall daily yield twelve pence in Valencian money. And we promise, in the matter of your heirs and successors, that the right of patronage will come to you and yours, with or without a last testament. [We will] provide perpetually without any obstacle an issue of twelve pence to one priest, who daily is to celebrate Mass in our church for the soul of yourself and your relatives.[17]

The cathedral parish, which was the chapel of St. Peter, was located where today the chapels of St. Francis Borgia and St. Michael, and the canons' vestry, stand.

The bishops resident may often have been traveling; no visitation records survive to check on this. However, they would surely not have wandered like the vagabond English bishops, because their support apparently lay not so much in far-flung manors as in tithes, which were gathered by officials into central depots and cellars for marketing.[18] Despite their loud outcries, the financial position of the bishops seems to have been relatively enviable. In any case, a bishop's residence in those days was a center of authority "far more stable than that of the king and his agents" who were forever on the move.[19] When at home, the bishop lived in a "palace" to the right of the cathedral.[20] This was probably nothing majestic. At first it would have been a complex of buildings converted from secular uses. The bishop may have acquired them in the multiple purchases of houses fronting on the cathedral in 1242.[21] An important settlement between clergy and Knights Hospitallers in 1255 was signed "in the houses of the bishop." A similar document has the singular "house."[22]

A bishop's household of this period might be expected to include a legal staff—Official, penitentiary, advocates, and the like with their clerks; an ecclesiastical staff, especially a chaplain and a theologian; and a secretarial staff—accountants, auditors, estate stewards, and bailiffs. Peter Savior "notary of the lord bishop" appears in action as early as June 1240.[23] A legal staff for the bishop of Valencia handled trials for usury, sacrilege, blasphemy, assault on clerics, marriage problems, and "similar" cases.[24]

The "Official of the Lord Bishop of Valencia," a delegate and judicial substitute for the bishop, appears almost from the beginning but formally from 1243.[25] He is named in 1263, when the Hospitallers appeal from him to the pope; in a tithe document of 1272; when he is interfering at St. Vincent's in 1284; and again in 1284 when a parent asks him to protect his son, a fugitive Dominican, from forcible return.[26] The penitentiary, who exercised jurisdiction over confessional or other cases "reserved" to the bishop, turns up in documents of 1241 and 1242. He had been one of the first functionaries appointed however as early as 1238. The office was then held by Matthew of Oteiza, archpriest of Teruel and canon of Valencia.[27]

These are only stray documents, giving no idea of the press of business which assailed the ecclesiastical courts in Valencia almost as soon as the city fell. One suitor was to recall going to court when the metropolitan was the acting authority in the city (1238–1239); "and he found there many litigants" already waiting, with a cleric busily hearing "all" the cases of the city. Another witness was to recall that the archbishop often appeared at this time to hear a run of cases personally; one day he watched him through two such cases involving clerics.[28]

As for the domestic staff, a chaplaincy was founded in 1260 under the invocation of St. Paul. But the palace already had possessed from 1243 a *de facto* resident chaplain. The "chaplaincy of the bishop's palace" and the "chaplain of the bishop's palace" are in the crusade tax lists of 1279 and 1280, paying the modest assessments of 22 and 24 solidi.[29] The bishop's bailiff appears a number of times in the records, though often he seems to be a transient tax farmer.[30] There is also an unspecified familiar in the records,[31] and a "Master Bartholomew of Garleyn, physician of the said bishop."[32] The "six dining tables, one of which is round, and twelve benches and three sitting chairs" in the inventory of Bishop Arnold (1248) suggest a sizable staff or else great expectations of company.[33] Mixed into the same inventory, perhaps to dust the tables and wash the pots enumerated, is the bishop's slave, a Moslem woman.[34]

All in all, the frontier bishops in Valencia succeeded in creating a fairly imposing central mechanism during the first sixty years. By the end of the century, when requesting a cardinal's hat for his realms, James II will not be ashamed to begin his list of the foremost suitable candidates with the name of the bishop of Valencia.[35]

∾ THE EPISCOPATE

A diocese reflects the man who rules it. An understanding of the evolving frontier church would not be complete without some examination of the individual bishops. They were five in all for this period, if we include the incumbent whose long reign began in the year James I died.[36] The first, who never passed beyond the status of "elect," was Berengar of Castellbisbal. He had taken part in both the Majorcan and Valencian crusades. As confessor and familiar of King James, he was a reliable man from the point of view of royal interest. He was also a Dominican friar of experience and spirituality. Vincke suggests indeed that James chose him for these latter gifts, with deliberate intent of making less reasonable the claims and interference of the Toledo metropolitan. There was no question at this date of direct, official intervention in the election of a bishop; still, the men favored by king and metropolitan would naturally have the strongest chances.

One of the crusaders, in testimony given at a trial shortly after the city's fall, recalled the election. The witness "saw how the said archbishop came out of the council he was at with his bishops, with the Franciscans, and with the Dominicans." To the observers standing there the metropolitan proclaimed: "We choose as bishop of Valencia Berengar of Castellbisbal." A few years later, losing the Valencian office during the jurisdictional wrangling between Toledo and Tarragona, Castellbisbal received instead the diocese of Gerona. He died in 1264.[37]

Ferrer of Pallarés (1240–1243)[38] turns up as bishop-elect quite suddenly in records of May and June 1240, apparently in full course as governor of the Valencian church.[39] The papal commission of April 1239 had reached a decision favorable to ownership of the diocese by the metropolitan of Toledo, only to have it appealed by Tarragona; this would account for Ferrer's consecration appearing in the cathedral constitutions under the date of June 22, 1240. However, he may have been consecrated in mid-October of that same year. Historians have expended a good deal of energy in useless speculation as to the implications of the words "elect" and "bishop" in his documents, but since the terms were interchangeable at this period, they prove nothing.[40] The exact date when Ferrer changed from administrative precursor to full bishop of Valencia cannot be ascertained.[41]

He certainly possessed administrative ability, in view of the important offices he exercised at Tarragona and which he retained during his incumbency as bishop of Valencia, and in view of his having previously been left in charge at Valencia by the metropolitan.[42] He was also, and the fact may be significant, a Catalan rather than an Aragonese. He had been at the king's side on a number of important occasions, acting as official witness to a treaty with Genoa (1230) and to the surrender of Minorca (1231).[43] As a warrior cleric he had led a sizable contingent, including a ship, on the Majorcan crusade.[44] The abundant rewards he received there indicate that his group had been prominent in the fighting. The organization of these properties, or other duties, apparently kept him from crusading in Valencia.[45] Like his predecessor, he was surely a personal choice of the king.[46]

During his reign an episcopal household was organized; a practical compromise was reached by which the king paid an endowment sum; a considerable amount of rentals, sales, and exchanges of property was undertaken so as to stabilize the financial basis of the diocese; a sensible division of revenues was arranged (1240); some vigorous disputes were brought to a compromise; the diocese was divided into two archdeaconries; and a general regulation of the divine services was worked out (by 1242). Judging from this evidence, Ferrer seems to have been a man of ability, a man with important connections before his election, a man equally at home in the saddle or in the chancery. This was a happy combination of qualifications during the disorganized initial years of settlement, when strangers were coming into the realm from all sides to seek their fortunes.

One glimpse of his personality is not reassuring. He weakly allowed the king to absorb all the tithes and rentals on mosque properties, except for a third; that is, he signed away to the crown the bulk of the revenues which the infant church would need for proper growth.[47] It is quite possible that Bishop Ferrer was, though not a tool of the king, at least too subservient. After all, the canons who were first installed at the capital were the king's creatures, according to the complaint later brought by the chapter against James.[48] This fiscal action of Ferrer, perhaps only a desperate expedient, inaugurated a long struggle between diocese and crown, concluded in favor of the former only in 1273.[49]

On the other hand, St. Peter Nolasco cherished Ferrer as a friend. While the bishop was on his way to attend a provincial council at Barcelona, he was ambushed by a party of Moors in the badlands north of Tortosa and taken prisoner. Nolasco "was extremely grieved" to hear of this; he did his best to ransom the bishop. No time remained. After a three-day captivity, the first bishop of Valencia was "wickedly slain" (April 30, 1243). In view of his combat record and the rebellious state of the conquered country, there is little excuse for the local tendency to regard Bishop Ferrer as a martyr.[50]

Arnold of Peralta (1243-1248) was unanimously elected to succeed him, the choice being that of six representatives designated by the Valencia chapter (June 1, 1243).[51] Arnold was a hardheaded Aragonese, from a noble family of Ribagorza. He had previously held the very important position of archdeacon in the diocese of Lérida. His electors introduce him as a man decent and educated ("honestum, literatum"), discreet in affairs spiritual as well as temporal, and capable of defending the rights of the church. His five-year tenure as bishop of Valencia left a strong imprint on the young diocese, whose southern portions at the time of his accession had not yet been conquered. Two vigorous struggles now began whose clamor would continue to the subsequent reign. The first was a determined effort to recover from the crown the revenues Bishop Ferrer had signed away; Bishop Arnold may even have carried this fight to Rome.[52] The second battle was against the claims of Segorbe to be an independent diocese, a complicated episode which will be discussed in the next chapter.

Bishop Arnold continued the work of organizing the diocesan revenues, especially along the lines of converting real properties into rentals. He it was who first created twelve officials, the priors or *prepositi*, to oversee the collection of the capitular share of those revenues (1247).[53] In 1243 or 1244 he seems to have convoked the first diocesan synod, in the series of twelve Valencian synods during the thirteenth century.[54] Thus he began that work of applying discipline, so necessary to counterbalance the effects of ignorance, adventurous effervescence, and disparate traditions in the newly forming clerical body. He set the number of possible cathedral canons at twenty, created in 1248 the archdeaconry of newly conquered Játiva (1244), and promptly fell into a serious legal quarrel with Játiva over respective jurisdictions. The metropolitan finally had to be called in to settle this last difficulty.[55]

Bishop Arnold continued on a large scale the regulative work of adjusting with each religious Order claims to revenues or jurisdiction. This last work was important in a young diocese which hoped to recruit skilled helpers from the local reserve of the religious. Thus the reign of Bishop Arnold marks a second stage in the organization of the diocese. Without introducing novel policies, except for the firm opposition to the king's raid upon church revenues, Arnold pursued the aims of administrative centralization of authority, combined with specific delegation of that authority to diocesan officials. The rate of progress was definitely accelerated during these five short years.

Bishop Arnold was strangely unsatisfied with his position and soon asked to be transferred. An opportunity came in the summer of 1248; Arnold was removed to Zarogoza, the capital city of Aragon proper.[56] One may only guess as to his motives—ambition, the interminable conflict with the neighboring diocese of Segorbe, or unhappiness over Moslem prerogatives. (He had been the major supporter of the king's proposal to exile the Moslems, or at least a substantial number of them.)[57] Perhaps, having backed the king so strongly on the Moslem question, and having proved so useful an ambassador to the pope when James had been excommunicated for cutting off part of Castellbisbal's tongue, Arnold was simply reaping the rewards accruing to those who befriend the powerful. Or, as an Aragonese he may have experienced a sense of friction in dealing with his Catalan co-workers and population. He left behind an interesting assortment of oddments for which an inventory was drawn.[58]

The Dominican prior Andrew of Albalat (1248–1276), one of nine candidates proposed to the chapter, was elected third bishop of the diocese early in December 1248.[59] His was easily the most important of these early episcopates. It lasted almost thirty years (he was to die in 1276, the same year as King James), as against the previous episcopates of three and of five years. It was able to build too upon the foundations so carefully laid by its pioneer predecessors. The new bishop belonged to a prominent Catalan family. His brother was a celebrated bishop of Lérida and from 1238 to 1251 metropolitan at Tarragona for the realms of King James.[60] Andrew Albalat, as brother of this luminary, naturally went from grace to grace.

Bishop Andrew convened no less than eight diocesan synods: in 1255, 1258, 1261, 1262, 1263, 1268, 1269, and 1273. At these synods the constitutions which would govern and form the Valencian church were worked out. Uniformity of ritual, instruction of clergy, reform of easygoing frontier habits and of morals, rules for residence and for clerical life, and regulation of revenues constitute the major themes of these meetings. There is a particular concern for the sacraments of the church.

Bishop Andrew also captained the clerical forces in the tithe dispute which resounded in the kingdom until settled by the crown. He pursued the barons of the realm who refused to pay tithes in full; in this connection he succeeded in filing away many a formal contract which preserved at least the principle that these tithes belonged inalienably to the church. During his incumbency, the great tithe settlement of 1268 was achieved.[61] In June 1262 he laid the cornerstone for the Gothic cathedral, whose construction he encouraged and labored over. He took much trouble to found the monastery of Gate of Heaven (Porta Coeli) and to secure for it a settlement of those prayerful recluses the Carthusians.

During his reign all the parish mosques except one were pulled down and bright new Gothic structures substituted. Bishop Andrew made further changes in the system for gathering revenues, creating twelve new offices or priorates to help in this work, one for each month. This proved to be a clumsy device, destined to cause problems.[62] By an appeal to Pope Clement IV concerning the extreme poverty of his diocese, Bishop Andrew brought pressure on James to remedy that situation through tax provision and through gifts. Andrew also created the deanery and twelve canonries to augment the splendor of the cathedral liturgy. His surviving records are filled with property transactions and rentals. They include the expected measure of lawsuits and the usual adjustments of conflicting interests between the diocese and religious Orders. There are privileges like the right of asylum by the king, and special faculties from the pope to deal with confusions arising from the mingling of two religions here on the frontier.

Andrew grew in stature as a national figure. This must have reflected some prestige onto the young diocese. He became a confidant of King James, ambassador, chancellor of the realms with custody of the royal seal, and an agent for the crown at Rome. He was sent by the pope in 1258 to reform the Augustinian canons of Montearagón near Huesca. In 1263 he served on the commission which drew the Valencia-Castile boundary. In 1274 he attended the second ecumenical council of Christendom at Lyons. Shortly thereafter he acted as papal envoy to dissuade King Alphonse of Castile from his aspirations to the crown of the Holy Roman Empire. Journeying to Italy to report on this affair, he suddenly died at Viterbo (November 25, 1276).[63]

The latter circumstance allowed the pope, by a canonical technicality, to appoint the next bishop of Valencia. A happy choice for the post was at that moment in Viterbo, one Jazpert of Botonach. He was a Catalan of noble family and of some reputation as a lawyer, who had already risen to be sacristan at the cathedral of his native Gerona as well as abbot of St. Felix. His episcopate (1276-1288) was to last thirteen years and was to consolidate the work of his predecessor, filling in the structural outlines and continuing the general policies. He was "a big, handsome, well-endowed, jovial, largehearted individual," gifts which surely contributed to his success in this work.[64]

He called diocesan synods in 1278 and 1280, and he refers in general to at least one previous synod. Jazpert created two more archdeaconries in 1279: Murviedro and Alcira, both near the capital. He added five canonries at the cathedral; and he made a determined effort to clear up the remaining unpleasant quarrels concerning tithes and first fruits. Bishop Jazpert seems to have had unusual literary gifts; he is thought to be the author of one of the greatest medieval histories, the chronicle of Bernard Desclot. It was to him that Arnold of Vilanova dedicated in an introductory letter his *De improbatione maleficiorum.*

Jazpert was also a prominent adviser to the crown, more especially during the quarrel with the papacy and during the French crusade against Aragon. His counsel as to the juridical position to be assumed by the king of Aragon may have influenced Philip the Fair in his later conflict with Boniface VIII. When King Peter lay dying, "he called to his side the bishop [Jazpert] of Valencia, whom he loved much," and reminded him "that I have ever cherished thee at all times and that I have continually relied upon thee and have entrusted to thee many of my affairs and . . . thou didst guide me faithfully and well."[65]

The last decade of the century was filled by his successor, also a papal appointee, the Dominican Raymond Deçpont (1289–1312). He was an important figure at Rome, both as a learned official of the pope and also as governor of the march of Ancona. He was equally important in the kingdom of Aragon where he was chancellor and an intimate of the king. As a diplomat making peace between France and Aragon, for example, or as one of the most active figures at the ecumenical council of Vienne he remained prominent in affairs of state. More to the point, he was a greathearted priest devoted to his people. His revenues he turned to the service of the poor. He made the rounds of the city hospitals alone every week, in the early dawn, to console the sick and aid the poor. His synodal legislation includes a careful exposition on the sacraments. Raymond is perhaps the most attractive of all the interesting bishops of this century in Valencia. His story really lies just over the horizon and must serve only to put a border to our summary view of the pioneer episcopate.

All of the pioneer bishops of Valencia were able men, well suited to their responsibilities—though Ferrer was something less than admirable in his surrender of the revenues to King James. All seem to have come from prominent families, products of the higher echelons of the feudal world, men accustomed to power and moving easily among the dignitaries of church and state. Strangely enough they will stay aloof from the baronial struggles in Valencia against royal encroachment. So clear is this that a modern authority can say (in terms too sweeping): "unlike the clergy of either Aragon or Catalonia, the Valencia clerics took little part in governmental affairs."[66] He suggests that this was because all except one bishop from 1234 to 1348 were Catalans rather than Aragonese. A more important reason may lie in the nature of diocesan economic support, which was monetary much more than by estates.

The two qualities marking the bishops—administrative competence developed by experience, and social background—must have been of great use for the task confronting them. These same qualities help explain a certain coldness in the records, a preoccupation at the synods with externals and behavior, a superficiality in the approach to the problems of intensifying the religious life as opposed to mere elaboration of mechanisms designed for that end, and the reservation of enthusiasms until relatively unimportant questions of jurisdiction or property arose to stimulate them.

Knowing the needs of the time and place, seeing the jealousy between diocesan and religious clergy, aware of the ignorance and lack of instruction in the masses, one looks not only for competence and head but for sanctity and heart. Perhaps this is expecting more than the surviving records can be expected to yield. The first bishops seem at least to have been good men, experienced, dedicated to their administrative responsibilities, learned enough (especially Andrew and Jazpert), and well thought of by their contemporaries. In the end these qualities may have been just what was needed by a diocese in embryo, a chaos of immigration, adventurers, confused customs, and Moslem rebellion in an alien environment.

⭗ ADMINISTRATIVE-ADVISORY: THE CANONS AND DIGNITARIES

The cathedral chapter was in general the cathedral clergy. But it was a body quite separate from the bishop's household, and juridically separate from the bishop. It was a community not so much of brotherhood as of service. By the thirteenth century its forms had been profoundly influenced both by the new monasticism of the Gregorian Reformation and by the legal renaissance. Above all they were influenced by the numerous communal and associative experiments of contemporary Christendom. Like the university and the commune, the chapter was a full-fledged legal corporation. A body politic, with all the attributes of individuality and immortality in law possessed by other corporations, it deliberated democratically in its chapter house, passed its own laws binding on members, acted under its own seal, owned and exploited properties, took its grievances before the law, and jealously cherished its several rights and duties.

The chapter personnel were canons, diocesan clerics without vows. Each had his stall in the central choir of the church, a voice and vote in the chapter house (at Valencia, apparently the sacristy), usually some function or job, and an enviably substantial endowment or prebend as well as shares or dividends from a common fund. The canons or their choral vicars (voteless) gathered together at prescribed times throughout the day to chant with solemnity the liturgical hours. This service alone justified the existence of noncathedral chapters, those at collegiate churches regular or secular. And the huge medieval cathedrals, towering over the small cities of that day, were primarily intended to accommodate the chapter in its daily, corporate devotions.

But at a cathedral the liturgical function was overshadowed by the canons' role as senate and general staff to the bishop. Beyond the advisory and administrative duties, and of course the electing of new bishops, the chapter had to provide a loyal opposition as defenders of diocesan rights. The bishop was bound to seek their counsel on a number of administrative details, and their consent on others. This close connection was well summed by the chapter of Valencia (1263): "the chapter is in the bishop, and the bishop is in the chapter."[67] The immediate context of this wording was juridical, indicating that the cause of the one involved the interests of the other. It also had a wider application. In practice, the powers of the chapter cut sharply into those of the bishop, and there would be some disputes. Here again was an institution preshaped, with evolved traditions, waiting only to be assigned a personnel.

Immediately after the city's fall a brisk organization of this body began. Within twenty months it was completed. Revenues had been assessed and divided; the principal dignitaries and the body of the canons, at least thirteen, appointed; labors assigned; and an agreement worked out as to the method of electing canons and dividing new revenue to come. The document which confirms all this presupposes, by its detail, considerable inquiry and discussion.[68] By the endowment document of 1241 the crown obliged itself to supply each canon with a house and small farm or garden—the latter probably just beyond the city walls.[69] This seems to have been provided for by special purchase, at this time, of fourteen buildings fronting on the cathedral.[70]

The original body of canons, less than a decade after its organization, applied to the Holy See for the high privilege of immunity from disciplinary action by legates or delegates from Rome. There seems to have been no particular necessity for such a privilege; but the new corporation probably coveted it as a mark of favor and esteem such as older chapters had acquired. Pope Innocent IV duly granted the request for three years in 1246.[71] At the end of the century when the new kingdom of Valencia has its own parliament, the cathedral chapter will receive a separate invitation from the king to participate.[72]

At the period immediately following the surrender of the capital there were at least five canons.[73] Later the contemporary bishop of Gerona was to recall the original group set by the metropolitan as "some seven or eight."[74] This number increased within the year to over a dozen.[75] The housing endowment of 1241 supposes fourteen canons. By January 1257 the number had officially been fixed at fifteen, and approved by Rome.[76] In 1277 and 1279 due to augmented revenues this official ceiling was raised to twenty.[77] This quantity of canons equaled the number in ancient, established sees.[78]

The competition for the lucrative, honorific posts was undoubtedly keen. One cleric, who had been properly appointed, was refused admittance for a number of years for some reason. "The cleric Dominic Matthew has set before us a complaint," wrote the metropolitan in 1247; although "in the organizing of the church after the taking of Valencia city, we created him a canon of that church," difficulties had been made. "The case was brought to court, and on account of the objections, his rights [were] called into doubt." The archbishop settled the matter by testifying that Matthew "had been received by us into the body of canons of the Valencian church at the first creation of canons done by us there."[79]

Some of the canonical number, invested with administrative responsibilities, enjoyed the revenues and rank of dignitaries. In the initial stages of the organization, these were limited to four: sacristan, precentor, and two archdeacons.[80] One of the canons acted as notary to the bishop. It is difficult to describe the offices of the dignitaries or the functionaries in detail because these varied from diocese to diocese and from time to time. Even the great contemporary Catalan lawyer Raymond of Penyafort refused the task in his *Summa*: "I shall not pursue the subject because, in these dignities and functions, there are just about as many varieties of custom as there are churches."[81]

The sacristan was not a minor caretaker as in modern usage, but a very important figure in the medieval diocese. Even in secular affairs he not infrequently fielded a respectable body of knights for the king's service. He guarded the liturgical treasures (a common name for him was treasurer) and the archives; he also saw to the purchase of valuable reliquaries, chalices, vestments, art work, and other ornaments. In a liturgical age his duties were central. In Valencia the office was established as soon as the city was conquered, the archdeacon and the sacristan being chosen from among the first canons.[82] A decree of June 1240 arranged for him to have 10 solidi from the first fruits and defunctions of the cathedral parish, plus supplementary salary to bring the total to 400 silver besants, a sum very soon increased to 600 besants.[83] Five years later the source of some of this supplementary salary is specified. It is to be taken from the first fruits and tithes of Ruzafa, Melilla, and Benimasot, and from the "rental pennies" which the bishop has in the capital. Half of this sum, however, was to be spent regularly for church furnishings (*ornamentis*).[84] The sacristan not unreasonably had the highest salary of anyone on the cathedral staff—considering the function alone—paying 400 solidi tithe in the annual taxation.[85]

The precentor or chancellor of the chapter dictated and sealed all the chapter's official documents. For the organization of the canonical choir and its liturgical assignments, he was the central authority. He was also responsible for education, procuring and examining schoolteachers, whence his alternate title *magister scholarum*. A statute of June 14, 1242 confirmed the arrangement for his salary in the recently formed chapter of Valencia: 300 silver besants a year from the bishop's own revenues, plus the first fruits of a parish to which he was to be appointed.[86] He paid tithes of 415 and 334 solidi respectively for the years 1279 and 1280.[87]

Within the cathedral body the dean was supreme. He officiated liturgically when the bishop was absent, had jurisdiction and a kind of court for disciplinary problems involving the canons, and in general acted as director and disciplinarian, as well as intermediate at times between bishop and pastor. Strangely enough, this office was not formally established until June 1260, thirty years after the fall of the capital, when the dignity was decreed and the revenues of the churches of Segorbe and Altura were attached to it.[88] Later, in September 1277, the revenues of four churches were substituted—Chelva, Tuéjar, Benagéber, and Sinarcas. To these were added the tithes of other churches such as Domeño, Andilla, Canales, Arcos, Aras de Alpuente, and Alpuente.[89] Nevertheless, an acting dean actually existed before this time, perhaps without status as a dignitary.[90] To the dignity of the deanery was annexed, as a gift from James of Jérica, the first fruits and two-thirds of the tithe for the castle and country of Domeño.[91] This had represented the local lord's own share from ecclesiastical taxation in that region. The dean's office or salary-tax is not included in the tithe lists of 1279–1280, because he himself was a tax collector for those years.[92]

Only one other dignitary need be considered, the archdeacon. At this moment in medieval history the archdeacon's office had attained its ripeness of power. He loomed in the diocese, "the bishop's eye," a figure of vague but sweeping powers, only less portentous than the bishop himself. After the conquest of Valencia he was the first dignitary chosen from the new chapter.[93] This functionary was usually not a priest,[94] nor properly active in the chapter; indeed, he was early warned away from interfering in the Valencian chapter.[95] Rather, he was a kind of alter ego of the bishop in his own archdeaconry, holding full jurisdiction, right of visitation, power to convoke synods, to approve new parishes, to collect taxes, to examine and present candidates for ordination, to impose discipline, to confer benefices, and to hold court for cases in his archdeaconry.

The "major" archdeacon was in the cathedral city. He was a much more significant figure than his rural peers like the archdeacon of Játiva. He lived directly behind the cathedral until about 1286, when his residence was changed to a building nearer the front. The southern or Játiva archdeaconry was planned by the authorities from the very beginning (January 1240); but, until that area was conquered, nothing could be done. The busy Bishop Arnold erected this lesser archdeaconry in mid-1248. Most of the revenues immediately around Játiva were assigned to it. The Játiva archdeacon was to provide clergy, give the care of souls, divide revenues, and so on.

In Valencia, as elsewhere at this time, the bishop and archdeacon came into conflict. According to the metropolitan's revision in 1242 of the first constitution drawn for the Valencian diocese, the archdeacon had rights of visitation and correction, receiving for this a modest payment as hospitality (*cena*). The bishop retained superior jurisdiction over all the churches.[96] Where legal jurisdiction could be delegated within the city the archdeacon was to receive it, appeal being allowed from him only to the bishop. This latter arrangement was a compromise designed to still the quarrels in the Valencian church; it was to cease upon the death of the incumbent archdeacon. The subsequent struggle in Valencia soon narrowed to two key complaints: the jealous exclusiveness with which Archdeacon Martin refused episcopal intervention in legal cases within his jurisdiction; and his determination to usurp the bishop's own legal powers during the latter's frequent absences. There were also side issues, such as the archdeacon's refusal to part with certain fines and his opposition to the bishop's having an Official or vicar in legal cases.

After a lengthy period of "quarrels and discord" the two parties submitted the case to the metropolitan, renouncing their rights of appeal. As elsewhere in Europe the bishop came out rather the better, securing the power of delegation of cases throughout the diocese of Valencia, an Official, and half the fines.[97] Still, the income for the function of archdeacon was alone tithed at 250 solidi per annum in the years to come.[98] The agreements at Játiva must have followed the Valencia pattern. A jurisdictional quarrel was settled by the metropolitan. At the close of King James's rule the diocese erected further archdeaconries at Alcira and Murviedro. It is interesting to note that Barcelona had but one archdeaconry throughout the thirteenth century, three more being added only in 1324.

There were moments of tension, some of them serious, between bishop and chapter. But in general their relations were amicably adjusted according to a series of agreements arrived at by the two parties and incorporated into laws. There were revenues held in common and annually divided between the two bodies according to the agreements; and there were properly episcopal and properly capitular holdings, to say nothing of individual properties. Thus, an occasional contact between the two corporations can be found in the archives.[99] The communal life of these first canons in Valencia was at a minimum, for each lived in his own house with his own retinue.[100] Each canon was probably expected to maintain a certain show of state, as was the case in contemporary England, out of his own pocket.

A fairly numerous aggregate of assistants was required by a chapter. The cathedral of Huesca at this time (from 1266), for example, had ten *portionarii*—four priests, three deacons, and three subdeacons; though not canons they assisted at the services and received a prebendal share of the cathedral revenues. There was also at Huesca a staff of "servitors" including bell-ringer, notary, teacher of grammar, and two choir boys "of docile nature and tuneful voice."[101] Valencia cathedral had such servitors from the beginning; provision is made for "all the servitors" in the revenue document of 1247.[102]

Most of the canons were probably not priests; four of the twenty at Huesca had to be so by a law of 1291. There was usually a numerous body of laymen employed by a chapter as administrators, tithe gatherers, bailiffs, and the like. A bailiff of the chapter of Valencia cathedral, receiving monies from the bishop, appears in 1255.[103] Several functions could be filled by a single man. The archdeacon of Valencia, for example, is listed three times in the crusade assessment of 1280: 23 solidi from his canon's portion, 260 from his salary as one of the ten overseers of revenue, and 248 from his own office. Similarly, the sacristan paid a total of 658 solidi from his functions as canon, overseer, and sacristan. The 1280 list gives almost thirty cathedral or episcopal functionaries by name, and a number of others anonymously.[104] In this list and that of 1279 special mention is made of a succentor (i.e. subcantor), two deacons, two subdeacons "of the diocese," two hebdomadarians, and by indirection a group of boys under the care of the school master. Some of the many entries were surely absentees; but they would be more than balanced by the minor functionaries exempt from contributions and from listing by reason of minimum income.

The personalities of the canons are less easily discerned than are their official selves. They included a decent scattering of academic men, and one illiterate. Of more significance, a large number of them were men of substance and importance. A closer examination of the individuals who comprised the chapter will emphasize this point. The names of most of them are known. During the brief reign of the first bishop (1240–1243), the following dignitaries and canons commonly appear in manuscripts: the archdeacon Master Martin of Entenza; the sacristan Arnold Piquer; the precentor Peter Dominic; Rudolph or Ralph Lemosin; Bertrand of Teruel; John Monzón; Matthew of Oteiza; Roderick Díaz; Bartholomew of Busquet or Boxadós; Master Bernard of Soler, Berengar of Targanova; Gerard or Gerald; Benedict of the Queen; Bernard of Vilar; Berengar the son of Raymond Vidal; and J. Vives.[105] About ten of these had been chosen and installed by the metropolitan, in the year after the fall of the city of Valencia.[106] Somewhat later (1245), in one of the more important documents of the early history of the diocese, the incomplete list of canons consists of ten of these sixteen names. Two years afterward (1247) a document formally arranging the collection of diocesan revenues lists nine of them, adding Gonzalvo Pérez.[107] There was also a Peter of Portugal in these early years, and several names or initials which are probably variants of those given.

These names appear again as the years pass, others gradually supplanting or supplementing them. Thus, Berengar of Boxadós is replaced as archdeacon of Játiva by William of Romaní before 1260; Peter Michael in turn succeeds him. Others in these middle years include Michael of Alcover, Peter Gomar canon and Official, Master William of Arbea, William of Arenys, and Benedict of Leduy. Forty years after the conquest of Valencia city, the names of many of the canons are inserted in the crusade-tithe lists (1279–1280): the archdeacon William of Alaric (succeeding Constantine), the sacristan James Albalat, the precentor Raymond of Morera or Morara (succeeding Peter Michael), the dean Raymond of Bellestar (succeeding James Sarroca), Peter Pérez of Tarazona, Dominic Matthew, Bertrand, Arnold of Rexach, Andrew, Benedict, Gerald of Albalat, Oliver, Pontilian (Garrígues), Master Ralph, Bernard of Vilar, Arnold Busquet, and Peter Cambrer.[108] To these should be added Master Vincent, William of Arenys, Nicholas of Hungary, and some others. Yet more names appear in the run of documents, men like the sacristan Peter of the King, the Valencia city archdeacon Bernard of Canet, the Alcira archdeacon Arnold of Riusech, and William of Mollet (canon in 1280, dean by 1299). Some men like Bernard of Vilar span the development of the chapter, in a continuing series of documents for decades.

Turning to individuals on these lists, one is further instructed as to their social origins. The lawyer James Sarroca, who was to advance to the dignity of dean, was able to buy castles and extensive properties, to accumulate benefices, and eventually to become the major power behind the throne in the declining years of James the Conqueror; he rose to be the king's royal secretary, favorite confidant, treasurer, and unofficial chancellor. Eventually he became bishop of Huesca.[109] Benedict of Leduy was a royal chaplain; he founded a chaplaincy by the purchase of properties bringing in over 200 solidi annually. Giles Garcés of Azagra, son of a crusading baron, and canon of Valencia just after mid-century, purchased two towns for 4,000 morabatins in 1258 and received from the king in 1260 Perpunchent castle.[110] Arnold of Rexach was chaplain to the prince; he was to become archdeacon of Játiva and a bishop.[111]

The sacristan William of Alaric once made a loan to the prince of 1,000 solidi of Jaca. He and his retainers were to cause a disgraceful tumult in Gerona (1262). He collected the bovage of the realm in 1280 for the king, and his brother James acted in 1259 as crown bailiff of Almenara. The James of Alaric sent by King James as ambassador to the khan of the Mongols may be his brother; if so, both are from a wealthy burgher family of Perpignan.[112] Peter of the King, holder of a second canonry at Lérida and prior of St. Vincent's, was probably an illegitimate brother of King James.[113] William of Romaní, archdeacon of Játiva, seems to be a member of the powerful knightly family of that name in Valencia. Nicholas of Hungary may well have been a royal in-law, and he had financial dealings with the king's son.[114]

Gonzalvo Pérez, canon (for example in 1247), then capiscol (by 1254), then city archdeacon (by 1256), was the brother of the knight Roderick Pérez; he was secretary to the king since before 1250. He continued to exercise this latter office at Lérida and elsewhere, even after he became archdeacon. He also acquired the dignity of the archdeaconry of Calatayud. He was a custodian of Murviedro castle, was named by King James to arbitrate a dispute between Aragon and Castile, and appears as one of two executors and presumably friends in the last will of the great baron Simon Pérez of Arenós. In a document of 1268, he gave to the son of that baron as a gift "my castle of Alventosa located in the kingdom of Valencia" including all the revenues, jurisdiction, and inhabitants he controlled there. An unabashed pluralist, he later became bishop of Sigüenza.[115]

Martin of Entenza, the first archdeacon of Valencia, was chancellor to Prince Alphonse. From the prince he received as a gift the town and castle of Foyos in Valencia. He also had a crown subsidy of 1,000 solidi a year to be taken from the saltworks. One finds him in various places and times as a signatory to important public documents, as at the treaty of Almizra in 1244 and at the pact between the king and the prince at Biar in 1254. He founded two benefices at the Valencia cathedral in 1252, and seems to have died around 1257. He was related to the future archdeacon Gonzalvo Pérez, and also to King James.[116] The archdeacon Constantine seems to have been a friend of the king; James thus refers to him when granting Constantine's nephew the secretariat of a town in Aragon.[117] Even the illiteracy of Roderick Díaz, in the position of canon, smacks more of the influential knight than of the deserving cleric.[118]

The canon Peter Michael in 1258 was able to buy houses and shops in Valencia city to the value of 1,000 solidi; and he purchased privately a former Moslem cemetery. He was precentor at least by 1270, and with others represented the king in a financial suit involving 100,000 solidi. He finished by becoming archdeacon of Játiva.[119] Master Vincent also held the office of precentor of Majorca; Matthew of Oteiza was also archpriest of Teruel; and Berengar of Soler was a papal subdeacon as well as notary to the king.[120] Gerald of Albalat had the name of a most prominent family. Michael of Alcover was a notary in the service of Bishop Andrew, in the latter's office of chancellor to the king; as such Bishop Andrew had him drawing up official documents at least from 1245 to 1259 at various places in the king's realms.[121]

Bertrand of Teruel left a last testament revealing something of his background and character. A wealthy man of the warrior class whose business instincts had led him to gather varied estates in the new realm, he bequeathed "my castle at Espioca"; "my armor"; "all my vineyards"; "my converted slave," whom he frees; "my red horse"; "all my arms"; 3,600 solidi for the establishment of a chantry, naming his nephew to the post; his wine cellar;

2,500 solidi to the Dominicans; many buildings and corrals; and so on.[122] A number of lesser names in the lists have a knightly ring to them, though evidence to confirm this impression is lacking.[123]

Peter Pérez of Tarazona was the brother of Roderick Pérez and the son of the justiciar of Aragon; he was thus directly connected with the most influential single baron of that province or kingdom. He seems to have been among the first canons named, and to have died about 1280. He held a number of estates and houses, some of the latter fronting upon the cathedral in Valencia city. In his last testament of 1279 he disposed of properties to the value of 15,000 solidi; he also left 4,000 solidi for a cathedral chaplaincy, his brother Roderick to hold the patronage. Items include 400 solidi for a fine tomb, and 200 for books and other gifts to another brother.[124]

All this evidence leads to the suspicion that the higher clergy of Valencia suffered under the blight of "feudalization," with the avaricious families of knightly or high burgher status crowding into the positions of prestige and power. This would be in keeping with the general trend in Europe at the time. Many churches as a result held a majority of nonpriests in the chapter, men who kept a door open for a good marriage in the family interest or for a return to secular life.[125] Valencia too may have been a dumping ground for friends of the mighty, who could thus confer the rewards of friendship with the powerful at the expense of the church and to the loss of the community.

Numbers of the canons may well have been absentees, delegating their liturgical responsibilities to vicars. It is difficult for instance to find documents in which all the canons are at Valencia. During the arrangements for the election of a new bishop in 1248, those of the canons "who were then on hand" were present.[126] When the canon and the royal notary Michael of Alcover lay dying, he was in Tortosa and had to make provision for one of his two "animals" to carry his corpse to Valencia.[127]

Since so much documentation has survived in the cathedral archives, it would be relatively easy to compile a directory of these canons and dignitaries from 1238 to 1280. The analytical survey just given will probably be more suggestive. It is not a heartening thing to contemplate, this capture of ecclesiastical influence by the class of men whose interests and mentality ought rather to have been curbed and instructed by that counterbalancing authority. One suspects that the result was to clothe the status quo in the garments of pious respectability.

Still, considered as an element in the assimilation of the frontier, such a body of men must have been invaluable. They gave many a feudal family a stake in the pioneer community. They brought the energy, talents, and social connection of their class to the task at hand. And they could deal as equals with the turbulent or selfish knights of the new realm, since few of them could be dismissed as "a clerk and a base person."[128] Conversely, the frontier offered to king and prelate a golden opportunity to reward service or merit; so that a number of admirable figures, like James Sarroca, brought some energies to bear upon this far corner, when otherwise the ecclesiastical organization might have lacked their contribution. And, at the most conspicuous level of canonical life, the daily service of the altar, the chapter with its accompanying assistants would have had a continuing impact upon the local population.

III

NEIGHBORS, AND INTRUDERS

Above the Valencian bishop stood his metropolitan, the archbishop of Tarragona. This subordination bypassed the claims of the Toledo primate to be metropolitan over the new conquest. James had cannily reserved Valencia to his own Aragonese metropolitanate as early as 1228, when the Moslems still ruled the whole kingdom of Valencia from end to end. The king had formalized this connection early in the crusade, in a document drawn up at Lérida in 1236.[1] King James had no authority at all for assigning the diocese to a given metropolitan. He had ample reasons of state, but the reasons he gave in the document were more discreetly drawn from motives of gratitude and charity.

∞ THE METROPOLITAN FOUNDS HIS DIOCESE

The bishop of Valencia soon promised obedience to the metropolitan.[2] Under the presidency of the metropolitan the suffragan bishops of the province, including the new bishop of Valencia, would meet regularly in the springtime at an annual council to discuss common problems (nineteen times in the thirteenth century).[3] The metropolitan also enjoyed some authority over a suffragan's people but only in areas clearly defined by law.[4]

How extensive this authority could be, however, can be seen by the results of the metropolitan visitation of Valencia early in 1242. A surprising range of diocesan policies seems to have come under scrutiny on that occasion, and important corrections were introduced.[5] Most of the decisions have as common denominators jurisdiction, revenues, and liturgy. But they also touch upon the parishes, the powers of the archdeacon, the schools, divine services, and diocesan and parochial boundaries.

The preparation and inception of the crusade against Valencia owed much to the metropolitan Spargo Barca (1215–1233), a relative of the king.[6] Subsequently, during the earlier stage of the crusade, the metropolitan was William of Montgrí (1234–1238) a good man "of no great lineage," conqueror of Ibiza and Formentera. He is always referred to as "elect," apparently because he was never confirmed by Rome and perhaps not even consecrated. It was to William that King James in 1235 made his promise to unite Valencia, when conquered, to Tarragona. In 1238 William renounced his prelacy, though he retained other dignities and lived on until 1273.[7]

His successor was the capable Peter of Albalat (1238–1251). As bishop of Lérida (from 1236), he had created a diocesan inquisition and had played a prominent role in the ecclesiastical affairs of the newly conquered Balearics. As metropolitan he contributed five thousand silver marks, a goodly contingent of knights, and his personal services to the crusade against Valencia. He began the organization of the Valencia diocese and did more than any man to keep the Castilian church from securing metropolitan jurisdiction over it. Peter multiplied provincial councils; the first of his ten councils was occasioned by the Castilian claims to the Valencia diocese. He also took an active part in the ecumenical council at Lyons in 1243. His brother Andrew was bishop of Valencia during the critical decades from 1248 to 1276.[8]

Next came Benedict of Rocaberti (1252–1268), a Catalan noble of rowdy temperament.[9] A considerable portion of his energies Benedict devoted to quarreling with his chapter and with King James. He led an armed assault against the chapter in a spectacularly scandalous episode (1256), and frightened away the papal legate sent to investigate; all parties were summoned to Rome where a settlement was imposed (1260). The tumultuous archbishop in crusading mood also dispatched a fleet against King James's ally, the Moslem king of Tunis, who promptly sued for damages. This latter affair was settled by papal arbitration in 1259, the three commissioners including the bishop of Valencia. After a long delay, Benedict was succeeded by a Mercedarian, previously bishop of Tortosa, Bernard of Olivella (1272–1287).[10]

As far back as 1228, King James had prudently granted any future diocesan rights in the Valencian region, under the titles of Denia and Orihuela, to the bishop of Barcelona. On that occasion he had pointedly warned away any other "archbishop or primate" from establishing a diocese there. It was hardly a needless gesture. Toledo had been keeping a wary eye upon Denia and seems to have appointed some titular bishops both to that see and to Valencia.[11] Besides, Toledo had been the active agent behind Jerome of Périgord who had been briefly bishop of Valencia under the Cid and who had died less than a century ago (1125).

The king's choice of Denia and Orihuela, both situated considerably to the south of the city of Valencia, might at first seem singular. Underlying it was an ancient concession (1058), by which the Moslem ruler of Denia entrusted the supervision of Christian affairs in his kingdom to the bishop of Barcelona. It was now possible to argue, as the Aragonese were to do in court in 1239, that the more southerly jurisdiction included the intervening space.[12] Moreover, in Visigothic Spain there had been dioceses of Valencia, Játiva, and Denia, where James meant to plant only the diocese of Valencia; a title to one could be evolved therefore into a title to more.

As for the jurisdiction going to the bishop of Barcelona, the Aragonese crown could say that "at the time, he acted as representative of the ruined and abandoned [metropolitan] church of Tarragona."[13] The Denia king's concession had involved the Balearics; King James's recent conquest of those islands further strengthened his claims to Valencia. The Moslem privilege was at least useful as indicating prescriptive rights during Mozarabic times; as a legal title it needed the support of King James's independent grant, based on his *ius patronatus*.[14]

During the crusade the dispute between the metropolitans of Toledo and of Tarragona—respectively Roderick Simon of Rada and Peter of Albalat—smoldered warmly. It burst out now and again into legalistic acts of jurisdiction by each side, aimed at establishing legal precedents. When the city of Valencia fell, bitter scenes ensued between the two powers.

Even before the king and queen made their formal entry into Valencia, the bishop of Albarracín had slipped into the city with his clerics as representing the archbishop of Toledo. He chanted vespers "loudly" in the main mosque, and hastily purified and consecrated it. "Who told him to do that?" exclaimed the archbishop of Tarragona. "Curse him! What right had he coming here?" Albarracín had also appropriated St. Michael's, inside the walls, where he offered the first Mass in the conquered city and pursued a busy course of baptism, marriage, burial, installation of rector, and the like before ever the bemused metropolitan could forestall him. In an access of silliness, the metropolitan laid St. Michael's under interdict. After the bishop of Albarracín had taken leave of Valencia later, his work for the claims of Toledo accomplished, the archdeacon of the city caused his altar to be pulled down, and his resident cleric Justus hauled forcibly out into the street. These demonstrations had gone on since the beginning of the crusade. They reached their climax at the cathedral shortly after the conquest, when a Toledo cleric "snatched a missal from the altar" and was treated rather roughly.[15]

The metropolitan had retaliated grimly in kind. He locked the door of the main mosque so that at least the first Mass might be his own. Then he made up for lost time, occupying himself "in the church and out of it, in affairs temporal and spiritual, among the clergy and laity." He already had his clerics collecting offerings for the making of altars and other furnishings, and he had overseen the placing of the altar. "It doesn't look good here," John the Painter was later to recall the metropolitan fussing, "put it in that other place."[16]

The Tarragona prelate had busied himself in the choice of a bishop-elect even "before the city surrendered." There being no chapter as yet, he had held a meeting of the suffragan bishops to whom he joined the Franciscans and Dominicans.[17] His choice was also of course the king's.[18] Berengar had been "the most honored among your [the king's] eminent personages."[19] It is to the credit of King James, however, that he did not install in the see of Valencia some relative. His contemporary King Saint

Ferdinand, with less wisdom, fondly put his son into the episcopate of the conquered city of Seville, at first as procurator since he was too young to be ordained; King Ferdinand even seems to have delayed endowing his diocese as pressure to insure the success of his plan.[20]

Within Valencia the metropolitan, rather than the bishop-elect, took the lead. With his suffragans he "ceremonially purified" and consecrated the main mosque on Saturday, the day of formal entry; he chanted Mass the following morning.[21] His consecration of the cathedral did not consist in the farcical scene described by later chroniclers of Valencia, where the king and his armies set about smashing the Arabic carvings, finishing with a benediction.[22] The contemporary manner of consecration is described at some length by the Dominican James of Varazze, archbishop of Genoa (1298), in the closing chapter of his *Readings on the Saints*. It involved a hallowing both of altar and of church. The first consisted in tracing crosses on the four corners of the altar with holy water, then circling and sprinkling it seven times, burning incense upon it, anointing it, and spreading linens over it.

As for the cathedral building, the archbishop circled it three times processionally. Each time he stopped to knock on the main door. Then he sprinkled it inside and out with holy water, made a pattern of cross and letters in sand and ashes upon the floor, and, painting crosses upon the wall, anointed them and lit candles before them. All this took place along with appropriate prayers and solemn chants. The ceremonies were freighted with liturgical symbolism, as well as with added strata of popular symbolism, as Bishop James narrates at tedious length. Reminiscences of these ceremonies may be found in the testimony of the Valencian witnesses during the trial between Tarragona and Toledo over Valencia.[23]

The metropolitan next proceeded to set up a chapter, amidst petitions of benefice-hunting clerics.[24] He appointed for the diocese, "as much as the Christians held," rectors and parishes.[25] Then he was off around the city, with assisting bishops and auxiliaries, personally to "make mosques into churches and . . . decide parish boundaries for them." One crusader later recalled going along with the metropolitan at this parochial delimitation, "showing him the places and advising him."[26] All the rectors of the city now made formal submission to him as metropolitan (in which capacity he was careful to perform his activities), and also as bishop until confirmation could come from Rome for consecrating their own.

An ecclesiastical court was set up and a full calendar of cases briskly attended to. The crusaders seem to have carried a store of church furnishings with them. A bell was hung in a church, and vestments blessed.[27] Rectors inside and outside the city were installed in their parish churches, each with the proper documentation. Enthusiastic crowds witnessed all this. "So thick was the mob" at the election of Castellbisbal that one witness "was unable to get close" enough to be sure of the details. Well-wishers and petitioners swarmed about the metropolitan in these first days, "kissing his hand, and asking favors from him, and requesting benefices from him, and carrying out his orders."[28]

Castellbisbal, candidate or bishop-elect, seems to have been only a figurehead, a part of the legal furniture being frantically shifted into place before the question of diocesan ownership could reach the courts. He soon drops from view, probably having returned to Barcelona where he was prior of the Dominican house; his designation as bishop was either quietly forgotten, or possibly annulled as uncanonical in view of Tarragona's lack of clear title. In 1229 James had tried to make him bishop of conquered Majorca[29] but had been balked. His reward came in 1245 when he was named bishop of the important see of Gerona. Meanwhile, the metropolitan of Tarragona, Peter of Albalat, turned to other affairs, including the trial over Valencia being held at Tudela in Navarre, which he personally attended late in 1239. His *locum tenens* was Ferrer of Pallarés, archdeacon for twenty years past at the metropolitan see and dean of its chapter.[30]

The childish tug-of-war between Toledo and Tarragona did not ease until the spring of 1239, when Pope Gregory IX, having heard the arguments of both sides, instituted a commission to investigate. This commission was either to settle affairs definitively or else to choose a suitable candidate. Gregory feared "lest a lengthy vacancy hurt" the "newly planted church which requires meticulous solicitude."[31] As a result, Valencia had no proper bishop for over two years.

‡ THE NORTH: THE DIOCESE OF TORTOSA

Attention has been concentrated thus far on the diocese of Valencia. This is understandable, since it was the only frontier diocese organizing itself in the new kingdom. The tiny Segorbe diocese was an abortive organism. And Tortosa, covering much of the northern part of the kingdom, was only partly a Valencian or frontier diocese. Some attention nevertheless must be paid to the diocese of Tortosa.

Tortosa represented an earlier frontier, reconquered and tamed now for some time; its diocesan institutions had been developing for nearly a century (from 1148). From its beginning, however, it had been looking to Moslem Valencia as an area into which to expand. Several reasons lie behind this. As a diocese small and relatively less settled, it desired more resources. As a recently consolidated frontier, it held a livelier crusade tradition as well as a more immediate responsibility for its neighbor Valencia. Finally, it could logically claim all the area in the Valencia kingdom formerly comprising the Moslem "kingdom" of Tortosa.

This last point deserves reflection. It explains why the dividing line with the Valencia diocese fell as it did. The northern Valencian area, in short, had nuances of development and history which set it apart. These differences probably rested on deeper and more ancient foundations than the passing political connection with the kingdom of Tortosa. Ramón Menéndez Pidal, studying the linguistic evolution of the Christian kingdom of Valencia, was struck by the sharply defined difference even of dialect between the north and the south. He could not explain it; he could only proclaim the fact, insisting that "by an inexplicable coincidence, it is the ecclesiastical jurisdiction[s] which correspond in this region to the linguistic frontiers."[32] Actually the Tortosa–Valencia diocesan line was the old southwestern frontier of the Moslem Tortosa kingdom.[33] As early as 1151 the bishop of Tortosa had called for restoration to his new diocese of all the land which had ever belonged to Moslem Tortosa. King Alphonse I spoke of the "ancient limits" as including areas like Nules and Onda. In 1178 Alphonse encouraged the Tortosa diocese with some Valencian pre-grants including the castles and territories of Miravet (near Cabanes) and Zufera.[34]

Bishop Ponce of Tortosa subsequently assisted in financing the risky earlier stages of the crusade. He was present in armored person at the unfortunate first attack against Peñíscola in 1225. Here young King James in gratitude confirmed and extended the pre-grant.[35] Bishop Ponce was active during the hard fighting of the crusade, at the sieges of Burriana and Valencia city; again he won substantial gifts for his diocese.[36] King James appreciated both the physical sacrifices ("more than our other realms" undergo),[37] and the real need of the diocese for ampler territory. The end result was a broadly sited diocese, based along the seashore from the Almenara country in the south (the present provincial boundary for Castellón and Valencia) up to Pratdip just below Reus in Catalonia.

Did diocesan reorganization progress in the Tortosan section of the realm much as it did in the south? Aside from the obvious differences to be expected in this case of an already functioning diocese undergoing an expansion, there were other important changes in the pattern. It is possible that the Moslems in the north retreated almost en masse out of the country. If this is true, the economic loss in seignorial tithes alone would have been considerable; the psychological position of the Christian authorities, faced with an empty rather than a hostile land, would also have been different from that in the diocese of Valencia. This thesis of mass emigration, though strongly defended, is at best debatable.[38] More to the point, anyway, is the slow rate of Christian settlement. Early large-scale replacement of Moslems with Christians took place only at conquered Burriana on the coast and in the mountain-fief of Morella held by Blaise of Alagón. Elsewhere the pace of settlement was slow. The main resettlement will be in the southern diocese.[39]

The nature of the land in the north encouraged the king to block out great areas for magnates and religious Orders. The exploitation and re-settlement would therefore resemble the Castilian pattern in Andalusia rather than the small-holder or scattered pattern in the Valencia diocese. Blocks of land went to the Hospitallers in the northwest and to the Templars below them, for example, with sizable estates to other religious groups like St. Vincent's and Benifasá. There was considerable activity here in sheep raising.[40] There was more in the way of resettlement projects than the Orders are commonly credited with. The churches of such areas, however, came under the patronage and administration of the Orders. The bishops of Tortosa would fight for their share of tithes and jurisdiction; but much of the direction including the building of churches fell to the Orders. This complex socio-administrative background helps explain why Tortosan documenta-tion for Valencia is relatively scanty and the episcopal activity sluggish.

The Tortosa diocese had but three bishops during this entire period.[41] Ponce of Torella ruled from 1213 to 1254. He was active in the crusade, assisted at provincial councils, presided over the sudden expansion of his diocese into Valencia, and reorganized the canonical regime at his cathedral. With a supporting bull from the pope (1235) he struggled to retain the lands given to the diocese. Above all, he fought to protect his rights in the huge areas controlled by Orders. The next bishop was a Mercederian who had been archdeacon at the cathedral; he was in office until 1270 when he be-came metropolitan of Tarragona. As bishop he carried to a successful con-clusion the fight with the Orders and others for tithes. As metropolitan he crowned James's son Peter king of Aragon.

Arnold of Jardí took his place in Tortosa (1272–1306). He is especially known for his work in codifying the celebrated feudal *costums* of Tortosa. He presided over the reformatory synods of 1274 and 1278, the earliest recorded medieval synods for this diocese. These bishops of Tortosa, be-sides delimiting the Valencian section of their diocese, planting parishes, building churches, and vindicating claims, had to work out an equitable distribution of the new Valencian revenues with their chapter. This com-plicated argument was finally arbitrated by the metropolitan in 1250 and 1266, with further adjustments in 1287.[42] The diocese also arranged settle-ments in Cabanes (1243) and Benlloc (1250).[43]

∞ ALARUMS AND EXCURSIONS: A DIOCESE OF SEGORBE

A diocese was like a kingdom. It might be strong or weak, wealthy or poor, large or small. The diocese of Valencia, called into being on the fron-tier, with ambitions beyond its primitive means, begrudged from the be-ginning any substantial diminution of its territory. Nor was there really any need to return to the multiple Valencian dioceses of the less developed Visigothic church. These were practical considerations. Underlying them

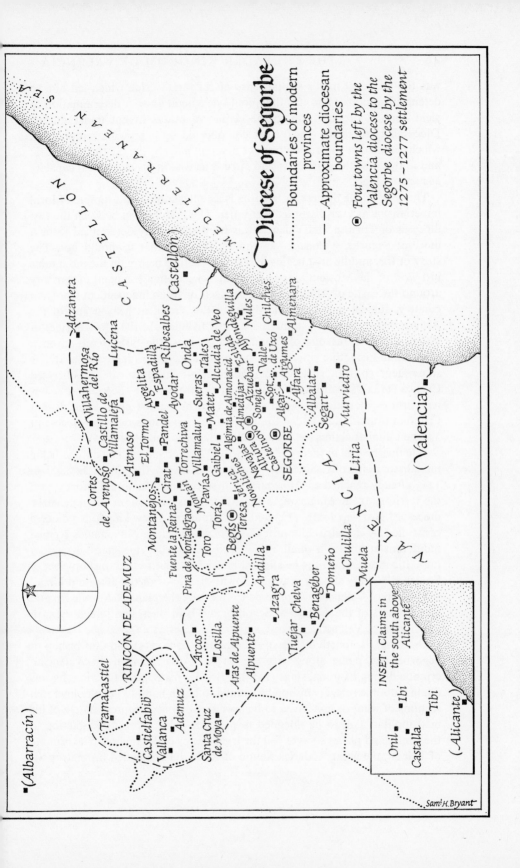

Diocese of Segorbe

.... Boundaries of modern provinces

– – – Approximate diocesan boundaries

◉ Four towns left by the Valencia diocese to the Segorbe diocese by the 1275–1277 settlement

MEDITERRANEAN SEA

CASTELLÓN

(Albarracín)

Adzaneta
Villahermosa del Rio
Castillo de Villamalefa
Lucena
Arenoso
Cortes de Arenoso
El Tormo Argelita Espadilla Ribesalbes (Castellón)
Pandel Ayodar Onda
Cirat Tales
Montanejos Torrechiva Sueras Alcudia de Veo
Fuente la Reina Montán Villamalur Matet Eslida Alfondeguilla
Pina de Montalgrao Pavías Gaibel Algimia de Almonacid Nules
Toro Torás Argimes Almenara
Begís Navajas Almedíjar Valle de Uxó Chilches
Teresa Jérica Altura Soneja Alfara
Novaliches Castelnovo Azuébar Algar Albalat
Andilla SEGORBE Segart
Azagra Murviedro
Tuéjar Chelva Liria
Benagéber Domeño
Losilla Chulilla
Arcos Muela
Aras de Alpuente
Alpuente
RINCÓN DE ADEMUZ
Tramacastiel
Castielfabib
Vallanca
Ademuz
Santa Cruz de Moya

VALENCIA

(Valencia)

INSET: Claims in the south above Alicante

Omil
Ibi
Castalla
Tibi
(Alicante)

Saml H. Bryant

was the medieval man's strong sense of corporate pride which led him to defend his diocese; and this duty could degenerate into a determination to yield neither jot nor tittle to the claims of others except under duress. Diocesan chauvinism was further complicated by a growing nationalism, which resented any intrusion into the new conquest by the Castilian primate; and in this case the primate would intrude as well in his more local capacity as metropolitan.

The case of the diocese of Segorbe is as entertaining an example of local imperialisms as ever disrupted a frontier. The middle area between the two dioceses of Tortosa and Valencia was itself stubbornly determined to be a diocese: Segorbe. Valencia was equally resolved that it should not. The story of this middle area begins over half a century before, in the mountains just west of the Moslem kingdom of Valencia. Here a fragment of territory around the castle of Albarracín had set itself up as an independent Christian country, subject only to the lordship of the Virgin in heaven and of the Azagra family on earth—though discreetly tributary to the Moslem ruler of Valencia.[44] For reasons of morale and politics, the bishop was given a traditional Visigothic title by his metropolitan, the primate at Toledo. A subsequent shift in ecclesiastical boundaries sent this title to liberated Cuenca (1182), substituting for it the equally traditional "Segobriga." Contemporaries identified this latter with Segorbe on the coast. The distant Castilian primate thus added to his metropolitan claims over the diocese of Valencia similar claims to "the church of Segorbe and of Jérica."[45]

Whether he was in theory right or wrong, the prelate of Toledo was being unrealistic politically. Since the Tortosa diocese by the gift of James I in 1233 already reached to Almenara, and since Valencia would shortly gain the territory from Almenara to Biar, there was little room for a Segorbe diocese.[46] Nor was James prepared to tolerate in his new kingdom a diocese controlled by a metropolitan in Castile. Nevertheless, King James seemed indifferent at first to a small Toledan diocese in the Valencian hills; in an impolitic moment in 1235 he allowed himself to refer to the "bishop-elect of Segorbe."[47] Very shortly, however, "with the favor of the aforesaid king," the bishop of Valencia will proceed to "occupy the place of Murviedro and many others of the diocese of Segorbe, and held them and joined them to the diocese of Valencia."[48]

Dominic, the fourth bishop of Albarracín (1223–1235) and thus bishop of Segorbe, had come along with the lord of Albarracín on the Valencian crusade during its initial stage (1233).[49] Besides his warrior function, he was filling a double role. As bishop he wanted to be on hand to acquire liberated sections of what he conceived to be his diocese; and as representative of his metropolitan Toledo he intended to perform public acts of jurisdiction in the conquered places so as to foil the legal claims of Tarragona. The primate of Toledo, the great Roderick Simon of Rada, had extended his metropolitan jurisdiction vastly by insisting that ancient sees, when liberated, be returned to their primitive jurisdiction.[50] At the fall of Burriana, Bishop Dominic of Segorbe made gestures of taking ecclesiastical possession for Toledo. Similarly, he took care to offer the first Mass said in conquered Almenara and Olocau.

His successor, William (ca. 1235–1237), was determined to make good his title to Segorbe and its surrounding Valencian lands. Apparently at William's initiative, Pope Gregory IX wrote urging King Ferdinand of Castile to help William recover Segorbe from the Moslems. In another letter the pope requested alms for Segorbe from the prelates of Castile—"such help [that] he be not forced to beg, to the dishonor of the episcopal office" (1236).[51] Help of a dramatic nature came from another quarter. The ex-king of Valencia Saʿīd, under his new Christian name Vincent and in virtue of his *ius patronatus* as a conquering ally of James I, granted the Visigothic diocese of Segorbe to William.

In a document drawn in 1236 in the presence of the lord of Albarracín, Saʿīd specified the towns rounding out the central Segorbe grant: Arenoso, Montán and Castielmontán, Tormo de Cirat, Fuente la Reina, Villamalur, Castillo de Villamalefa, Villahaleva [Villahermosa?], Cirat, Ayódar, Arcos, Bordelos [?], and Bueynegro; off toward the coast, Onda, Nules, Uxó, and Almenara; and, to the south, Alpuente, Cardelles [Canales?], Andilla, Tuéjar, Chelva, Domeño, Chulilla, Liria, and Murviedro. Essentially this grant conveyed the towns of the Mijares and Palancia river valleys all the way to the coast, and the towns of the Guadalaviar Valley down to Liria almost at the gates of Valencia. It put squarely in the center of James's proposed kingdom a Toledan diocese in the shape of an egg or flattened wheel with the town of Segorbe as its hub.[52] The response of King James, toward the end of this same year, was a declaration subjecting all the Valencian conquest past and future to the metropolitan overrule of the archbishop of Tarragona.

The stage was set for a battle royal, though King James's town of Segorbe itself, solidly Moslem, was to remain without Christian church or presence for another decade. Bishop William's successor, Simon (1238–1243), immediately armed himself with another grant from Saʿīd reconfirming four strategic towns in the upper Guadalaviar Valley (Alpuente, Tuéjar, Domeño, and Azagra). Bishop Simon also had played a prominent part in the critical stages of the crusade. He helped at the long siege of Valencia city and signed the document of capitulation. During the siege he took care to offer the first Mass at St. Vincent's, a celebrated shrine in the suburbs. He has been described already, challenging the metropolitan of Tarragona both in the army and later inside the conquered city at St. Michael's church. He countered indulgence with indulgence, prayer with prayer, burial with burial.[53] King James awarded him the usual estates given to barons and warrior prelates, but turned a blind eye to his jurisdictional claims.

Simon appealed to Rome. In reply, Gregory IX set up a commission of three Castilian archdeacons in May 1239 to investigate the region by personal visit; they were to draw up a boundary for the diocese of Segorbe. The pope also dispatched a stern letter to the king of Aragon, sympathizing with Simon's sufferings, and another letter to the barons of Aragon.[54] Five years of near silence ensue. In 1242 there seems to be an echo of the dispute, when the Tarragona metropolitan takes special care to single out the Murviedro area, on the occasion of his first formal visitation of the Valencia diocese, declaring that the Murviedro churches belong fully to the bishop of Valencia "just as the other churches of his diocese belong to him."[55] But, on the whole, the Segorbe affair seems to have been temporarily shelved. Most probably this was because the principals were devoting themselves to the larger struggle between the Toledo and Tarragona metropolitans for control of the diocese of Valencia. Obviously the Segorbe question could be settled easily if Toledo won.

This larger quarrel seems to have ended in a negotiated victory for James of Aragon in the spring of 1244. The forces of Segorbe were isolated and thrown on the defensive by this outcome. In 1244, moreover, the secular lordship of the Segorbe region passed by arrangement from Saʿīd or Vincent and his Moslems to become crown property. James I subinfeuded the area, in effect preparing it for Christian settlement.[56] In the light of these developments, the latest bishop of Segorbe apparently felt it necessary to regain the initiative. It seemed logical to attempt to take possession of his city. But the city of Segorbe boasted only three Christian residents in 1245. The first ringing of the church bells roused the Moslems to fury; they rioted and drove the bishop out.[57] To make the bishop's discomfiture complete, Saʿīd in February 1246 revoked the gift of many of the Segorbe towns. By this time King James seems to have acquired a conqueror's title to other Segorbe towns by having had to reconquer them himself.[58]

The latest in the line of hapless bishops of Segorbe, the Cistercian Peter (ca. 1246–1271), appealed to Rome.[59] Pope Innocent IV came to his defense with a strong letter to King James and another to the barons of Aragon and Castile (April 1247).[60] In the same month Innocent presented the bishop with a most important document, confirming him in the possession of Segorbe. And the pope busily set up a new commission to arrange boundaries for a Segorbe diocese. He also sent a bull approving Peter's election as bishop of Segorbe and Albarracín. Peter took heart. He traveled down to Segorbe. There he purified a mosque for use as a cathedral and began alterations (November 1247). He also gave attention to a church of St. Peter in the suburbs, created an archdeaconry of Alpuente, looked into tithe questions, and busily set about building a diocese.[61]

This was too much for Bishop Arnold Peralta of Valencia, a man who enjoyed a personality "algo bellicosa."[62] His legal appeals to the *ius patro-*

natus of King James and his denial of the identity of Segorbe with ancient *Segobriga* had failed to impress Rome. If ever he was to vindicate his claim to the upper Guadalaviar Valley, some direct action was indicated. Early in 1248, enveloped by a clutch of supporting clergy and armed retainers, Arnold stormed up to Segorbe. Peter fled to his little cathedral where he locked himself in. The indecorous scene which ensued is vividly described by Pope Innocent IV in his letter of rebuke (April 22, 1248). Bishop Arnold rode in "with hostility"; proceeded to "break down the doors in sacrilegious defiance"; and offended the Segorbe prelate "with many insults and contumelies". Finally, "unmindful of episcopal decency," he "violently laid hands" upon Bishop Peter and "maliciously threw him out of the church"—along with the cross to which he continued to cling. The bishop's residence was then plundered.[63]

Such interludes of violence were not unprecedented in that vigorous age. A few years later (1256), the metropolitan of Tarragona was to head a band of retainers into his own cathedral on Holy Saturday, breaking up the services with an unseemly brawl. Then, having collected a modest army of rioters, he returned crying out angrily that he would kill all the canons. He directed his crew as they broke down the choir doors with a log, forced the dormitory entrance, and set the canons scattering with a fair amount of bloodshed. Expressing his hearty satisfaction, the prelate then decamped. By an irony of history Valencia's bellicose Bishop Arnold, by that time transferred to Zaragoza, was present in the city of Tarragona during this tumult.[64]

Civil authorities stood aloof in Segorbe as Bishop Arnold of Valencia retook almost all the churches of the upper Palancia and Guadalaviar valleys by direct military action. King James had his own problems at the time, since the great Moslem revolt was under way in the kingdom of Valencia. Poor Bishop Peter of Segorbe had to flee back to Albarracín and appeal to the pope again. Innocent IV bade the king restore Peter to his see (April 1248); then he instituted a commission to go to the kingdom of Valencia to investigate the violence and require satisfaction from Bishop Arnold. "We do not want to leave such viciousness unpunished, lest others imitate its example."[65] An excommunication, reserved to the Holy See, was about to descend upon the hasty Arnold's head.

Despite Rome's severity toward Arnold, the bishop of Valencia has his defenders today. Sanchís Sivera, for example, refusing to yield an inch in the defense of his diocese, sees only Arnold's "zeal for the glory of God and sanctification of souls, and the prudence displayed in all his episcopal governance." He flatly rejects the papal letter as a forgery, for no better reason than that it is housed in the Segorbe archives. Warming to his subject, he even comes to suspect that Rome had previous knowledge of Arnold's intentions and occultly approved what was about to happen. Diocesan loyalty can hardly go further.

Arnold had his contemporary defenders as well. Not for nothing had platoons of lawyers been returning from Bologna's lecture halls these many years. A countersuit by Valencia was tabled at Rome. On February 24 of the new year, the bishop and chapter established "you, P. William, rector of the church of Carayana, as our agent" at Rome.[66] Further to confuse the issue, Arnold was transferred to the important see of Zaragoza (1248), which had fortuitously fallen vacant. Moreover, the metropolitan of James's realms (who happened to be the brother of the new bishop of Valencia) in a fit of family loyalty excommunicated the bishop of Segorbe for persisting in episcopal gestures. Almost reflexively by now, one would think, Peter appealed to Rome. Pope Innocent demanded that the metropolitan and the bishop of Valencia plead their case before him within three months.[67] But the pens of the lawyers only moved the faster.

By 1258 the new Pope Alexander IV seems to have lost patience. He ordered King James "to see that everything is given back which [Peter] complains he was despoiled of by the aforesaid bishop and archdeacon."[68] For Pope Alexander the case seemed to be closed. He set up a commission of dignitaries who were to cite the bishops of Valencia, Tortosa, and Zaragoza to a hearing on the precise boundaries of the diocese of Segorbe. He soon acceded also to an appeal from Bishop Peter, that Segorbe and Albarracín be established perpetually as two distinct yet inseparable episcopates; they would share a single bishop, chapter, customs, and privileges (1259).[69]

Even King James retreated before the vigorous papal actions. James composed a heartfelt and petulant defense of his own past activities, being careful to explain to Alexander that he had really obeyed papal directives on Segorbe but had become confused at contradictory orders issuing from Rome. Now, if the pope would make himself clear, the king concluded, he could count on James's support. In fact, however, James refused to help Segorbe. An element in his stubborn anti-Segorbe stand was undoubtedly the new political orientation of Bishop Peter's overlord in Albarracín, which became anti-Aragonese from 1257; Albarracín moved into the Castilian orbit, and became more fixed there from 1260. Indeed, the new papal initiative may well have been stimulated by the intervention of Toledo and Castile.[70]

Bishop Andrew of Valencia, nothing daunted, embarked upon a generous program of distributing the revenues and rights in Segorbe diocese to sundry beneficiaries. The town of Segorbe became a vicarage supporting the dean of the Valencia chapter (1260). The bishop of Segorbe set off for Rome in 1266 to see the new pope, Clement; but both bishop and pontiff soon afterward died. On the eve of the council of Lyons (1274), the primate of Spain called the attention of the new pope, Gregory X, to the anomaly of "a bishop without an episcopate" whose jurisdictions were unjustly held by the bishops of Valencia, Tortosa, and Zaragoza.[71] It might have been possible to manage some agreement at this time. King James's own son Sancho was the incumbent primate-archbishop of Toledo; and the latest bishop of Segorbe, Peter Simon of Segura (1272–1277), enjoyed great personal influence at the court of Aragon.

At this promising juncture the Segorbe worm turned and, in so doing, made a tactical error. The long-suffering chapter of Albarracín apparently had elected young Peter Simon, scion of a distinguished baronial family of Teruel, to inject some life into the Segorbe affair. A quarter-century had gone by since the Valencia diocese had violently taken over the Segorbe regions. Popes and lawyers seemed impotent in the face of a *fait accompli*. In an access of brashness Bishop Peter Simon now put himself at the head of four hundred armed knights of Teruel plus a contingent of Alpuente stalwarts and marched on Segorbe in late 1273. He expelled the four priests who administered the place for Valencia, then seized Pina, Jérica, and other places. It hardly seemed the apostolic thing to do. Worse, it evened the atrocity score and destroyed his psychological advantage.

Pope Gregory ordered Peter Simon to desist, and to surrender the area until judgment was made. He committed the whole unhappy situation into the hands of the outstanding jurist of the region, Bishop Arnold of Tortosa. Neither side really wanted Arnold's help. Nor would young Peter Simon release his properties into the custody of Tortosa. Bishop Arnold, therefore, as papal delegate excommunicated him. King James froze his revenues. Bishop Andrew, back at Valencia from the ecumenical council at Lyons, prepared lawyers for new campaigns. A graceful retreat was managed, nevertheless, all hands submitting to arbitration (1275 and 1277).[72]

Valencia emerged still clutching thirty-two of the thirty-six localities comprising the diocese of Segorbe.[73] Peter Simon was left with just four places (Segorbe, Begís, Altura, and Castelnovo) and no money. Somehow it didn't seem right. He departed for Rome to make this point. Peter never got beyond Teruel, where he died late in 1277. About the time of his death, a series of documents was filed at the cathedral of Valencia, where they may still be seen; they formally incorporate into the Valencia diocese the towns which had been named in the final compromise.

Some idea of the predicament of Segorbe may be gathered from the crusade tithe of 1278. From all the ecclesiastical incomes in those parts of the Segorbe-Albarracín diocese which fell under the king of Aragon, a total of only 251 solidi could be garnered. This is about the tithe one would expect from a single dignitary at the cathedral of Valencia. In the next year this contribution fell to 166, but was made good in 1280 by a total of 435—that is, about 300 solidi for each year. In fact, the collector of the tax felt it necessary to mount a mass excommunication against the canons of Segorbe for refusing to pay at all; the 1280 total seems to be restitution reluctantly offered by the insolvent diocese.[74]

Segorbe could only yield now, so as to salvage what she might. Peter Simon of Segura was succeeded by the Navarrese Michael Sánchez (1278–1288). But the new king of Aragon, Peter III, had no patience for the Segorbe problem. He brusquely intruded as a dubious bishop the superior of the Franciscans at Valencia, his personal confessor Peter Zacosta, while Bishop Michael fled to Castile.[75] In the opening years of the fourteenth century, when finances were in better order, the Segorbe bishop took care to include the renewed Valencia fight among his major lawsuits. He did not live to see the qualified victory, which only came after mid-century; even this victory would be frustrated for a long time by the disturbances of the Western Schism. In 1318 both Segorbe and Albarracín fell under the newly created Aragonese metropolitan of Zaragoza, thus losing the support of Toledo. On the other hand, Pope Innocent VI soon qualified the settlement of 1275–1277 as "unjust," and many of the lost places returned to Segorbe, including (1347) Jérica, Alpuente, Chelva, and Andilla.[76]

If the dream of the bishops of Segorbe had ever succeeded, and all their claims had been vindicated, a diocese of considerable extent would have emerged. Excluding the enclave of Valencia city and its environs, the base of the diocese would have run from the Guadalaviar river valley to the Mijares river valley and beyond. In terms of towns appearing in the documents, it would have centred on an axis or corridor running from below Albarracín, in the mountains, all the way to the sea. Looking in from the seacoast, it would have begun from Nules and the Mijares River in the north, and from Murviedro (Sagunto) on the border of the municipality of Valencia in the south. The southern boundary would have bent down to Liria, just behind Valencia city, and then have run due west to Chulilla and Domeño on the Guadalaviar River; it would then have proceeded along the northern bank of the river, taking in places like Chelva, Tuéjar, and Alpuente, finally entering and claiming the large Ademuz–Castielfabib sector. The northern boundary, starting again from the sea, would have gone west to Eslida, then have climbed ambitiously north to Tales, Onda, and Ribesalbes, and have continued in a deflected northeasterly direction to Castillo de Villamalefa and Villahermosa del Río.

The hinterland is filled with names of places claimed by Segorbe in the dispute. But there was more. Below the Guadalaviar, far to the south, a separate sector comprising towns like Castalla, Onil, Ibi, and Tibi was claimed. If one examines closely the pattern of the cities in dispute, it becomes apparent that the base of power for the diocese lay directly along the Murviedro–Teruel highway. This was the invasion route for the main drive of the Valencian crusade. It had also represented the area controlled by, or partly loyal to, the converted Moorish king of Valencia, patron of the bishops of Segorbe. Northward the diocesan base of power extended roughly to the modern Castellón–Teruel road, omitting the small area of coast at Castellón and Burriana. The extension to the south of this Segorbe highway was ambitious in its theory, but shallow when one reflects on the strength of the Valencia diocese opposing it.

Of all these claims, some would be better than others, and some would be canny devices of overreach, designed for use in arbitration. Compiling the actual places claimed in the dispute, and attempting to disentangle them from the medieval orthography, the following names may be suggested as substantially the main identifiable towns and places of the abortive diocese: Ademuz, Adzaneta, Albalat, Alcudia de Veo, Alfara, Alfondeguilla, Algar, Algimia de Almonacid, Almedíjar, Almenara, Alpuente, Altura, Andilla, Aras de Alpuente, Arcos, Arenoso, Argelita, Arguines, Ayódar, Azagra, Begís, Bellida (? Bellota), Benagéber, Castalla, Castelnovo, Castielfabib, Castillo de Villamalefa, Chelva, Chilches, Chulilla, Cirat, Cortes de Arenoso, Domeño, Eslida, Espadilla, Fuente la Reina, Gaibiel, Ibi, Jérica, Liria, Losilla, Lucena del Cid, Matet, Montán, Montanejos, Muela, Murviedro, Navajas, Novaliches (? Berniches), Nules, Onda, Onil, Pandiel (near Cirat), Pavías, Pina de Montalgrao, Ribesalbes, Santa Cruz de Moya, Segart (? or Zucaina: Sijena), Segorbe, Soneja, Sot, Suera, Tales, Teresa, Tibi, Torás, Tormo, Toro, Torrechiva, Tramacastiel, Tuéjar, Vall de Uxó, Vallanca, Villamalur, and Villahermosa del Río. Each of these areas, of course, included its surrounding district.

A frontier is no place for the weak, individual or corporate. Too many elements had conspired to defeat the pretensions of Segorbe. Economic strength was at stake, and jurisdictional powers, and the prospects of a more princely diocese. There was the fierce, local patriotism of the new and growing area to consider, and the deeper antipathy toward Castile. King James viewed the church in a reverent perspective; but somehow the dimensions managed to shift and merge until the spiritual happened to buttress the temporal. The church was, after all, his major transforming agency on the frontier. Surely Rome must have been misadvised; legal dodges would have to serve until the period of formation had safely passed.

IV

THE PARISH AS A FRONTIER
INSTITUTION

Unhappily there would be elbowing and unseemly noise when the moment came to plant a Christian church. But there would be no uncertain movements, no need to experiment. The diocesan mechanism in all its functions—financial, legal, social, spiritual, and liturgical—could begin evolving in 1238 with a minimum of time and effort. Like a blueprint, evolved by generations of men in divers lands, it lay ready.

०० FUNCTION

The parish network represented the combat front, from both a religious and a social point of view. It had to be set up in rudimentary form immediately, before the cathedral and diocesan mechanisms. Within the city of Valencia king and metropolitan would organize the parishes even before the municipal government. This was no accident but farsighted policy. The procedure constituted "an element of prime importance for transforming provisional occupation into definitive organization."[1]

By modern standards the parish system was primitive. It could not deliver to its people an educated clergy nor a decent supply of sermons. It could not always control the appointments of men to its service or, once appointed, command effective discipline. Quarrels and lawsuits shook it like a fever. Scandals frequently rocked it. The changing temper of the times wore irritably against it like a friction. Yet it was capable of surprising adaptation. And it could, after initial conflict, cooperate with those auxiliary institutions which had evolved to meet modern needs.

Above all, it was admirably suited to do the one essential: it could carry to every corner of the new realm the sacraments, the liturgy, and the whole range of para-liturgical ceremonies and customs. Each separate church of the far-flung system was thus able to create its own atmosphere, an added dimension of symbolism by which the ordinary was clothed with sacramental significance. The liturgy, pageantry, and customs transported to the frontier a religious world of sight and sound, the daily public office and sung Mass, the procession and the ceremony, the votive lamp and the wayside shrine. It was an Old Testament world of tithes and theocratic overtones. It was a world which somewhat neglected preaching (though this was now changing) but which fed upon the chanted service and occasional confession, the blessing of crops, the solemnities of the current marriage, baptism, or funeral, and the recurrent feast days in the cycle of ecclesiastical seasons. These set the mood and temper of the people. It was an ecclesiastical world somehow Byzantine, in many ways prescholastic, and only incipiently Franciscan or Dominican in tone.

In remoter parishes where the appurtenances might be few and shabby, the caliber of appreciation in art and symbolism was correspondingly less discriminating; thus the impact of the ceremonies, while suffering a measure of diminution, might still be considerable. This complex of ceremony was so fused into the details of ordinary living as to be, to a degree, inescapable. In such a context experience and feeling managed somehow to convey considerable instruction. At the same time, they reinforced the convictions of the participants, joined the parishioners in the solidarity of a group, related them to a sweep of history, and emphasized for them both the objective and subjective dimensions which characterized the Christian way of life.

How deeply such roots would strike or how firmly hold against a hostile wind is another question. When suddenly cut off from them and immersed in the counteratmosphere of Islam, Spanish Christians too often gradually lost their spirit and eventually drifted as material advantage and environment urged.[2] The identifying of religious and social observances of a society into a communal whole, however beneficial it may temporarily be to purely religious values, may also compromise and even destroy those values. There is danger that a façade of conformity to the group may conceal a slowness to move from the external perception to a true engagement, and to a personal and individual commitment. But as a conditioner, an atmosphere, an auxiliary, this complex of ceremony and symbolism was invaluable.

The Roman liturgy had been well established for over a century among James's subjects.[3] Its direct, logical, restrained nature would commend itself even to the simple, in the more official acts of communal worship. The very calendar of the new realm was Christian. The conquered majority might retain their Moslem Friday as the most important day of the week; but, by Valencian law, they had to show open respect for the Christian minority's Sunday. By law all public baths and ovens in the Valencian kingdom closed on Sundays and on Good Friday, even for Moslems. When the priest carried the Host through the streets, the Moslem too must fall on his knees or else vacate the locality completely, under pain of heavy fine or whipping.[4] The liturgical feast days became the public holidays and festive seasons; each one seemed to gather about it an impressive corona of legend and fascinating local custom.

The muezzin would still call from the minaret. But now his sound was challenged and overborne by that clangor so hateful to the Valencian Moslems: the ringing of the church bells "by day and by night."[5] There are bitter references by Moslem authors to the blasphemous din of the bells, which deafened pious Moslem ears in the conquered kingdom of Valencia.[6] In Segorbe the first ringing of the church bells had precipitated a serious anti-Christian riot.[7] There was reason for this. The bells spoke the language of the Christian conqueror. The parish bells tolled over the village for the dying, and for the dead; they marked the progress of the Mass; they rang out interminably in honor of a vigil, of a feast, of a marriage. The bells "do much to perpetuate the sense of community," remarks a modern observer of the Catalan scene; "it is incredible how many rhythms and sentiments two miserable bells can be made to express . . . ; [they] impose emotions on you; thus the whole village hangs on their words and possesses a unity dictated by them."[8]

In the more important parishes of the realm, and especially at the cathedral, the round of plays and dramatic programs in church would have been a popular adjunct. At this date they were probably in the vernacular; and in this mobile time they would have been readily accessible to many Valencians. Unlike Castile, a modern authority on the medieval liturgical drama comments, Catalonia was "one of the great centers of the liturgical drama in the Middle Ages," with an ancient dramatic tradition and deep roots in the Roman-French rite. The plays here, he says, had an "extraordinary success." Gerona and Barcelona were important dramatic centers. "In few churches of Europe it seems were liturgical plays more popular" than in conquered Majorca, whose history so closely parallels that of Valencia.

Unfortunately, the lack of thirteenth-century Valencian records, in contrast to the richness of later documentation, has misled modern researchers. It has been all too easy to assume that King James found the Mozarabic rite in possession in Valencia, so that drama had no friendly soil. The argument from silence and the argument from a ghost community of Mozarabs might combine to persuade one that the liturgical drama was a late import, exploding "in triumphant fashion" in the late thirteenth and fourteenth centuries.[9] But Valencian records have suffered wholesale destructions, and Mozarabism was insignificant and perhaps nonexistent at Valencia in 1238. Even had the Mozarabic rite flourished, the dominant Catalan religious groups which immediately flooded in from the north would have carried the liturgical play with them, just as they brought in their other religious forms.

Implicit in all these religious values and symbols was a specific set of additional secular and cultural forms. The very mood or measure in which expression was given to the former was native to the latter. Other secular forms comprised a context in which the religious or religious-social forms coexisted, so that to recall the one would be to invoke the other. The ringing of a village church bell could thus evoke—in an instinctive, penumbral fashion—the whole world of juristic ideas and usage, of ethic and moral, of personal and social values, of artistic, political, and community activities. Heredity and immediate environment may seem decisive in setting the forms of a society, but even more important is this hidden environment: one's history and traditions, an inheritance tied intricately into particular sensile forms.

The clerics who surrounded King James—the first Valencian canons were from his curia—knew the parochial system. He had only to let these men go busily to work on the Moslem milieu, and in a trice his people would be breathing their native spiritual air, as at Barcelona, Zaragoza, or Montpellier. Part of the achievement loosely attributable to James therefore, the swift assimilation of people to country, should be credited to an institution, the parish.

It is in the perspective of parochial liturgical aims, which required a staff in each small parish, that one must view the plaint of the Valencian bishop and chapter, a plaint otherwise absurd, that the diocese was suffering from a lack of clergy. Outside help must be sought "because of the newness of the land and the scarcity of priests."[10] The patronage of a prebend was sold because the bishop and chapter desired "to afford, with respect to the ministers of Christ, more ample worship of the divine name, having weighed the need and utility of our church and the scarcity of clergy."[11] The same formula appears in a later transaction;[12] yet the cathedral alone had by this date long been able to support the services of fifteen canons with their assistants.[13]

In contemporary England (1238) the celebrated bishop of Lincoln, Robert Grosseteste, expected to find in each parish a priest, deacon, subdeacon, and helpers, and in the poorest parishes at least an assisting clerk. The Oxford council of 1222 would have liked, for the suitable service of the altar, two or three of the clerics in each parish to be priests. Out of three million population in England at this time, a modern authority estimates forty thousand clerics plus seventeen thousand monks or friars. He suggests an average of four or five clerics per parish, "something like one in twelve of the adult male population." Yearly "some thirteen hundred boys in England" became clerics.[14]

In the realms of King James of Aragon a general air of religious revival, stimulated especially by the appearance of the new Orders, was combining with the economic progress in town and countryside, to effect a large increase in endowed benefices in the thirteenth century. King James and his successors enthusiastically shared in this movement, but not necessarily from motives of purest piety. There were more immediate advantages for the founding patron, and for the heirs who inherited the rights of patronage to chantry or chapel. Consequently, Vincke can speak bluntly of the crown's "self-interest," and even of an ecclesiastical-political "Patronatspolitik," in founding such benefices in Valencia and elsewhere.[15]

Parochial staffs are only infrequently glimpsed in records of Valencia. In 1277, for example, Bishop Jazpert admonished the rectors that they should provide legacies in their wills to servitors in their churches, throughout the diocese.[16] Such a staff supposedly would grow quite slowly during this period, the shortage of clergy making it probable that they would at first spread out widely. Near the end of the thirteenth century the basic staff at the parish church of Murviedro (Sagunto) would include no less than three priests and three "scholars," together with "the other personnel proper to the church," all in permanent residence. The number is not deemed excessive; in fact, the document containing this information is complaining that the church is thinly staffed.[17] The priests administering the parish of Segorbe for the bishop of Valencia and the dean, who was absentee rector, numbered by 1272 no less than four: Dominic Valls, Peter of Tárrega, Bernard Finestres, and Peter Zacapella.[18] In 1275 there were two priests at the church of St. Mary in Játiva besides the presumed lesser clerics.[19] The will of Peter of Barberá in 1258, leaving five solidi to the parish of St. Stephen in Valencia, adds two more for its "clerics."[20]

The seriousness of the liturgical idea represented by this multiple clergy is emphasized in one of the earliest disciplinary decrees for the diocese (1255); it warns the Valencian clerics that they imperil their souls by missing, for a few days in a month, the chanting of the office in their country churches. It insists that, even though the pastor visits the capital city and returns the same day to his parish, he is to see that his abandoned flock are provided with these usual ministries. This is hardly the picture of a diocese without clergy, unless we remember that liturgy is here paramount. In this context, too, it is clear why it was not necessary for the bulk of the clergy in Valencia to be priests. Other legislation of that year required the pastors of the diocese to conform the rubrics of their daily chant to those of the cathedral at Valencia; it imposed a fine for those who did not secure a copy of these customs within six months, or for country parishes within a year. This legislation indicates that the people attended the chant, though not how many did so nor how regularly. In 1273 the clergy of the diocese were admonished, when they come to the *Pater* and the *Credo* in the office, to chant them slowly and loudly for the instruction of the laity.[21]

In the same liturgical mood King James—to whom gifts to the churches "do not seem loss of patrimony but gain"[22]—made it one of his cares, after conquering Játiva, to endow a castle chaplain there who should chant the hours.

> Since we James . . . have wrested from the hands of the infidels the castle of Játiva located in the kingdom of Valencia . . . the divine office ought always to be celebrated in it. Therefore . . . have we instituted one chaplaincy for the chapel of the Blessed Mary in the above castle of

Játiva, in which one priest will continually celebrate the divine office by day as also by night.[23]

In another Valencian document, James gave as his general purpose in endowing "religious places": "that the divine office be celebrated there unceasingly."[24] The general enthusiasm for endowing perpetual votive lamps, perpetual chantries, and the like, as seen in the gifts and last testaments of Valencians at the period, also reveals something of this liturgical and paraliturgical mood.

The significance of the parish becomes even clearer when one adds the moral ties, the aspect of a common meeting place, the parish council collecting and managing the tax of first fruits, and the role of the parish as a center of social life, of alms for the needy, of asylum for justice, and of gathering for associations and confraternities. The parish harnessed the strong, divisive localism of the period, elevating and universalizing it to help construct a cell of the common Christendom. This was more true of the country parish in King James's realms, where few competing institutions or distractions existed. Here, and much more so on the frontier, it was the major single unifying factor.[25]

৩৩ EXTERNAL STRUCTURE

The parish network, insofar as it can be visualized, displayed a certain symmetry. A large number of units were scattered broadcast throughout the new realm, each performing similar functions, each apparently controlling subordinate nonparochial chapels like satellites. Except in the cities, this parish was a far different unit from its modern namesake. It was as Gratian had called it "a little diocese" in itself, whose dominant church among a group of chapels held a variety of ancient rights and jurisdictions, sole claim to the parochial revenues of this whole area, and sometimes even a court. Its rector, often surrounded by a pseudo-collegiate body of clerics, made the appointments to benefices in the area and conducted visitations. For baptism and for some big feasts like Palm Sunday the people had to attend this central church, receiving in return a visit by the rector and his retinue on the respective patronal feast of each church.

Although this was the hallowed outward form during the period, the modern parish was imperceptibly evolving within it. Spurred on sometimes by local repugnance to the tithes leaving the neighborhood, or to their vicar's being sent them from afar, and perhaps not hindered by bishops who saw the rector as an intermediate and rival, the lesser churches in the parish had been acquiring ever more autonomy, more and more of the functions proper to the central church. In law the hierarchical façade of the parish group remained; in fact, from the point of view of social and sacramental life, there were at this time two kinds of parish. The term parish indeed already had been used by Gratian to denote the area served by one of the lesser churches.[26]

A significant case of this kind seems to have come to a head in the diocese and city of Vich in Catalonia in 1241, where the "rector" of the church of St. Mary's was fighting the "rector" of St. Columba's. There was only one parish, that of St. Columba's, and so it remained. But, with the help of the two lay patrons of the suffragan church of St. Mary's, the following concessions were forced from the parish of St. Columba's in an out-of-court settlement. The pastor was to leave the celebration of all services at the chapel, even on great feasts, to the chaplain; only twelve solidi of Barcelona yearly need be paid to the parish, nothing else; no St. Columba's people were to attend the chapel, but if they chose to be buried there with the St. Mary's people, a mere third of all they gave to the chapel was to go to the parish.[27] At Castellón in the northern part of the Valencian kingdom the pastor refers to his church in 1298 as the "matrix ecclesia" of the town; his was the only parish, and perhaps not too much should be read into the phrase. It is used again for the Murviedro church.[28]

The impetus to local autonomy could operate more freely on a frontier, where jealously guarded prerogatives and petrified traditions had not yet grown up, and where practical needs kept the institutional patterns fluid. The Valencian frontier showed a tendency to organize by a rapid proliferation of delegated authority. The first generation would create four autonomous archdeaconries, where the Barcelona diocese at this time could boast of only one and Tarazona of only two. One suspects therefore that the phenomenon would have its counterpart at the local level. Along this line of development, one charter of settlement in the Valencian diocese assures the pioneers "that your sons may always be rectors in the churches of the said places, on condition that they are suitable candidates."[29] This was obviously a lord yielding the right of presentation, but it shows the liking of the people for having local men serving them.[30]

It indicates too that the word "rectors," here applied to the incumbents of unimportant plural churches in a restricted country area,[31] was used, like Gratian's "parish," in connection with nonparochial churches. "Rector" is certainly employed in this sense in another document of the time.[32] Reversing this usage, Valencian documents not infrequently term a real rector a "chaplain." Sometimes the head of a nonparochial church held by religious (or even the resident priest of a tiny chapel such as the one at Eslida where there were neither parishioners nor parish) is called a "rector." The bishop of Tortosa in a settlement concerning his Valencian parishes correctly uses the term when ordering a patron to present "vicars or rectors, suitable secular clerics."[33] The lists for crusade taxes in Valencia called the priests in charge of churches attached to hospitals "chaplains" correctly in 1279, and "rectors" improperly in 1280. Since local notaries worked on this project, the looseness of terminology was native as well as contemporary. It was probably influenced by the vernacular use of chaplain for pastor or clergyman, a term deriving from the Low Latin *capellanu.*

In view of this confusion in the documents themselves, historical comment must be similarly imprecise. Juridically, however, a "rector" should be the officially constituted head of a real parish. He was also called "pastor," a title emphasizing the more spiritual *cura animarum*[34] (this usage has survived, for example, in the United States). A "chaplain" might be a cleric sharing jurisdiction in some lesser way, or acting as a chantry priest, or in charge of some outlying church or of some chapel in a home or institution. "Vicar" is the substitute appointee for any of these posts. The difficulties are not more than verbal, since most of what is said in this book applies *mutatis mutandis* to either kind of "parish"; but the clarification may afford a nicer appreciation of some of the documents quoted. On the Valencian scene, therefore, one need not expect to discern clearly a large number of parishes in the technical sense of the word, nor be surprised to find that lists give a fraction of the real chapels staffed by permanent clergy and serving the daily spiritual needs of their districts.

Valencian evidence is not clear on the parochial status of the churches. With the contemporary background in mind, however, some concrete cases of possibly multiple, and of scattered, parishes may be reviewed. It is not easy to distinguish the parish with multiple sub-churches from the parish serving a flock scattered among several settlements. The latter may in fact sometimes be a component of the former. Many "churches" appear in the documents for areas which seem too inconsequential to be central parishes even in expectation; and charters of settlement even for small areas sometimes look forward to several churches, as at Aras and at Villahermosa in 1243.[35]

An interesting pattern appears in the suburban parish of Roteros outside Valencia. It included Castellón near the Albufera, Raytor, Rafalaxat, and Ort.[36] The parish of Cullera included the dependent territory (*terminus*) of that town.[37] The Valldigna, or Alfandech de Marignén, church of Rafol included the entire valley: Simat, Benifairó, Tabernes, Alcudiola, Zarra, Alfulell, Ombria, and Masalali—as Christians arrived to settle these places; yet there was only a single church standing in the valley by 1298.[38] The royal grant to the Roncesvalles Order of "all the churches of Roteros," and to St. Peter's in Calatayud of "all the churches of Boatella," fit the contemporary parochial pattern.[39] Ternils is a late but illuminating example of the scattered parish. In 1316 its rector would petition to be allowed to reside at Cogullada, which was also in his parish, and which was both more populous and more central for visiting his far-flung flock. A document of 1317 reveals that the people of Carcagente also were under the parish of Ternils, and that their religious obligations were fulfilled there. Only in 1434 will they be allowed their own church, with bell and Mass, though still under Ternils.[40]

At Guadalest, the whole valley seems to have been the parish, with the church located in the castle even as late as 1574. Chiva included Cheste until the latter was separated from it in 1336. Adzaneta, which had a Christian settlement, may always have been dependent upon the parish of Albaida. The detached port of Gandía had its church of St. Nicholas under the parish of St. Mary in the city. Albalat dels Sorrells was similarly related to Foyos; only in 1426 will it attempt to become a parish, the lord of the place appealing to the pope. Confrides seems to have ministered to Christians in at least eleven other settlements. The castle of Madrona included in its parish Dos Aguas and the castle of Otanel. In King James's neighboring conquest of Majorca, where circumstances were analogous, the parish of Pollensa was conterminous with the municipal boundaries and comprised no less than thirteen geographical zones such as coast and valley; these zones surely held some dependent churches. The legal code devised especially for the kingdom of Valencia just after the capital city fell gave a privileged status to the one major church of each place (*loch*) of the realm of Valencia, probably referring to the central rural parochial church.[41]

This network of parishes had a varied origin and development. King, knight, and monk rushed to begin the work, their enthusiasm not damped by the consideration that a parish church brought a certain importance to the hamlet and kept at home the ecclesiastical fees it paid, but especially that a very large portion of the church's revenues would find its way into the pockets of the founder and his descendants.[42] More commendable motives predominated in all this, we trust, but the fact remains that it was far more advantageous for a lay or religious lord to found than to see founded. On the frontier the opportunity for doing so was everywhere present.

ECONOMIC BASIS OF THE PARISH ON THE VALENCIAN FRONTIER

By feudal custom and by his promise at Lérida (1236) after the crusade parliament in Monzón,[43] and again by his formal transfer of title at Valencia in a document of October 1238, King James was obliged to endow the parish churches. This included transferring to the parish the Moslem religious properties: mosques, oratories, cemeteries, and the lands or rents which had supported them.[44] Involved were cemeteries large enough to hold more than a dozen bodies; but one great cemetery in the capital was retained by the crown for conversion into a market place for the city. Mosques held by private groups like the Templars or St. Vincent's were likewise excluded.[45] An interpretative decree retained for the crown mosques in the form of a fortification or tower, or those adjoining such a construction.[46]

The Moslems very often kept their mosques by treaty. The settlement charter of the Vall de Uxó, for example, left mosques and mosque properties to the Moslems, as seems to have been usual in fully Moslem areas.

At Murcia, to take an example recorded only because of the dispute over the mosques down there, King James took only the major mosque at first. He left to the Moors ten others, all apparently of fair size; "we Christians should have a great place for worship, since they themselves had so many." The episode seems to illustrate King James's general policy further north, in the kingdom of Valencia. At Valencia city, where the remaining Moslems had soon been thrust into a separate suburb, mosques in that suburb seem to have been plural; at any rate, the cathedral authorities had acquired at least one, possibly by purchase, which in 1277 they rented to a Christian.[47] In the city of Alcira only two mosques seem to have been required by the Christians at first: a secondary mosque which became St. Mary's by 1244, and the major mosque which became St. Catherine's by 1246.[48]

At Benigánim near Játiva, the church of St. Michael was a former mosque. This arrangement continued for a century, until in 1391 the mosque became a cemetery, and a church was built. At Chiva the Christians had their own church and chapel, while the Moslems retained the major mosque and presumably other secondary mosques. Carpesa, which has a rector in the crusade-tithe lists of 1279–1280, had a mosque for the Moslems too. Carlet seems to have been in the same situation, the mosque becoming a chapel in Morisco days. A document of 1251 speaks of the major mosque at Lombar near Calpe. At Mirambell near Valencia city the mosque remained, to become the church for the converted Moors in the sixteenth century.[49]

In much the same manner, the celebrated center for ceramics Manises seems to have retained its mosque until the middle fourteenth century, and then to have converted it to a church; only in the sixteenth century was it ordered replaced as compromising Christianity and keeping old loyalties alive.[50] In Navarrés, which had a church named on the 1279–1280 crusade-tithe list, a small mosque was also kept in use by the Moslems until Morisco times, when it became a church. At Pardines there was not only a church, and by 1316 a parish, but a mosque as well. Similarly, there was a mosque at Petrés besides the parish church; it later became a Morisco church and was replaced in 1603–1608.[51] One even finds small villages where there was only a mosque, so that the few Christians had to travel to a neighboring hamlet for Mass. In Valencia city, at least one new mosque was created for the Moors from a private building; but we do not know whether this was to replace all the others or, as is more probable, to supplement the small number still held by the diminished Moslem community there.[52] Where the Christians had not yet settled, the Moslems apparently kept all their mosques, as in early Segorbe. From extant documentation one has the impression that in general the Moslems retained more mosques than they lost.

Knights, religious, and laymen managed to acquire mosques. One such property became the town hall of Valencia.[53] Another was the town hall of Játiva (1271). A mosque in Valencia city became someone's stable. Yet another was presented to the physician Guy.[54] Bonet Fuster took a perpetual lease on a mosque in St. Bartholomew's parish (1260).[55] What seems to be a separate mosque in the same parish was rented four years earlier by Bernard of Camarasa; the building was gone and its site was near other buildings he owned.[56] In St. John's parish a mosque, similarly dismantled by 1270, left a lot measuring just under 50 by 15 feet.[57] A Moslem oratory stood nearby. In 1240 the bishop, "at the urging of petitions from the Franciscans stationed in Valencia," gave Ramona Torpina, wife of Ponce of Soler, "a mosque with the cemetery belonging to it" and adjoining buildings.[58] In St. Lawrence's parish, besides the mosque used as a parish church there, a former mosque was converted into a complex of animal pens.[59]

In St. Andrew's parish and elsewhere still more mosques were in clerical hands.[60] The diocese rented out many mosques, to gain revenue; these are discussed, more appropriately, in the chapter on diocesan finances. Other mosques went unrecorded, their existence being betrayed only by late documentation, as at St. Martin's parish in 1303. A number of mosques, not designated as such, may be hidden in prosaic rentals of church property. In contemporary Huesca, an established diocese, such a "hidden" mosque was given to a priest as late as 1250, to be converted into a church, now that one was needed; the priest had the right to the revenues, but first had to bear personally the expenses of repair and conversion.[61]

The king apparently owned a mosque in Valencia city, as did the alcalde of Begís. Two men on Chepolella Street (modern Trinquete del Caballeros) lived in a mosque. A troop of soldiers remodeled a mosque for living quarters and were given the shops it had owned. Ten mosques in this city alone were converted to public housing.[62] In all, one way or another, the church seems to have acquired a good half of the city's mosques, including the ten converted to parish churches, the major mosque used as a cathedral, and those either in the possession of religious or subject to rental as a source of church revenue. King James could hardly have done less, even had he been initially reluctant to give the mosques, since the transfer of mosques had become traditional in Aragonese frontier warfare.[63]

In the Castilian city of Seville, also conquered at this time, it is possible to locate some seventy distinct mosques, even if one excludes others which may or not be the same buildings.[64] It is improbable that the Valencia or Seville mosques, including those which have escaped mention, really were mosques in the popularly accepted sense of the word. Many were certainly shrines and burial places of holy or notable men, designated by the Christians as mosques not out of ignorance but for convenience. One contract of exchange (1242) granted a mosque and its adjoining cemetery, which fronted immediately upon "a similar mosque" and had along its side still another cemetery, in the city of Valencia.[65] Texts like these, especially when taken in the context of so many other "mosques" in the city, and of such a plethora of "cemeteries" both in city and diocese, suggest that the words are inclusive technical terms covering every sort of mosque property or open place.

This impression of varied religious establishments, inclusively tagged as mosques, is reinforced by an examination of the size and quality of the buildings involved, as indicated by the uses to which they would be put by the Christians both at Seville and Valencia. Some, for example, were substantial edifices capable of being converted into church, hospital, synagogue, or warehouse; others were small and poor affairs better suited for residence, shop, or stable. In general, however, the secondary mosques of the city seem to have been more numerous by far than the churches of a Christian town, and somewhat smaller.[66]

Did the parishes also acquire the accompanying mosque revenues? "All the buildings and estates belonging to the former mosques" were included in the 1238 gift to the church. This grant was applicable to churches "within and without the city walls," an ambiguous localization which in fact denotes the diocese as well as the city area.[67] These the king gave in free alod. As with King James's endowment of the Valencia diocese, the previous grant of Alphonse II gave to the bishop of Tortosa, in the large territories of Valencia belonging to him, unequivocally "the mosques of the entire diocese . . . with all their alods and holdings."[68] King James later confirmed this gift. In 1243 the Tortosa bishop claimed both the mosques and mosque properties of the town of Burriana.[69] In 1241 at Valencia city, cathedral authorities gave "a mosque and the houses of the said mosque" to a layman in exchange for an inn.[70]

The mosque properties may have been widely seized, however, both by the king and by others. The endowment document of 1241 has a concession by Bishop Ferrer, weakly turning over "to you [the king] and to all those who possess [them] all the estates, buildings, and farms which in Saracen times belonged, or ought to have belonged, to any of their mosques in the entire kingdom of Valencia." He went on to revoke and disallow any previous gift of these "possessions of the mosques" ever made to the diocese by the king.[71] But the successors of Bishop Ferrer refused to acquiesce in this. The city parishes also held houses from an early date, either as private grants or as the promised rectories.[72] The cemeteries—all the plazas, patios, fields, or lots covered by that rather ambiguous term—seem to have been numerous. They were regarded often as ordinary real estate. Just outside the capital city there had been four or five important Moslem cemeteries.[73] It is probable that at least a good many of the appurtenances of the mosques were kept; they would have helped supply property and capital used for the rapid initial expanse of the parochial system.

For a number of rural parishes the outlook was bleak. In the castles and lands of Peter of Montagut, that lord had kept the mosques and their supporting possessions. He never surrendered the latter, though he finally offered the bishop a token jovate of land.[74] This procedure seems to have been adopted as a face-saving formula in such cases, as when the lord of Chiva castle presented to the bishop "for all the holdings formerly belonging to the mosques: one jovate . . . frank and free in the aforesaid castle territory, on the marginal lands."[75]

James was a sincerely religious man according to his lights. But the lights never shone dimmer than when revenues were in question. He was as industrious in seizing a full third to a half of the frontier's tithes as he was nimble in everlastingly dodging the full burden of endowment. The Valencia clergy put up a stubborn, even a rowdy, fight. They clung to their principle of no altar unless first a minister,[76] and no minister unless first an endowment.[77] In agreements with individual lords they gave what they had to, and seized what they could. For example, they reclaimed mosques and cemeteries from the lord of Carlet and Alfarp and from the powerful lord of Chiva and Turís,[78] and insisted on retention of the first fruits.[79]

In areas where the bishops of Segorbe and Valencia disputed wide districts, the barons had slyly seized the local mosques. This situation could only be remedied after the diocesan dispute had reached a tentative settlement (1275–1277). In the course of recovering mosques in Segorbe, the crown intervened to support the bishop of that diocese:

> We are informed by the bishop-elect of Segorbe that certain men of Segorbe persist in holding some places on which in Saracen times mosques and cemeteries stood. Wherefore we order that you [the justiciar at Segorbe], on reception of this document, cause them to be restored to the said bishop-elect or else to be answered for properly at law.[80]

At any rate, a widespread movement of mosques into diocesan possession in the kingdom of Valencia was taking place, whatever the exact proportions of this movement. Even so soon as a year after the surrender of the capital, the metropolitan could speak of "all the parochial mosques of the diocese of Valencia" which he held.[81]

The usual endowment on this frontier comprised the necessary living quarters, probably a small house and farm building, together with a grant of land "for the support of the pastors there."[82] King James early issued such a concession for the parish of Corbera: ". . . that hill which stands before the castle of Corbera, for erecting a church, and buildings, . . . and a garden four fanecates in size adjoining the aforesaid houses, and two jovates of land alongside the said hill, with entrance rights and appurtenances."[83] Or again: "We command that you assign to Ferdinand of Ort, pastor of the church of Pego, buildings and a farm in the valley of Pego for the estab lishing of that church, just as is usual when planting other churches in the kingdom of Valencia." The date 1280 on the document indicates that the closing generalization is based on past policy and is not merely a pious wish for the future.[84] In 1241 the landlord Peter of Montagut set aside on his estate "a house and its farm for the support of the chaplain in active service there."[85] This was the usual grant here from a local lord, or from the king on crown lands. It appears as formula in a number of documents and also in the Valencia privileges.

In the cathedral and diocesan endowment of 1241 this very principle was confirmed by the king: "to assign an individual residence, and a garden belonging to it, to every chaplain serving in the parish church to which he has been appointed."[86] And, as early as 1225 at the abortive first siege of Peñíscola, King James had provided buildings and properties, belonging to the Moslem Zuleima Bolahan, for the future church and pastor in the town.[87] Probably similar pre-grants of parish properties had been assigned in other regions. The Tortosa diocese took care to endow its Valencian parishes properly. In yielding patronal rights over potential parishes on Hospitaller lands here, for example, the bishop of Tortosa instructed the Order to provide every parish church with the usual "parish house, farms, buildings, and cemetery."[88]

Within twenty years of the fall of Valencia, the original sources of endowment seem to have been exhausted. In the year 1268 the king decreed that purchase or gifts of land might be allowed for future churches up to a limit of twenty-five parishes; he specified a total of one hundred and twenty jovates, but only four to a parish. It would seem that a preliminary period of diocesan construction had passed, and that plans were going forward for orderly expansion. The implications as to energy, application, and able executive direction are impressive, considering the magnitude of the task these pioneers had to face.[89]

Besides this basic support, the pastor was entitled to a complex of small service fees and the tax of first fruits. Allowing for local differences, this latter revenue in the kingdom of Valencia consisted of a thirty-ninth portion of many crops.[90] The first fruits bulked fairly large and attracted the greed both of some civil authorities and of the cathedral churchmen. The diocesan endowment by the crown (1241) had reserved the first fruits of every parish for the support of the pastor and for his church.[91] The archbishop of Tarragona early took a stand on this point and laid it down firmly for the diocese of Valencia that these first fruits were to be left to the individual parishes, "so that their pastors may be properly supported."[92] This ruling was not always respected by the cathedral chapter.[93]

Some first fruits in Valencia were with difficulty prized from the strong fists of local nobles.[94] King James himself successfully attached the first fruits of some places, a privilege his successor Peter was careful to preserve.[95]

Most often, however, they were respected. The lord of Ladrón writes them into his charter of settlement, "for use of your churches."[96] So do William of Anglesola,[97] Blaise of Alagón ("the first fruits to your [parish] council"),[98] and others,[99] even when the tithes are retained. A tithe contract of 1242 has the bishop of Valencia stipulating that "the parish chaplain, to be installed by us [after presentation by the lord], is to get the first fruits and other [revenues] just as the other chaplains get them in the diocese of Valencia."[100]

On the other hand, the claimant to the diocese of Segorbe, who was having special difficulties with that small section of the kingdom of Valencia, made a long-term lease of the first fruits of the Segorbe region for 30,000 solidi (1280).[101] He had previously been unable to collect some of the first fruits; probably he meant to keep at least a good part of them. The bishop of Tortosa received the right to first fruits in his Valencian sector from the king (1258). When the parishioners resisted, King James effected a compromise (1263) by which two-thirds went to the diocese, the parishioners retaining one-third for the necessities of their churches. The Knights Hospitallers, after a long dispute with the diocese, retained much of the tithe and first fruits on their holdings.[102]

In many cases, first fruits went under the administration of the local council. One might take this to indicate the lack of a cleric; yet the tithe was set aside for "the church." As will be seen later, the parishioners through an elected council regulated the financial affairs of their parish, and the first fruits were generally received by them.[103] An illuminating document in this connection is the list of taxes or crusade tithes in 1279-1280. Nothing pertinent appears in the lists for the diocese of Valencia itself; but, for those parishes of the kingdom of Valencia which fell under the jurisdiction of Tortosa, the collector has jotted down some valuable notes. A long series of taxes upon the first fruits of the diocese is given, and in each the usual wording "from the chaplain" has been changed to "from the people" (hominibus).[104] Even in the mixed list of this collector, the title of the payee is changed to "the people" when first fruits are in question.

The impression one gets from the documents is that, where a church does not exist, the first fruits went to finance its construction. Sometimes the obligation of building by the settlers is openly stated, as at Pulpis and Alfandech.[105] But the normal purpose seems to have been maintenance, parish expenditure, and charity. Thus, the Morella first fruits in 1263 were designated "for work done on the church or for other needs of the men of Morella."[106] One charter stipulates the repair of the town walls as an item covered by first-fruit revenues.[107] The responsibility for actual collection of the first fruits seems to have rested upon the local pastor.[108]

An irregular stream of small windfalls also came to the pastor from free will offerings or on the occasion of such a sacrament as baptism or marriage, or during the Mass, or most of all in connection with a parishioner's death.[109]

From this sort of minute revenue—candles and lamp oil and pennies, bread and wine, small legacies, novena dues, anniversary "fees," a funeral coverlet, or a pig taken by way of death duty—the Knights Hospitallers alone gleaned in fifteen years, from their clients among the early pioneers resident in and around Valencia city, a resounding 4,000 solidi. This, complained the local pastors in a state of considerable agitation over the situation, did not include legacies, horses, and armament.[110]

From all these parochial revenues came the salaries of domestics and possibly of the liturgical assistants. A sixth of the first fruits throughout the diocese of Valencia was to be applied to the furnishings of the parish church.[111] Complete neglect of the kind of church then built, for a period of forty years, would have resulted in its ruin.[112] Linens, vestments, service books, bells, instruments for processions, images, banners, and similar appurtenances prescribed by the statutes had to be acquired and kept in repair. Taxes had to be paid on the occasion of visitations by the bishop and archdeacon, at synods of diocese and archdeaconry, for poor relief, and so on.

That important revenue the tithe was only rarely seen by any pastor of the diocese of Valencia. In this respect Valencia fell behind contemporaries in the Seville conquest, who reserved a third of the tithe for parish upkeep and a third for the clergy, a final third going to the bishop.[113] For a brief time during the diocesan organization, the pastors of churches in the Játiva archdeaconry, on the far southern border, seem to have been supported from a small share of the tithe.[114] The endowment document of 1241 significantly gave the pastors only the first fruits. The first bishop of Valencia and his chapter, with the approval of the metropolitan of Tarragona, decreed that the ecclesiastical two-thirds of the tithe should go to themselves. What began apparently as an emergency measure was soon consolidated under the second bishop. Arnold and his chapter petitioned Innocent IV for papal confirmation of this statute. This the pope conceded in a bull of October 1245 from Lyons.[115]

On the local scene a lord is found yielding a fourth of the tithe to the rectors of a number of churches he has founded. This was a case of the Valencian bishop intruding into the Segorbe diocesan claims, and so the canonical model is cautiously being followed: a fourth to the bishop and the chapter, a fourth to the rectors, and a generous half to the patron. The bishop's share of this, 200 solidi, was justified as visitation fees, the rest going to the chapter.[116] Another lord agreed to add a lump sum of 35 besants annually to the parish income.[117]

There seems to have been some confusion between personal and parochial ownership, perhaps somewhat as there was in civil society between the kinds of ownership exercised by a king. For many years throughout the diocese, the property of deceased rectors was simply seized—whether by the patron or by the parish council, we do not know. To put a stop to this, Bishop Jazpert finally promulgated a condemnatory statute in 1277. Removing even the occasion of such confiscation, he and the chapter decreed that the rectors could each make a will, and that personal income could include even gifts given to the rector precisely in his capacity as rector.[118]

Once the local church was endowed, the bishop or the patron (perhaps a religious Order or even the village community[119]) would assign a cleric and such staff as could be managed. The new pastor would be fortified in true feudal style by yet another contractual charter:

> We give and grant you, John Gutiérres, relative of our faithful secretary Bartholomew Thomas, all the days of your life the church of Villarreal near Burriana. In such wise that you hold the said church with all its rights and serve it day and night at all hours just as a chaplain or rector of a church is obliged to do. Ordering bailiffs. . . .[120]

A feudal due might be required. Sixty solidi were paid each year by the pastor "of the town and district" of Cullera to the Hospitaller castellan of Amposta.[121] And from Arnold, the chaplain of St. Julian, to the bishop every Christmas went "a pair of capons by way of recognizing our lordship, and as rent."[122]

Many of the Valencian parishes belonged to (or—if one prefers—were under the patronage of) "religious, nobles, [or] knights."[123] Perhaps most of the churches were held to some extent in this manner; but there is no way of assessing the proportion. A bull of Pope Urban II, today usually considered a forgery, gave to crusaders of Aragon a right of patronage (*ius patronatus*) over the churches they would found or endow or even liberate.[124] This complex of patronage enjoyed by crown and nobles was an amplification of similar powers supposed to have been conferred by Alexander II and Gregory VII. In former times, a lay guardianship of the local church had been a desirable thing in frontier regions, if only to ward off bandits. Defense, and the privilege of presenting a candidate, easily slipped into domination over church and revenue, into spoliation and investiture. The bulls had previously been useful, both to founder and to church; their utility to the church was now somewhat more dubious. The science of canon law was already well developed, and canonists were attacking the document with heavy juridical artillery. Legists in turn defended them. The bulls were especially useful to the latter in arguments over lay ownership of tithes.

Obviously such claims would have a remarkable repercussion in the newly liberated realm of Valencia. The bishop did not think of denying these bulls. In fact they formed a most important argument in equity, offered before a papal commission, for the gift of the diocese by the king of Aragon to Tarragona rather than to the Toledo metropolitanate.[125] But the bishop did strive to limit the right of patronage severely in Valencia, at least in its theory. He clung to the position that the churches of his diocese belonged to him alone, and "pleno iure"—a phrase applied to all the churches of his diocese.[126] He insisted that no part of the church tithe could be alienated, permanently and as a matter of law, to laymen for their private purposes;[127] all concessions were merely for *ad hoc* reasons and without violation of the bishop's sweeping ownership.[128]

Sometimes the bishop retained for himself the right of appointment involved in lay patronage. The Tortosa bishop claimed this right for all the parishes in the Valencian part of his diocese.[129] In general, the Valencian bishops strove to interpret patronage, not too successfully, as allowing only a right to present to these churches suitable candidates.[130]

Here is the confirmation of one such privilege by the bishop and chapter in 1260, giving "as to the proper lord of the place and the founder of its churches, the right of patronage in all the churches of the Mijares river territory, existing or yet to be built, and in the church of the town of Andilla, whenever these or anyone of the aforesaid shall chance to lack a pastor."[131] The perpetual beneficiary or patron Simon of Arenós had to defend these churches, help them in their needs, and do "homage" for them as "vassal" of the Valencian "church." The financial returns were particularly favorable, apparently because of the dubious status of a region still vigorously claimed by the diocese of Segorbe. Already this pattern had been established for the area, and for the Segorbe diocese, in the original grant of Saʿīd to Segorbe. Saʿīd kept the patronage and half the tithe, did homage as a vassal of the diocese of Segorbe, could present candidates (except at Tibi), and gave a fourth of the tithe to the rectors. At the time, these churches were only claims, since few Christians had settled here yet.[132]

Early in 1246 the bishop made a like concession to the Knights of Calatrava for their parishes "in all these churches and in others of other places which the said brothers shall, please God, acquire, wrest, and free by themselves from the hands of the Saracens, or elsewhere even, with or without fighting."[133] Elsewhere the bishop defines an apt candidate:

> By aptitude or suitability we understand that the man be of upright life and acquainted with the divine office, that he be a priest or such as can be shortly (or at least within a year) advanced to priestly orders. Nor do we wish or intend that he be permitted to be ignorant of the arts of grammar.[134]

Since this is not the hopeful promulgation of a general statute, but rather a specific directive to a canon enjoying a *ius patronatus*, such candidates may have been less scarce than one might expect. On balance, however, it seems probable that priest candidates were rare enough.[135] Certain clerics functioning as pastors seem never to have been candidates at all. Adventurers, wandering in to establish their own churches, they had set themselves up as spiritual guides; this abuse was sharply attacked.[136]

King James took his own rights of patronage seriously (and realized from it no little profit).[137] Immediately after the fall of Valencia he took care to secure from Pope Gregory IX the confirmation of his patronage over "certain churches and monasteries of the realm of Valencia."[138] There is a passage in the royal endowment of the diocese where James formally hands over all the churches inside and outside the city walls; this is an action stemming from the crusading king's right of patronage.

All these problems of lay control are a mark and effect of the frontier. They remained in the social and economic structure of the kingdom of Valencia, just as they remained in the structure of the older provinces, as a permanent souvenir of former frontier status.

V

THE PARISH IN ACTION

Only when the incumbent had received from the bishop the *cura animarum* or care of souls—the complex of rites and obligations which constituted the legal essence of the parish—did he become "henceforward a legitimate pastor." His duties would then include: "to officiate at divine services, baptize his parishioners and absolve or refuse them in the internal forum, hold nuptial festivities also, legitimately conduct funerals, and confer all the sacraments of the church which are duly conferred by other priests in the diocese of Valencia."[1] Or, more simply, he is "to celebrate Mass, . . . with the other religious ministries and the ringing of bells by day and night."[2]

⬩ THE MINISTRY

The pastor must offer the bishop the obedience required by canon law, "attend the episcopal synod and chapters at the accustomed times," carry out the bishop's decrees, and observe his excommunications.[3] He is to instruct his people,[4] provide for the poor,[5] and bury the dead.[6] "With care and diligence" he should seek out public sinners, warn them three or four times, and then forbid them the sacraments.[7] He is the confessor, who hears and judges and forgives the people's sins (confession was becoming more frequent and popular, though communion was much rarer). Through his hands, during the Mass, the Son of God is to enter the confines of the grubbiest of Valencian hamlets.

It was to the pastor that the infant was brought for baptism. It was to him the young people came to be married. Finally, it was by him that the dying were anointed and their obsequies later conducted. For these occasions he kept a careful register. Often enough he seems to have acted as civil notary.[8] As a social function alone, or as an office of registry, or in its deeper relations to the common faith, the local pastorate was a significant contribution to the frontier. The pastor was a ubiquitous presence, giving a measure of form and unity to the inchoate settlements in remote places. Even the least personable, or the most sinful, of the rural clerics would be all of these things. Men of piety or of presence could easily be more in their respective little worlds.

Each parish had a cemetery, as had some religious Orders and hospitals; this often adjoined the main building. The floors of the churches themselves

73

were ever more widely excavated as time passed, to hold the corpses of men of distinction, members of pious brotherhoods, or substantial families of the locality. In time the open cemeteries by the churches in the capital city would invite passers-by to take short cuts, to dump rubbish, or to set up a convenient market or playing field, as the bishop had to complain by the early fourteenth century.[9]

"The one major church of each place of the realm of Valencia" shared with the cathedral that peculiarly Old Testament institution, the right of asylum.[10] By special decree of the king it was extended as well to the shrine of St. Vincent. Asylum applied to all but a few specified crimes like murder in or near a church. It moderated the medieval urge to a precipitate action or to mob violence; thus it affords a good example of social institutions or customs, involved in the ecclesiastical structure, which helped stabilize the frontier.

Many contemporaries looked upon benefices or pastorates not as spiritual responsibilities but as properties and sources of income. The incumbent might wander off to live upon his revenues as an absentee, casting the care of the parish upon a salaried vicar. A lesser species of vicar, really a resident curate or assistant, would be appointed for the outlying dependencies of the parish. The "vicars of the churches of the city and suburbs of Valencia" early appear beside the rectors.[11] In King James's lifetime there was a long struggle to change the city parish of St. Thomas into a perpetual vicariate, a project which achieved tardy success before the century was out. Each Christmas this vicar was to pay the titular absentee rector 200 solidi, and at St. John's day in June 200 more, as well as ten pounds of candles on the patronal feast of St. Thomas.[12] The church of St. Mary at Játiva, and indeed all the churches of the city and countryside there, present and future, were served by salaried vicars presented to the post by the Játiva archdeacon; the latter pocketed the first fruits and all the revenues (1248).[13] A parish was similarly attached to other cathedral dignities; in 1260 the dean was given Segorbe and Altura with the obligation of placing vicars; in 1277 a number of other churches were substituted on the same plan.[14]

The prosperous parish of Alcira was held by Raymond of Montañans, counsellor to the king, canon of Lérida, archdeacon of Tarragona, and eventually chancellor to the queen of Aragon.[15] Cullera had as rector in 1279–1280 one William Thomas, surely too important a man to have resided personally in that village.[16] The pastor of Holy Savior in the city was granted, as a personal benefice for life, the outlying nonparochial church of St. Julian; this would require a vicar or assistant (1250).[17] At the end of the century, when the king was repeatedly requesting the parish of the town of San Mateo for his secretary's brother, Berengar March, as soon as the present incumbent died, he cited as his reason a principle which reveals much as to the pastors of those days: "because it well befits the bounty of the king to reward his servants and friends according to their merits."[18]

A pastor in those days could sell his parish, or rent it out for a time, without a qualm of conscience. But, in 1274, the bishop of Tortosa inveighed against the abuse of selling one's church to a layman who then could appropriate all the fees and income, installing for the ministry any cleric of his choice. The bishop decreed that one must sell only to a priest, and that the priest must seek episcopal approval before taking up the care of souls.[19]

A remarkable document of 1273, hitherto unnoticed, illuminates the approved practice in the diocese of Valencia.[20] It involves the church of St. Stephen in Valencia city. The pastor was Hugh or Huguet of Lavania, son of the powerful Albert of Lavania. Albert was one of the handful of men closest to King James, so much so that a modern expert seriously discussed him as the possible redactor of the king's autobiography. A Provençal patriot, Albert had been one of the two principal leaders of the Marseilles revolt in 1263 against Charles of Anjou; fleeing into exile, he had soon become one of the most important men in King James's realms.

Master Albert, who signed himself "doctor of laws" and "professor of laws," functioned as judge in the king's traveling curia during the last decade of James's life. He was involved in most of the king's important cases during this period, received a castle and town in 1268 for his services, and was specially recommended by James on his deathbed to his successor King Peter.[21] Master Albert's own procurator negotiated the parish contract. The judge, his procurator, and a Micer Simon pledged their goods as surety for the agreement. Micer Simon of Monbru, a Valencian from Genoa, was a man of substance; when his brother Pascualino of Monbru, owner of Alcira estates, outfitted a ship and leased it to the king for an abortive crusade to the Holy Land, Simon gave surety to the crown.[22]

The contract was thoroughly businesslike. The procurator "sells to you William of Trencard and to yours" the revenues of the parish of St. Stephen's. This included all property and possessions of the parish insofar as they yielded income. The revenues, profits, fees, taxes, "and all else which will accrue through the devotion of the faithful" went to William. The vicar was bound to meet all expenses; but "Albert of Lavania and his aforesaid son," the pastor, agreed to provide the episcopal visitation fee as well as the crusade tithe and similar extraordinary "aids." Vicar William would own such revenues as might exceed the sale price. The contract was to run three years, during which time William was "bound to serve the said church" and to "do and fulfill in all things what the rector is obliged to do."

The price paid was 2,700 solidi, at 900 per annum. The installments came in two equal payments (450 solidi), at the beginning of each year and on All Saints' day; but the first year's down payment was to be 600 solidi with 300 on All Saints' day. St. Stephen's was one of the wealthiest parishes of Valencia. Six years after this contract it returned a crusade tithe of 152 solidi (1279), and in 1280 one of 173 solidi.

William was about to make a tidy profit.[23] The new vicar entered the document to record his "purchase of the said revenues during the said years for the said price in the aforesaid form," promising honest payment of the price.[24] The capitular precentor, acting "in place of the lord bishop of Valencia," signed the contract along with James, Simon, and William.

The problem of appointing vicars also arose in parishes held by military and religious Orders. The Orders often held parishes and their revenues, agreeing in turn to present proper candidates to the bishop and to provide a decent share of the income as pastoral salary. Some of these appointees retained the perquisites and even the dignity of pastor, depending upon whether they resulted from patronal presentation or from rectoral choice of a vicar. A sample case is the Hospitallers' candidate John who received the church of Cullera in the Valencia diocese in 1256, "with all its appurtenances and rights existing or to come."[25] And in 1263 the Temple lost a long struggle to retain the first fruits of their Valencian parishes in the Tortosa diocese.[26]

Other clerics were abroad in the diocese, some perhaps as settlers. King James at the Monzón parliament had promised that not only bishops but all "clerics" helping in the conquest would receive "rewards."[27] Just as clerics of his curia subsequently received Valencian canonries, so other clerics probably won parishes. Crusading clerics appear in the records from time to time. James the Chaplain came with "the men of Perpignan and Roussillon" and shared their grant; a subdeacon was among the contingent from Navarre that was rewarded.[28] Clerics would have come also as members of the baronial households—men like "William of Caceria priest and familiar" with one of the king's counselors in Valencia.[29] Chantry priests and their vicars abound in Valencian documents for religious houses, parishes, and shrines.

✠ DISTRIBUTION OF PARISHES IN VALENCIA DIOCESE

To fashion an ecclesiastical map of the kingdom of Valencia during its formative period, one must sort and evaluate a variety of fragmentary clues. At first sight the task seems too difficult, even hopeless. The diocesan archives of Valencia were destroyed in 1936–1937 in the civil war; the Valencia cathedral archives are specialized in nature; the collections belonging to civil and religious entities furnish only scattered bits of information; and the materials on parish organization for the Segorbe and Tortosa dioceses are disappointing. King Peter in 1280 ordered a list of all the "ancient" parishes, probably to check their charters; but it has not survived.[30] A later list by Peter is dismally lacking in detail. Only a few parishes appear there by name: the rectors of Murviedro and of St. Martin's and St. Andrew's in Valencia city. All the other rectors and vicars of the realm are given only as a group, with a number of dignitaries.[31]

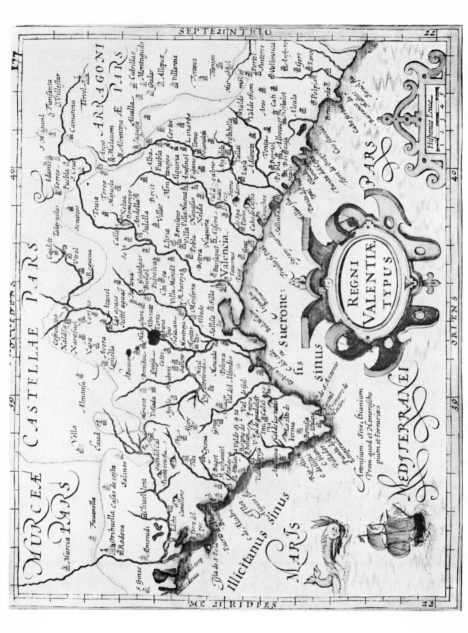

The Kingdom of Valencia (map by Mercator, 1512–1594)

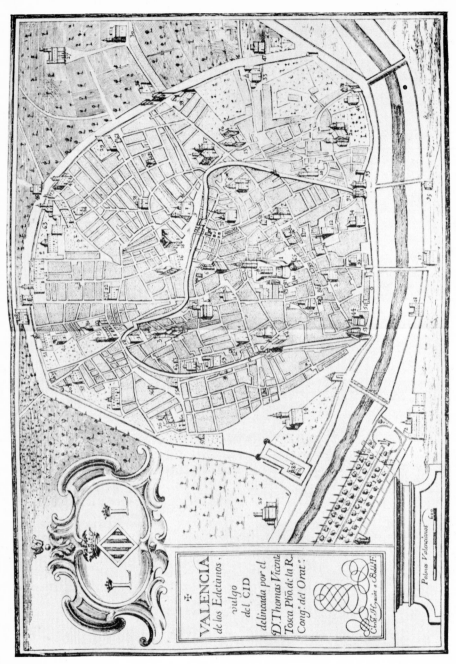

Valencia, showing medieval city within inner walls (by Tosca, probably from his 1704 map)

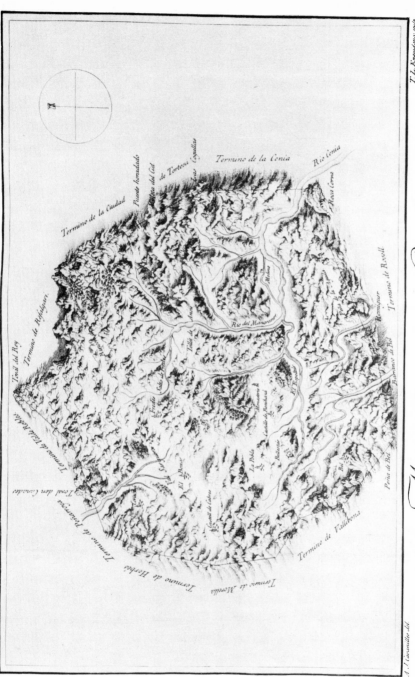

Mapa de la tenencia de Benifasá.

The Benifasá "countryside" surrounding the monastery (1795 map)

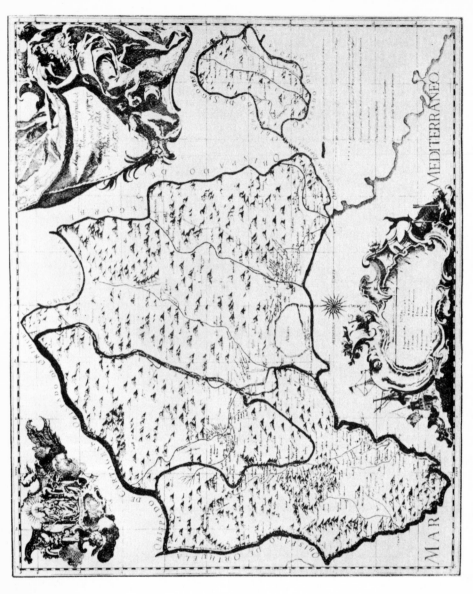

Archdiocese of Valencia and bordering dioceses, 1761

The taxation lists for Christendom's crusade effort furnish the most satis-factory general picture, contemporary though not really complete. A four-teenth-century list at the cathedral counts some one hundred and twenty parishes for the diocese of Valencia.[32] The organization of cathedral revenues in 1247 names the rural parishes of Puig and Foyos specifically, with per-haps the implication that the other forty-and-more names are also parishes. It is possible, as Beuter asserts, that a mass Christian immigration took place just after the Moslem rebellion in 1248; if so, this would have caused some reorganization of the parish system as seen in the document of 1247. In any case, it would be interesting to know whether an artificial system had been preimposed, or whether the diocese followed a shifting and unplanned pattern of growth. The parish network must have been fairly established by 1268, when the king issued that document which allowed limited financing of future parishes up to the number of twenty-five.

It would be wrong to assume a parish wherever an organized Christian community is found, as Sanchís Sivera would have us do.[33] But common sense does suggest at least a church to service such a group or cluster of groups.[34] Conversely, no real "church" seems to have been planted unless at least a small Christian settlement was found in a given locality. Thus, there was no church at Eslida during the thirteenth century, but only "a kind of chapel inside the castle . . . because no one lives there except Sara-cens, nor are any Christians there except the castellan [alcaydus] and some keepers of wine shops."[35] Room should be left for exceptions: for example, to establish juridical precedent in areas disputed with other dioceses; to continue a promising center of conversions from Islam; to please a powerful lord; or simply in expectation of immediate colonization as the symmetrical grants and infeudations continued. Thus, there was a rector before 1280 at Chulilla, a town dominated by Moslems to such an extent that divine services shortly ceased to be celebrated. The bishop could only redeem the demora-lized town by expelling all Moslems and infusing enough settlers to increase the few Christians, bringing their number to a hundred.[36] Again, rights to "churches" might warmly be debated for regions where no actual church building, and few or no Christians, existed; thus there was dispute over future possession of churchless Segorbe.

The preliminary limits of the diocese of Valencia, drawn by King James in a formal statute, were soon incorporated into the municipal law. It was to run north up to the boundary dividing the territory of Almenara castle from that of Murviedro (Sagunto). To the south it reached "down to Biar or beyond," as far as the king would conquer.[37] The southern limits of that conquest had been set in advance by the kings of Castile and Aragon in the treaty of Almizra (1244).[38] This treaty affected the diocesan limits eventually, especially when Alphonse X of Castile set the northern limits of his new diocese of Cartagena here (December 11,1266). In a formal statute of 1240,

4—1

the bishop of Valencia spoke of the southern limits of his diocese as being temporarily at Puerto de Biar and Alcalá below Lorcha, and then from these two points southeast to the sea, including the town of Alicante. This was a greedy estimate, going beyond what the diocese would ever possess; but the statute stubbornly adds that even more may be expected, as far as the king will conquer.[39] At that time there was talk of collecting the tithes up to a northern boundary closed only by the territory of Burriana.[40] The Valencia diocese therefore fluctuated in its outline, especially along its bottom and where it disputed with the Segorbe diocese at its top. After 1250 a certain stability prevailed in the south as the first bishop of a diocese of Cartagena held Alicante and its country over to Villena in the northwest, with a salient up the Ayora Valley to Cofrentes.[41]

The troublesome southern border of the Valencia diocese may be substantially delineated by a line from Calpe (later Villajoyosa) on the coast, inland to Jijona and up to Biar, then north-northeast to Játiva, again sharply west through Enguera (for a while Ayora), and finally north to Cofrentes at the juncture of the Cabriel and Júcar rivers. Along its western side the diocesan line excluded Utiel and Requena, thus setting off a poor enclave which would belong to the diocese of Cuenca. Above that and along the northern frontier, almost to the sea, was the area disputed with Segorbe diocese. In brief, the external line of the diocese did not differ greatly from that which modern times inherited.[42] It covered the modern province of Valencia, but surged across the northern border somewhat into Castellón and south into the province of Alicante. It was an extensive diocese. Later, when King James II was ambitious for a second metropolitanate, to be achieved by a division of ecclesiastical territory into new dioceses (1317), he could suggest to the pope both Tortosa, as being large, and Valencia, as "exceptionally large and extended."[43] He proposed the formation of a separate diocese of Játiva, running from Alcira down, while Valencia itself was to be modified to run roughly from Alcira northward to Castellón, at the expense of Tortosa diocese.

In 1248, four years after the conquest of Játiva, the diocese was divided into two archdeaconries, one continuing at Valencia and the other centering upon Játiva.[44] An archdeacon being a powerful personage of great authority in the diocese in those days, this step effectively created a semi-autonomous entity on the southernmost frontier of Valencia, under a special personnel. It concentrated here a large measure of attention. It also supposed a pre-existing organization in the area which had already advanced beyond the stage of a mere mission. Thirty years later a more thorough adjustment to the needs of the prospering new kingdom resulted in the creation of two more archdeaconries, at Murviedro (Sagunto) above the capital, and at Alcira just below.[45]

The tax lists by the papal collectors of 1279 and 1280 for the crusade may be made to reveal the framework of the diocese at just this time.[46] It shows the organization substantially as it had evolved during the years after the conquest up to the death of King James in 1276. This tax was the "first truly universal and fully organized" crusade tax upon clerical income; it was gathered from 1274 to 1280 by order of the general council of Lyons.[47] Christendom was divided for the purpose into twenty-six collectories, each controlled by a collector-general and his subcollectors. One of these divisions comprised the Aragonese realms and Navarre. Each taxee had to submit, under severe penalties, a notarized and exact declaration of all his ecclesiastical income.[48]

The resultant lists are by no means complete;[49] they represent perhaps two-thirds of the entities constituting the diocese.[50] Religious Orders, for example, might have been left out by special privilege rather than by reason of juridically exempt status. An income below the minimum taxable amount dispensed many clerics, a circumstance one would expect to find rather more often in the rural areas of frontier Valencia than in more settled dioceses. This was more true of Valencia where by papal permission the parish share of the tithes went to the bishop. Some places in the kingdom of Valencia are therefore omitted. Others are explained. "Because its revenues, after expenses, were not worth seven pounds of Tours, it gave nothing" (Oropesa, La Jana, Villores). "It paid nothing because the place was destroyed by the Moslems" in the recent uprising (Bechí), or because "it has nothing" (Buñol), or because "it has nothing but [must] receive support from the rector of the church of Morella (Cinctorres).[51] Where only Moslems lived, the crusade tithe would have been exiguous or nonexistent.[52]

When all allowances have been made, the picture of a given diocese which emerges from these lists is substantial enough to be of the highest value in reconstructing the parochial network. The Valencian lists (see Appendix III) are the result of four separate previous catalogues. They were drawn up in the last two years of this first series of taxes, at a time when the listings were more rigorous and complete than before.

The archdeaconries of Valencia and Játiva are separately grouped, the latter as "the church beyond the Júcar River," a phrase recalling the parallel system of civil government then existing in the realm. Under the Valencian archdeacon are over thirty churches important enough to be taxed, excluding those of the capital city. Each church has its own town or village in the diocese and is probably the main parish of its respective region. Only twelve appear in the first list as having rectors, the others being down as under chaplains or merely as churches; but the list for the subsequent year supplies fifty such rectors. Insofar as one can rely upon the sums collected in each as being indicative of the importance of that church, there were prosperous churches at Murviedro (Sagunto), Alcira, Foyos, and Carpesa. Somewhat less wealthy were the churches of Masamagrell, Albalat, Villamarchante,

Carlet, Toro, Albal, Algemesí, and Sollana. Lowest in this scale come the churches of Chulilla, Aras, Espioca, Benaguacil, Arcos, Paterna, Museros, Ruzafa, Moncada, and the rest. Beyond the Júcar River there are well over thirty localities, each boasting a central parochial church with its rector. The sums collected were understandably smaller. In relative ability to pay, Cocentaina, Corbera, Canals, Onteniente, and Gandía were important.

No one has been bold enough to attempt a parochial map of postconquest Valencia. Later maps are not much help due to successive reorganizations of the inner structure and to adjustments as Moslems became Christians. From present information, however, a fairly satisfactory map can be devised. Patient analysis and comparison of the two main lists will reveal at least a basic skeleton of the organization. For practical purposes the churches in each list may be considered as parishes—if not in the juridical meaning, at least in the sense of being the important ecclesiastical center for each locality.

The list of 1279–1280 for the crusade tithe, however incomplete, furnishes perhaps seventy financially well-established churches outside Valencia city. The fourteenth-century listing of some one hundred and fifteen pastors or vicars, attending the diocesan synods from the thirteenth century on, serves in three ways. It is far more complete. It represents a sampling of the parishes under a different formality. Especially, as close examination reveals, it groups the parishes by regions; for example, Albalat in both lists is necessarily Albalat de la Ribera; and such forms as "unxen," "racuna," and "saxona," must be Onteniente, Rótova, and Jijona. There is something yet more striking. If the lists are broken down alphabetically and contrasted in detail, the two overlap exactly, allowing for the greater extension of the later list. An incomplete list of synodal attendance and an incomplete list of financial returns thus concur to indicate that a representative sampling of the Valencian parishes of 1279–1280 is actually to be had in the crusading tithe lists.

There may have been other churches, identical or not with the remainder in the synodal lists; but the thirteenth-century list is not unbalanced or skimpy. This impression is fortified if one projects a map and studies the pattern of the extra parishes which appear only in the synodal list; they reveal no special change of direction in diocesan evolution or any very remarkable elaboration of the parish network between 1279 and 1350. If to all this is added the information which may be gleaned from local histories,[53] archeological traces, and occasional asides in other documents, the general picture remains unchanged.

A consideration of population figures tends to confirm this. If King James's formal estimate of thirty thousand settlers at Valencia in 1276 is accepted, and if these are assumed to be households, the population could have been no more than one hundred and twenty thousand, a figure confirmed by the monage tax rolls in the next century.[54] The parishes at the capital absorbed perhaps twenty thousand of these.[55] Of the remainder, roughly a third, or perhaps forty thousand in all, would be at this early date in the northern part of the realm; this included Burriana (the second most populous city) and over fifty parishes. The remaining sixty thousand settlers, or fifteen thousand families, would fall into the diocese of Valencia. The figure represents an average of one hundred and fifty families to a parish or parochial region. Statistically considered, this is not unreasonable, considering the urban centers involved; communes like Alcira, Játiva, Murviedro, Denia, Liria, and the like would have absorbed the larger numbers. Parishes within Valencia city at this time averaged two hundred and fifty families, as we shall see, so that the lesser population of a parish of scattered hamlets is adequately offset.

A startling confirmation of these theories comes from the small library of books filled with land grants, listed by King James in 1270.[56] These compilations, one for each major sector of settlement, have long since disappeared; but their titles allow the pattern of settlement to be traced. There were other collections, such as those for Valencia city and its environs and for Burriana and the northern part of the realm. The present list is mostly for the south, from Cullera-Alcira down; only four are above this line. Almost all of the twenty-three regions listed here occur also on the list of parishes for 1279–1280. The two exceptions, Liria and Cullera, are on the synodal list; in any case, parishes adjacent to them, like Villamarchante and Alcalá are on the tax list. Five apparent exceptions require comment: Almiserá which is equivalently the Finestrat–Villajoyosa area of the tax list;[57] and Segorbe, Onda, Peñíscola, and Almenara, which were not within the Valencia diocese.

The areas covered by these books may be rearranged under these headings: Albaida, Alcira, Alcoy, (Almenara), Almiserá, Bocairente, Calpe, Castalla, Cocentaina, Corbera, Cullera, Denia, Guadalest, Játiva, Jijona, Liria, Luchente, Murviedro, (Onda), Onteniente, (Peñíscola), Rugat, and (Segorbe). Thus, the parochial network, even in its incomplete listing for the tax of 1279–1280, is coextensive with the settlement pattern. If this is true for the south, it probably holds as a picture of parish distribution for the north as well.

Besides the land grants everywhere to individuals and groups, formal settlement charters were issued to a number of places on the list of 1279–1280: for example, Algimia de Almonacid, Bocairente, Carlet, Carpesa, Chulilla, Masamagrell, Moncada, Museros, Planes, Puzol, Sollana, and Torrente.[58] Others coincide with those on the second list: for example, Almedíjar, Andilla, Biar, Cuart, Chelva, Finestrat, Pego, Silla, Tárbena, and Villahermosa. There were forty Catalans in the Jalón Valley, and other small groupings at relatively obscure places like Albaida, Alcoy, Carbonera,

Cocentaina, Enova, Guadalest Valley, Luchente, Parcent, Perpunchent, Rugat, and Senija.[59]

It will be no easy task to relate this information about land grants and settlement charters to parochial organization. Some settlements were never properly begun; others failed or soon disappeared; others must be reckoned as included under the parochial jurisdiction of one of the castles or villages in the ecclesiastical lists. And numbers of places under religious Orders would have been absent from the tithe list and perhaps not openly counted in the synodal catalogue. Finally, since the lists are admittedly incomplete, perhaps they may best be filled precisely by adding places of probably high population which are otherwise unaccounted for. The final answer on the problem of the Valencian parish is inseparable from the problem of settlement patterns, though it may not be related to settlement alone. Perhaps it had as well a wider dimension of its own, including an artificial symmetry designed to give a wide general coverage of the diocesan map.

The lists of 1279–1280 may be reorganized alphabetically as follows, after having been identified and transposed into more modern spelling,[60] or into an equivalent location: Albaida, Albal, Albalat de la Ribera, Alboraya, Alcira, Alcoy, Alfafar,[61] Algemesí, Almonacid, Alpuente, Aras de Alpuente, Arcos de las Salinas,[62] Benaguacil, Bocairente, Calpe, Canals (near Játiva), Carbonera, Cárcer, Carlet, Carpesa, Carrícola, Castalla, Chella (?), Chirivella, Chiva, Chulilla, Cocentaina, Corbera de Alcira, Denia, Enova, (Benifayó de) Espioca,[63] Foyos, Fuente Encarroz, Gandía, Gorga, Guadesequies, Jalón, Játiva, Jérica, Jijona, Luchente, Madrona, Masamagrell, the churches of the Mijares River,[64] Moncada, Murviedro (Sagunto), Museros, Navarrés, Ollería, Onteniente, Palma de Gandía, Parcent,[65] Paterna, Picasent, Pina, Planes, Puzol, Relleu, Rótova (with Palma), Rugat, Senija,[66] Sollana, Ternils, Toro, Torrente, Torres-Torres, Turís, Valle de Alfandech de Marignén,[67] Valle de Guadalest, Valle de Seta, Valle de Perpunchent, Villalonga, Villanueva de Castellón, and Villamarchante.

Almost all of these names are on the synodal list though they do not exhaust it. Identified and reassembled, these extra parishes within the synodal list are: Almedíjar, Andilla, Bañeres with Serrella,[68] Bélgida (with Carbonera), Benisuera, Biar, Buñol,[69] Canales (near Andilla), Castillo de Villamalefa, Chella with Bolbaite, Chelva, Confrides with Abdet,[70] Cortes de Arenoso, Cuart de Poblet, Cullera, Domeño, Enguera, Jávea, Liria, Orcheta, Pego (but before 1280),[71] Penáguila, Polop, Prado (near Villamalefa), Puig, Segarra (?), Silla, Tárbena, Valle de Alcalá with Valle de Gallinera, Valle de Ayora with Jarafuel, Valle de Pop with Valle de Laguart and with Murla, Valle de Travadell, Villahermosa del Río, Villajoyosa with Finestrat, and Villamalur. Of these, several are known to antedate the fourteenth century, and might just as well have been added to the tax list of 1280: Canales, Cullera, Carbonera, Bélgida, and Liria.[72] Other places are known from odd

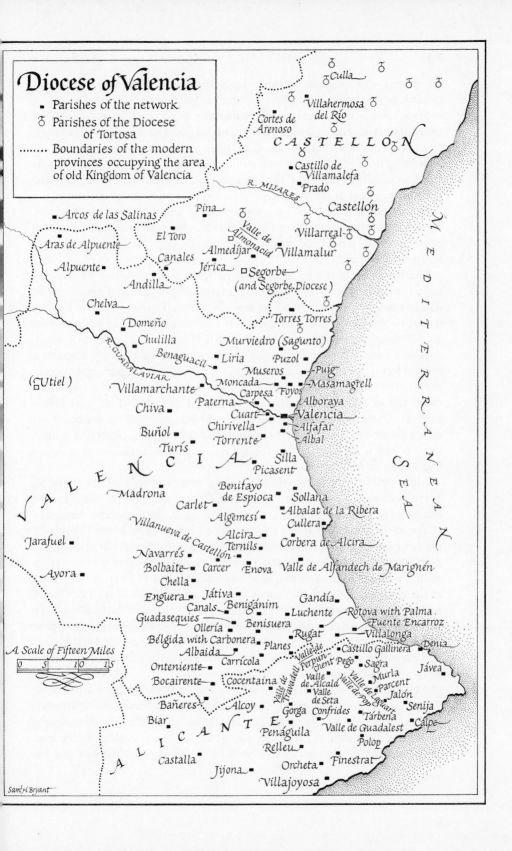

Diocese of Valencia

- **▪** Parishes of the network
- **♂** Parishes of the Diocese of Tortosa
- **.......** Boundaries of the modern provinces occupying the area of old Kingdom of Valencia

CASTELLÓN

Culla
Villahermosa del Río
Cortes de Arenoso
Castillo de Villamalefa
Prado
R. MIJARES
Castellón
Arcos de las Salinas
Pina
Villarreal
Aras de Alpuente
El Toro
Valle de Almonacid
Almedíjar
Villamalur
Alpuente
Canales
Jérica
Segorbe
(and Segorbe Diocese)
Andilla
Chelva
Torres Torres
Domeño
Chulilla
Murviedro (Sagunto)
Benaguacil
Liria
Puzol
R. GUADALAVIAR
Museros
Puig
(Utiel)
Moncada
Masamagrell
Villamarchante
Carpesa
Foyos
Paterna
Alboraya
Chiva
Cuart
Valencia
Chirivella
Alfafar
Buñol
Torrente
Albal
Turís
Silla
Picasent
Madrona
Benifayó de Espioca
Sollana
Carlet
Albalat de la Ribera
Algemesí
Cullera
Jarafuel
Villanueva de Castellón
Alcira
Corbera de Alcira
Ternils
Navarrés
Ayora
Bolbaite
Carcer
Enova
Valle de Alfandech de Marignén
Chella
Enguera
Játiva
Gandía
Canals
Beniganim
Luchente
Rotova with Palma
Guadasequies
Benisuera
Fuente Encarroz
Olleria
Rugat
Villalonga
Bélgida with Carbonera
Planes
Denia
Albaida
Valle de Perpun-chent
Castillo Gallinera
A Scale of Fifteen Miles
Ontiniente
Carrícola
Pego
Sagra
Jávea
0   5   10   15
Bocairente
Cocentaina
Valle de Travadell
Valle de Alcalá
Murla
Parcent
Jalón
Valle de Seta
Valle de Laguart
Valle de Pop
Bañeres
Alcoy
Gorga
Confrides
Tárbena
Senija
Biar
Penáguila
Valle de Guadalest
Calpe
Relleu
Polop
Castalla
Orcheta
Finestrat
Jijona
Villajoyosa

MEDITERRANEAN SEA

VALENCIA

ALICANTE

Sam H. Bryant

documents—for example, Enova, whose priest is discovered in a document of 1296, or Penáguila, which was a church at least before 1280.[73]

These places in general cluster along the coast, and inland along the rivers Palancia, Guadalaviar, Júcar, and Serpis. The number of parishes, and apparently their settlement, diminishes as one goes inland, the hinterland being relatively bare. An apparent exception to this is the scattered network west of Segorbe and the impressive concentration throughout the southeastern part of the diocese.

Other evidence suggests that these represent scattered rural populations, with poor communications and heavier Moslem environment; a special effort seems to have been made here, through multiple units, to effect a liturgical presence.

The broad pattern seen in the general lists can be clarified by drawing upon the fragmentary, supplementary information in scattered documents.[74] Alacuás near Valencia, settled by crusaders from Teruel, was a real parish perhaps only from 1300; in 1354 it was to become a perpetual vicariate under St. Nicholas' in the city of Valencia with Dominic Gil as its first vicar. Alasquer near Alcira had Christian settlers but until 1343 no church; it was subject to the Alcira vicar. Alboraya (see lists) formed part of Almácera parish; the two were separated in the fourteenth century. The important commune of Alcira (see lists) had St. Mary's church at first, and before 1248 St. Catherine's church which was the adapted main mosque of the city; a document of 1268 speaks of the latter as being in a plaza on the main street of town.[75] From 1277 (perpetual from 1327) the archdeacon of Alcira had a vicar at Alcira.

Alcoy (see lists), a fairly settled town by 1256, had a small church of St. Mary built next to the castle. Alcudia de Carlet (see lists) probably had its church of St. Andrew from 1251; Peter Montagut, the lord there, received a statue of the Virgin for it in 1276 from Pope Innocent V. From the time of the conquest, there was a small hermitage and a resident priest at Aras (see lists);[76] but the parish itself came only in 1299. At Benejama, to the west of Alcoy, a chapel and baptismal font was granted only in 1341, to be erected in the castle; Christians previously held the castle (Giles Martin of Oblites had it about 1276) and probably kept up a private chapel of sorts. Benimaclet was under the parish of St. Stephen in Valencia city. Burjasot seems to have had a nonparochial church of St. Michael. The Callosa (see lists) settlers had no parish, their church belonging to the Polop parish (see lists); only in 1338 was a baptismal font conceded here.

At Castillo de Villamalefa the settlers had as a parish the chapel of St. Lucy in the castle. Chiva (see lists) had a chapel or sanctuary in the strongest tower of its castle, but its parish church was St. Michael's. The commune of Denia had its church in the castle, apparently from the beginning and even as late as 1335; its cemetery was near the sea until 1334 when a new one was allowed near the church. Finestrat and Relleu, separate institutions according to the fourteenth-century synodal list, had only a single priest offering separate Masses on Sundays as late as 1336. The Finestrat church was in the castle, as was that of Guadalest Valley (see lists). The important town of Gandía had the parish of St. Mary and a chapel of St. Nicholas; the latter moved in 1343 to be a sub-parish at the port, Grao de Gandía.

Játiva (see lists), ecclesiastical center in the south, had its major church of St. Mary in the purified main mosque (probably from 1244), the Mercedarian church of St. Michael (before 1251), and the original castle chapel or church of St. Felix; there were also several houses of religious Orders, probably with chapels. The Játiva castle chaplaincy was a post endowed by James I; the crusade tithe of 1280 speaks of the chapel of St. Margaret, perhaps referring to this. The *Repartimiento* lists churches of St. Peter, St. Thecla, and St. Michael.

Jávea (see lists) has no early documentation, though its church was to be visited in 1343. Liria (see lists) was an important settlement, given in full dominion to Prince Ferdinand in 1238; perpetual vicars served the church until the Porta Coeli monastery assumed it in 1273, at which time the Gothic edifice was already in use. The church of Luchente (see lists) became a center of pilgrimage, because the miraculous linens connected with a battle of the Valencian crusade (1240) were honored here; a chapel was built on this spot in 1335, but a previous or separate church also had existed. Llombay developed early, but before 1329 it was part of the church of the Valle de Alcalá (see lists). Meliana near Valencia was one of the settlements given to crusaders from Barcelona (1238); it was not to achieve independent status until 1309 when it received permission from the crown to build a church. Murla near Pego emerged as a long-established parish in 1317, when a new church was under construction; its title seems to have been St. Michael's.

Navarrés (see lists) must have been a castle-church parish; centuries later, in 1534, it was to appear again as a new Morisco parish, its church an inadequately small ex-mosque. Onteniente (see lists) had a church dedicated to the Virgin; there would be a second church under the invocation of St. Michael in the fourteenth century. Palma de Gandía (see lists) also had its St. Michael's. Pardines developed so rapidly that its church had to be separated from that of Albalat de la Ribera (see lists) and made into a parish by 1316; the church here may have been named St. Peter's. Penáguila had its own priest at least before 1280.

Petrés was another castle-parish from the beginning; until 1603 it was to have no other church except the Moriscos' ex-mosque. Rebollet (see lists) had its castle extensively improved after its conquest in 1239, and a church of St. Nicholas as well as a village built inside the fortifications; ruined by war in 1344, the place had to be rebuilt in 1368. Ribarroja may have had a castle-church for its Christians. The faithful of Rocafort, however, had to make their way to the Moncada church (see lists) for services for nearly a century. At Sagunto (then Murviedro; see lists) the major mosque became the church of St. Mary during the crusade; in 1273 it was given to the Valencia archdeacon who put a perpetual vicar here. There were also churches of St. John and of Holy Savior,[77] and the churches or chapels of the Franciscans (1294) and Trinitarians (1275).

At Simat de Valldigna there may have been a small church of St. Michael. The Tárbena church (see lists) seems to have been a converted mosque within the castle precincts, the center for the population of what was then called the valley of Tárbena. Tibi apparently had no church or regular ministry until the next century, when the lord of the area received permission to have Mass and other functions regularly in the castle chapel (1337); meanwhile alms were collected for building a church (1339). Villahermosa del Río (see lists) was a colony or expansion of Castillo de Villamalefa (see lists); its thirteenth-century church was probably under the invocation of St. Bartholomew. Though the lists show that Villanueva de Castellón, near Játiva, had a church in the thirteenth century, no further documentation survives before 1358.[78]

The names of many of the parochial clerics have come down to us. Some, like Ferdinand of Ort at the village of Pego, have already been mentioned; others will appear in later chapters. Most of the names are preserved quite by accident; thus, Arnold Darcol, "chaplain of the church of Cullera," wrote up the agreement closing a lawsuit between the communal authorities of Cullera and the religious of the Temple and of the Zaidia at Valencia city, over water rights; this document, and the chaplain therefore, are referred to in a subsequent agreement in 1266. With some industry and patience a large roll call of such clergy could be assembled.[79]

The tax list of 1247 may or may not relate to the parishes. It is interesting, however, that over half of the names clearly or probably[80] identify with places on the other lists, or with places where a church already existed. Thus we have: Albalat de la Ribera, Albaida, Benaguacil, Chulilla, Cullera, Liria, Lullén, Madrona, Murviedro, Paterna, Picasent, Puig, Puzol, Ribarroja, Torre de Espioca, Torrente, Torres-Torres, Valle de Alcalá (including Aledua, Alfarp, Carlet, and Llombay), Villamarchante, and several dubious names like Segart and Cortes. Does this mean that the remaining places also had churches? These include Alcácer, Almusafes and its region, Catadau, Catarroya, Cheste, Macastre, Manises, Monserrat, Montroy, Náquera, Pedralva, Serra, Terrabona, Tous, Tuéjar, Turís, and ambiguous names like Agües and Sallaria.

᛭᛭ DISTRIBUTION OF PARISHES IN TORTOSAN VALENCIA

The separate network of parishes projected by the diocese of Segorbe came to naught. The Tortosa diocese had its base along the seacoast from Almenara to Pratdip, and its interior holdings defined by a great crescent (through Onda, Culla, Ares, Morella, Peñarroya, and Tivisa).[81] Here too a parochial network evolved, related to the well-established older portion of the diocese. Working largely from the crusade-tithe list, one can reconstruct the basic parish groupings of the Tortosa diocese insofar as it fell within the kingdom of Valencia.[82]

Churches are indicated at Adzaneta del Maestre, Albalat, Albocácer, Almazora, Almenara, Ares, Bechí, Bel, Benasal, Benicarló, Bojar, Borriol, Burriana, Cabacer, Cabanes, Cálig, Canet, Castell de Cabres, Castellfort, Castellón de Burriana, Catí, Cervera, Chert, Chiva de Morella, Chivert, Cinctorres, Cuevas de Vinromá, Culla, Forcall, Herbés, Herbesét, La Cenia, La Mata, La Jana, Lucena, Morella, Nules, Onda, Oropesa, Ortells, Peñíscola, Portell de Morella, Puebla de Benifasar, Rossell, Salsadella, San Mateo, Serrañana, Sierra Engarcerán, Tírig, Todolella, Toga, Traiguera, Vallibona, Villafamés, Villafranca del Cid, Villarreal, Villores, Vistabella, and perhaps a few other places.[83] Occasionally an unimportant hamlet boasts a pastor; thus, Berengar Puig is "rector ecclesie Xerer" (Mas de Xirosa) in a 1267 Hospitaller document; but the word rector perhaps is used loosely.[84] It is significant that the churches, once they are identified properly and drawn up in a list, are seen to include twelve of the fourteen Christian settlements brought into the Morella fief of Blaise of Alagón: Albocácer, Benasal, Castellfort, Catí, Cinctorres, Cuevas de Vinromá, Forcall, Herbés, Ortells, Villafranca del Cid, and Villores; of the other two, Olocau del Rey could have been served from Forcall, while Culla may have received its clergy from the military Orders claiming it.[85]

These lists demonstrate how widespread was the ecclesiastical establishment for both dioceses by the time of the Conqueror's death. Each had its own incumbent and revenue; each probably had its small staff and network of subordinate churches. In terms of sheer activity—recruitment of personnel, building or at least adapting churches, outfitting for the liturgical ceremonies, arranging for the support of each church from local sources, and so on—the implications are impressive. This had all been consummated, and the diocese had taken its equal place among other Spanish dioceses for purposes of crusade taxation in the short (and disturbed) span of thirty years after the fall of Játiva.

The parishes of each diocese may possibly have been grouped into rural deaneries or archpresbyteries, each under an archpriest acting as agent of the archdeacon. The archpriest was supposed to gather his pastors into a rural convocation from time to time, visit the parishes, keep the bishop informed on local affairs, adjust lesser problems, and supervise his small area. We have no information on such divisions for the Valencian area. Perhaps they did not exist. As for definite boundaries for the rural areas, again we have no information; they may frequently have corresponded to natural or traditional localities, without distinct borders.[86]

ΙΩΙ ECCLESIASTICAL ARCHITECTURE

Both dioceses represented an architectural frontier. Sifting of archeological evidence indicates a widespread urge to replace the mosques with
something larger and in the Western manner. This suggests expansive and
relatively prosperous communities, not at all abashed by their Moslem
milieu. The rural settlements, naturally, were less prosperous than the
communes. Even in time of crisis the tax expected from all of them together
("the other rectors of the bishopric and diocese") was only as much as the
ordinary cathedral canon paid or as much as a wealthy city parish was
assessed.[87] If less prosperous, the country places were nevertheless affected
by the building movement.

The parish church at San Mateo, a Valencian town founded by King
James in the Tortosa diocese, began as a Romanesque structure of one
nave, with an octagonal tower and a fine main door. As wealth increased, it
was expanded and transformed into a Gothic structure. A document of 1257
mentions it. Today it is designated by law as a national monument.[88] The
parish church of Castellón de la Plana in the Tortosa part of Valencia, St.
Mary's, was erected sometime between 1251 and 1288 on the same site as
the modern edifice. A simple Gothic structure with a wooden roof, it was to
burn down in 1337. The very earliest notice surviving about this church
comes from 1272, when the Castellón resident Bernard Zamora willed it
ten solidi, leaving as well five solidi for its rector Luke (who owed Bernard
10 solidi besides).[89] At Alcira stood another St. Mary's; it may have been a
fine new building beyond the ordinary, since King James in 1276 designated
it as an alternative to the cathedral to be a temporary burial place for his
body.[90]

The church of La Sangre at Liria, boldly rising on a hill at the western
fringe of the Valencian huerta, has also been declared a national monument.
Originally a rectangle ninety feet long, it had a single nave, with four Gothic
arches supporting a wooden roof; built perhaps around 1260, it was used for
worship at the latest by 1273.[91] Basically the same as Liria's boxlike Gothic,
though somewhat smaller, is St. Peter's in Segorbe, probably built around
mid-century.[92] Murviedro's rectangular St. Savior is another example of
this species.[93] The king was to sign a tithe document in 1305 "on the porch
of St. Mary's of the church of Murviedro," a new title suggesting perhaps a
previously rebuilt church.[94] "One of the most interesting Gothic churches
of the Levant region," and a national monument today, is the parish church
of St. Mary's at Morella in the Tortosa diocese. Dominating its region from
a remarkable hilltop site, it has been called a landlocked Mont-Saint-Michel.
This Gothic gem was begun in 1265, consecrated only in 1318, and completed in 1330.[95]

Puzol had a Romanesque church; its entrance, dating from the first half

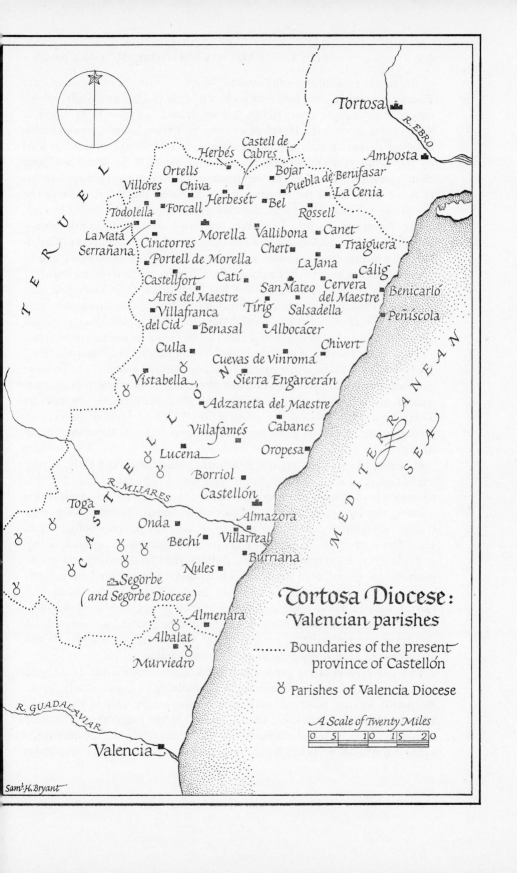

Tortosa·
R. EBRO

Tortosa

Amposta

Castell de
Herbés·   Cabres·
Ortells·   Bojar·
Villores·   Chiva·   Puebla de Benifasar·
Todolella· Forcall· Herbesét· Bel·   La Cenia·
                                    Rossell·
La Mata·   Vallibona· Canet·
Serrañana· Cinctorres· Morella· Chert·   Traiguera·
        Portell de Morella·   La Jana·
Castellfort·   Catí·   Cálig·
Ares del Maestre·   San Mateo·   Cervera   Benicarló·
Villafranca·   Tírig· Salsadella· del Maestre·   Peñiscola·
del Cid· Benasal·   Albocácer·
Culla·   Chivert·
                Cuevas de Vinromá·
Vistabella·   Sierra Engarcerán·

Adzaneta del Maestre·

Villafamés·   Cabanes·
Lucena·   Oropesa·

Borriol·
R. MIJARES   Castellón·
Toga·   Almazora·
        Onda·   Villarreal·
        Bechí·
                Búrriana·
        Nules·

Segorbe·
(and Segorbe Diocese)

Almenara·

Albalat·
Murviedro·

R. GUADALAVIAR

Valencia·

T E R U E L

C A S T E L L O N

M E D I T E R R A N E A N   S E A

Tortosa Diocese:
Valencian parishes

.... Boundaries of the present
province of Castellón

☿ Parishes of Valencia Diocese

A Scale of Twenty Miles

0   5   10   15   20

Saml. H. Bryant

of the thirteenth century, still remains, "a lovely example of the Aragonese Romanesque style."[96] There was a church of St. Roque at Ternils; of this only a Romanesque door, simple but impressive, survives.[97] At Chert in the Tortosa diocese the Hospitallers seem to have adapted some available building, perhaps a mosque, for a few years; as settlement increased, at least by mid-century, a church was planned and begun.[98] At Alcoy a Gothic church seems to have been started shortly after the conquest (around 1253); in April 1276, when the Moslem rebels attacked the town, most of the Christians were in this church assisting at the Mass being offered by their priest Raymond Torregrosa.[99] We hear also of the thirteenth-century church of St. John in Albocácer, a primitive church of St. Nicholas in Castellón, a thirteenth-century church at Villarreal (all in Tortosa diocese), and so on.[100] Churches built in the reconquest era, in fact, are fairly numerous.[101]

The church of St. Felix in Játiva has been called "the prototype of a Valencian church of the thirteenth century." It is neither large nor particularly beautiful, but it has a solid simplicity and an intriguing regional character of its own. It is admired today as an historical document in architecture, one of the few of its period saved "from the frenzy of the restorers." There had been a Visigothic church here and later a mosque. The mosque was torn down just after the conquest of the city, and a larger edifice was erected on the same site. The ex-king of Moslem Valencia, the convert Saʿīd, contributed toward the construction.[102] These Gothic churches in general were derivative, even imitative, as is only to be expected on the frontier.

St. Felix, like its counterparts at Segorbe, Murviedro, and Liria, hardly seems Gothic at first. In floor plan it resembles a rectangular box. There is no vestibule to distract from this simplicity. More exactly it is a parallelogram 67 feet by 45, more like a room than a church. But three very solid Gothic ribs spring out from the walls to support the peaked roof of wood. The effect is of cryptlike solidity. The exterior is attractive, especially along one side where an ample porch runs, distinguished by a striking and severe Romanesque portal. St. Felix too has been declared a national monument. Lavedan sees in the Játiva church, as in those at Segorbe, Murviedro, and Liria, a kind of native tradition, perhaps harking back to Mozarabic antecedents, or perhaps representing in architecture the political turning away of the Aragonese realms from Languedoc.[103] This search for a new national destiny could most freely express itself on the frontier.

Two last aspects of the general parochial organization in the dioceses of King James's realms were significant in the building of a new society. First, the parish was an accepted social and administrative unit in the towns. Secondly, it was a remarkable source, at least in the kingdom of Valencia, of civil revenue. Often the words "parish," "church," and "commune," were synonymous.[104] When King James decreed that counselors were to be chosen to assist the Valencia city justiciar, he arranged to have one drawn "from each parish" every three months.[105] He ordered a similar election of two from each parish to form the town government.[106] Tax collectors for regalian and municipal fees were similarly elected, two or more from each parish throughout the realm.[107] Under James's successor, the city fathers in each commune of the realm of Valencia were to elect one man from each parish annually as the official nominees for the office of justiciar.[108] Houses in the official listing of grants were sometimes by parish, as happened also in grants for other parts of James's dominion.[109] Contracts often located properties according to parish. To pay a debt King James assigned his creditor the rent of four shops in the district (*partida*) of Holy Savior.[110] Castellón, a century later (1385), referred to its use of parishes for administrative civil units as a custom dating from "ancient times" and operating "as in times gone by."[111]

The country or small-town church also served to some extent as political center and meeting place. In 1289 at Castellón, for instance, the magistrates and people gathered in the church of St. Mary to swear homage to their feudal lord, the abbot of Poblet.[112] The celebrated chronicler Muntaner, a delegate from the city of Valencia to the coronation of King Alphonse IV of Aragon early in the next century (1328), describes how "each parish brought its bull, decorated with the royal devices" from Valencia city to the bullfights in the Zaragoza arena.[113] The parish was the focus for a kind of district patriotism. It enjoyed "a certain autonomy" in civil organization and "concentrated the whole life of the district."[114] This would have been more than ever true on the frontier, where other corporations and groupings as yet offered no rivalry and where the population elements had dissolved the traditional ties with their homelands.

Even as a source of civil revenue, especially in frontier circumstances, the parish system can hardly be overestimated. It is difficult to imagine King James sustaining the military and organizational programs in his frontier state without the assured, considerable income afforded to the crown by the parish tithe. The tithe was an all-embracing tax on income. It cut into every productive human activity, sometimes as deeply as 10 per cent. It touched everyone from king to peasant to (indirectly) slave. It was backed by the sternest of ecclesiastical penalties. And the share of king or noble was a half or a third of the total. Where in a kingdom could an equivalent revenue, or one so comprehensive and effective, be found?

CITY PARISH LIFE: THE PARISH OF ST. THOMAS

During the primitive stages of parish development in the cities, as the new organism was asserting itself in strange surroundings, what is known of its inner history? Little enough remains to serve as parish records. In any event these would have been largely administrative, with the small dramas decently interred. It is possible, nevertheless, to gather some ideas. Despite the strong hierarchical pattern framing the system, the active unit was practically autonomous in its ordinary affairs. The rector, who was probably appointed from the crowd of clergy forming part of the crusading host, was at the head of this parochial organism. He cared for the endowment properties, chanted the daily Mass and office along with his other spiritual duties, and ruled his household and flock.

He did not rule his parish by himself. There was a strong admixture of medieval commune in it. The parishioners elected a lay organization to represent and execute their own wishes. The lay council also had a financial function. The elected parishioners were responsible for the parish economy and property. They considered applications for burial and for founding altars. They planned and organized the frequent public feasts. They had a voice in the selection of sacristan, acolyte, organist, bell ringer, and other officeholders. They imposed and collected a tax for the upkeep of the church. And they took charge of building the new churches.[115] The best surviving records of this kind of lay activity come from the following century. Thus it was the town council, operating through three functionaries, who rebuilt the Castellón church in 1341 after a fire; they also had charge of guarding the liturgical treasures at Castellón and supervised expenses connected with worship.[116]

Unlike his modern counterpart the Valencian pioneer did not merely possess a church, or support a church, or attend a church. To an active degree difficult to appreciate he *was* the parish church. He created a tiny parish community, "completely laic,"[117] and felt himself to be a part of its strength, a trustee or an elector whose opinion should be courted. In many documents he identified himself as "a parishioner of St. Andrew's" or "a citizen of Valencia of St. Catherine's parish."[118] The concept of lay community as self-administrating parish adds another dimension to our view of the church as a frontier institution, as an essential in the rapid development of the Valencian frontier.

From the beginning there were ten such communities within the city walls of Valencia.[119] Three more stood just beyond the walls, and there were others not far away.[120] They had been plotted and assigned immediately after the surrender of the city.[121] These churches seem to have been small mosques, abruptly converted to Christian use. Picturing the city roughly as a square, with its northern end based on the Guadalaviar River and its southeastern corner flaring out to form a large salient, let us quarter the square and briefly locate each parish church in turn. In the northeast quarter near the river are Holy Savior and St. Stephen's. Continuing in clockwise fashion, St. Thomas appears in the southeast segment; St. Andrew's stands within the deep salient here, and St. Martin's to its west just clear of the salient. St. Catherine's is encountered next, in the southwest quarter of the city. In that area is St. Nicholas'[122] and below it St. Bartholomew's (the former mosque of Beb Alcántara). Finally, in the northwest quarter near the river lies St. Lawrence's. At the cathedral, which sits in the center of the city like a hub, the side altar of St. Peter, in the left or Gospel nave of the church, serves as center for the smallest parish.

Sanchís Sivera denies territoriality and true parochial status to St. Peter's.[123] Perhaps he was misled by the custom of allowing any citizen to be baptized, married, or buried at the cathedral parish.[124] But an organizational decree of 1240, in assigning revenues, gives the sacristan the first fruits and small offerings "in the whole parish assigned to the major church of St. Mary"; these are expected to be few, and the bishop must supplement them when they fall below the sum of 40 besants.[125] A cathedral document of 1270 locates a shop "in the city of Valencia in the parish of St. Mary of the [episcopal] see" near the bishop's buildings.[126] The "chaplain of St. Peter of the see" is taxed 54 solidi in the 1279 crusade tithe and 52 solidi in the 1280 tithe.[127] In 1276 the wife of Blaise Peter of Fuentes leaves a legacy of 10 solidi to this chaplain of the Valencia see.[128]

The parish of St. Peter Martyr presents a knottier problem. The sixteenth-century historian Escolano makes this the tenth city parish, growing out of a previous oratory of St. Nicholas "before 1278." His colleague Diago puts it down as an oratory to St. Peter Martyr which soon evolved into a parish, only later acquiring St. Nicholas as copatron. The eighteenth-century antiquarian Teixidor refutes both positions without really clarifying the problem. In the present century Chabás concludes the discussion by erecting St. Peter's as an eleventh parish; it appears toward the end of the century and disappears in the fourteenth by incorporation into St. Nicholas'.[129] Actually the St. Peter Martyr parish seems to be St. Nicholas' under a new (or perhaps double) invocation. The St. Peter Martyr church and its rector appear in the crusade-tithe lists of 1279 and 1280. It is one of the richest parishes in the city. The lists account for every other city parish except St. Nicholas', indicating that only a title-change is involved.[130]

Is it possible to establish an earlier date for St. Peter Martyr's? In his will, drawn up on March 1279, García Pérez of Biel chooses burial "in the cemetery of the church of St. Peter Martyr of Valencia," giving 40 solidi to its fabric (opus) and speaking of its rector Peter Ferdinand.[131] More important is a deed of sale in the cathedral archives, locating a property "in the city of Valencia in the parish of St. Peter Martyr." It bears the date 1258.[132] It would be difficult to find a date much earlier since Peter Martyr, a Dominican of Verona, had died only in 1252. Canonized in 1253, he was being regularly honored by the Valencia public before 1257 in the Dominican church.[133] Already progress has been made beyond the position of Beuter, who attempted on a loose tradition to place the foundation of the church of St. Peter

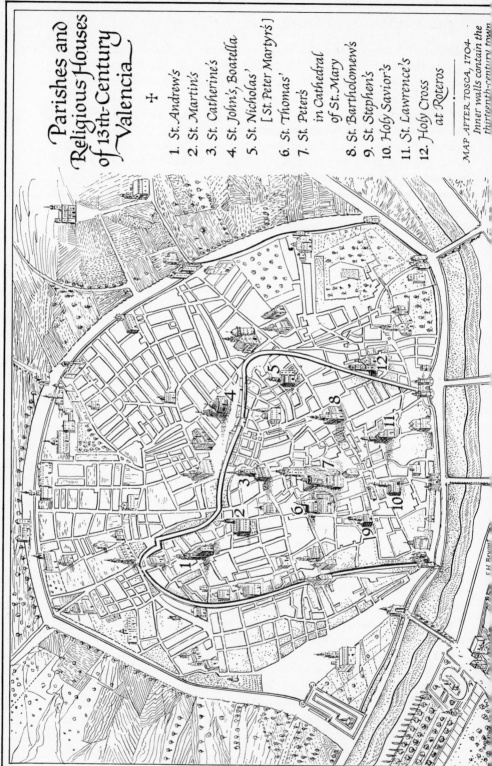

Parishes and Religious Houses of 13th-Century Valencia

✝

1. St. Andrew's
2. St. Martin's
3. St. Catherine's
4. St. John's, Boatella
5. St. Nicholas' [St. Peter Martyr's]
6. St. Thomas'
7. St. Peter's in Cathedral of St. Mary
8. St. Bartholomew's
9. St. Stephen's
10. Holy Savior's
11. St. Lawrence's
12. Holy Cross at Roteros

MAP AFTER TOSCA, 1704. Inner walls contain the thirteenth-century town

S.H. Bryant

Martyr between 1259 and 1268 after a local miracle had turned Valencians toward this devotion. But the gap can be further narrowed, for one Bartholomew signed an important agreement as rector of St. Nicholas as late as 1255.[134]

What happened between September 18, 1255 and the fall of 1258? A document drawn up a decade later gives one terrible glimpse. Accused and convicted of homosexuality, Bartholomew had fled the country, and his lands in Almenara and in the valley of Pego had been confiscated. Allowing two years for this scandal to erupt, and for the bishop to counter it partially by retitling the church, gives an initial date for the name change (late 1257), and an understandable motive.

Why should Peter Martyr have been chosen? Perhaps it suffices to say that Bishop Andrew was a Dominican and this was the latest Dominican saint. But normally such titular patrons were more traditional and ancient; this was an unusual departure from the pattern. The career of Peter Martyr gives a clue, for it called to mind Bartholomew's crime and in a symbolic way countered it. To the mind of the western Mediterranean townsman of this period, Bartholomew's homosexuality carried a strong suggestion of the Albigensian heresy. In Valencia the crimes of heresy and sodomy were linked in the same statute and drew the same terrible punishment, burning at the stake. The sodomite, like the heretic, was an outlaw in the Valencian *Furs*; any man might arrest him "without a court order." His goods, like those of the heretic, were confiscated. Valencian contemporaries knew Peter Martyr as a man born of Albigensian parents, who had spent himself in inquisitorial pursuit of the deliberately homoerotic Albigensians and of other heretics, and who had finally been cut down by Albigensian assassins. The very name of Peter Martyr conveyed the extreme opposite of all that the pastor Bartholomew's crime evoked.[135]

The parish was to keep its new invocation for a generation, past the turn of the century. But the name St. Nicholas seems to have persisted in popular usage; at any rate Nicholas was destined first to join and later to supplant his young colleague as patron.

Ten parishes in one city was a generous supply for that day and place. The Moslem population had left the city of Valencia en masse, a circumstance not true of any other Valencian city except Burriana where surrender conditions had been equivalent. Moslems remaining behind would mostly have been in the suburbs around the city. Thus there was need for no more than a single mosque for the natives, with perhaps a shrine or two. The Moslem minority was soon transferred outside the walls; incidental to this removal, apparently, was the suppression of a parish church named St. Michael's. Its pastor Peter signed a document of 1245 along with other pastors; but the church appears on neither the 1279 nor the 1280 crusade lists. Its position inside or near Valencia city is something of a mystery.[136]

Just beyond the walls, upstream or to the west, was Holy Cross parish in the suburb of Roteros. Directly south of the city was St. John's in the suburb of Boatella. A liberal choice of more independent churches and chapels supplemented the parish centers. Most of these were held by religious communities. The king's chapel at his Valencia residence was within the boundaries of St. Stephen's parish; its major incumbent in 1272 was John Martin.[137] Worthy of special note are the chapels of St. George (treated below in Chapter X) and St. Thecla—respectively a center for a confraternity of crossbowmen, and a shrine to honor the spot where St. Vincent had been martyred. St. Thecla's apparently stood a short distance to the southeast of the cathedral, on the east side of today's Plaza del Reino.[138]

Each city parish extended into, and was responsible for, a rural district nearby. Down by the ocean was the port suburb, Villanueva del Grau (Grao). James named it Villanueva del Mar and began to wall and improve it (1249). The church here was Our Lady of the Sea. The will of Raymond Morella in 1251 left twelve pence to this church; Peter Armer in 1251 left it two solidi; Peter Oller, a draper, in 1249 left it five solidi for upkeep and lights.[139] One hesitates to attempt a delimitation of these wider rural boundaries for the city churches; but illustrative notes are at hand. The Benimaclet church was under St. Stephen's; Mislata belonged to St. Nicholas'; Patraix, it would seem, belonged to St. John's; Campanar had a church under St. Catherine's.[140] Within the city, the delimitation made by the metropolitan just after its conquest was confirmed again by him during the incumbency of Bishop Ferrer.[141]

Parish sizes and shapes would have depended upon many factors, such as the natural disposition of city sectors, the collective prosperity of each segment lest revenue and burdens be disproportionate, the predominance of residences as against shops or public buildings, the promise of future expansion in a district, the presence of large colonies of settlers from one region or language group, the collaboration and rivalry of nearby religious Orders, and all those errors of judgment, those accidents and immediate small problems which influence action but are hidden from the historian. Examining on a map the plotting of parishes after the conquest of contemporary Seville, one is struck by the disparities of size and the vagaries of shape. Some are small, a few huge, some moderate in size, others larger; in contour they recall the modern art of gerrymandering.[142]

At some remove from the city certain other suburbs enjoyed their own pastorates. St. Valerius', for example, was the parish center for the suburb of Ruzafa, a short walk away to the southeast of the city. It was attached to the office of dean (1242), whose vicar ran it. Though other cities in the frontier kingdom were equally well organized, their parishes were understandably far less numerous.

At least half of the city parishes were prosperous, returning a crusade tax of 100 solidi or better. The parishes of St. Stephen, St. Catherine, St. Lawrence, and St. Martin were wealthiest, with those of Holy Savior, St. John, and St. Andrew close behind. The pastors of St. Thomas', St. Bartholomew's, and St. Peter's can have had few economic worries, but their income was appreciably lower.[143] The names of all the first pastors of the churches of the city of Valencia have been preserved in a document of 1245.[144] The order of signature is: Peter of Romaní (St. Peter's, at the cathedral), William Ferrer (St. Martin's), John of Campol (St. Andrew's), Thomas (St. Thomas'), Peter (Holy Savior's), Raymond (St. Nicholas'), Peter Ferdinand (St. John's), John Michael (St. Catherine's), Peter (St. Michael's), Lope (commander of the Roncesvalles hospital, for his vicar at Holy Cross), Peter Simon (St. Lawrence's), William of Pelagals (St. Stephen's), and Dominic (prior of the canons of the Holy Sepulchre in Aragon, Majorca, and Valencia, for his vicar at St. Bartholomew's). The order followed in the prefatory section of the document differs somewhat.

Not much more can be said about the individual pastors. They appear now and again, affording brief glimpses of their activities or personalities. The legal holder of the pastorate of St. Peter's at the cathedral was Bernard of Vilar, priest and canon, apparently from 1241 to 1280; the vicar, after Peter of Romaní, was Bernard Ferrer.[145] At St. Martin's, William Ferrer is still pastor in a document of 1255,[146] and again in 1266 when a judicial decision was handed down in his favor against an attempt by the city fathers to usurp the cemetery lying along the city wall near the Boatella gate.[147] He appears under the title of rector in cathedral documents of 1270 and 1272.[148] At St. Andrew's, John of Campol was still the incumbent in 1252;[149] the previous year he had been cogranter of a settlement charter for three hamlets of the Carlet area.

The rector of St. Andrew's, perhaps the same man as in the 1245 list, went on crusade and was dead by 1279; there was a new rector in 1280.[150] At Holy Savior's one Arnold had succeeded Peter by 1250.[151] At St. Michael's, Peter supplanted the cleric Justus at least by 1242, but he was apparently the last rector before the suppression of this parish.[152] At St. Lawrence's in 1280 the incumbent was Dominic of Biscarra.[153] At St. Catherine's, Raymond of Bellestar was rector in 1252 and as late as 1261.[154] At St. Nicholas', Bartholomew had replaced Raymond by 1255.[155] Very little is known about the assistant clergy serving at these churches; in an analogous situation in contemporary Seville at the end of the century, there were generally at least three to a parish church.[156] Were the rectors of all the parish churches of the city grouped together in a collegiate alliance or corporation, with their own customs and president? When they act in union there is no hint of such a formal organization.

It speaks loudly for the vigor of these small communities at the capital city that before the death of James the Conqueror every parish save one (delayed by litigation) had torn down its mosque to replace it with a sizable church "in a Christian style."[157] This involved the election of parish treasurer, notary, and procurator-general. These functionaries would decree a building tax to be collected on such occasions as marriages, baptisms, and funerals.[158] They would hire an architect and—if they followed the example of the cathedral—contract for the services of a wandering troupe of builders. They would also seek royal permission to buy extra land for the expansion.[159] They already had in the cities a royal privilege of free circuit around each church. No buildings could touch it, the streets must remain wide and unbridged around it.[160]

Any number of last testaments in Valencia during this period leave money for the *opus* of their parish. It is dangerous to argue from a single Latin word, especially one which may refer loosely to conservation or decoration of an existing building; but these gifts may well have been part of a fund for building the first churches and furnishing them. King Peter in a codicil to his will in 1285, leaving money for the *opus* of the Valencia cathedral and for churches elsewhere, provides for using the money as alms in those churches not having such a program ("in quibus opus non fit"). The phrasing suggests that other gifts to Valencian parish *opera* were for construction and substantial improvement rather than for upkeep.[161]

The parish of St. Thomas was probably as typical as any. Dedicated to the doubting apostle, medieval patron against dogbite, it was off in a corner of the city. Enclosed within its borders was the Jewish synagogue and district with its money tables. The pastor, suitably named Thomas, was installed at the conquest in 1238. He appears again as incumbent in 1245.[162] In the division of the city the mosque called St. Thomas' received the house of Mohammed Annagar, and in the delimitation of the parish a set of boundaries which would remain substantially the same into the nineteenth century. As with most parishes in Valencia city, St. Thomas' had a rural section outside the walls dependent upon it, including the harbor suburb.[163] The popular church of the Knights Hospitallers was located in this parish.

By modern times the St. Thomas parish boundaries would hold over twelve thousand souls; but they contained little more than a twelfth of that number, in some four hundred houses, when Valencia was a renowned and prosperous sixteenth-century port. In the thirteenth century it seems improbable that St. Thomas' could have held a great deal more than half that total. In 1239 the parishes of Valencia taken at an arbitrary average would each have numbered two hundred and fifty families or some thirteen hundred people.[164] Using a somewhat different methodology, one finds an average of over eleven acres or four and a half hectares per parish, with one thousand five hundred and sixty souls in two hundred and sixty-one houses, plus whatever rural population belonged to each parish.[165]

An even more useful set of figures comes from the monage lists of 1355, only a lifetime after the close of the period examined in this book. The number of taxpayers may be multiplied by five to arrive at a parish population: St. Andrew's 310 taxpayers, St. Bartholomew's 243, St. Catherine's 605, St. Stephen's 547, Holy Cross in Roteros 385, St. John's in Boatella 723, St. Lawrence's 187, St. Martin's 634, St. Nicholas' 352, St. Peter's at the cathedral 315, Holy Savior's 289, and St. Thomas' 139. This gives a fair idea of the respective population size of the parishes. The numbers fluctuate in the next monage list (1361), St. Thomas' being 193 or almost a thousand souls; there was perhaps some imprecision as to parish boundaries, especially beyond the walls. In any case, St. Thomas' was one of the three smallest parishes.[166]

St. Martin's, the only parish for which a certain figure survives from the thirteenth century, contained two hundred and eighty-two houses, though the meaning of house (*domus*) in the records is ambiguous. This would probably mean a parish population of over twelve hundred for St.Martin's.[167] Using Lot's methodology of figuring four to four-and-one-half souls per hearth, there were less than 1,269 persons in St. Martin's. Thus the city parishes of Valencia were both far fewer and far larger than those of big cities of contemporary England. Contemporary Seville, just conquered, was organized into twenty-four parishes, double the Valencian number; since this number was not needed, problems arose.[168]

Pastor Thomas may have entertained ambitions of building a fine new church, as every one of his fellow pastors was planning to do. But this project must have been submerged in the uproar following upon his demise.[169] The cathedral chapter proposed to annex the parish to their office of sacristan and by this device drain away its revenues. The bishop stood stubbornly against the plan. Bishops die, however, and the corporate body survives. In 1276 the chapter, in a complaint against the policies of the deceased Andrew, insisted upon the annexation of St. Thomas'.[170] Oddly enough, this did not take place for another twenty years; in 1294 the cathedral sacristan James Albalat took over the parish, naming as his resident vicar William of Castellnou.[171] By the thirteenth century the traditional control of chapter over parishes was breaking up; the unity of ministry had become a diversity in Europe. Chapters tended to cling to remaining prerogatives; but probably popular pressures were working against the monopolies of ministry. Meanwhile, the parishioners had been able to get on tardily with their building program, buying houses to clear away.[172] Soon a Gothic structure in stone was up, consisting of a single nave and containing a simple main altar.[173]

Of the assistant clergy nothing is known. Bartholomew Despont founded in the chapel of St. Francis (February 1285) a benefice to the honor of St. Barnabas. Shortly afterward Peter of Prades established at the main altar a benefice in honor of the parish patron St. Thomas.[174] This Peter, a pious layman of the select confraternity of St. James at the cathedral, supplied the Valencian common people with a horrendous bit of ecclesiastical folklore. His tombstone was removed to the outside of the church at the next remodeling, and the legend prevailed that he had been a priest of the time of the conquest, walled up alive for breaking the seal of confession![175]

St. Thomas', like all parishes, had its adjoined cemetery, its annual patronal festivity, its daily Mass and chanting of the hours, its electioneering for civil office at stated times in the year, its great processions on funeral or feast days, its round of marriages and christenings, its absorption in the progress of the new church going up—all quite important to the relatively few families who comprised this little world. No doubt it also had its share in the wordy struggles with the religious Orders and with the tithe-gatherers. St. Thomas' was the new realm in microcosm. Of such minutiae was the frontier kingdom patiently built up.

VI

THE SCHOOL SYSTEM IN VALENCIA

In fitting Christian institutions to their frontier home, diocesan authorities early gave attention to the problem of education. This was the age of the universities. It was also heir to a long development in secondary schooling. And it was a period which, for all its faith and its violence, placed emphasis upon rationalization and legalism to the point of naïveté. Faced with a massive program of parish organization and of church building, and immersed in countless struggles over revenue and jurisdiction, the Valencian church nonetheless boasted a precentorship and a municipal school by the summer of 1240, a cathedral school in 1259, and even the beginnings of a university by 1245.

⋈ A University

Because the university ultimately proved abortive, its practical influence on the frontier state might seem nil. Yet its charter demonstrates that higher education was considered a need with priority. It shows once again how thoroughly and swiftly these people tried to carry their blueprint for a social order into the realm of fact. For, though the enterprise failed, it had nevertheless been conceived and in a legal sense born. It is one more note of enterprise and expansion, of assertion by a few settlers in creating their environment, of unity and self-importance in the new kingdom.

The kingdom of Valencia was conquered and reorganized during the golden age of the universities, those autonomous and mobile corporations by which the medieval European discovered how to institutionalize higher learning. From its small origins in the last decades of the twelfth century, the university movement was running broad and deep throughout the first half of the thirteenth century. Of the two archtypal universities, Paris had received its first code of laws in 1215, when James I was already king in Aragon; it had rallied after its critical great dispersion (1231), when King James was about to attack Valencia. The university of Bologna had been developing at about the same time and pace as her sister in Paris. By mid-century a dozen other universities had also sprung up over Europe from Oxford to Salerno, and the movement would swiftly spread. The speed and impact of the movement are reflected by Roger Bacon (1214–1294) in an enthusiastic outburst:

Never has there been so great a display of learning nor so much dedication to study, in so many [university] faculties, in so many regions, as
there has been these past forty years. Professors are scattered everywhere,
particularly for theology, in every city and in every fortified or commercial
town—especially because of the scholars of the two [mendicant] Orders.
Nor did this happen [before] but only during about the past forty years.[1]

One of the first and greatest of these universities was in the realms of King
James, at Montpellier.[2] King James had been born at Montpellier, knew the
city well, and was involved in its problems and turmoils. He was especially
concerned for the development of its university and intruded himself into
its affairs.[3] His subjects of Montpellier had come on the Valencian crusade;
they had stayed to settle at Valencia in numbers three times as great as those
from Lérida, and almost as great as those from Barcelona. A special section
of the conquered city was set aside for them.[4] Montpellier was the national
university, attended by subjects from all of King James's realms.[5] It was in
a stage of dynamic development at the very time Valencia fell, its statutes
being confirmed in 1239–1240. It had just won for medicine a place as a distinct university discipline; academic medicine would hereafter prosper. It
erected a faculty of the two laws before 1230 and a faculty of arts from 1240.

But the university of Bologna was an even stronger force in King James's
realms. Raymond of Penyafort, one of its most celebrated professors, and
any number of brilliant graduates like James Sarroca and Vidal of Cañellas,
were intimate advisors to the king. King James, more than any other monarch
of his time, surrounded himself with legists and promoted the Roman law
enthusiasm. Even the Barcelona cathedral at this time was a center of legal
studies. It is possible that the king's bishop of Zaragoza during the first
years of organizing the conquered city of Valencia was the great Bologna
professor Vincent of Spain. At any rate, the Catalan "nation" established at
the university of Bologna was sending a steady stream of university men
back to the homeland.[6]

There was, then, a strong university tradition among the Valencian crusaders. There was also a definite tendency in this general region toward
princely foundation of a university. Besides, King James's neighbors and
rivals had recently increased their prestige by opening universities of their
own. Toulouse had begun its lectures in three faculties with fourteen professors in 1229; by the time Valencia fell, it had survived its time of troubles
and was making steady progress. In Castile the same primate of Toledo who
was soon to clash with King James in a court fight over the metropolitan
jurisdiction of conquered Valencia, had already brought professors from
Italy and France to remote Palencia; here under the aegis of Ferdinand III
a moribund study center was changed into a national university (1220).
Castile had begun a second university at Valladolid (1228) and a third at
Salamanca (1243), and had pioneered with the first code of university

legislation.[7] It is not surprising therefore that James of Aragon projected a second university.

That King James should plan to install his new university on the partially settled frontier, however, is surprising, until two factors are considered. To begin with, Toulouse, "the first university that can properly be said to have been founded at all,"[8] had just set a successful precedent of a center of higher learning established as an intellectual and spiritual garrison, a deliberate, artificial bulwark against unfriendly and unorthodox currents. It received fuller privileges from Innocent IV in 1245, the same year the pope issued the Valencia university charter. Secondly, King James was deliberately fashioning a separate entity out of his southern conquest, a special kingdom with its own money, its own procurator and administration, its own parliament, its own progressive law code, its own "knights of the conquest"—in short, an artificial creation which could add luster to his name and serve to balance the power of his other realms. A university, simply by its existence, would strengthen the new kingdom. If it prospered, attracting a large student population and encouraging settlement, so much the better.

On July 10, 1245, in answer to an appeal from the king, Pope Innocent IV issued a charter for a *studium generale* at Valencia. It was to serve the subjects of the realms of Aragon, as well as any others who might come from abroad.[9] This document has been casually noted by historians of the university movement, who assume that it represented a paper university.[10] Rashdall even refuses to grant it this dignity or existence—it was merely a document. This is by no means certain. Paper universities were rare in the thirteenth century, and papal confirmations were not bestowed lightly.[11] In deciding whether a university existed, what should we look for during these early years at Valencia?

A university did not as yet require buildings and libraries; it was largely a juridical status, a complex of privileges and intentions. As for physical evidences, the total professorate of a new university might run from one up to ten masters, and these mostly in legal science. Thus, four years after its charter (1358) Huesca university was to have only one faculty member, and he had been there long before the charter. According to the *Siete partidas* in thirteenth-century Castile, a *studium generale* should have a master for civil law, one for canon law, and one each for at least the three most important of the seven arts. At Salamanca, Alphonse X had three canonists, one legist, two logicians, two grammarians, and two masters in physics—though the last six together had a salary total not much bigger than the individual salary of any canonist or legist. Lérida was to have four masters in law, one in medicine, one in philosophy, and one in grammar. Toulouse began grandly with fourteen masters. Salamanca had two salaried chairs in civil law, three more in canon law, two in medicine, two in logic, two in grammar, one in music, one in pharmacy; local Dominicans taught some theology. Law was the leading faculty "in by far the greater number of medieval universities"; in Spain and in southern Europe generally "law was driving theology out of fashion."[12]

The most sanguine settler in the newly Christian city would not have expected the necessary faculties to emerge at once. The best that might be hoped for some time was to attract scholars to the new land, develop university men among the clergy, cultivate the growth of preparatory schools, and set attractive conditions for the university lecturer. And that was precisely what was achieved during the early years at Valencia city. This had been the manner in which the university at Montpellier had been encouraged. Even in a settled prosperous community the process might be expected to last some time, as the faculties grew slowly toward the day when they might hope to amount to a true university.

There would be Montpellier and Bologna graduates among the crusaders to advise the king on this. There was a plentiful supply of "masters" in Valencia from which to draw lecturers. Over twenty appear in the *Repartimiento* of land grants; three were in the pioneer cathedral chapter of the early forties; and others appear in the records from time to time.[13] In individual cases the title might carry no academic meaning, but during the thirteenth century it commonly designated a degree, often legal or medical. Did these men take up residence and become available as professors? In any case, the goodly supply of masters, in what are meager and scattered records, suggests an academic stratum among the colonists generally. Men trained in the university Roman law were particularly common in Valencia, so that their activities and fees had to be curbed by a series of Valencian statutes.

Others could more easily be brought in by King James than they had been by the king of Castile for Palencia. Or the king and bishop might have hoped that the cathedral school would develop eventually into the university, as had happened in so many other places. If so, the academic legislation by the bishops in 1240, 1242, 1254, 1258, 1259, and 1345 should be linked to the university project. Or, finally, certain masters organized as a *studium particulare* may have been installed here on salary, as had been done elsewhere, with the hope that eventually the institution would grow larger.

What evidence is there that these were the general lines along which the project had been planned? The very grant indicates things were so. It would otherwise be an absurdity to confer such a privilege for a far corner of Christendom, upon a motley crowd of crusaders, while fighting was still going forward, and before revenues, churches, town governments, or the probability of a large permanent immigration had been finally and properly settled. But if we see the charter as an academic call to arms, as a practical stimulus and a vote of confidence, as a reflection of the optimistic *gaudium* which rang through the western Mediterranean when Valencia fell, then the document assumes intelligibility. The "great exaltation" of all Christendom at the capture of "the kingdom of Valencia" is expressed in this university chartering; and the spread of the faith on the frontier is adduced in it as the motive for placing a university in Valencia.

The wording of the charter clearly establishes the Valencian institution canonically as a *studium generale*, intended for students from all over Christendom.[14] It includes a practical privilege giving to clerical masters, coming from any place in James's dominions to teach in Valencia city, their full benefices just as if they were still resident in their home dioceses. Yet another privilege, separately issued, broadens this: "the scholars of your realms and of every other land subject to your rule" who study at Valencia may also keep their benefice revenues, "as do other scholars in Spain giving themselves to study elsewhere."[15] A further document appeals to Valencian scholars to preserve the privilege and not allow anyone to impede it.[16] All this adds up to a very practical encouragement both to prospective teachers and to prospective students. It would be surprising if no one took advantage of it.

In the original charter Pope Innocent made special reference to James's enthusiasm for this university enterprise. This is pertinent, since James was not a flighty man, nor was he inexperienced in university affairs. Besides, was not a Valencian university clearly what the educational statute in the *Furs* prepared the way for? In the statute, the legal cornerstone for educational development in Valencia, the king decreed (1245): "I grant that any cleric or layman may, freely and without any service or tribute, conduct a school of letters, and of all the other arts, and of medicine, and of civil and canon law, in any place throughout the whole city."[17] Villanueva conjectured that the strong language of this law must have indicated serious opposition to be overcome. But the wording was more likely another indication of the strength of King James's determination to lure teachers to Valencia.[18]

Why then, after these promising beginnings, is no more heard about the university of Valencia? Surviving documentation on thirteenth-century Valencia being as scanty as it is, there is nothing remarkable in a lack of records for the embryo institution during its first decade or so. After that brief time—not having fulfilled its early promise, for reasons which became more obvious with the passing years—authorities probably ceased to hope much for it. A clue to these reasons may be found in the manner in which the crown of Aragon next established a university, fifty-five years later (1300), this time at Lérida.

First, Lérida was endowed with tax funds; previous artificial universities, when unendowed, had not survived. Secondly it was placed at Lérida, central to the populations of both Aragon and Catalonia; settlers had refused to come to the kingdom of Valencia in great numbers, as King James complained in 1276. Finally, a full monopoly on higher teaching was given to the new university (Montpellier by then being under the king of Majorca); it is possible that those pioneer Valencian clerics who did take up university studies had preferred the prestige and adventure of Montpellier. In founding Lérida, moreover, nothing was left to the chance of natural development; the university was put into full operation that very year, with statutes drawn and promulgated—all with unprecedented efficiency. "No university, indeed, was more entirely the creation of a monarch's will."[19] It is reasonable to look for at least a partial explanation of all this in the failure at Valencia of an existent, but very disappointing, embryo university.

By this time there may have been no lecturers left in the barren academic groves of the south, or at best a few unimportant clerical hacks who kept up the pretense of a university. The decree of 1300 establishing Lérida university destroyed whatever ambiguous remnants of the earlier Valencian university remained. This may even have been the main purpose of the decree of monopoly. In the next century, however, the Valencians were to erect a *studium particulare* (1374); they countered the Lérida monopoly by citing the laws of James I from pioneer days. The people of Valencia had not forgotten their university beginnings.[20]

ᛥ SECONDARY, ELEMENTARY, PROFESSIONAL, AND CLERICAL EDUCATION IN THE REALM

In June 1240 a genuine municipal program was founded, quite distinct from the later cathedral school, or from whatever purely private tutoring there might have been in the city, and distinct also from the education of the clergy or choirboys. This was almost immediately after the conquest. The cathedral precentor Dominic superintended this "school of the city."[21] He also gave teaching licences, and apparently examined the masters. This is to be expected, since the office was equivalent in academic matters to that of chancellor in northern Europe.[22]

In 1242 a statute of the metropolitan ordered some changes. His decree was in force at Valencia and a copy was filed away in the cathedral archives: "Anybody who wants to teach children the psalms and chant and grammar may do this without a license from the precentor. But the examination of these masters belongs to the bishop, as has become the custom in some churches already."[23] It would seem that, as was quite common in the Middle Ages, clerics and seculars in Valencia were teaching for a small fee the elements of Latin, reading, and writing. The *Decretals* of Gregory IX had ordered every priest to have a clerk to teach parish boys; these papal laws were not remote and foreign, but had been compiled at this very time by the ecclesiastic of Barcelona and adviser of King James, Raymond of Penyafort.

The Valencian diocesan synod of 1258 ordered a permanent fund to be set aside for a master of grammar. His primary function was to train candidates so that they might be successfully examined as to "whether they chant, or read, or can pronounce Latin words . . . and how they ought to bear themselves in the house of God." This is probably the choir school to provide choristers and to instruct potential clerics. Sanchís Sivera reads this, and the prohibition against promoting anyone "unless he knows how to speak Latin," as implying a "very complete" education, including the ability to "converse" in Latin. But the statutes really only require the ability to pronounce the words properly and to have the rudiments of grammar; *conversari* means to conduct one's self or to behave.[24]

More ambitious plans were afoot. In 1179, sixty years before Valencia fell, when secondary education was popular but expensive, the Third Lateran ecumenical council had ordered each cathedral to set aside funds to support free teaching for the young clerics and, as a charity, for the local poor boys. In 1215 the Fourth Lateran council had extended this to all other churches which could support a master. Raymond of Penyafort explained this obligation for contemporaries as involving "separate masters of the liberal arts—at the least, of grammar." It would be simony to charge a fee of "clerics and other poor students" who attend, "because knowledge is the gift of God and therefore cannot be sold"; but offerings could be demanded to supplement an insufficient salary.[25] In 1219 at Lérida the provincial council formally put the conciliar legislation into local effect, though this amounted to no more than a strengthening of older traditions here.

The diocesan synod of Valencia decreed, in the Easter season of 1259, that a cathedral school would be formed along these lines. It was to consist at first of "one master who is to conduct the grammar classes in the church" at the expense of bishop and chapter.[26] In the crusade-tax lists of 1279 and 1280 the chapter functionary Master Vincent appears, in charge of the Valencian students, with a modestly substantial income. Vincent may have been the teacher, or a liaison officer between chapter and school, or a combined administrator and teacher of advanced subjects.[27] At contemporary Vich the *magister scolarium* in the chapter assigned teaching duties to another master, along with control of the school, at a yearly salary of 60 Barcelona solidi.[28] Vincent did not bear this title at Valencia, and licensing here belonged to the precentor. But just after the end of the century (1308) one Raymond Algarra, *doctor scolarum*,[29] is found at Valencia. His job may be analogous to that of the *magister scolarium* or *scholasticus*. If so, supervisory functions at Valencia had already passed from the hands of the precentor to that of a special capitular functionary. In 1317 William Cortés will resign the Valencia cathedral school to become vicar of Liria; a Master John will succeed him.

What of the numbers of smaller schools, those conducted by laymen or clerics in the city and diocese? Such lower schools were common enough in other cities. The legislation at Valencia points to their existence here, though legislation may be wishful. The provision that teachers be free from civil fees or from the precentor's licenses may be meant to regulate, though the laws are from rather too early a date for this. On the other hand, they may be meant only to stimulate. That there were such schools is probable; but their beginnings would be so informal that documentation cannot be expected. One can only say: here is a zeal for schools under difficult circumstances; here are attractive concessions to teachers; and because many documents show evidence of a class of men with university degrees, here presumably was also a proportionate body of educated men without these formal titles.

Having viewed the problem from the *terminus a quo*, it will be useful to approach it now from the *terminus ad quem*, gaining from the later results some understanding of the previous evolution. In the early fourteenth century, the Játiva city fathers complained to the king about his prohibition against teaching philosophy, law, or medicine anywhere in his realm except at Lérida; they said this hurt the teaching even of "grammatical and logical subjects" at Játiva far to the south of Valencia city. The king assured them that he had in mind only the professional subjects, and that grammar and logic may be "taught and studied" at Játiva or elsewhere.[30] These subjects must have been taught on a fairly advanced basis, to have been so shaken by the university decree. If at Játiva, surely there was similar activity at the capital, with its longer history of secondary schooling and its university privilege.

Very early in the fourteenth century, schools run by laymen and clerics were numerous in the realm of Valencia and stood in need of reorganization. In the town of Murviedro, just above the city of Valencia, two doctors had to be appointed to examine masters wishing to teach in that town, because the situation was getting out of hand.[31] Besides a salaried episcopal lecturer in grammar and logic, "some scholars both clerical and lay" were teaching there, not always with sufficient knowledge (1336); two years later the official lecturer, John, was given a rival, Peter, so that scholars had a choice even of these.[32] A town as small as Jérica had two schools by 1334, when the vicar of the church there was licensed to begin the second one.[33] In all, eight important secondary schools outside the city of Valencia are documented for the fourteenth century. Rashdall even lists as *studia particularia* at this time the schools at Murviedro (Sagunto), Morella, Sueca, and Játiva.[34] By 1329 the city of Valencia had set up at royal command an examining board for practitioners of medicine or surgery in the kingdom and had forbidden nonlicensed physicians to practice.[35] Such early fourteenth-century evidence involves an uncomfortable time-lapse from the period discussed in this book. However, this is a difficulty native to investigations from a *terminus ad quem*. In the absence of documentation for the inter-

vening period, these somewhat later evidences of a wide cultivation of
schools may not be irrelevant to a knowledge of the situation during the
preceding generation.

Mere literacy, as distinguished from education, may have been rather
easier to achieve than one might imagine. Raymond Lull, a contemporary
courtier in the Catalan regions (and eventually a philosopher and mystic of
note), was an enthusiastic composer and writer of troubadour poetry, but,
because he knew Latin grammar only a little (*un poc*), he considered himself
"illiterate."[36] Notaries who composed in Latin were very common in the
city and realm of Valencia, the names of many being known. One of them, a
Berengar of Ripoll, notary of Valencia city, received a license from King
James to train assistants: "that you may install under your care a student
[*discipulum*] or students, whomever you may wish, who may draft and copy
wills for you from memory."[37] Scattered evidence of a professional and
artistic leaven in the population glints in the records from the start: physicians, painters, silversmiths, troubadours, a plethora of legal men, interpre-
ters, notaries, makers of manuscript books, and so forth.[38]

Clerical education at the universities of Europe was encouraged also by a
constitution introduced into the Valencian church in 1254, providing for
dispensation from residence for benefice holders who attended universities.[39]
That this was not an idle gesture can be seen from a subsequent statute
which protests that, though learning be an excellent thing, Valencian
canons must not quickly rush off into it; a residence of six months is demanded after acceptance as a canon.[40] The canons always included among
their number some masters; most of these would have taken the arts course
or the legal training.[41] The country clergy had fewer opportunities as boys
or as clerics; they probably had only that minimum, spoken of above, required of the parish priest. To his even more ignorant peasant parishioners,
however, the local cleric must have seemed erudite as he performed his
liturgy or returned from the synod with new theological gleanings.

There was no chair of theology in the cathedral until 1345,[42] though
Escolano and Beuter attempt without evidence to install a theology master
here in 1275. But from the beginning (to speak again of antecedent pro-
babilities) the Dominicans would have had lectures open to the clergy and
laity of the city. The Dominicans deliberately fixed their headquarters at the
university world-centers, and their main houses "from the first assumed the
form of colleges."[43] Their activities at Oxford and elsewhere during this
period, like that of the other Mendicants, are well known; it was an essential
part of their vocation to bring Christian scholarship from the universities
out to the provinces. They commonly erected an informal *studium* of
theology in the big towns. Barcelona, which was behind Valencia in a number of innovations at this time, before 1299 had such a Dominican faculty
with two chairs.

At least one of the Dominicans present at the fall of Valencia, and forming part of its first Dominican community, was a professionally trained theology teacher.[44] Within a decade after the conquest, in fact, the Dominicans were operating a *studium* of oriental languages in Valencia city and assigning teachers there from other localities. True, this was with missionary purposes in mind, for the converting of the Valencia Moslems, but it shows how quickly the Order could act.[45] It seems probable that their normal theological preoccupation would similarly have found expression.

The archivist Sanchís Sivera proposed, mainly by way of conjecture, that the hospitals of the thirteenth-century city of Valencia furnished an informal apprenticeship to beginners in medicine, that similarly informal schools in nonecclesiastical music existed, and that convents of nuns and religious houses were generally centers of instruction in letters and science.[46] Some religious houses probably did give instruction. A land document reveals an interesting example of this elsewhere; King James endowed a "studium theologie" for a Cistercian monastery in the Agde diocese, to be used by the monks and "others" (1263). The king allowed the Carthusians at Mont-pellier to set up a similar *studium* that same year. Convents of nuns at this period commonly taught upper-class girls and even young boys; we have no information on the educational activities of the several Valencian convents. There are a number of "scholares" in the records; the Latin term is am-biguous without a context, however, and easily bears a nonacademic mean-ing.[47]

Taken all in all, a surprising concern for education characterized these early years. The several projects and the hints of further educational activity reveal yet another aspect of the church's activity as agent of social progress and Westernization on the Valencian frontier.

VII

FRONTIER PASTOR AND PEOPLE

The character of a body of clergy, or of a body of laity, is difficult to appraise. The surviving Valencian documents shed some light especially upon the clergy; though what is seen by that light is not always reassuring. Of course, to criticize clerical shortcomings may be only to criticize the times: saying in effect that, where every age has its faults, here are the faults which shadowed medieval times, exacerbated perhaps in the Valencian situation by the circumstances of a frontier environment. The earliest remaining disciplinary decrees for the Valencia diocese date from the year 1255. There are no synods in the thirteenth century for Segorbe. The synodal materials for Tortosa are exiguous and, because of the dual nature of that diocese, ambiguous.

The Cleric

One of the Valencian decrees is concerned with keeping the suburban priests in their parishes, far from the lively capital. Defrauding the parishioners by their absence, and with peril to their own souls as well, "they enter the city more often than is suitable, participating in prohibited and unbecoming actions."[1] They stay overnight and miss the public recitation of the office at their parishes. From now on they are to come in only twice a month, return the same day, arrange for a substitute to provide for the people in their absence, and while in the city attend, properly habited, the chanting of the various hours at the cathedral. One rather doubts that these country priests were enjoying a rousing time in the city, or the legal vocabulary then available would have supplied this rebuke with phrases much more lurid. It is a scene of life, then, and little else.

Specific prohibitions laid down in 1258 draw a composite portrait of the worldly cleric in Valencia, though it would be unfair to fuse all these vices into a single person. He favored the latest in clothing fads, drank in taverns, patronized the budding theatrical life of the frontier ("shows or women singers"), took part in a floating dice game, wandered about the streets and squares, frequented the market place, and was not above the popular diversion of watching thieves hang, heretics burn, or malefactors suffer interesting and sanguinary ends.[2] Supposing this composite subject to have had little interest in spiritual things (not at all a necessary deduction), his

vices are not yet spectacular; if anything he seems a bit of a bumpkin. This
impression is strengthened by the nature of the pastoral admonitions furnished to his companions at this synod. They must not stare into the faces
of penitents making their confessions, especially if these be women. They
are to show penitents "sympathetic kindness," and they must never "express
consternation over the sins however base they be."[3] The doctrinal instructions received here are on the same practical and elementary level.

Elaborate dress had been frowned upon by the synods of 1255 and 1258.[4]
"Many," however, were still uncanonically garbed. From 1268 on, a
determined effort to dress the clergy more soberly achieved a measure of
success. Red, green, and yellow outfits with ermine trimmings had to be put
aside, though the wearer might get a year's use out of them since clothing was
expensive.[5] A special cape was to be worn by the priests; this order was
later extended to deacons and benefice holders. Similar injunctions were
issued in the following year, again in 1273 because "not all" had obeyed,
and by the new bishop in 1276.[6] Some clergy favored "weapons of different
kinds, especially daggers, and swords bigger than laymen carry," to the
scandal of the Christian community. When traveling outside the city the
cleric should wear a sword only of reasonable size, a "Segovian" being
recommended.[7]

Dicing, a universal passion at the time, was not without its clerical clients.
After 1268 a heavy fine was imposed. In 1273 this was qualified by the sly
device of remitting a third of the fine to fellow clerics informing on the cul-
prits.[8] A more serious lapse, reported only once (in 1268), was that "some"
clerics "shamelessly get drunk, and their drunkenness results in the grave
scandal of many." A severe fine was decreed, "no mercy to be shown as to
its payment," and canonical punishment threatened besides.[9]

A sinister note, not unfamiliar for those times, was sounded in the synods
of the early 1260's. Between a regulation about clean altar linens and the
propriety of consecrating a new host weekly for reservation, comes the
prohibition "that priests may not associate their children with them in the
service of the altar because of scandal" (1261).[10] And there is the indignant
revelation that "a number of the clergy of our city and diocese use the goods
of the church they are in charge of, to buy possessions and property to
provide for their children; these they ought to thrust entirely aside if they
have any regard for the dignity of their calling."[11]

Such rebukes almost surely concern the obligation of celibacy. In interpreting them, nevertheless, allowance must be made for the legitimate
married status of the more numerous lower clergy. These men were often
placed in charge of a church, or subsequently promoted to the priesthood,
thus being exposed to the temptation of using their office to their children's
advantage. (Perhaps allowance should also be made for a proportion of
priestly marriages, illicit yet valid due to some quirk of local custom law.) It

is possible that the second text applied only to the legitimately married lower clergy. In any case, one should not condemn out-of-hand men like "the priest Gerald of Massoteres with his daughter Berga" who received property in Valencia, nor the married clergy at the cathedral of Valencia.[12] Again: when the synods warn Valencian clergy to take a companion as they visit women of dubious reputation, the mild phrasing and the context of concern for clerical reputation show that these were pastoral and not social visitations.

The severe tone of other regulations, however, as well as the context of the times forbid the minimization of clerical immorality in Valencia. Ambiguity disappears in this decree of 1268:

> Since we have very often thought it well to warn the clergy, in synods and in visitations of the churches, to cast their concubines wholly aside and live decently as they ought; and since not many of them have bothered to reform because of these admonitions; we decree that whoever were found in public concubinage from the time of the siege of Murcia, or will be so found from now on, incur automatically a penalty of thirty morabatins.

The statute also says that "children born in future from such damnable intercourse, we think ought to be put aside."[13]

The evil was rooted and of long duration, though its exact extent cannot be determined. Some Valencian clerics concealed their mistresses in another parish.[14] The *Furs* provided that clerics with women were to lose the benefit of clerical justice and be treated in court as laymen.[15] The next bishop passed legislation similar to that of his predecessor, though this may have been routine; its interest lies in the fact that it specified "that any deacon, subdeacon, or priest" (the orders on whom the obligation of celibacy fell) who "presumes to keep his illegitimate offspring in the house he inhabits" was to pay a fine of 10 gold morabatins.[16]

All this undoubtedly relates to the traditional practice of *barraganía*, a form of lay and clerical concubinage peculiar to the kingdoms of the Spanish peninsula. This was in no sense a marriage, nor yet quite prostitution, but a semi-permanent arrangement which enjoyed (by way of a necessary evil) privileges in law. Its antecedents lie possibly in the concubinage of ancient Rome. Clerics bound to celibacy did not share in the legal toleration accorded; but they were influenced by the custom and by its degree of social acceptability. The thirteenth century saw a determined campaign to reduce and stamp out clerical *barraganía*. This raised echoes not only in the lower diocese of Valencia but in the northern part of the frontier kingdom as well.

In 1278 the bishop of Tortosa took up the problem in synod. He reviewed the efforts of popes and Spanish bishops so far in this century against "the disease which brings such infamy upon the clergy of Spain." Apparently needing more practical weapons against too widespread an evil, he commuted the standing penalty of excommunication into a severely punitive money fine. Clerics in minor orders were of less concern; their concubinage cases were each to be handled separately. Still, as late as 1343 the Tortosa bishop was to complain of "very many" clerics, tonsured and in minor orders, who keep women despite the efforts of his several predecessors.[17]

Confidence in the clergy of the new diocese as a group is not restored by reading the case of the homosexual pastor of St. Nicholas' church in Valencia city.[18] Misgivings are further increased when one encounters the case of a high cathedral dignitary, the sacristan William of Alaric. Charged in court with the abduction and rape of A. March's wife, William arranged for a royal waiver of prosecution. It is not likely that a formal charge of this magnitude, especially where a waiver of prosecution rather than a clearing trial is sought, would prove to be merely slander; slander would have produced a vigorous rebuttal, or at the very least some indication (as happened in similar waivers sometimes) of lack of evidence. William, a very rich man, was probably a priest as well as a major cathedral dignitary.[19] The episode did not prevent his rising even higher; he soon became archdeacon of Valencia. William was more fortunate than his colleague holding the same dignity at this time in the metropolitan cathedral, whose colder passions directed him rather to counterfeiting (coins of copper covered with gold leaf) and thence to jail for life.[20]

The financial position of the Valencian clergy seems to have been satisfactory; but "some clerics" were not satisfied. The synod of 1262 had to take drastic measures against those who sought to have what was not theirs, and who went so far as to "conceal and hide and transfer to their own purses sometimes the very money left by deceased persons in restitution for injuries or to pious causes for the sake of their souls." By lengthy court action these mean clerics deferred the day when they had to make compensation. This happened "a number of times to our certain knowledge." A "base impiety and horrible sin," it continued so long that by now it had almost been adopted as a custom, according to popular outcry. Therefore, all executors of wills, under pain of excommunication, were to conclude their business within a year of the client's death, meanwhile depositing the legacies "in a religious building." A salaried "patron" was appointed by the bishop to act under oath as defender-at-large of justice in the execution of wills. Sharp lawyers had stimulated the dishonesty, which mirrored some of the *furor legalis* of the age.[21]

From the beginning there was trouble with certain clerics' selling or pawning chalices and church goods.[22] Others—the evil seems widespread—descended like vultures upon the property of their deceased predecessors.[23] Still others negotiated to acquire "several chantries,"[24] farming out the duties to salaried vicars. "Many" irresponsibly swore oaths in connection with contracts and then, from avarice or forgetfulness, neglected the obligations thus shouldered. To uproot this last practice, no one in the diocese was allowed any oath of the sort for a full year, under pain of loss of benefice or, alternatively, excommunication.[25] In the tithe dispute, settled in 1268, one notes an intemperate urge to take every penny.[26]

The bishop dared not leave for the ecumenical council at Lyons in 1276 until he had settled the "many dissensions and scandals [which have] sprung up in our church." The canons in charge of collecting sections of church revenues, at a fixed lease price, had gathered the revenues belonging to others also, and refused to make restitution.[27] Some canons appropriated more of the living quarters owned by the chapter than they really needed, then loaned or rented them to laymen or to families of lower clerics ("clerics with wives").[28] What seems to have been an undignified scramble for extra houses and rents likewise required regulation.[29] The clergy was forbidden to demand or receive anything for ringing the church bell three times to announce a parishioner's death; nor could they keep the chains or goods of Moslem slaves who fled to the church to be baptized. Certain minute offerings were not to be taken unless freely tendered. Elaborate rules were promulgated to regulate funerals.[30]

A number of poor corpses were the subject of windy dispute, though the adjective "poor" is perhaps ill-chosen. The Moslems had not been long conquered when William Ferrer, pastor of St. Martin's in Valencia city, was locked in litigation with the Mercedarian church of St. Mary's at Puig, over the body of their *donné* Boniface and the bodies of his two young sons. No doubt Pastor William felt affection for them as being among his first parishioners; besides, they had given the Mercedarians over 2,000 solidi in burial fees. The pastor won the case in 1256 and was allowed to recover the 2,000 solidi and cart away the three corpses.

This sort of thing was not uncommon, nor was the fault on one side. An occasional litigation of the kind would even be expected, to adjust jurisdictions in the new diocese. But as a pattern—and the many quarrels over revenue in Valencia indicate pattern—it betrays a malaise, a worldly preoccupation with every petty right or claim. Pope Gregory IX was referring to this kind of greed-inspired litigation, on the scale of a great plague, in his appeal of 1234: "the abuse of litigation would extinguish the law binding men together, and exile harmony beyond the world's frontiers."[31] Into this same category falls the childishness of the St. Victorian monks, who systematically slandered the Mercedarians as having bribed the king so that Mercedarians might supplant the monks at St. Vincent's.[32] And the first diocesan synod had to order "that the Friars Preachers and Friars Minor be received with honor by the clergy."[33]

There was trouble with absenteeism, a problem "in our Valencian diocese."[34] There was also trouble with wandering clerical guests and adventurers. These clerics, and all others who claimed to be clerics, had to register at the cathedral, according to a regulation of the new bishop in 1276; they had to have a tonsure and wear clerical dress.[35] The bishop had made worldly and turbulent clerics the subject of public rebuke during his sermon at the cathedral. The present regulation had been introduced, he told the synod later, "because of the many scandals and frequent quarrels which come before us, very often, on this score."[36] This suggests a migration of unbeneficed clergy toward the frontier. In view of the many churches staffed adequately by the time of King James's death, with vicars to supply for the luckier holders of the profitable pastorate, Valencia would seem to have been a land of clerical opportunity. Small wonder if a fringe of enterprising clerical rascals or floaters had been borne in on this tide of settlement![37]

Our curiosity is intrigued by a brace of clerical murder victims. The first was William of Caceria, a priest in the household of the royal counsellor Raymond of Montañans; he was gravely wounded at Alcira by James of Canals. When the victim died, James was apprehended, convicted, and dealt with.[38] Had this priest been fulfilling some duty, secular or ecclesiastical, with a consequent unpopularity? A Brother William of Talamacha also came to an untimely end; in 1284 a roundup of his assaulters was in progress.[39] Was he an overzealous Dominican? A vicious person? A Hospitaller collecting the rent? A brave monk rebuking sin? We do not know.

Some general conclusions may be drawn from these documents, but with caution. Synodal bodies were not given to temperate language. They dealt with the darker side of clerical life. Some of their decrees would be formal and routine, repeating metropolitan or general church statutes. The mere repetition of decrees was not significant, because the modern idea that decrees stand until repealed did not hold; they would need repetition from time to time to stay in force, and the traditional formulas would recur in them.[40] Other laws would be illuminative of local affairs, but applicable to relatively few or else to matters of little real importance for an estimate of clerical character.

Perhaps most of all our understanding of the word "cleric" needs adjustment. The modern "cleric," chosen and trained by his church and with a substantial measure of authority and responsibility, would be the medieval bishop and priest and in a measure the deacon or subdeacon, though the elements of choice and training were often at a minimum. The other orders would best be understood today if termed "liturgical assistants." Their share of spiritual powers was usually minute. Their qualifications and discipline were a matter of much less control and their morale was consequently lower. If they had no benefice there was no leverage for disciplinary action against them. A few dozen such adventurers who had contrived to acquire some clerical order as a step to better things could distort legislative records, making it difficult to see how the average diocesan cleric did his job. An examination of the kingdom's clergy is concerned not with the wandering rowdy nor with the young pluralist in his city chambers or his castle, but rather with the *de facto* incumbent—the pastor, the vicar, and the like. In any event, this less edifying element may be balanced by those few clergy of sanctity and dedication who graced this frontier and whose reputation was to continue down to our own day.[41]

Bearing all this in mind, one is left with a clerical society which sheltered a disturbing number of men unworthy of their calling, but in which the majority performed their round of difficult duties with some sense of dedication. This majority stands quietly behind every statute lashing out at the "some" or "several" or even "many." They are present in the document as loudly by their silence as they would be if listed by name. What was the proportion of unworthy men? As high as 30 percent? As low as 10 percent? What was the intensity of dedication in the average decent cleric? It was enough to keep him chained to a monotonous and exacting liturgical routine at an obscure post, to keep him subject to obedience and rebuke, and to keep him (the three major orders) celibate. He may have been much more, but he was not less. Were his sacrifices compensated proportionately by economic security, by authority, and by self-importance, so that his continuing dedication would lose its quality of the admirable? It seems improbable, especially on that expansive frontier.

The taint of greed and the self-righteous legal strife had roots in contemporary society and patterns of life. These and similar defects perhaps reveal the over-all situation in the new diocese as unhealthy. On the credit side of the ledger stand the vigorous legislation, the high concept of the clergy implicit in the lay indignation when reporting some of the defects, and the concern for liturgical prayer-life throughout the diocese.

In judging the character of the majority, it is even risky to assume a gradation from wicked to good; there may well have been, in the circumstances of patronage and frontier opportunity, a contrasting black-and-white. Nor can one argue, as Michavila has recently done, from the state of the higher clergy to a proportionately worse condition of the pastors.[42] The canons and dignitaries were the trained university men, the ambitious or talented, and those who knew the proper people, plus a solid corps of men from the feudal families. They were not drawn off, like cream, from the lower clergy.

All in all, though the Valencian clergy were not untouched by the "pride and greed" of contemporary Europe,[43] as a body they do seem to have been adequate to the parochial tasks (as then defined) so important to this frontier.

6—1

ᴥ Last Testaments in Valencia

It is easier to analyze the activities of the clergy or to review administrative history, owing to the nature of the documents which would usually be preserved, than to reach a judgment as to the quality of the mass of laymen. Any assessment of the "church," however, must include the laity. Much of what is classed as ecclesiastical institution or custom exists primarily in and through the layman. It is he who gives them vigor and application, or allows them to decline into formalism. He supports or neglects them; he is passive or responsive or indifferent or ambivalent; rejects, vaguely respects, or enthusiastically mirrors and promotes their inner meaning. The individual layman is not only within the institution, he is within it as a constituent, creative cell. He makes the difference between a living institution and a dead one. In this context it is important to remember that even the reluctant, the apathetic, or the rebel in a society will in turn be shaped by its institutions— as long as these institutions retain their traditional position among the majority, or their vitality among a dynamic minority.

A theological excursus is probably required at this point. One of the fascinating aspects of medieval life is the tension between ideal and reality— the one exalted and in the stars, the other often a prey of malice and primitive brutalities. To watch medieval people climb the stairway to the stars, and tumble down, and climb again is an instructive exercise in the study of man. These ideals were sometimes fixed, and almost always modified or influenced in some way, by theological notions.

To the medieval man the church was not simply a religious corporation or an institution of fellowship, socially structured and hierarchically organized. It was not only a tribal people of God, a community or Christendom bound into unity by the New Covenant. It was primarily a spiritual "person," whose soul was the Holy Spirit. In this "mystical body" Christ existed, through it He acted, and by it He incorporated into Himself the individual Christian. The visible organism with all its functions was not a different and separate reality, but another mode-of-being of this inner mystical thing, and simultaneously an instrument by which the latter was realized. Theologians like Aquinas, Albert, Bonaventure, and the other thirteenth-century scholastics gave contemporary expression to this ancient doctrine.[44]

The Christian thus possessed an interior second nature, infused into him and fused with his proper nature, by which he communicated in God's own life and was in a sense divinized. He was now to live, suffer, and triumph within his own local context, not merely as consecrated morally to Christ, but as another Christ by virtue of this new and higher life-principle. The medieval man, therefore, embraced a dizzying paradox. He was at once the weak sinner in peril of his soul, inclined to evil and damnation, constrained to walk warily and in penance through his time of earthly trial, and yet even now partaker of Christ and triumphant heir to all creation.

It was precisely to promote this unique kind of identity with Christ, and to intensify one's growth into Him, that the liturgical formation of the medieval man, with its ever-changing cycle of ritual, existed in each parish. And it was in the light of this mystical incorporation that the liturgy was centered around sacred history, unfolding the story of creation, redemption by Christ, and fellowship of the earthly community with the saints and martyrs. The para-liturgical ceremonies worked to the same end, as did the popular forms of devotion and celebration, and even the luxuriant hagiological mythology and symbolism.

The historian is often able to do little more than portray the visible structure of the church, with its evolving shapes. The nature of spiritual activity within the medieval community or individual is a relatively inaccessible object of study. The historian, therefore, contents himself rather with the more prosaic external activities, with good works and bad, with generalizations on moral standards, and with tantalizing glimpses of souls caught at single moments in their unceasing change and growth. In an age of strong clerical supervision, the layman may thus appear more as an object, and the active role he played may be obscured. But his permanent, inner life-pattern and function must never be forgotten, otherwise one loses the key to understanding the medieval layman's psychology. Even those who fell ludicrously short of the ideals implied by their divinized status could not completely escape the mentality and forms induced. This mentality and the devices which promoted it had significance both as cultural conditioner and as cultural manifestation. The significance would be shallow but comprehensive for many, profound and intense for others.

The lay people played a role in the administration of the parishes. They centered their guild life on the churches of the religious Orders. In their last testaments they supported the divers institutions of the diocese liberally. And they rapidly multiplied chantries in the churches. Even the ecclesiastical structure was modified by a sort of public opinion or popular pressure. Reactionary or conservative organizational principles yielded before the people's initiative and enthusiasm, as can be seen for example in the popular support of the Mendicants and in the increasing autonomy of the individual parish church in Christendom during the thirteenth century. The phenomenon of a numerous clergy predicates also a very wide base of relatives and neighbors who in proprietary mood could make known their discontents and needs.

The pertinent documents which survive for Valencia often fall into two classes: those recording unusually bad deeds, and those recording unusually good ones. In the mass of the people one can discern also a few currents; there are examples of heresy and of apostasy to Islam, and of sharp disputes between clergy and laity. When it comes to specific individuals, the documents more usually concern the urban than the rural population. As a whole the people were probably not much worse nor much better than their contemporaries elsewhere, since an excess in either direction would have deposited traces in the not overly discreet documents at Valencia in this period. One may begin by attributing to the populace the characteristics, stupidity, wisdom, good-heartedness, cruelty, shortcomings, and virtues common to people of all times and places, as well as the intense amalgam of all these proper to the medieval man located in the more advanced—that is to say, southerly—regions of Europe in the thirteenth century.

These were a religious people as a group, rather ebulliently so, as the general run of Valencian documents demonstrates: the preludes and formulas of the documents, the enthusiasm for church construction at the capital and throughout the realm (when a place as settled as Huesca was still managing with a mosque for its cathedral); the people's religious guilds; their concern for the sick and the poor; their dowering of maidens and building of bridges from religious motives; their preoccupation (when they can afford it) both with a proper funeral and with a steady supply of prayers to follow their departed souls; the indications of so many rural shrines, and so on.

In building their new kingdom the people of Valencia responded to the offer of indulgences. These provided a powerful stimulus for building programs, as in the case of the Dominicans at Valencia city, or in the rebuilding of a bridge there across the Guadalaviar after the destruction during the siege, and in projects for community good generally.[45] No really dramatic stories of the use of indulgences survive for Valencia; since indulgences were used so effectively in Valencia, however, it may be helpful to insert such a story from King James's recent crusade against Majorca, where conditions were so similar. The dead, remaining in great numbers after the battle, had raised the fear of plague. The bishops therefore offered an indulgence of a thousand days "to every man that should cast out from the city the body of a dead Saracen; then the soldiers, by means of horses and mules and nags, thrust out and dragged from the city all the dead bodies gladly, for the sake of the indulgence; and they made a great pile of firewood and burned them, and in this wise gained their pardon." The incident illustrates the use of spiritual means to serve the commonplace temporal needs of a society; and, while showing the church supplementing for a lack of civil institutions in a specific case, it also demonstrates the esteem of King James's people for indulgences.[46]

In the memoirs of King James one may discern something of the spirituality of his people and, by indirection, of the Valencian portion of it: its touching naïveté, its virile energy, the shrewd eye somehow never straying far from the material opportunities, and finally (decently interred by shame at times) the violent sins which scar it. There is also evidence that the intellectual foundations of the faith, especially on the part of the uninstructed masses, were shallow, and on the part of those with more advantages a shade too arrogantly rationalistic.[47]

The last testaments of well-to-do Valencians reveal something of their authors. Direct clerical influence was at a minimum in the making of Valencian wills, for the clergy were forbidden by local law the office of drawing up these documents.[48] Most of the wills provide for the poor and the church. Many of them especially remember the wretches carried off to Moslem slavery—"aware," as the king puts it, "that the ransoming of captives holds chief place among the other virtues."[49] King James's own life reflected this virtue. In 1276 when one of his household had been made captive, he did not hesitate to stop the royal feeding of a hundred beggars daily to divert this revenue to the captive's release, even though at the time James was close to death and concerned to multiply works of charity.[50] Earlier he gave a Valencian grant to Ramona Cospin, "houses in Játiva free and frank so that she can sell them right away in order to redeem" her captive husband Dominic.[51] In his autobiography the king even rebukes a crossbowman for cowardice during a Valencian skirmish by telling him that, if the Moors had captured him, he could have been rescued easily for only 150 to 200 solidi.[52]

Valencian last testaments include such works of mercy, along with works of piety and prayerfulness, as a normal pattern. One citizen, "seized with a serious illness from which I fear I shall die," leaves "fifty solidi for redeeming one captive." He makes provision for his parish church, for each of the other parishes inside the city and in the near suburbs, for the cathedral, its sacristan, two hospitals, five religious Orders, his pastor, and (a lump sum to be spent at the executor's discretion) 150 solidi for other pious causes. Like many of his fellow citizens, he takes care of his debts, lest he be unjust, and sets aside twelve pence for every pastor of the city who appears at his funeral. He is not really a wealthy man, and has family claims to consider, so the proportion of his property given to good causes is generous. He asks to be buried at the cathedral.[53]

"A citizen and resident of Valencia" leaves small sums to every city parish, a special gift to his own parish and to several religious houses, and something to insure an ornamental tomb in the Hospitaller churchyard.[54] Another, requesting burial in his brother's grave in the cathedral, arranges for "two clerics to offer requiem Mass for my parents' souls" at their burial place in Zaragoza; 50 solidi are for the poor, 90 more for several religious houses and hospitals, the same amount to the cathedral building fund, and the same to buy a fine bier cloth for his funeral—later to be sewn into a liturgical vestment, a chasuble. He furnishes 50 solidi for redeeming captives, but looks to a mass freeing of poorer slaves. A typical item, besides the twelve pence for every priest at his funeral, is ten gifts of 10 solidi each to be given to the "embarrassed poor," that is, to people who had come down in the world but would be too humiliated to descend further to begging in public.[55]

A knight of large property gives his saddle, bridle, and war horse to the Mercedarians of Arguines, and arranges to be buried at their church in a splendid tomb. Sixteen hundred solidi go to his parish St. Bartholomew's, from rents on houses in the parish, largely to be used for anniversary Masses. There are smaller gifts for five religious houses and for each of the city parishes, including a special gift for St. Mary of the Sea; he had already given great tracts to Merced.[56] The wife of another knight, having provided for her debts, a proper burial by the nuns of St. Elizabeth's convent, a chantry, a perpetual vigil lamp, and a chalice of silver, leaves 100 solidi to the cathedral, 200 to the Franciscans, five solidi "to every parish" in the city, and her bier cloth for a vestment.[57] A parishioner of St. Stephen's remembers the parish and the pastor and leaves sums for five religious Orders and the cathedral. His funeral must be done "splendidly."[58] A great noble disposes of large sums, with a general direction to divide it "among the Templars, and to other religious Orders and the redemption of captives and the dowering of maidens and the care of the poor, especially the embarrassed poor."[59] A lady of the city, expressing her desire to be put away "into a tomb of rock" of no mean price (300 solidi), also leaves bequests "for dowering maidens" and "for clothing the poor." She orders bread for the poor on her burial day, many Masses for her soul, twelve pence for every priest at the funeral, a vestment made from her bier cloth, and her beds to be given to the hospital. Each parish, nine religious houses, and two hospitals share from her 100 solidi, and the cathedral receives 200.[60]

Citizen Lazarus of Vilella, glumly admonishing that nothing is more certain than death and nothing more uncertain than its hour, provides in this his last illness for burial at the cathedral, naming one set of executors for his Valencia properties and another for those in the region of Zaragoza. Besides 30 solidi to the cathedral, he leaves 10 solidi to its canons, and 10 solidi to five different religious houses, as well as twelve pence to every parish and twelve pence to every priest present when he is buried.[61] The knight William Ochova Alemán in 1255 bequeaths two silver marks for a chalice at the cathedral, 10 marks for prolonged ringing of bells at his demise, and 300 solidi "for making one Bible."[62]

It was not unusual in those days, once one found one's foot to be inescapably on the high road to the future world, to assume the habit of a religious Order. The status of these *conversi in extremis* was something of a puzzle for the canonists, who nonetheless tended to hold the vovent to his vows if he recovered. Some people even assumed this status partly to insure themselves of the superior medical service at the monastic infirmary during their final days. In Valencia the custom led to some sharp conditions being dictated by the bishop to the hospital of the Trinitarians; piety was one thing, but a dead layman was of more value to cathedral revenue than was a dead religious.[63] King James himself in 1276 would pass from the city of Valencia to the heavenly city garbed, down all the old warrior's nearly seven-foot length, in the robes of a monk of Poblet.[64]

CIVIL AND ECCLESIASTICAL LEGISLATION

The laws codified in the *Furs* of the city and realm in 1245 and 1276 have a more universal relevance than the wills. These laws were not royal impositions but the product of a legal commission, presented for criticism and approbation to the nobles, clergy, and townsmen of Valencia.[65] They were intended to fit the needs of this one kingdom. In matters of daily living they bore the stamp of habits or customs. In general, a disciplinary law should indicate, aside from the common permanent needs of men, either prevalent faults or those not easily tolerated. They may point to either of two extremes, then: public laxity or public reaction and vigilance. No matter which is true of a given law, something of contemporary society can be seen in it, at the very least a sense of engagement with the subject of the law.

The laws against blasphemy, for instance, were severe. Such detailed legislation usually indicates a population who take religion with some seriousness. A distinction was made between thoughtlessly "speaking evil of God or the Holy Mary" (for which a fine of ten solidi or a light whipping was imposed), and a businesslike blasphemy for which one must expect to lose no less than 100 solidi. This latter fine diminished to 50 when apostles were the subject, and to 20 for martyrs.[66] There must have been a brisk activity in blasphemy-fines, which were handled by ecclesiastical courts, because one of the specific points of friction between the bishop and the archdeacon in the earliest days of Valencia was the possession of such fines.[67]

Perjury, involving a false oath before God, was deemed so terrible as to require no legal punishment at all: "it is enough that Our Lord be its avenger, for a sufficient penalty on perjury is the one which he must expect from Our Lord."[68] The taking of solemn oaths by high and low was a widespread custom in James's realms and often a legal proof of innocence. This law would therefore have been an absurdity on the part of the authorities unless it reflected a general state of mind at the time.

There was a strange prohibition against publicly fashioning the "faces or images of God or of the saints, or making or painting them in the streets, or placing or carrying them to sell there," with a penalty of 20 solidi. Had this some relevance to the frontier situation, representing Moslem influence or reflecting a desire to avoid occasions of conflict? Was it designed to control inept or even disrespectful rendering or to protect a monopoly?[69] On Sundays and on Good Friday public baths and ovens were to be closed, and respect for the day shown by all subjects, "for Our Lord Jesus Christ wishes that people so abstain on these days."[70] (The law added, while on the subject of baths, that men and women were never to use the same public baths on the same days.) On holy days shops had to close, and no one was allowed to work in the fields.[71] There were restrictive laws for Jews and Moors, either curbing irreverence or compelling an outward conformity to certain modes of reverence. A physician summoned to the bedside of a fatally ill citizen was not to give his services if the patient refused to prepare his soul properly too.[72] In this connection, the settlement charter for Villahermosa (1243) provided that inhabitants were to be freed from the death duty of one-fifth of their goods if they died fortified with the sacraments or else suddenly; but, "if one will have died in illness without confession and the reception of the body of Christ, by his own negligence, let his possessions be taxed."[73] The author of this condition was the former Moslem king of Valencia; it undoubtedly issued from the proverbial zeal of the convert. Exaggerations often point to some more moderate common attitude, however, which in this case would be an appreciation of the last sacraments.

There was no mercy in the *Furs* for heresy; burning with confiscation of all goods was the punishment.[74] Even aside from specific statutes like this, the very tone of the code in its expressed general motivation and habitual formulas reveals an attitude of intense seriousness toward religion and an urge to engage it with affairs of practical life. Even allowing for the probable influence of clerical draftsmen and canon law, this tone is striking.

Ecclesiastical legislation yields its valuable items. The diocesan synods were concerned not only with clerical but also with lay discipline. They reveal that as late as 1273 "there are many in our city and diocese who do not know the Lord's Prayer, that is, the Our Father, or else do not know it well; and there are very few who know the Creed."[75] While this reveals nothing of the people's devotion or morality, it speaks volumes for their lack of instruction, since the *Pater* and *Credo* were then the basis of what instruction existed. The clergy were told to chant these slowly and loudly during the office, and to teach parishioners their meaning. The legislation against embezzlement of testamentary funds predicates an even more widespread trust in the clergy, inasmuch as they were obviously so often designated as executors.[76]

Gambling at dice, a passion for the layman at Valencia as elsewhere in the Middle Ages, was forbidden by diocesan synods, partly from puritanical motives and partly because the game easily passed the limits of self-control. Violence and blasphemy were, not rarely, concomitants of this sport. The situation seems to have been a problem of the new urbanism which the clergy were unable to meet with anything more intelligent than a universal ban. There is no record of gambling houses in Valencia such as had to be regulated by Alphonse the Learned in his realms in 1276.[77] These houses soon must have existed, however, because by 1301 James II had introduced legislation for Valencia prohibiting the public licensing of gambling houses.

Public adultery was a problem, though perhaps uncommon enough. Bishop Andrew had arranged to have such people denounced in church as excommunicates, on every Sunday and feast day. Yet the decree had to be insisted upon later, because the sinners had succeeded in casting doubt upon the intention of the law.[78] Public sinners, duelists, "those who die in tournaments," and usurers were forbidden ecclesiastical burial.[79] Some superstition existed, especially sortilege with baptismal water, and divers conjurations by witches at marriages, condemned in a decree of 1258. Was it chance that the celebrated Arnold of Vilanova, who grew up in Valencia during this period, later dedicated his work on magic to the bishop of Valencia?[80] A recent student of Valencian life, as it was reflected through the office of justiciar during the century after the Christian conquest, was not at all impressed by the moral tone generally revealed in his sources; but perhaps some allowance must be made in this instance for the fact that police records are always depressing.[81]

As for the people's devotional practices, the favorite saints for whom they named churches and chantries reveal a catholic taste. They included the warriors Michael, George, and Martin; the persecuted Christians at Valencia in Roman times Valerius and Vincent; the patron of seafaring peoples (today's Santa Claus), St. Nicholas; those favorites of the western Mediterranean, the penitent Magdalene, Lazarus, and John the Baptist; the protomartyr St. Stephen; and some apostles like Peter, Andrew, and John.[82] One historian sees in this choice a proof of dominant settlement by Léridans, and presumably a Lérida pattern of piety and devotions.[83] In the rural and noncapital areas, the Virgin and St. Michael were favorites. The choice reflects the choosers—a seafaring, warfaring, militantly Christian, frontier people, who appreciated the need for penance, were mindful of their continuity with Valencia's Christian past, and could not afford to be unmindful of martyrdom.[84] Their most sacred days, when even the Jews had to close their shops, were Christmas, Easter, Pentecost, the feast of John the Baptist, and certain feasts of Our Lady.[85] Rental contracts often specified one or more of these days, or else St. Michael's day, for payments. Valencians carried candles and a cross in the general processions. They tolled the parish bell thrice to announce a male parishioner's passing, twice for a woman, and "over and over and over again" for a priest.[86] They fasted twice a week. At confession they accepted severe penances: pastors were ordered to "impose fasts, alms, pardons, prayers, pilgrimages, and the like."[87]

The "unspeakable public sins," which may have been rare, indicate something of the time and place; they are murder, violence to one's parents, running arms to the Moslems, homosexuality, and heresy—all reserved to the bishop's forgiveness.[88]

A number of guilds or brotherhoods existed in Valencia city, religious in aim rather than occupational, though usually organized around a trade.[89] They seem to have formed here on the frontier from the very first; a law of James the Conqueror soon controlled their number and perhaps even suppressed them briefly. At this early stage of their evolution they were not so much guilds performing works of charity, as charity expressing itself through the handy form of professional groupings. By 1283 fifteen of them—including fishermen, tailors, barbers, and notaries—won a powerful place in municipal government. At the turn of the century, King James II will suppress the lot. Apparently fearful of intrigues and monopolies, he left only the prayer brotherhood of St. James. The later charters of a number of guilds proclaimed that they were revivals of similar organizations well established in the immediate past.[90] They may even be survivals, if the suppression had involved only a revocation of recognition as a public organization.

In May 1268, King James I allowed the formal and legal existence of the furriers, under Dominican tutelage: "We James, . . . to honor the Dominican house in Valencia, St. Dominic's, grant that the skin processors of the city of Valencia may establish and cause to be established . . . lawfully and without any impediment a brotherhood."[91] This is a valuable document, in view of the almost total lack of documentation of the early confraternities. A similar precious glimpse into the existence of this organization, in a Valencian will of 1252, shows that it had been flourishing sixteen years before this charter of foundation; it may have been organized during the decade after the conquest of Valencia city. The will was made by Dominic Calderón, who left "to the confraternity of furriers of Valencia five solidi"; he ordered "that to the same confraternity the twelve pence which I owe them be paid." The Dominicans also seem to have had a brotherhood in honor of St. Peter Martyr from 1269.[92] There was a brotherhood at St. Bartholomew's fairly early. In a will of 1261 Bernard of Nausa left it five solidi.[93] Another Valencian, García Chicot, in his 1279 last testament spoke of it: "I leave to the Brotherhood of St. Bartholomew, of which I am a brother, five solidi."[94] A noted brotherhood was that of St. James, a spiritual and benevolent association of a hundred select laymen, and probably their wives, together with a body of canons and clerics. Their center was the altar of St. James at the cathedral, where King James gave some of his rents to found a chaplaincy.[95] They soon had a little house near the back of the cathedral just off to its right. Peter of Barberá left 20 solidi to them in his will of 1258, one of the two largest items in that will.[96] Their origins go back to a clerical brotherhood begun at the cathedral in 1246. In 1263 King James gave his official blessing to their formal organization:

Seeing the charities and alms and sacrifices which you canons and clerics, and your companions, perform in the brotherhood you have recently formed under the title "St. James," we grant . . . that you and the hundred laymen aforesaid may construct and build, and cause to be constructed and built, an altar of St. James in the Valencian cathedral.[97]

And in a codicil of 1276 to his last testament the king applied to "his" altar and chapel of this confraternity a shop and its rent.[98]

The Hospitaller church in Valencia also had its brotherhood; Teixidor thought this the oldest for which a document exists, but earlier evidence has been seen above. The Hospitaller group appears in the will of Bernard Dalmau in 1273: "I admit and profess that I am a co-brother of the house of the Hospital of St. John of Jerusalem, and I choose and determine my burial in their cemetery of Valencia." Bernard was a lawyer, who in 1259 had won from the king as remuneration for his services a pension of two hundred Valencian solidi.[99] Guilds were not confined to the capital; for example the crown confirmed an existing brotherhood of artisans at Murviedro in 1289. But documentation is richer at the capital.

Pious lay corporations, professional and nonprofessional, were no novelty in Christendom. In the thirteenth century, however, they were emerging in new forms, often closely associated as participants in the prayers and merits of a religious Order, and with a remarkably varied field of action. Besides the expected devotions and the works of mutual benevolence and charity, one finds them fending off wolves, fixing roads, erecting installations against threatened floods, running small hospices, acting as lawmen, fighting usury, caring for strangers, collecting and distributing alms, and so on.

No field of social aid, however bizarre, seems to have been foreign to the brotherhoods of medieval Europe. At Toulouse, just north of the Aragon kingdom, one confraternity fielded five thousand militia for a campaign in the Albigensian crusade. A Valencian confraternity consisted of converts to Christianity—presumably from the Moslem majority. Information is lacking as to the work being done specifically by the Valencian brotherhoods, though the movement is well documented elsewhere in Europe and Spain. The value of such organizations for a frontier area is obvious, both for the social activities of each group and for the more pervading contribution they would make as framework to the lives of participating citizens. They also cut across the arbitrary parish lines to unite professional or other groups arriving on the frontier from many regions.

In all times and places, scoundrels abound; only an excess of them in quantity or intensity would be pertinent here. Thus, that Roderick of Montoro waylaid the merchant Hugh Robert at Alcira in 1268, robbing him and abusing him and "pulling out his teeth" so that he died, is really of little interest to the history of social morality.[100] Sometimes, however, the solution of a crime reveals a strong sense of family honor in the population.

At Játiva in 1273 one Simon is to be set free by the court if his defense be shown true: that "you found your wife the defunct Tolosa, and A. Sarcedel defunct, committing fornication or adultery together, and you killed them both."[101] We may disregard the more colorful vices and violence, where they seem to have no connection with the generality of the population as such.

The red-light district, for which the city of Valencia was shortly to become notorious among the floating population of the maritime world, may not have existed yet. However, there is evidence of prostitution from the time of the crusade. In the book of Valencian land grants, which seems to have something for almost everybody, a house in the respectable Tarragona quarter is conceded to "Mary the Portuguese, prostitute." She may charitably be considered a repentant sinner, or at least retired from her profession. She has as neighbours the houses of two archbishops and of two bishops, as well as a church. There is a grant also to the "king of the harlots," but the literal meaning of *arlot* is "youth". This functionary may be the superintendent of court troubadours and entertainers, as Vincke believes; or he may already have become what he certainly was in Valencian legislation of the early fourteenth century, the municipal master-pimp.

Legislation on the subject of prostitution began in Valencia with the reform law of 1311; by that time severe measures were required to discourage the business, and this reflects on the preceding decades as well.[102] It is probable that during the thirteenth century the prostitutes had been gathering already into that pleasant spot just beyond the walls between Roteros, La Pobla, and the Moslem quarter.

The institution of slavery, with its inevitably corrupting influence upon the owners, merits at least a passing notice. It was not uncommon in the realm, though not yet so very widespread as it was to be in the next century.[103]

The nobles of the countryside assay a certain percentage of shabby personalities. They mounted a sustained opposition, for instance, against the conversion of the Moslem workers, even when the latter were freemen. The reason lay in the consequent diminution which the ecclesiastical tithe would make in the owner's own revenue.[104] One also discerns an instinct in this gentry toward insinuating a hand into the revenues of church and monastery. Among those who "do not fear God nor honor man,"[105] as King James complained, there was a rowdy delight in damaging religious houses.[106] These were general conditions, and Valencia may even have suffered less from them than did other realms of King James, though the charters of protection frequently given suggest otherwise. A number of papal and local ecclesiastical decrees, condemning those who misused or unjustly held church property and dating from this period, are found in the archives of the cathedral of Valencia. King James thought knights "bad people" in general "because there are no people in the world so arrogantly highhanded [*sobrer*] as are knights."[107] But James was not as objective an observer in this matter as one might wish.

To curb such violence, the king gave his charter of protection freely to churches and churchmen in Valencia. Those holding it could carry royal pennants and fly them on their houses. A breach of such a charter could bring swift retaliation from the king. The *Furs* demanded restitution and double damages from the culprit; the charter often specified a severe fine besides; and the king would take such further action as his wounded dignity required and his limited armed forces allowed.[108] One such charter (1254) to the bishop and canons of Valencia set the fine at 1,000 morabatins and secured the beneficiaries from seizure of goods for various legal causes.[109] Some of those charters given to clergy or religious in the realm of Valencia are short and formal, others impressively elaborate.

The unpleasantries of the nobility against clergy can more usually be ascribed to such origins as feudal rivalry for property or grievances over the tithe, rather than to spiritual dissatisfaction. This may be why James, in giving to the church the town of Puzol, promised to guard them in the holding against all opposition but "particularly against William of Entenza and his supporters."[110] Considerable numbers of nobles could be generous, a number of them even to the point of heroism. Some landowners of the kingdom joined the Order of Merced, bringing with them their properties. A man in Villarreal gave up his estates in his own lifetime to found a hospital. The high noble William of Cervera, one of the king's closest friends and advisers, became a Cistercian (his brother was already abbot of Poblet).

The appearance of a few people eminent for their attempts to recreate Christ's personality under a form suited to their times and environment betokens a segment of population religious enough to discern their merit (for canonizations then depended as much upon popular advocacy as upon intrinsic merit) and to be influenced by them. On the other hand, the rise of such men to prominence may seem less a tribute to a society capable of producing them than a measure of reaction by part of that society to contemporary wickedness. The Valencian saints, separately discussed in an appendix, were not products of the Valencian scene in this early period, but shapers of it.

A number of relevant topics have not been touched, such as the violence and even fanaticism of religious feeling among the masses, or the attitude of Christians toward converts from Islam and toward the Jews, or the unhealthy influences of urban poverty and clerical inadequacies. It suffices, for the scope of this undertaking, to have seen the mutual causality of people and institution. That is, the institutions were not just outside the people, directing them; they were rather a body to which the people were a soul. The institutional mechanisms could not properly operate on the frontier unless one supposes this financial and moral support, this esteem and active cooperation and participation by the laity. Through these institutions the populace or a considerable portion of it was both answering a need it felt and expressing itself. Through activities, laws, generous legacies, and compliance with restrictive ecclesiastical injunctions, it manifested underlying aspirations and principles which formed a recognizable mentality, a climate of public opinion.

The foundations may have been weak. A lack of instruction is evident, a strain of materialism, and a sufficiency of clerical and lay scandal. The interaction of populace with institution nevertheless persisted; through this interaction the people were as much creative agents of the institutions as they were its acquiescent instruments. Despite the small number of settlers the intentions and spirit of the frontier people, incarnate in their institutions, were adequate to the task of imposing the Christian pattern of society, the communal personality, upon the conquered land.

VIII

ECONOMIC FOUNDATIONS
OF THE DIOCESE OF VALENCIA

The overriding problem of a frontier diocese was to stabilize its economic base. Everything else depended upon this. The Gothic façade of a parish church, the brightly costumed procession in the streets or field, the strong chant of clerics, or the sounding of the bells—all the many externals which were helping to wrest Valencia to the semblance of a Christian society—reposed in turn upon an economic foundation. This was equally true of the extensive system of charity and social work. In Valencia the economic base involved three problems: firmly to move the king from promises to action; shrewdly to administer, invest, or convert current holdings; and especially to define the tithes and enforce their collection.

These prime objectives were pursued simultaneously with lesser campaigns. Accords must be negotiated concerning church properties held by the king, nobles, other bishops, and religious communities. A division of revenues must be arranged between bishop and chapter, among chapter dignitaries, and between diocese and parish. There were problems of constructing and elaborately furnishing a cathedral, housing the dignitaries and canons with their staffs, transporting, storing, and marketing the tithe produce, and so on.

All this was to be done in such a manner as to support the largest number of clerics possible, on a scale decently comparable to that of other dioceses. There was a clerical dignity to maintain; in those somewhat barbarous times, this could best be managed in conjunction with a certain outward show. Only under special circumstances, and for special types like the Mendicants, could the stark appearances of apostolic poverty serve. The majesty of God grew vague where splendor dimmed. Thus, in Valencia the bishop of Segorbe-Albarracín became a figure of fun, "scorned" by Valencians because he had to live in a small room just off the church. A proverb grew common: "the bishop of Albarracín—two mules and a nag."[1]

Besides this obligation of splendor, the bishop of Valencia had to provide for the usual legal, educational, charitable, and other functions of a diocese. And the expense of litigation alone must have been a frightful waste. The Valencian church had a sort of reverse Midas touch, transforming any difficult situation into a ferocious legal quarrel, a fair number of which had to be settled at Rome. However, the rest of Europe was resounding enthusiastically with like quarrels.

It is not correct to say, as do historians of the stature of Chabás and Sanchís Sivera, that money from abroad and especially from Languedoc was used to establish the diocese of Valencia. Funds did come south from Languedoc.[2] Chabás is surprised that no trace of them remains; a closer look at the documentary context dispels the mystery. The money was required for the continuation of the crusade. To collect it in Languedoc for this purpose was normal enough; to have asked it for diocesan endowment was neither normal nor necessary. Endowing the new diocese was the duty of the crown of Aragon.

ཀྵ THE KING'S DEFAULT AND COMPROMISE

King James was obliged by tradition, and especially by the promise made at the parliament of Monzón and drawn into an official document at Lérida (1236), to finance the diocese "first and before everything" during the most costly initial stages of its organizational development. The king's strict laws against buying or inheriting or receiving property made direct crown support even more imperative. Still engaged in the expensive latter stages of the conquest more to the south, however, the king was unable to do more than a bare minimum. There was the expected formal endowing of the church with mosques and mosque properties in a document at Valencia in 1238.[3] But in April 1239, when Pope Gregory IX was arranging for a decision as to which metropolitan was to receive jurisdiction over Valencia, he closed his letter with a strong admonition to King James on the matter of endowing the new church:

> We seriously exhort our beloved son in Christ, the king of Aragon, according to the wisdom given him by God, that he should devoutly meditate on how everything put aside for the praise and glory of the divine name is amassed as treasure in heaven; [and that he should] assign to the future bishop, and to the cathedral and other churches of the city, a fitting endowment . . .[4]

In November 1241, under pressure from the Valencian church, King James finally amplified his initial gifts to the new diocese. Besides confirming to the diocese all the mosques and Moslem cemeteries, he agreed to hand over a lump sum of 10,000 silver besants.[5] The manner of endowment was to be decided by five arbiters: the archbishop of Tarragona, the masters of the Hospital and Temple, Prince Ferdinand, and the viscount of Cardona.[6] It is quite possible that some of this endowment was paid by the king's assuming responsibility for diocesan expenditures up to an agreed sum. Most of it, however, seems to have come in properties, or in monies which could be invested in properties so as to yield a permanent income. The award included a hospice near the cathedral, two jovates of land, houses, a tower, and a tenth of all that the Moors paid to the king; and it incorporated also the previous promises and gifts of the king to the diocese. A crown privilege was separately provided, since the church had been forbidden indiscriminate buying in the realm of Valencia.[7] The agreement was regarded as a second endowment, a supplement to the preliminary charter by which the church had received the mosques. In all, it was not a princely sum. The salary of the Valencia sacristan for ten years would surpass it, so that its value as capital was considerably less than that single salary. Before the end of the next year, the bishop had 5,000 silver besants, or perhaps their equivalent in property, and had written a receipt for this amount.[8]

A few days later the king turned over buildings in front of the cathedral, in lieu of the other 5,000 besants, the transaction taking the form of a sale to the bishop.[9] Judging from this equivalence of value, the previous 5,000 besants could hardly have purchased any grand estates. Among these buildings were fourteen "houses or lodgings, which are crown property." They were intended for the chapter, "for your personal residences." A special privilege was supplied to permit their purchase.[10] If the houses constituted the bulk of the purchase, this would imply a sales value of 350 besants or over 1,000 solidi apiece. Each building probably included a small farm or garden outside the city walls.[11]

James was soon to be accused of having packed the early chapter with favorites, and by this means craftily to have insured himself against having to sign a stricter compromise.[12] In his favor should be counted a number of privileges, tax exemptions, and smaller gifts over the years such as the houses in Murviedro or the park at Játiva.[13] The wrangling only increased, and the case had to be brought to Rome. In 1274, in a lengthy and irritable charter, James made a final settlement.[14] These documents and several others—especially one in 1249—are more valuable for the allied problem of the king's share in the tithe.[15]

Before plunging into detailed documentation, a crown record which throws a good deal of light on the end result of the many negotiations should be described. Drawn on May 28, 1285, almost fifty years from the day when the Moslems surrendered the capital city, it lists the contributions expected from the various ecclesiastics of King Peter's realms, to help resist an invasion from France. The bishop must give 60,000 solidi; the dean 30,000; the archdeacon of Murviedro 15,000; the archdeacons of Valencia and Játiva and the precentor 10,000 each. The rectors of two of the city churches, those of St. Andrew and St. Martin, are assessed 2,000 each— though probably not in their capacity as rectors. "The other rectors of the episcopate and diocese" seem to give 2,000 solidi as a combined contribution. But "all the canons of the church of Valencia each" must pay 2,000.

In the Tortosa diocese area of Valencia, the abbot of Benifasá is put down for 10,000, and the rector of Morella for 5,000.

The general impression, especially after comparing the Valencia list with those of other dioceses, is of a fairly well-endowed cathedral and a diocese relatively poorer but adequately provided for.[16] Earlier lists (1279–1280) for the crusade tax also indicate that the finances of the cathedral and its personnel were sound, and that the diocese was reasonably supported. The diocese prospered despite the difficulties which assailed it. Forty years after the final settlement of the diocesan endowment by King James I, his grandson James II could report to Rome that the Valencia diocese was "wealthy," as was the diocese of Tortosa, and that each would "remain wealthy" even if it were to suffer serious amputations of territory to form an extra diocese.[17]

∞ PROPERTIES AND ESTATES

The archives of the cathedral are cluttered with contracts of purchase, sale, and exchange, and with a supporting documentation of homages, promises, and previous bills of grant. This activity, along with the acceptance of legacies and gifts, sometimes ran counter to Valencian law. As early as 1240 statutes forbade the Valencian church to inherit or acquire land. This would have reduced the diocesan economic base largely to gifts originating from the king's largesse; with so many other claims upon his resources, this was bound to prove inadequate. The diocese consequently opposed the onerous limitation.

King James had not been able to impose such a limitation upon the more established older dioceses, though he had tried. His failure was underlined in 1235, when an ecclesiastical parliament in his realms decreed the liceity of alienating or willing one's property to churches anywhere in Aragon or Catalonia.[18] Valencia seemed to offer the king a better chance for success in his restrictive policy. Yet, as early as June 1240, Valencian church authorities could speak about their properties "throughout the whole diocese, and outside it."[19] Only five years later, King James found it wise to ratify all illicit acquisitions by the Valencia church to date; he sternly forbade them for the future. The next year (1246) he had to content himself with ruling that such lands were unprivileged and must therefore pay their proper taxes.

In 1251 he reconfirmed this position; clerical and baronial property must not increase. From time to time he permitted exceptions to segments of the Valencian church. In 1266 he allowed the cathedral chapter to purchase or inherit land. In granting this boon the king added a clause allowing simple exchanges with holders of crown land, but he insisted that the properties exchanged be of truly equal value.[20] Finally, at the general revision of Valencian law in 1271 the whole royal position collapsed. Admitting defeat,

James put no barrier to the church's acquiring land and retaining it with tax privileges.

In a land market so swiftly moving as that of Valencia, it is impossible to fix a clear picture of diocesan holdings for any given time. Nor is it easy to decide which items were purchased, which were obtained by barter or by gift, which pertained perhaps to a mosque, or which specify substitutes for lands promised but never given by the king. A few odd documents in the cathedral records may conceivably have been deposited for safekeeping and may have no reference to church lands.[21] And, when one is about to total up the royal donations to the Dominican nuns at Alcira (to take a handy example), one finds that the bishop of Valencia has already appropriated them in great part, alienating them for his own needs.[22] But some sense can be wrested from the disordered documentation.

Some fifty records of sale and purchase exist in the cathedral archives, for the first fifteen years after the conquest, ranging from sizable hamlets to a few houses or scattered plots of land. When compared with other sources, a few of these prove to have become in time church property: the rural area of Puzol, for instance, or the city property of John of Silla. Did all these records represent gifts or sales to the church? They do not appear in the elaborate fifteenth-century codex, the *Book of Legal Documents*,[23] where a multitude of similar small transactions are recorded. However, the codex seems to be concerned rather with exchanges of land, rental contracts, infeudations, and the like; perhaps simple buying and selling, especially of smaller lands, required less care or less permanent care than would important properties or those with a mixed history. Or the book may be limited largely to revenues applied to the support of the cathedral and its personnel; the diocesan archives, had they survived, might have given fuller information on other charters.

That there must have been serious buying of land may be deduced from the fact that the Valencian church was assigned substantial sums of money for this purpose, with the royal provision to do so despite the laws of the realm.[24] In many cases the church does not seem to have been successful in claiming her Moslem inheritance. Recognizing the difficulties and aware that several contracts may belong to a single piece of property, some generalizations may be attempted from what are probably incomplete records.

The items are most often on a modest scale, such as a field,[25] or houses— sometimes with land attached,[26] a farm or odd bits of land,[27] or rents.[28] Some castles intrude in one document.[29] A countryside with its central hamlet appears in two cases.[30] Occasionally the land is defined: the park of the father of King Zaiyān,[31] another park,[32] a corral,[33] two jovates, or eight, or six, or four.[34] Once the rents are specified as a shop.[35] In short, the records deal with numerous houses and small holdings, and a few larger pieces of land, besides the towns of Benimaclet and of Puzol.[36]

One notes an expected preoccupation with the area around the cathedral, perhaps with an eye to its subsequent rebuilding. There are documents dealing with the houses of John Anglés on the cathedral plaza;[37] the expensive shops and buildings hard by the cathedral (bought from the king and queen);[38] houses purchased from Giles of Hungary and his wife Milia near the cathedral;[39] the acquisition of "a part of our buildings, namely two arcades, to extend your buildings";[40] those "houses in Valencia city in the parish of St. Mary, of the see of Valencia," for which a 1258 secular contract exists in the cathedral archives;[41] the houses of John of Lasceyles, acquired by exchange (1242);[42] and lesser items. Some of the buildings in this area also came by gift.[43] Since a remarkable number of properties lie "before" the cathedral, one assumes they must be on various sides, "fronting" the cathedral or being close to it. Some documents probably deal with the same object as previous grants, perhaps by way of copy or of confirmation. In a general confirmation of 1242, the king "concedes, delivers, and sells to you our venerable and beloved Bishop Ferrer . . . forever as your own free and frank alod, all our shops and buildings located in Valencia city before St. Mary's cathedral."[44]

Few of the properties recorded are very far from the city of Valencia. Supplementary grants given directly by the king include a special farm beside the king's park,[45] an important park in Játiva,[46] houses in Liria,[47] shops near the cathedral,[48] two jovates of land in Mislata, houses in Valencia,[49] a large group of houses fronting on St. Mary's church in Játiva,[50] the town of Puzol,[51] the town of Bolulla,[52] houses and barbican in Murviedro,[53] the village of Losa del Obispo,[54] the castles of Gorga, Carrícola, and (after some wrangling) Chulilla.[55]

Storage properties were bought in Gandía, Alcira, Onteniente, and Cocentaina: "buildings for your project of granaries and cellars."[56] The township of Albal, near Torrente, was purchased by the chapter in 1244 from its lord, Giles of Atrosillo, for 2,200 Alphonsine gold pieces. The village of Albuixech near Valencia was granted to the Dominican Berengar of Castell-bisbal on September 17, 1238, apparently in his official capacity as bishop-elect of Valencia; whether it subsequently reverted to the crown, or was sold by the chapter, is unknown.[57] Near the end of this century the town of Benaduf and its neighbor Villar del Arzobispo passed from the family of Liori to the diocese; the bishop issued a settlement charter here in 1313.[58]

The small scale of many of the purchases should not be surprising. This was an infant diocese whose expectations of property lay in the leisurely future. There has been question, so far, only of the documentation for common funds. Properties seem also to have been assigned directly to individuals, as a stipend for life; these would have been cared for by the individual, accounting to no one.[59] The bishop might have had estates specifically episcopal whose records would have been contained in the diocesan archives.

The cathedral archives are more concerned with the communal fund, half of which went to the chapter, half to the bishop.[60] But familiarity with the documentation both at the cathedral and elsewhere leaves one with the impression that the bulk of diocesan holdings of all kinds is known. And the papal concession of tithes to the bishop, rather than to the parish, tends to confirm the suspicion that episcopal income from estates was relatively small.

There are no detailed records for such revenues as synodal fees, episcopal or archdiaconal procurations, quadragesimals, see-dues (*cathedraticum*), hospitality (*cena*), fines from the various law-courts, and so on, though some of these appear occasionally. For example, Simon Pérez of Arenós signed an agreement in 1260 giving the episcopal procurations to the pastors of Andilla and of the Mijares River churches; in compensation the bishop received 200 solidi yearly. This is a considerable sum from one fee in one area.[61] But the overwhelming share of episcopal, as well as capitular, revenue derived from the "temporals" just described and the tithes. The capitular *mensa* or share had to furnish the prebends, the "portions" thereof belonging to the cathedral personnel for subsistence, and the daily "distributions"—the latter being a complex of variable fees and foods awarded to insure constant attendance at choir, Mass, and chapter meeting. The rental surplus was commonly divided semi-annually among the canons and others. Benefices and chantries, multiplying in Valencia as elsewhere, were a separate revenue; some idea can be gained of their value only insofar as they enter into the total income of the individual Valencian cleric.

One class of documents from the cathedral archives reveals a lively business of renting and of exchanging properties. In 1240 a mosque in the Barcelona section of the city of Valencia, near the Boatella gate, was exchanged for the houses of the queen's porter Raymond Seguí.[62] A farm was given to Peter Ruiz in return for a vineyard.[63] The knight John Lasceyles, who had received some houses close to the cathedral in 1238,[64] exchanged them with the bishop and chapter for a mosque and a cemetery "near the burnt tower" in Roteros.[65] The bishop left these houses wholly in the hands of the chapter, in return for their rights in another cemetery.[66] In 1241 the diocese acquired a building from Bernard of Huerta in the quarter of the men of Lérida at Valencia city, giving him in return as a free alod a surplus mosque and houses "on the street of the bridge."[67]

The stronghold and township of Puzol first belonged to the knight Assalit of Gudal in 1238;[68] he gave a charter of settlement four years later,[69] but almost immediately sold the whole thing (now worth 18,000 Jaca solidi) to King James.[70] The king promptly divided it equally among the Order of Roncesvalles, the bishop, and the chapter.[71] The chapter in turn, sensibly realizing that "what is held in common is usually neglected by many," sold its rights to the bishop for the duration of his life at an annual 430 solidi.[72]

In 1240 six jovates of land were granted in Senqueir and Benisanó to a certain Peregrin;[73] Peregrin sold them to the notary of the king Bernard of Soler (1244); as a canon of the cathedral, Bernard must have given or exchanged them to the church.[74] The dates on the documents are not always a positive indication of when the church came into possession, however; this is especially true of last wills and of original deeds preserved as part of the property's legal history.

ꙮ RENTAL INCOME

Small properties were most profitably managed by renting them out.[75] The rents seem inconsiderable and at times a formality. But custom probably dictated that, in addition, a definite share of the tenant's profits be given to the owner, as was the case in mass colonization projects in Valencia at this time. And even a city property rented at a small fee seems to have involved an extramural patch of productive farm land. Again, "house" often conceals an industry or shop with profits. Equally important is the consideration that a low rent can conceal a capital improvement; this is stipulated several times in both ecclesiastical and nonecclesiastical documents in Valencia, and was a not uncommon device even in a well developed foreign diocese like Lincoln in England.[76]

Thus, the rental of a mosque at Fortaleny in the diocese of Valencia in 1256 involved not only the small service of a pound of pepper yearly, and probably a share of profits, but required as well that the tenant "effect works and improvements worth ten solidi of Valencia" yearly.[77] A rental document for a mosque at Játiva in 1273 stipulated an annual sum "for improving the said mosque"; it set the interesting condition: "and it is not permitted to you to sublet to anyone the said mosque at a greater rental than has been said."[78] Such clauses had been common also in Languedocian rental and enfeoffment contracts toward the end of the previous century. A piece of land of Andarella was sold to William Ratera forever, for two gold pieces yearly, but only if he "keeps it well cultivated and settled," and improves it.

Another mosque, adapted to secular use, was rented out in 1265 at only eight solidi yearly; but it carried an obligation to put in 120 solidi worth of improvements during the first two years, 60 solidi in each year.[79] The main mosque of Lombar rented for a pound of wax yearly, but with a proviso that, within two years, 30 solidi be expended for "works and improvements."[80] A mosque site, or perhaps its patio or a square hard by (*platea mezquite*), at Alcoy in 1273 was rented to a neighboring property-holder named John Escuder for two pounds of wax every Christmas, plus the obligation that he "construct there one roofed building" within the year.[81] Similarly, the precentor Peter Michael arranged to have the cleric Arnold

Pellicer build a shop on the diocesan land he rented just outside the Boatella gate. Tenant Arnold was to pay 2¼ gold Alphonsine morabatins a year for his shop, plus the ground rental already coming in. The high rent is understandable since this was a market area.[82]

The process of renting out the properties began slowly. There was a Christian population in the town of Puzol, so that the bishop enjoyed a good sum simply from the secular third of the tithe he collected as owner. Besides, each residence had to give him as rent five solidi of Jaca every year, two chickens, and a seventh of all the produce—to be reckoned by number or by measure, according to its nature. The renters had to provide cartage to deliver all this.[83] In September 1240 the bishop and chapter rented to Peter of Balaguer "a certain mosque we have in the street of St. John at the Boatella gate," for which he was to pay "for rent each year on the feast of St. Mary in September six pennies of Jaca, and besides that rent no other rent or usage are you to pay for it."[84] This mosque was soon destroyed, for it reappears as a long and narrow piece of ground being leased again in 1270.[85] A nearby oratory of the Moors—it does not seem to be the same mosque—was sold to Arnold Bertrand in order to connect two flanking properties of his brother William Bertrand; the rent was a pound of good wax each Christmas. He recognized bishop and chapter as his "lords or over-men."[86]

In 1243 a man and wife from Barcelona rented a Moorish "cemetery which we [the bishop and chapter] have in Andarella."[87] There was a condition attached: "provided that you and your successors maintain it well-managed and settled, and improve and not deteriorate it."[88] This cemetery seems to have reverted to the church, for one was rented to William Ratera, notary and bailiff of the king, in 1249 for a yearly piece of gold.[89] He in turn sold it within the year to a Tarazona man.[90] In 1240 a mosque was rented, or perhaps given outright, to a benefactor of the Valencian church, the wife of Ponce of Soler who may be a relative of the canon; it included an adjoining cemetery and houses, and was situated just outside the city on the path to the Dominican church.[91] Within the Moslem quarter itself, at least one mosque was held by the bishop and chapter; it was rented to a Christian in 1277, with all its appurtenances, for one gold piece yearly.[92] In 1265 the cathedral authorities rented out perpetually "some animal pens [which] in Moslem times used to be a mosque, [and] which are in the city of Valencia in the parish of St. Lawrence."[93] The rent was eight solidi a year.

A Valencian notary in 1244 put down ten years rent—three gold mazmodins a year—for a piece of land in Roteros on the Mislata road.[94] The same year, a mosque and its houses in the Barcelona sector of Valencia city were rented to a man and his wife. This may be a different mosque from that given in 1240 to the queen's porter in exchange for houses; or was it the same mosque, reclaimed for some reason?[95] Yet another mosque, it would seem, was rented in this Barcelona part of the city, to G. of Lousach and his wife Benegunda; only two-thirds of it was actually rented, for which 100 solidi were paid to the bishop and chapter.[96] The pastor of St. Martin's held the Moor cemetery near the Boatella gate at perpetual rent for over fifteen years,[97] finally selling his right to the cathedral chanter Peter Michael.[98] The municipal authorities tried to seize this property in 1266, on the pretext that it had held less than twelve Moslem graves and therefore was not included in the king's endowment of the diocese. The pastor won his case, so the cemetery must have been small. By 1271 this property, which lay along the city wall and was distinct from the parish cemetery, had come to be called "fossarium beati Martini."[99]

Shortly after the conquest of Valencia city, the crown had built an inn or hospice on a Moslem cemetery in the suburb of Roteros.[100] One A. Bertrand rented "a cemetery outside the Boatella" gate in 1248.[101] In the same year the sacristan of the cathedral and the prior of St. Vincent, as administrators, rented to Peter of Copons a field in Campanar which had been donated by laymen.[102] Two mosques were rented out in 1250, one of them in the town of Játiva to the knight Arnold of Sant Celoni for two gold pieces yearly.[103] In 1251 a mosque was rented in the Valencia suburb of La Xarea,[104] as well as a field apparently belonging to the mosque which had become the church of St. Michael in Játiva.[105] In 1252 some houses near the cathedral were rented to Mary for a silver besant every Christmas.[106]

Also in 1252 church authorities rented a Moslem cemetery near the city wall of Murviedro to Lucy, the widow of William of Agramunt.[107] That same year three mosques were let, one with adjoining buildings in Murviedro at eight solidi a year,[108] one in Játiva,[109] and one at St. Andrew's parish in Valencia which went to the pastor John of Campol and his sister.[110] The rentals of 1254 include a cemetery and a "destroyed mosque" in Poliñá del Júcar,[111] a field near Játiva,[112] and a Moor cemetery near Castellón.[113] The Franciscans were still renting their Játiva mosque from the chapter as late as 1252, when they lost possession of it.[114] The tenant Constantine shows up quite suddenly as holding at rent houses as well as a field which had formerly been a Moslem cemetery in Roteros.[115] In 1242 a property in Almazora, given by the king, was being rented from the church by Bernard Rochet.[116]

These can be considered as only illustrative transactions, since a number of them were single stages in a multiple transfer, or are known almost in passing. Many other examples might be added. Thus, in 1255 there was a mosque rented to Bernard Reig in Murviedro,[117] another in Játiva to John Pérez at a pound of wax yearly,[118] another—with a smaller mosque added for a hundred pence—to Giles of Fraga in Liria,[119] and another again at four solidi yearly to A. Roquet which had previously been rented to John of Palau.[120] A number of times the diocese cleared away a mosque to prepare a building site; this resulted in plots of ground like that in St. Bartholomew's parish (1256), another in St. Lawrence's (1265), and a third in St. John's (1270).[121] The Valencia city mosque of Bonet Fuster rented in 1260 for a pound of wax at Easter along with the task of making improvements.[122] A plot of ground which was formerly a mosque was rented in 1256 in the city to B. of Camarasa.[123] Other mosques were sold at Fortaleny,[124] at Carpesa,[125] at Nacla near Corbera (1260),[126] and so on.

Seven fanecates of cemetery land were sold at Alcoy, with the obligation of improvements and a rental of half a pound of wax yearly.[127] To the rector William of Coll at Espioca were sold "three pieces of land" from former cemeteries there, at a rent of two solidi yearly on St. Michael's day (1279).[128] Other mosques appear in various documents as boundary markers, but nothing is known of their owners or fate.[129] Many others had become parish churches. Some of the mosques may have been quite solid and comfortable buildings for, when the Moors surrendered Almenara, they lodged King James in what was "formerly a mosque."[130]

A special office existed for the rental of mosques and Moslem cemeteries—particularly the latter, to which may have been added other pieces of land, perhaps former mosque properties. For a long time, at least from 1250 to 1280, the canon Bernard of Vilar held this office; Bernard, who was also pastor of the cathedral parish of St. Peter, acts in the name of the bishop or the chapter, or of both. A different name intrudes in the negotiations very rarely, and then usually as procurator for Bernard.

Thus, the canon Raymond of Grau acted as his procurator from 1260 to 1263, though Bernard remained independently active. The canon Dominic Matthew turns up as procurator briefly in 1273. As early as 1256 such a procuratorship had been exercised by Bernard Ferrer, who was also vicar:

> Let all know: that I, Bernard Ferrer, vicar of the altar of St. Mary of the see of Valencia, and procurator for Bernard of Vilar canon of Valencia, for the use and convenience of the lord bishop and the chapter of Valencia, with written contract do establish to you, Raymond of Almenara and your heirs forever, for renting and improving, a cemetery which is in Alcoy.[131]

Bernard of Vilar is listed in the crusade-tax list of 1279 with the rubric: "for the daily support of Vilar and for the rental of the cemeteries, 119 solidi." Next year, these offices are separately listed and are tithed at 16 and at 62 solidi respectively.[132] Though this sum is considerably less than he must pay from his priorate of tithe receipts, 267 solidi, it is still one of the larger items of income listed.

No conclusion as to diocesan revenues can be drawn from the large salary implied; but as cemetery manager Bernard is obviously holding a responsible post. The same office appears quite clearly in a late document (1341), when its holder describes himself in a rental contract:

> Let all know that I Raymond Ferrer, canon of Valencia, [am] ad-
> ministrator and governor of the rents of the mosques and cemeteries
> formerly belonging to the Saracens in the whole diocese of Valencia, and
> of the [revenues] coming from them. [I have been] specially delegated by
> the [bishop] . . . and by the honorable chapter of his church, as may be
> seen by a public document drawn up on April 13, 1341.[133]

This office also existed in the thirteenth century in newly conquered Seville,
where a canon had charge of rentals and exploitation with the title of con-
troller of the mosques.[134] It is difficult to believe that Valencian *fossaria*
were all real cemeteries. Despite the name, some at least may be thought of
as mosque properties, plazas, patios, or fields.

Though enough full information to project a developing pattern is lacking, there are ample indications of the direction events were taking. There
was a certain amount of buying, mostly in the environs of Valencia and
mostly of small properties yielding small rents. This was supplemented by
the rental of mosques and their supporting lands, a task carried on by delegates from the chapter and by procurators throughout the diocese. The job,
although a large one, would have been rendered easier by the circumstance
of the properties being advantageously located. This activity, as revealed in
the surviving records, would have been heavier in the early period, tapering
off thereafter.

COLLECTION AREAS

To supervise the collecting and auditing of capitular revenues, and more
easily to distribute them among the canons, Bishop Arnold had established
twelve priorates (*prepositurae*) in his chapter as early as 1247.[135] These
priorates offer some clue as to the geographical location of capitular properties and their relative value, so they deserve a brief notice. Each priorate
was worth 800 solidi a year. Each included the tithes on wheat, wine, animals,
and vegetables, together with large fines and legacies. The regions of Alcira,
Corbera, Sumacárcel, and all holdings in the diocese below the Júcar River
were divided into three priorates, collectively valued at 2,400 solidi. Another
six priorates collectively valued at 4,800 solidi included the Valencian
huerta, the parish of Foyos, the Albufera lagoon, and sea-fishing along the
coast. Three final priorates, at a total value of 2,400 solidi, included all other
areas above the Júcar. Almost fifty places are named in this particular section; the spellings provide a challenging exercise in identification.[136]

The first three priorates were put under the charge of the archdeacon
Master Martin. Three more went to the precentor [Peter] Dominic. One each
went to the sacristan Arnold, to Bertrand of Teruel, and to Berengar of
Boxadós. And the last three described above went to Bernard of Soler,
Berengar of Boxadós, and the precentor again. The charges were to be held

for a period of four years; they covered all capitular income in the diocese. Each prior could sublet his priorate to one or more tax farmers, for a year at a time. From these figures it appears that the huerta of Valencia brought almost a fourth of the total capitular income; the same would be true of the episcopal income. The huerta was understood to be the area immediately around the city, since in this document it excludes such places as Picasent, Alcácer, Espioca, and Puig. It also appears that three-fourths of the income came from the region above the Júcar River. It is not clear whether rentals are included; their collection seems to have been an independent function, probably not subordinated to the priors.

The project proved abortive. The next bishop, Andrew, completely revised it. His revised priorates were in operation by 1259.[137] At first there had been only six of the collectors, three in the Valencian huerta and three for the region below the Júcar River.[138] But the acquisition of more extensive properties soon made necessary the full twelve. They were named after the months, and their jurisdictions indicate the localities of high or low revenue. Thus, the collectors named after February, March, and April drew most of the revenues below the Júcar. Above this river the collectors of May, June, and July had the generality of income, except for Cullera and for what must have been the richest area of revenue. The latter was a tight arc of territory around Valencia city, based on the sea, and running in from Puzol and Puig to Museros, Foyos, Moncada, Burjasot, Paterna, Manises, Torrente, and back to the sea. This area was cared for by the remaining six months together. The priorates were to account for all the revenues belonging to the chapter, including the tithes and even the besants which the knights of Calatrava and Santiago paid.[139] If after six years these revenues had increased, the surplus was to be applied to increase the fees of the canons, or their number, or else the number of cathedral assistants.

The region below the Júcar must have been the most unproductive. The three priorates in charge are not even mentioned in the crusade-tax lists for 1279; the lists for 1280 simply give a token tithe of five solidi as received "from Bertrand for the three priorates," in the section below the Júcar River.[140] The other wide collectorate, that above the river, is included in the nine given in the 1279 list, and in the ten[141] given for 1280. For the region around Valencia all the priorates are expressly mentioned in 1279 except August, which is included among those listed according to their holders. These five yield the highest income, tithed at 265, 249, 261, 282, and 291 solidi; the other four yield respectively 218, 366, 159, and 156 solidi.

This is as much as can be learned from the tithe lists; but even this must allow for a margin of error due to agricultural fortune of the current year, or to underpaying or overpaying the crusade tax in a given year. Where comparison is possible, between the payments of 1279 and 1280, Andrew (July) gave 218 and 293; the sacristan 156 and 208; Benedict 366 and 278; and

Ralph 159 and 184. It may be conjectured, then, that the revenues were richest in the immediate vicinity of the capital, fair in the remainder of the upper part of the diocese, and very poor below the Júcar River. It is difficult to say what part, if any, the individual canons played in the actual process of collecting.

The capitular income was much higher than these sums indicate, since other choice revenues had been reserved to dignities and lesser officers. A crusade tithe of about 4,700 solidi was paid by the combined posts and chaplaincies of the cathedral in 1280; in the same year the bishop paid 2,750 and for his unpaid tax of 1279 another 2,750. When increased from tithe to original income, this amounts to a cathedral revenue of at least 75,000 solidi per annum. This was well over a quarter of the revenues actually falling under the crusade tax, since the total crusade tax of about 20,000 solidi means a minimum of 200,000 solidi diocesan income, including bishop, chapter, parish, and all. Almost a third of this 75,000 may have come from diocesan tithes.[142] The figures represent a minimum, since the tax may have been considerably below the strict 10 percent. It did not fall necessarily upon all income, and some sources may actually be omitted;[143] it represents also the gross income without, for example, the share of the tithe farmer himself. There is no way of knowing what the ecclesiastical income in the diocese would total if one could add in the monastic lands, the hospitals and charities, the military and other Orders, and all the small or exempt incomes.

A document has recently come to light, indicating something of the scattered nature of diocesan properties in Valencia, and perhaps something of their value. In December 1273, King James ordered a cautionary seizure of Valencian episcopal and capitular properties and revenues. Located in eleven regions, these were assigned to eleven respective bailiffs, alcaids, or justiciars of those regions to seize: Valencia-Liria, Murviedro, Biar, Castell, Castalla, Cocentaina, Alcoy, Jijona, Denia, Tárbena, and Valle de Gallinera with Alcalá (near Pego). Each was to make a list, and to guard these properties and revenues until further notice. General though it is, the document is valuable in its suggestion that diocesan resources in the poorer area below the Júcar were widely scattered, and therefore individually small.[144]

⋈ THE DIOCESAN TITHES

The greatest single revenue, and the solid base of diocesan growth in Valencia, was the first fruits (for the parish) and the tithe (for the diocese).[145] This was especially true for the earlier years when property acquisition was restricted. An examination of this tithe system is not only essential to understanding the Valencia diocese, but instructive in connection with general tax methods, kinds of crops, social and socio-religious tensions, and the intertwined structure of politics, religion, and economics. It also furnishes an exciting glimpse of the vigor and pace of the frontier economy.

The tithe was an income tax of 10 percent or less, enforceable at law. It fell especially upon agriculture, livestock, oil, wine, fish, game, mills, ovens, and personal income. Under the latter form, through the tithe upon the income of the crown and of the barons, most human activities, even those of Moslems or slaves, contributed in some measure. Transient or wintering flocks were affected. Thus the diocese, in selling the tithes of Almonacid and Benaguacil to Roderick Díaz in 1268, retained the tithe on "animals from outside."[146] Similarly, the Paterna and Manises first fruits (which fell upon the same objects as the tithe) were levied in 1263 on "alien" or "transient" flocks.[147] The Catalan canonist Raymond of Penyafort even solemnly pondered the question of tithing a prostitute's earnings; he concluded for the affirmative, lest tax immunity and consequently approval seem to be conferred upon vice.[148]

The documents give little information about the tithing of industry, commerce, or mines; Penyafort includes them all as subject to tithe.[149] Bishop Andrew and his successors in Valencia did collect a tithe even upon the tributes and fees paid to the crown from the Moslem quarters of the cities and countryside, and therefore upon commercial and industrial profit indirectly to a small extent. This information is revealed only after the bishop's death and quite by chance, though one might also infer it from the endowment charter of James I in 1241; thus, there may have been wider applications of the tithe than the run of records reveals.[150]

Again, industry and commerce would have paid something indirectly through a personal tithe like the following: "it should be remembered that the said tithe ought to be imposed not only on the [civil] tenths, but upon everything which you receive from Saracens of that region in any proper or customary fashion."[151] Sea fisheries and butcheries, and probably every industry in Valencia, paid as well a direct tithe. In the Tortosa segment such industries as mines and fishing explicitly came under the tithe.[152]

Throughout Christendom there was a common distinction made between "greater" and "lesser" tithes. The former affected the main source of revenue, usually wheat and wine; the latter touched accessory revenues, and might be subdivided into "green" tithes (on produce and such) and "blood" tithes (on animal increase, wool, and the like). One finds no mention of the distinction in Valencian documents.[153]

In principle, the tithes in Valencia were paid by every Christian, including king, baron, and cleric.[154] There would be exemptions, of course, such as the basic rectory property and certain monastic holdings;[155] but even the hospital of St. William in Valencia city had to pay the tithe on its revenue properties except for one farm. Priests in the diocese were to admonish their parishioners to pay the tithe and first fruits properly.[156] If a Christian sold his land to a Jew in Valencia, that land carried the tithe obligation with it; otherwise non-Christians were legally free.[157] There were rare exceptions to this, as with the Moors at Villarreal in 1280,[158] or the attempt by the bishop's bailiff to force the Jews to pay in the Murviedro settlement.[159] More often, the Moslem refused to pay the tithe on lands acquired from Christians. The bishop and chapter of Valencia complained of this strongly; eventually in 1314 church authorities received the active support of the crown on their side. As general rule transferred revenue was tithed twice, as original income and as transferred share; this made it more expensive to have Christian than Moslem tenants.

The kingdom of Valencia was a new one, with a number of different custom-laws and social pressures transplanted to it, so that one might expect to find a spirited quarrel concerning the tithes. And, since the king, many religious, and nobles claimed two-thirds or a half or at least a third of this revenue by right of conquest or foundation, all three would participate actively in the quarrel. The complete tithe ought to have gone to the church, if ancient Visigothic precedent had not been swept away by abuse and feudal chaos an immemorially long time ago; a tripartite division would then have assigned a third of it apiece to the bishop, the clergy, and the material upkeep of the churches. In thirteenth-century Valencia, the church retained at best only two-thirds of the tithe. In the diocese of Valencia, the two-thirds went directly to the diocese rather than to the parish, by special permission (1245) of Pope Innocent IV.[160] This diocesan share was split into two categories. The tithes of the area about Puzol, together with those of specified areas close to the city of Valencia and just below it, were to be divided equally between bishop and chapter for their respective expenses. Throughout the remainder of the diocese, the larger part by far, only a third of the common share went to the chapter.[161]

The *Furs* were explicit on the details of payment; but as in many medieval affairs, violence lurked below the legalities.[162] This law was actually a treaty of peace, an arbitration imposed by King James after the contention became unmanageable. A dilemma inherent in the tithe system was that, while it insured independence for the spiritual power, it could easily arouse opposition as the impersonal institution imposed its demands. This opposition had to be countered with severity by a church grown dependent on the tithe, thus raising more opposition. Worse, a good amount of the money the church fought for had to be transferred to some secular power.

Thus, the ecclesiastical authorities had to keep a sharp eye out for the "fraud and trickery" anticipated by some of the tithe agreements. And as early as 1247 one finds a hint of future trouble in the document organizing the collection; collectors are not to be held responsible for the full amount where "violently or in any manner whatsoever revenues are carried off or withheld."[163] In cases of nonpayment, it was sometimes provided that bishop and chapter could seize and put at pawn the Moslems and livestock until satisfaction was given. Some people in the kingdom of Valencia refused to pay the tithe; others maliciously threw aside the church's portion so that animals would be sure to devour it or neighbors bear it away. The more sophisticated—and the urban centers were the strong right arm of the opposition—sought out illogicalities and apparent injustices in the system and opened a delaying action in the courts. The question of olives and vines, which required a different working system than did other crops, and the condition of the soil (unbroken, or already in cultivation when acquired) occasioned loud complaints. A prededuction of salaries and wages was strenuously fought for.[164] Left to themselves, even those who paid the tithe peacefully could not be counted upon to give full measure.

In Valencia there was no evidence of opposition to the tithe as such by the body of the people, but rather a demand for reform. Indeed the extent and seriousness of opposition to the tithe in medieval Europe has been the subject of no little exaggeration.[165] Nor must it be thought that these rural Christian areas in pioneer Valencia offered dazzling sums to the collector. But the churchmen apparently felt that a clear stand should be taken, against the day when settlers would come in numbers; meanwhile, they had begun their campaign to insist on the tithes from Christian personal income derived from the Moslems. This mentality is seen when the diocese early infeuded to the king the fief of one-third the tithe of Alcira, with the proviso that the full tithe will be taken on all revenues received from Saracens there until such time as the place is populated by Christians.

The capital city was the seat of the disturbances. Both her bishop and the strongest civilian group were there. Her delegates and arbitrations were the ones more often recorded. The situation was nevertheless general and well organized. King James reported that the issue had united "the high nobles, knights, burghers, and other inhabitants."[166] Prominent among the communes which sent representatives to the talks preceding the agreement of 1268 were—besides Valencia—Játiva, Murviedro, Alcira, Liria, Denia, and Gandía.[167]

In Valencia the farm tithes were paid usually in kind, and at the moment of harvesting.[168] This precluded fraud in the quantity to be assessed. A crown order forbade the removal of crops to storage until the tithe had been taken.[169] The bailiff of bishop and chapter, and the bailiff of the king (officials sometimes called *decimarii* and *primiciarii*)[170] were to be notified so that they could be on the spot to make the assessment and collection, even where a tithe-owning lord was concerned.[171] For collecting the tithes, the kingdom of Valencia or at least its crown land was divided into "rectorates" or "titheships."[172]

Under the general responsibility of the canons who held the office of collectors or priors,[173] but under the immediate superintendence of the bailiffs or tax farmers, the tithe portion was gathered into diocesan granaries and wine cellars. The diocese commissioned suitable buildings for this purpose at Valencia, Gandía, Albal, Alcira, Onteniente, Játiva, Murviedro, and Cocentaina. This disposition suggests a strategic scattering of such posts throughout the diocese. Though ordered in mid-1242, however, many of these storage buildings had not been completed even by 1260, much to the bishop's distress.[174] This confirms the impression given by royal exemptions and privileges for the marketing of the tithes: that most of the collection was usually converted by sales into money. This process took time; consequently quantities of diocesan tithe stores, including wheat and wine, were available to help feed King James's army in 1276, and thus help defend the frontier.[175]

I X

ENDING THE TITHE WAR

By 1254 the situation demanded royal interference. King James wrote in March, urging the Valencians to be mindful of their eternal salvation and to cease defrauding the church. Contrary custom laws they had been citing were to be looked upon as void. No one was to gather his crops until the agents (*nuncii*) had assessed them. Payment in full was especially demanded "for olives, wheat, grapes, flax, hemp, and vegetables, and [the offspring of] animals."[1] The document hardly marks a stage in the conflict. Medieval burgher and peasant, pastor and bishop, were much the same. None of them could resist the arbitrament of a bellicose uproar.

ༀ THE CONTROVERSY

Resistance spread from eggs and chickens to pigs and figs, olives and grapes.[2] Where would it all end? Reports of unhappy scenes reached the royal ear. The cloth at the burial service, and candles at Mass and at baptisms, were "violently snatched away" from the lay participants. When no candles were brought, some clerics demanded money.[3] Feelings being what they were—and medieval litigants were not prone to minimize their grievances—the whole system of tithes and fees was on the point of breaking down.

After his attempted settlement of the tithe problem at the diocese of Valencia, James had turned to those parts of the kingdom of Valencia which lay under the bishop of Tortosa. Here too he had sternly imposed in 1258 the *status quo ante*. The bishop "can by your own authority force and put at pledge . . . all the men of the kingdom of Valencia of the diocese of Tortosa, to give you tithes on everything as they ought," with the help of the royal officials.[4] Now James turned his attention again to the diocese of Valencia (May 1260). He banned collection of the more disputed objects until he could come in person to settle the question. Meanwhile the usual tithe had to be paid on greens of all kinds, on rice, grapes, lambs, and the like.[5] The storm seems to have abated somewhat, possibly due to the exemption James cannily gave for eggs, chickens, hens, olives, and figs (1260).[6] But three months later he had to rebuke the men of Denia: "Because a Christian man is bound to pay God tithes on all fruits, therefore we wish and command firmly and severely that you pay in full, without making difficulties, the tithes on the figs and almonds which you dry or cause to be dried for sale."[7]

The Burriana folk were causing a similar disturbance, over first fruits, keeping back that tax and at the same time dispatching complaints to the king. They had some room for legal maneuver in the circumstance that, though they fell under the diocese of Tortosa, they belonged to the realm and custom of Valencia. In November, James made a personal and "diligent" investigation there, with the bishop of Tortosa present, and ordered the people to pay up.[8] An equivalent excitement in Morella—the bishop of Tortosa against the knights and people over first fruits—had previously been settled by the king in 1258. That settlement applied to all places in the Valencia segment of the Tortosa diocese except Burriana; payment was to be modeled on that of the Valencia diocese.[9] But the tithe problem remained a lively issue in the north in 1263.[10]

It was in the capital city that feeling about the tithe ran high. Unsatisfied with the last ruling in their favor, the citizens seem to have passed a regional law to their further advantage. Soon they were sending off a delegation to wait upon the king; these agents protested several points of the royal decision, especially the prohibition against harvesting and storing before an assessor had arrived. Independently the bishop had already sent a procurator bearing the clerical complaints. The king could effect no compromise because the bishop's man was not authorized to represent his principal to this extent. An exchange of letters ensued.[11] Finally, in July 1261, less than a year after his last judgment on the situation, the king in desperation ruled:

> We wish that all the aforesaid state of affairs should be returned to its original condition, until we can investigate it. Wherefore . . . you will pay the tithe and first fruits just as you have been accustomed to pay them hitherto; and if you have passed any law to the prejudice of these in Valencia, you will immediately cancel it.[12]

There is no record of this inquiry and decision.

Six years later the situation had deteriorated to the point of being an open "magnum scandalum."[13] Tithes, first fruits, sacramental stipends— the whole system needed drastic reorganization. Unreasonable appeals to the crown by the clergy were rejected. When James came to Valencia both sides, weary of the long strife, appealed to him to make a definite arbitration of "that quarreling and discord" during his stay in the city.[14]

ɾɤ THE SETTLEMENT OF 1268

It was no easy task; the king says he had to "discuss and converse with the one side and the other, laboring over the matters in dispute, and compromising and improving that which seemed ill done." With feelings run-

ning high, with ecclesiastical thunders imminent, with all social classes
from baron to peasant allied, and with every town in the kingdom represented, it is easy to imagine the tension at these parleys. James had personally experienced the painful consequences which followed infringement
upon clerical rights. On the other hand, he could not afford to alienate the
cities, which continued to be a support to him in his turbulent reign. This
whole realm indeed, upon which he relied for consolidating and strengthening royal power, was in crisis.

There was a brighter side. Neither of the parties involved could afford a
serious estrangement, and both had reached that stage of disgust over the
long strife which made the moment ripe for negotiation. The king's simple
arbitration would be welcomed. "It is better and more proper," he argued,
"to arbitrate than to use the rigor of the law." The subsequent agreement
was solemnly signed by a great concourse of representatives "in the palace
of the bishop."[15] This covenant, dated April 27, 1268, was later rendered in
Catalan and incorporated into the *Furs* as the law of the land.

Considering the almost painful detail of this document, not the humblest
leafy green vegetable can have been overlooked. According to the arbitration, the tithe fell mostly on farmers and stockmen. Why, then, were the
city folk so concerned? It cannot be on account of price rises, since the
great staples—wheat, wine, and oil—are given no relief. Therefore, the
average city man must also have been, in the kingdom of Valencia, a small-
scale farmer. This agrees with what is known of some other cities, like
Narbonne, where contemporary conditions were not dissimilar.

It would also account for the brotherhood of *agricultores* of the city and
countryside of Valencia early in King James's reign;[16] these latter may even
have consisted of bourgeoisie who rented farms to tenants on a crop-sharing
basis. What is more to the point, a generous plot of land was commonly
given to settlers in the city. Even when a whole section of town was assigned,
a corresponding segment of lands was added. The shoemakers got a street in
Valencia, plus forty-three fanecates of land and other bits, for instance; a
Teruel group got one hundred and fifty jovates along the Guadalaviar,
along with their own section in the city. Vegetables and fruits grown in and
about the city, within the walls of Valencia and in the immediate suburbs of
Roteros, Boatella, and La Xarea, are in fact covered by a special proviso;
one may sell them untithed, with no limitation of quantity or exception of
kind.

A more general series of exemptions, concerning the whole realm, draws a
picture of the small farmer. He raised a variety of vegetables and fruits for
his domestic needs. He kept a few pigs and chickens, perhaps a donkey or
doves or some bees, and some domestic cattle. He hawked a modest surplus
about the city streets. After this arbitration, he paid no tithe for vegetables
or fruits consumed at home, or for carrots, cabbage, turnips, spinach, or any

other vegetable. Onions and garlic, however, were tithed when in strings of eleven or more. No offspring of cattle or donkeys actually engaged in tilling the field could be taken from him. No chicken or chick, no pigeon or peacock, goose or duck or any kind of egg was to be touched. He could grow his own sugar (not a commercial crop in the realm then) and dry some raisins for home use untithed. Pigs were taxed when the sucklings of the herd reached fifteen. Cheeses and fleeces of wool were set at the same figure, beeswax at the level of thirty pounds per annum. Feed for draft animals or domestic stock was tax-free.

One might dabble in trade, selling in a casual way—not beyond a yearly income of a few solidi—pears, peaches, apples, pomegranates, nuts, mulberries, plums, quinces, sorb apples, and all other fruit from trees. The same was true for small amounts of fresh figs and almonds sold from a basket on the open squares. These items might also be eaten free at home in any quantity. Bowers of grape vines within the walls of any town in the diocese were free from tithe. Fishing in the marshes of the Albufera and snaring birds anywhere in the realm had been exempted much earlier, in 1250.[17]

It becomes clear why the clergy had been making tithe demands upon the city—and why the people of the city or the small rural farmers resisted these raids into their modest revenues. The small farmer does not have the most generous of natures; the clergy were in no dire need; and this kind of tithing assumes an unedifying aspect of niggling and harassment. The treaty, therefore, seems to have been in large measure a victory for the laity.

The commercial farmer could draw but slight consolation from the treaty. He was the man who marketed grains, wine grapes, or olives, or who raised the fruits in common demand, especially dried figs and almonds. Bread and wine formed the bulk of agricultural commodities grown just around the city of Valencia, vegetables and fruit being of lesser importance.[18] This serious farmer had lost every argument as to the manner of making the tithe. He was to wait upon the judgment of the tithe officers, and to leave his harvest where it lay for two full days (one day for millet) until their arrival. This meant in practice that the officials could take their pick of the crop, the choice wheat or grapes or olives, and in full measure, with all benefits of doubt. The point had been hotly contested and, despite this ruling, would raise its indignant head again.

All grains fell under the full tenth. Fourteen varieties were specified, including alfalfa, barley, flax, oats, blue vetch, and white wheat. Their tithe had to be paid on the field itself at harvest time. The few reductions amounted to little more than a deduction of expense, equitably made by law rather than left to the farmer's conscience. Olives were down to one-twelfth, but "no other expenses are to be deducted." Rice was similarly entered at a twelfth, saffron at a fifteenth. Dried figs dropped to a fifteenth; the tithe was to be given upon gathering, "before the figs are divided between the owner and his harvesters." The tenth on wheat was softened by allowing a deduction of the sheafage (*garba*) paid to the reapers. The arbitration swept aside the farmer's cherished distinction between sparse or nonsparse olive groves, and between land cultivated or newly broken. It rejected any deductions from grapes. And it shrewdly insisted that the tenth be given in the vineyard, from each individual plot; no one could slyly offer the collectors a moldy field as a geographical tenth! Warning was issued against another tax evasion: cows and donkeys were not to be untruthfully represented as work animals.

The stockman was not spared. The Valencia kingdom had been and would continue to be important in this type of enterprise. Horses, cows, donkeys, every lamb and ewe, any sizable herd of swine—all had to make their contribution. Their forage was taxed a full tenth. One gathers that the the horse, the lamb, and the ewe were not a normal possession of the small farmer, since even single animals returned a money tax: twelve pence for the former, an obol each for the two latter.

In sum, the basic tithes on oil, wine, grain, figs, commercial livestock, and large-scale fruit or vegetable farming were vindicated but slightly relaxed. The small farmer was almost completely freed from the nuisance—though he still contributed a personal share at the mill or the oven—as long as his produce was substantially for domestic consumption. The cities had won out; the rural areas under the feudal lords, who received a share of the tithe themselves, had been less fortunate. The result, on the whole, was not without profit for the church, though it involved a loss in connection with produce tithes coming from city parishes. From now on, church authorities knew, the tithe could not be disputed, or contrary custom adduced, or payment refused, without breaking the agreed and formal law.

Protests and deputations to the king continued, but in diminished measure. In 1271 the justiciar of Valencia Master Guy together with Mark of Tovia, William of Sarrión, Raymond of Castile, William Zaplana, and Arnold Sexiba acted as a protest committee to the king. They represented the knights, eminent citizens, "and whole community" of the city and kingdom of Valencia. In this capacity they raised problems as to the manner of collecting the grain tithe and as to first fruits. The Valencians were currently enjoying a "contention" on these matters with the bishop, who had sent off his own agent to the king.[19]

Opposition to the terms of the treaty was handled rather firmly by the crown. Very early in 1273 King James promised the bishop and chapter that he would make all inhabitants of the city and diocese pay their tithes according to the judicial arbitration of 1268; his officials were to give active help too.[20] The problem survived after the death of King James. The cities of the kingdom of Valencia sent delegates, fortified with documents clarifying their position, to plead before the new king. King Peter was not sympathetic. He warned that "we propose to continue exacting justice with regard to the tithe belonging to us and to the bishop of Valencia in the land of Valencia."[21] And the first document of the new king Peter in the corpus of municipal privileges concerned the manner of collecting tithes and first fruits.[22]

Later in 1278 King Peter worked out a form of "compromise" in co-operation with the delegates and the bishop. Ample notice was to be given to the tithe officials; the tithe was to be taken by them in the fields; and pre-cise instructions were supplied concerning collection of such items as rice and wine grapes.[23] Peter seems to have stood firmly on this. In 1279 he several times ordered coercion under heavy fine where necessary and punishments for fraud. He was particularly annoyed that some vineyard owners, when asked to identify their plots so that the tithe could be cut from them, simply pointed to a neighbor's vines.[24] In 1281 the king wrote to Peter Alçut the bailiff of Picasent, recommending the use of force "to compel [people] to pay and give to the church of Valencia its tithes and first fruits, as they ought."[25]

Two burning general questions remained to be solved, now that it was obvious no further concessions would be made as to the manner of collect-ing the tithe. Both concerned the first fruits. Could it be tolerated that "on all for which the tithe is given, let first fruits also be taken"?[26] And which came first, the tithe or the first fruits? After all, a crop undiminished by the tithe contributed more first fruits to the parish; the process in reverse favored the diocese over the parish; and a full tax of both on the original sum favored church over farmer! The customs of Aragon were supposed to be the guide.[27] But people were not of one mind as to precisely what had been the custom in Aragon. In June of 1271, King James applied the crown's authority and neutral arbitration to this problem.

Like the tithe difficulty, the problem of the first fruits was not confined to the diocese of Valencia. The Tortosa diocese had been experiencing similar difficulties with its Valencian towns. But the northern diocese does not have an ecclesiastical tax documentation on the scale of the Valencia diocese. Aside from quarrels in this matter directly with the religious Orders and with the tithe-holding king, only an echo is heard there of the more general disturbances. A major reason undoubtedly was the less extensive town life in the north and the wider extent of religious holdings. The two independent centers of town life, Morella and Burriana, were seething very much like their neighbors in the southern diocese. The king had to make a general tithe settlement up here in 1258,[28] and then include the north in the wider settlement of 1268. Separate agreements on the first fruits had been worked out with Burriana (1260) with Morella (1258 and 1263), and with Castellón (1260).[29] In the few places comprising the Segorbe diocese too, the people "refuse to give the first fruits to the venerable bishop-elect of the Segorbe diocese," and the king finally had to order officials of the crown to support the diocesan collectors.[30]

In the diocese of Valencia, Bishop Jazpert assaulted his first fruits problem with diligence. Letters of inquiry were dispatched at the hand of Dominic of Biscay, "a discreet man" and pastor of St. Lawrence in Valencia city, to the dioceses of Huesca, Zaragoza, Tarazona, and Tarragona.[31] One set of messages was directed to the ecclesiastical authorities, another to the lay authorities. The answer indicated that the laity in Valencia had not been quite honest in their scruples. The tenth was to be given first. But the reckoning of the first fruits was drawn from the original total, so that the abstracted tithe was mentally restored, to be computed once again "in the quantity of the first fruits," as the lay magnates of the commune of Tarazona pointed out.[32]

This presumably settled the question, but in those litigious days one fears that it did not. In any case, both the what and the how had been settled by the compromise of King James in 1268 with its subsequent modifications. And an unusually competent bishop was at hand to deal with difficulties.

ᐅᐊ THE KING'S SHARE

The king sat on the side of the angels during the Valencia tithe dispute, passing high and objective judgment. Was the objectivity complete? James was a just man by and large, and circumstances made an equitable arbitration imperative. But it must be remembered that the tithe was also a civil tax—among the most important because so universal and secure.

In Valencia the tithe assumed even greater importance. The estates of barons and religious Orders were owned free of land tax; royal revenues from land therefore derived from the king's own holdings in the new kingdom. These latter were extensive; but the process of infeudation took time, rents had to be lenient in order to encourage settlement, and from an early date King James had to waive even the 10-solidi entry fee. In short, Valencian land tended to be or to become alodial. As a result King James's exchequer counted heavily upon tithe income.[33] Thus, no matter what his personal sympathies, the king had to watch carefully over the collecting of what the crown bluntly called "the tithe owed to God and to us."[34]

It may also be significant that the king's share of the small farmer's domestic produce could more easily be waived than could the stake in the commercial farming. Three and a third percent of much of the food sold in the kingdom of Valencia, of the oil it was cooked in, and of the wine it was washed down with went into James's purse from the tithe alone. Wheat was affected by the tithe three different times: at the harvest, at the mill, and at the oven. James got certain first fruits as well, to say nothing of his direct levies on church income from time to time, much of which was reductively the tithe.

James was continually embarrassed for funds. He supported a frustrating series of petty wars and too often allowed his generous nature its head. His tribute and revenue system in Valencia limped badly, as succeeding documents in the *Golden Book* of municipal privileges reveal; the nobles and clergy were determined to pay as few taxes as possible, while the townsmen and merchants required exemptions and privileges in order to promote trade. Quite a number of the Valencian documents in James's archives have reference to the king's small debts and borrowings.

This introduces a struggle chronologically prior to the great tithe outburst of the late sixties: that between James and the church. James had a double tithe to consider. As the greatest landowner in Valencia he wished to attach to the royal purse the maximum possible share of the tithe. And, as the recipient of large revenues from commerce, feudal services, mines, industry, and the like, he wished to pay out the minimum possible. Almost to the end of his life King James kept, and allowed the knights and religious Orders to keep, a half of the tithes in the Valencian section of the Tortosa diocese.

This was the easier because, while the crusade lasted, the king had a real claim based upon a concession by the diocese of Tortosa. After the crusade the bishop was hard put to get even his half; in 1267 Pope Clement IV ordered King James not to disturb the Tortosa bishop in the gathering of his half-tithe.[35] Only in 1273, when the weight of evidence made it impossible for the king to deny that the crown had once promised the bishop of Tortosa "the tithes and first fruits in his whole diocese," did he reduce the intake by the crown, nobles, and religious to only a third "as in the Valencia diocese."[36]

Even then he insisted on retaining the full half for the important holdings of St. Vincent's hospital in the Tortosan part of Valencia. Previously, in a greedier moment, James had made a contract for the lion's share of the tithe, with the infant church being organized in Majorca (1238). "The lord king is to have in perpetual fief two-thirds of the tithes owed by divine law— that is, on bread, wine, and oil. But of the other things tithable, whether of animals in large or small number, or of sheep, wool, cheese, and fish, the king is to have only a half."[37] Struck with caution lest he be taken advantage of, he quickly added that "if the lord pope does not wish to ratify the accord here noted, neither the lord king nor the prince are under obligation to fulfill their part."[38]

James was not so fortunate in Valencia, though the canons were his own creatures and might be relied upon to be compliant.[39] In the first year after the fall of the city, however, he does seem to have captured half of the tithes then available.[40] An agreement was very early reached in 1240 and 1241. Bishop Ferrer and the chapter gave him, "in perpetual benefice and a fief to you the lord James by the grace of God illustrious king of the Aragonese . . . the third part of the fruits of things tithable . . . in the whole episcopate of the kingdom of Valencia."[41] This same contract, under the aegis of the metropolitan, was spelled out again in the document of endowment in November 1241.[42] In 1247 the bishop and chapter referred, in their organization of revenues, to this "arbitration" of the tithe between diocese and crown.[43]

The king had to tithe all his crown revenues (there was little distinction then, it seems, between public and private income of the king), including mills and ovens, sea fisheries and taxes from Moslems, and game and fish. He retained a third of this crown tithe. Specifically excluded was any royal claim to the third of tithes paid by knights or clerics. This would prevent the king from stepping into a power vacuum and seizing the thirds of weaker knights before the church could organize her own attack ("because, when we [the church] find ourselves in a position to reclaim these, we shall keep them for ourselves and our successors").[44] Perhaps King James respected this latter restriction; his son Peter was not disposed to do so.[45] There is evidence indicating that James took at least some of these knightly thirds, and indeed the inclusion of such a condition in the document suggests a royal lack of scruple in this direction.[46]

As a vassal of the bishop for his share of the tithes, James bound himself to be a defender of diocesan interests. When new settlers arrived the agreement was automatically to extend to those who were directly under the king. This same agreement would be written into future arbitrations, when settling the wrangles over the dowry of the church. As far as he was concerned, James simply surrendered (the word is "absolved") as a favor whatever other claims he had to church revenue. Church authorities, on the other hand, expressly introduced the principle that no layman could ever claim a tithe nor could the church surrender it. They viewed their concession as a convenient infeudation.[47] It was a moral victory. It also placed the king under feudal obligations.

Centuries later the infeudation remained, to embarrass constitutional theorists in early-modern Spain. The seventeenth-century constitutionalist Matheu y Sanz was to marshal arguments for royal possession of the third-tithe as a clear regalian property. He would argue for royal jurisdiction over all tithe cases because James I had alienated only the actual possession of the two-thirds. Even the recent diocesan historian Sanchís Sivera understands the church tithe as "profane and secular," a regalian gift to the diocese by way of endowment, given by the king in fief. This odd interpretation stems apparently from a wish to justify "nuestro piadoso Conquistador" and his right of patronage.[48]

Why did the metropolitan archbishop of Tarragona replace the bishop of Valencia in certain of these negotiations? It could have been routine confirmation; or perhaps in this way James felt more secure, foreseeing how he would later be accused of imposing his will through a packed chapter; finally, in some cases the problem of the disputed episcopate in the early days of Valencia city was a relevant factor. Thus, late in 1241 the metropolitan awarded James and his heirs "the third part of the tithes of the town of Alcira and its country," from the time when it should be conquered. The agreement was for the Valencia diocese, but meanwhile the king must hold the partial tithe in fief from the church of Tarragona.[49]

In 1245 the king reached an agreement with Bishop Arnold over the tithe of the Albufera lagoon near Valencia, a source of crown wealth from fishing and salt.[50] The bishop and chapter accepted a flat rate of 1,000 solidi annually, in lieu of the two-thirds tithe. The sum had to be paid by the crown tax-farmer, or by those currently leasing Albufera income, before any other disbursement from this source was made. When the king assigned the Albufera revenues to his son Prince Alphonse in 1253, he retained this 1,000 solidi for the church.[51] It was not always easy to collect on such promises. Nonpayment led to an appeal by the diocese in 1256; the king ordered the current tax-farmers to pay bishop and chapter their thousand for the preceding year.[52] Probably the sum given yearly to the diocese represented a fair tithe at first; it assumes a revenue from the Albufera of 15,000 solidi yearly, and in 1253 Prince Alphonse was collecting 18,000 from the Albufera plus certain Valencian rents. A hundred years later the crown interests in the lagoon would be sold for 120,000 solidi, the saltworks alone being worth 50,000.[53]

Bishop Andrew maintained a continuing battle against the facile concessions to the crown by his two predecessors. The case must have gone through the usual preliminaries of extensive negotiations, appeal to arbitrators, mutual recrimination, and the rest. At any rate, in the very year when James was reproving the settlers and solving their tithe problems, the king's own case came before the papal court. On August 13, 1268 James appointed two commissioners to act "as our advocates at the papal court ... for the negotiations we are conducting with the bishop of Valencia about the business of the third part of the tithe."[54] The fight continued.

Five years later (1273) it is apparent that these negotiations have not gone well with the king. A man grown fairly old now in deeds good and bad, he found himself on the brink of the future life, "wishing to provide for the salvation of our soul."[55] He was inclined from sheer weariness to put some conclusion to this interminable wrangle with the Valencian church; there is a snappish tone to the final document. Nor should one overlook the possible pressures—for the tone of the settlement is so far ungracious that one suspects pressures—of the international situation. The current bishop of Valencia was a powerful man at the court of Rome. A new pope, Gregory X, had recently replaced two successive French popes who for a decade had been pouring out money to promote the Angevin cause as against the interests of Aragon. A compromise candidate (indeed, he had not been a cardinal nor even a priest), his succession offered new hope to Aragonese

interests in the western Mediterranean. Besides, at this moment James
fancied himself as a strong candidate for Holy Roman Emperor and as the
leader of a great crusade to Jerusalem.

The agreement reviewed the whole case. James remarked that

> you claim, and often claimed before, that we were doing you injustice as
> to the third part of the tithe which we have kept until now, and are re-
> ceiving now in the city and diocese of Valencia from our castles and towns,
> and as to the endowments we promised to make . . . , and as to the pro-
> perties belonging to the mosques which we gave this church.[56]

In other words, Bishop Andrew had been insisting that the king surrender
his third-tithe in the realm, take care of the expenses and debts in the diocese, and reclaim for the church the lost mosques and their possessions.
Small wonder there had been a "long contention" on this subject! James's
defense had been that the transaction with Bishop Ferrer, by which all three
claims were waived in return for ten thousand besants, had put the third
"licitly" in his hands.[57] Bishop Andrew and his chapter had been pressing
their cause all these years, however, on the grounds that the document
"had not been signed, except only by Bishop Ferrer himself, deceased, and
five canons of their church who were at the time members of the royal
court."[58] Bishop Andrew also maintained that the nature of the exchange
had "enormously damaged the said church."[59]

Here the royal document catalogues the reasons impelling the king to a
settlement: affection for the church, regard for the honor of God, a dis-
inclination for further litigation on the subject, and "also the desire to shut
the mouths of many who might be able to say that we purposely and harm-
fully withheld the aforesaid rights of the same church."[60] King James is
careful to add—and the concession is a measure of the deep feelings aroused
in the controversy—that "according to our conscience, we do not believe
that we are bound to do this." Besides this appeal to a notoriously lax
faculty in his kingly personality, he also reproachfully recalls that "we
snatched [this church] from the hands of the pagans and gained it by our
own blood and restored it to Christian worship."[61] The long, petulant
document is moving and very human.

In the end, the king gave to the church "our castle of Chulilla and our
castle and town of Garg, situated in the kingdom of Valencia and in your
diocese, with their fortifications and men and women," including the king's
third of the tithe in these two places, plus justice and coinage duty.[62] A proviso was appended that, if ever the question of the king's third should be
raised again, or allied questions, this grant would become void. The church
happily accepted, this time mustering thirteen out of a possible fifteen
canons to sign the agreement. A companion document to these two by the
king and church announced a policy of severity by king and civil officials

toward nonpayment of ecclesiastical taxes of all kinds by other laymen.[63] The crown had not come away the loser. Seventy years later the king's third of the tithe on bread and wine, plus his third of the vegetable tithe for the lands in the environs of the capital city, alone amounted to almost 9,000 solidi a year. This almost equaled the great tax on salt, was three times what the king got from the Jews, and was surpassed by the revenues of only the largest towns.[64]

There is a final point, only indirectly pertinent to the tithe, about the king's financial interest in the church and his influence exerted through it. This is his right as patron over the houses of some of the important religious groups in the new realm. This patronage had been firmly established from the beginning, and confirmed by a special document secured from Pope Gregory IX early in 1239. Not only St. Vincent's church and hospital fell under it, but any "other churches and monasteries of the kingdom of Valencia which you built and endowed."[65]

King James gathered unto himself certain of the first fruits, a fact one learns from a document of his successor. James had renounced them in a general way in 1240; in 1282 King Peter was ordering payment in the Alfandech Valley "in those places where the said lord king our father receives these first fruits and ought to receive them."[66] And a document of 1278 reveals that the crown is corecipient of first fruits in the realm widely, though places are not specified.[67]

King James could handily use his share of the tithe or first fruits to pay local debts, as in May of 1262 when he mixed civil and ecclesiastical revenues of assigned places, without distinction, to make a grant to the abbot of Benifasá.[68] A decade later, to fulfill a promise of 1,000 morabatins left to the monastery in his will, James handed over forever his share of the tithe in these same places.[69]

Barons and Knights

Other powers were not less happy in their determined efforts to sequester church revenues for the family purse. Settlement charters granted by nobles often required payment of the tithe, even stipulating the custom law to be observed in its assessing. Many were discreetly silent as to the ultimate beneficiary.[70] But some name him quite candidly: "me and mine"; or, more piously, "me and Holy Mother Church"; or, more subtly, "according to the division" practiced on the lord's estates in Aragon.[71] The church in Valencia early set as a goal the reclaiming of the third-tithe from these nobles, advertising her intentions in the document in which she settled with the king.[72]

These lords included a number of outside bishops. The bishop of Zaragoza received the walled towns and castles of Ribarroja and Albalat del

Júcar where he held the "ius et dominium" until 1269, when he traded them to the king for Pedrosa in Aragon. The bishop of Vich in 1238 got Labeiren and Cunilare near Murviedro, houses in the latter town, and Alcudia and Benialcazim near Paterna—the latter soon traded for the castle of Sagart. The bishop of Segorbe had Borbotó, Coscolana, Piedra, Navajas, and Tramacastiel, or substantial parts thereof—though his situation, as we have seen, was unique. The bishop of Barcelona held the castle and valley of Almonacid, a valuable area the king soon tried to reclaim. Other crusading bishops, like Huesca, Narbonne, and Tarragona, received properties. The Zaragoza bishop acquired also from a local lord half the tithes of nineteen areas in the Segorbe diocese. The tithe claims of such prelates could be settled *pari passu* with those of other lords.[73]

The secular lordships included a number of ecclesiastical establishments as well, like the shrine of St. Vincent's which held Castellón or the religious Orders whose properties were far-flung. Unlike the case of the prelates, the Orders brought uncomfortable nuances to the situation. Some claimed to be exempt from diocesan jurisdiction or tithes, while others did not. Those with exemption sought to extend the privilege to vassals and villages. Some Orders had arrived to take an active, apostolic part in the work of the new diocese; whereas other Orders, or separate houses of an Order like Ripoll or Escarp, only held *in absentia* revenue-producing property to help their work elsewhere. Perhaps these latter eventually paid the tithe. But an absentee owner like the abbot of Montearagón, whose monastery held enough land in the Valencian kingdom as to be involved in military service here in 1277, nowhere appears in the tithe documents. The resident Orders were each the subject of special negotiations, in the course of which matters of revenue were worked out.[74]

The lord not infrequently won the third-tithe. Even then the church imposed the same admission of principle as in the case of the crown: the right of being paid tithes could not become invested in a layman nor was the church able to give it to a layman.[75] However, though the bishop retained in his power the legal and moral jurisdiction, the money or the grapes or the wheat went as a special favor to the lord. Somehow one feels that the latter was not dissatisfied with the arrangement. The lord could hope, in return for the release of mosques, cemeteries, first fruits, and the like, to retain some of the mosque's supporting properties and a third of the tithe. But he would have to accept the latter as a fief, doing homage to the bishop for it.

This concept of a tithe infeudated, in whole or in part, was a settled abuse throughout Christendom. The third ecumenical council of the Lateran (1179) had ordered the laity to return these tithes; the Fourth Lateran (1215) had forbidden them for the future—a prohibition unfortunately seized upon as a tacit approval of the current situation. In France at this time, King St. Louis counseled restitution; but his nobles were unenthusiastic. In the kingdom of Valencia, however, the infeudation of the captive tithe might be defended as the lesser of two evils and a hesitant step forward toward ecclesiastical liberty.

What was the formal process? A document would be drawn: "we grant to you Peter of Montagut and your successors, as a perpetual benefice and fief, the third part of the tithes" in all his territories.[76] By this "you are henceforward our loyal and lawful vassal and defender of our church, and you are bound to do fidelity and homage for these."[77] A supplementary document, by the lord, recorded the homage and ratified the conditions.[78] The infeudation normally seems to have been perpetual; but it would require the formality of renewal by subsequent possessors, at least where the same family did not continue to hold.[79] An ecclesiastical lord had some differences of form, in the matter of homage, from the lay lord; thus a provision in the perpetual fief got by the bishop of Huesca was that, if the successors in this holding were laymen, they were to swear homage as knights do. This may explain the appearance briefly of Miret of Ciutadella, doing homage for the bishop's land.[80]

This kind of document represented more than a church victory as to the theoretical owner of the tithe. It had the practical effect of assuring the lord's backing in collecting the whole tithe, so that the bishop as well received his share fully. It brought the matter under the feudal law—itself codified in a section of the *Furs*. It established firmly a principle which might later be vindicated against less strongly entrenched foes. And it provided an opportunity to define exactly the objects to be tithed. For security the church preferred that the collector in the first instance be the bailiff of the bishop.[81]

One after another, the great landowners entered the cluster of Moorish houses called the episcopal palace. There in colorful ceremony they made homage for their holdings and for all future acquisitions. Each set his signature to a properly witnessed document, perhaps before "the assembled chapter" and with other knights as witnesses.[82] Loose manuscripts survive for a number of these homages, and a fourteenth-century register of those past infeudations which still seemed important at the time of compilation. For the sake of fashioning some generalization, it may be assumed that these represent the bulk of the pertinent documentation. In them, perhaps fifty knights and barons accepted the fiefs of their third-tithes; occasionally the proportion received varied. At least once the church authorities, anxious lest this concession ever be construed as coming from their own two-thirds, emphasized in the contract that the grant left room only for one secularized third; "from our two parts, however, we intend to yield or give you nothing."[83] Though the infeudation was usually perpetual, the bishop could restrict it to a lifetime.[84]

Despite the automatic extension to future holdings, separate charters of infeudation were sometimes drawn to cover these different estates.[85] Most

of the documents were drawn up during the years just after the main crusade effort, indicating a brisk attack on the problem shortly after actual
possession of their lands had been taken by the various knights—if reasonable time is allowed for the first tithing to be refused and a subsequent
quarrel to develop. Before the end of 1242 the system seems to have been
regularized, and perhaps thirteen or more of the lords brought to do homage.
A number of the documents show that there was reluctance and then
arbitration. It is not unsound to assume that even pious knights would
demand the third as their due—as did the religious Orders, the several
crusading bishops, and King James himself. During the interim period before final surrender, there may have been many a knight who, like Artal of
Luna, saw to it that the church received none of this revenue "from him or
his Christians or Moors." In Artal's case (1257), past nonpayment had to be
specifically remitted for the rather long stretch of almost twenty years.[86]

The king's homage for Valencian crown properties had been given early
in 1240 to the bishop-elect of Valencia.[87] Vidal of Cañellas, the great
scholar and statesman who was bishop of Huesca, followed in June, for his
townships of Alboraya and Almácera. He secured the full tithe for any ten
jovates of the land, yielding the remainder.[88] The first of the secular lords
was brought in at the opening of the new year. This was Peter of Montagut,
the brother of the bishop of Zaragoza, doing homage for the tithes of his
castles and territories of Alcudia de Carlet, Alarp, and Carlet, and for his
lesser holdings (February 7, 1241).[89] A month later the Navarrese knight
López of Esparsa made an agreement for the Benisanó area near Liria and
for all future gains.[90] Before the year's end—another struggle and agreement
having intervened with the king over the diocesan endowment—one of the
greatest barons, Berengar of Entenza, had done homage in separate documents for his castles and territory of Chiva and of Turís.[91] The pattern had
been set. The infeudations continued now in a steady stream.

In January 1242 the knight Miret of Ciutadella signed for Almácera
which he had just acquired, apparently by sub-infeudation from the bishop
of Huesca.[92] The powerful Simon Pérez of Arenós, lieutenant of the king for
the realm of Valencia, swore homage on April 1, for his castle and territory
of Pedralba southwest of Liria.[93] In May, Peter Jordán of Alfambra received the infeudation of the third-tithe of Melilla and its country (a grant
"below Ruzafa").[94] Peter d'Or did homage for the Albalat territory not
far distant.[95] Peter Azlor, very possibly the same man, did so for holdings in
the same place and at Cinqueros;[96] Peter of Puig for his lands near Valencia;[97] Simon of Salinas for his Campanar estates;[98] and William of Espailargas for his lands there.[99] The warrior bishop of Vich, St. Bernard Calvó, was
represented in a settlement for his holdings (June 1242), places like Labeiren
and Cunilare near Murviedro, and Alcudia and Benialcazim near Paterna.[100]
In July 1242, the bishop of Huesca again did homage in general for all his

holdings; perhaps he had acquired important lands since his previous appearance; he also did homage for his town of Alboraya.[101]

A series of owners followed in August: the justiciar of Aragon Peter Pérez, for his lands in the Valencian huerta;[102] the crusader Roderick of Falz or of Salses, for Rafalaxat in the huerta;[103] Sire García for his Ruzafa lands;[104] and Sancho Pérez of Oblites for nearby property.[105] In September the royal functionary Martin Sánchez did homage for his lands near Valencia city,[106] Raymond of Rosanes for lands in Almazora,[107] and Arnold of Vernet for his place in the Valencian huerta.[108] Others followed, like Raymond of San Ramón for his Cuart possessions (1245);[109] Berengar of Montreal in 1248 for holdings present and future;[110] the powerful Artal of Luna for Paterna and Manises in 1257 and 1262;[111] the magnate Simon Pérez of Arenós again for "the land of the river Mijares" and for Andilla in August 1260.[112]

The latter two holdings were renegotiated in 1263 by the procurators of Simon's wife, Mary Fernández. At her death all rights "both as to Saracens and to Christians" were to revert to the bishop and chapter.[113] The tithes of Sot, Chera, and Villar were given to the Aragonese magnate Furtado de Lihori in 1271.[114] The lord of Rascaña and Algerós, William of Aguiló, made his homage sometime before 1260.[115] Roderick Díaz arranged in 1260 for the tithes of his castles and regions of Almonacid and Benaguacil for life.[116]

A list of thirteen men doing homage in 1272 for the third-tithes includes new names, some of them perhaps heirs or subsequent owners. They were substantial, even great, men: the knight and royal counselor Blaise Maza,[117] James of Oblites,[118] Simon Peter of Daroca,[119] Simon Zapata of Murviedro,[120] Sancho Ferdinand of Loriz,[121] Martin Roiz or Ruiz of Chelva,[122] the crown agent Simon Zapata of Játiva,[123] John Peter Zapata,[124] Peter Martin of Oblites,[125] and Lope Sánchez.[126] Others turn up in the *Book of Legal Documents*, including some of the greatest names in the realm, like Carroz of Rebollet, the admiral of Catalonia, who held Denia, Olocayba, Polop (to 1257), and other places.[127] In 1273 the Tibi lands of Sancho Pérez of Lienda were negotiated.[128] The now discredited *Trobes* of James Febrèr, which may nevertheless derive from some form of documentation, speak of an Agramunt from Navarre who "enjoyed half the tithes of Nules, which the bishop gave him," a Raymond of Seguí who kept all the tithes on his holdings, and a William of Salines who bought the third-tithe of Campanar from the cathedral chapter.[129]

Some areas have a less usual history. In 1243, Cuart in the environs of Valencia city lost the episcopal two-thirds to the king, who in return traded his third of the Puzol tithe to the bishop.[130] Raymond of San Ramón, who seems to have acquired a small fortification and a number of corrals in the region, secured the infeudation of the usual third: "but we grant you this in such wise, only if you shall be able to retrieve the third part from the lord king, because it is he who holds it as a fief for the bishop and the Valencian church."[131] The bishop and chapter, unoptimistic and wishing to be perfectly safe, explicitly forbade their share to be touched by the owner.[132] The rejected wife of King James, Teresa Giles of Vidaure, received a full half of the tithes for her castles of Jérica and Toro; this was a lease but such a permanent one that custom would surely congeal it into a right: three hundred years.[133] Exceptions to the latter infeudation were made for the offspring of cows, horses, asses, and goats, which the cathedral body preferred to retain.

The important official Simon Pérez of Arenós, though he had done homage in 1242 for his castle and country of Pedralva, struck a very different bargain in 1260 with the bishop and chapter for his later lands: a half of the tithe or, when it fell on his considerable Saracen revenues, all of it.[134] Simon's son Blaise kept these latter claims. He even attempted to transfer the homage to the bishop of Zaragoza, perhaps with an eye to a better contract. But the Valencian bishop and chapter sued Blaise, and a royal investigation confirmed their rights.[135] Artal of Luna had his tithe fief for Paterna and Manises restricted to his lifetime, and complicated by an annual fee to the bishop and chapter of a hundred silver besants (1257).[136] The Paterna lands were renegotiated in 1262 by his heirs, being again restricted to a lifetime and with certain animals retained.[137] Some lords drove a hard bargain. A son of King James, Peter Ferdinand, refusing to pay the tithe for his Saracen revenues at Buñol and Ribarroja, did agree during an arbitration to pay 300 solidi every Christmas, a concession of the tithe which was to end at his death.[138]

In the northern part of the kingdom of Valencia the bishop of Tortosa similarly sought to regularize the ownership of tithes. But documents of tithe homage here are rare, probably reflecting far less activity. Tortosa was a more established diocese, not so needy or so concerned to establish precedents at the outset. Again, a great deal of seignorial property up here belonged to the military Orders or to the Cistercians; and the Tortosa diocese did make strenuous efforts to diminish the Orders' ownership of tithes. One lay baron prominent in the Tortosa tithe records is William Raymond of Moncada, lord of Nules. In spring of 1250 he did homage for half the tithes of Nules castle and countryside. He and his successors held this forever, with the obligation of populating the area, of protecting the local church, and of seeing that the diocesan half was paid. His own revenues from Saracen tenants were included as under the tithe. (In 1306 a descendant, Raymond Moncada, renewed this homage.) A similar Tortosan tithe arrangement was made with Peter Simon (Eximénes) for the castle of Montornés in 1268. Simon of Urrea received a temporary grant of all tithes in his Alcalatén estates in 1282 at a price of 100 solidi yearly to the bishop. It was to run for his lifetime plus ten years, after which his heir must give half the yearly tithes to the diocese.[139]

Certain areas in Valencia are represented by documents of later date; it is difficult to relate these to the post-conquest period.[140] In the abortive Segorbe diocese there was understandably little opportunity for tithe problems to evolve. Even here, on the occasion of the first reorganization attempted (1247), Bishop Peter awarded half the tithes of Olocau, Adzaneta, and Chodos to Peter of Alcalá.[141]

What of the many knights whose names do not appear? There were several hundred newly created "knights of the conquest" alone, and documents disclose a large number of lords and lordlings not considered in the tithe records. For one thing, only the diocese of Valencia is here under examination. Crown lands and religious lands—an enormous extension— are not being considered, nor are those of city dwellers, nor probably some Moslem regions. This having been said, a puzzle remains. Were these the only secular lords powerful enough to claim the privilege of conquerors? Had other landowners given in, without leaving a trace of protest? These are not likely solutions, especially when one remembers the part taken by the barons and knights in the more general tithe conflict. It might be conjectured that the ecclesiastical authorities did not press their case against the others; but this would have been inconsistent with their inner urge to barratry. The piety of the majority would hardly have caused them to make a gift of these revenues to the church, though James of Jérica did so (1279) with the tithes and first fruits of Domeño castle and territory.[142]

A superficially plausible explanation might be that we are dealing with holdings to which the church itself had some claim, with the knights as vassals. This would explain why immensely powerful men did homage for relatively small territories; it is supported by a comparison of place names, because so many of the estates are near those listed for the church. To accept this hypothesis would mean greatly expanding our present understanding of the amount of land owned by the diocese. The theory seems unlikely, in view of the great poverty professed by the church, especially when the diocese had to employ this excuse to secure the tithes from the parishes by papal permission. And all the documentary evidence points the other way: that these lands were held by the individuals themselves with no reference to the church. Besides, some of the tithe-contracts refer to a wide sweep of holdings present and future of a given lord; it is not probable that only church-owned lands could be meant. Again, one might suspect that the records refer to lands whose tithes were to be applied to the cathedral, since the diocesan records have disappeared. But it seems most improbable that no indication of such a situation, or of other tithe arrangements, has survived in the many documents relative to the Valencian tithes and tithe conflict.

It is possible that these individual agreements represent owners of great power, especially from among men holding lands in the diocese *mero et mixto imperio*. Once the church settled with them, the other feudatories in the diocese could be treated as though on crown lands. This would explain why the church warned James away from claiming the thirds of the knights, and why she later clashed with the crown over this question. It would also explain why the barons and knights as a body were involved in the general tithe conflict and in the accord of 1268. It may be that the church first settled in principle the question of the king's third, then that of the third claimed by the very powerful nobles (especially where the farmlands were more settled by Christians?), and finally that of the tithes owed by the body of knights and citizens.

Speaking in a general context and as late as 1273, King James said plainly: "we and the knights and religious in the diocese of Valencia receive a third portion of the tithe."[143] The king intended this as a restatement of general policy, which he claimed to be applicable also to the Tortosa diocese holdings in the kingdom of Valencia. He revealed again the situation of general lay ownership of third-tithes in another plain-spoken document that same year.[144] Yet again, when the king assumed control of the third-tithe from lands of knights which he had come to hold, and the Valencia bishop protested the action, there is evidence—though not unambiguous—of antecedent possession of the third-tithes by all knights (1279–1280).[145] Cases also exist of the refusal by knights to transfer their right to the king.[146]

King Peter made it one of his first duties after his accession to cite Hugh of Baux to court (October 1277), assigning him a day to answer "about the demand of the third part of the tithe which the king required from the knights of Burriana."[147] In 1280, ordering the holder of the queen's flocks in Valencia to pay the tithe, King Peter told him to reserve the king's third. In 1281–1282 crown functionaries even attempted to seize the thirds belonging to the Templars at Burriana and Ademuz.[148] And in 1280 the king commanded an official "to see to it that the bishop of Valencia produces just reasons, if there be any, which could stand in the way of paying the king the third-tithe" of lands formerly held by knights.[149]

Some knightly estates paid no tithe; seven such places including a Valencian saltworks are listed among the holdings of James's son Peter Ferdinand. The tithe Peter Ferdinand actually did pay was considerably less than a mathematical tenth of the given income.[150] Possibly knights with more modest estates staffed only by Moslems owed too small a tithe to bother about; the bishop could hope in such a case for a mere two-thirds of a tenth of a previous Moslem rent. Among larger landholders enjoying a share of the tithe were ex-King Vincent or Saʿīd. He regulated the tithe in detail in his baronial settlement charter for Villahermosa, ordering it to be given "both to us and to the church."[151]

It can be argued that the majority of the important Valencian landholders did not submit to infeudation for their share of the tithe, nor yet formally surrender that share. This contention could be based upon the roll call of Valencian feudatories obliged to fight during the 1277 Moslem revolt, and upon the inexplicable silence of the tithe documents regarding most of its names. The listing is far wider than the names available from the tithe documentation. The disparity is partly in numbers (almost fifty men in the tithe documents, some one hundred and fifty in the roll call), partly in the circumstance that the two lists do not jibe. Some twenty-five of the 1277 warriors also appear in tithe settlements. Names which do coincide include some very important men, such as James of Jérica, Simon of Urrea, Carroz, Artal of Alagón, and Entenza. Of course, it is only fair to note that the military roll call has an extension somewhat wider than the combined dioceses of Tortosa and Valencia, and that changes of ownership in a rapidly moving real-estate market can account for some disparity between the two lists. A comparison of the two does tend to confirm the suspicion that the tithe settlements cover a minority, though a large and important minority, of the landholders.[152]

In conclusion, it seems that knights generally claimed the third-tithe, but that the church did not recognize their claim, and that a large number of them secured an infeudation to regularize this. There is no clear reason why only those named made such compacts. They may have been the most important landowners; or have held lands possessed of some unique quality—a connection with the crown, or with the cathedral, or utterly independent; or (feeblest supposition of all) all manuscript trace of further surrenders has disappeared. A general conclusion seems to be that the church did not recover the third-tithe from the knights, any more than she had from the king or the religious, but that for reasons difficult to stabilize firmly she had to be content with infeudating the third to a large minority of them.

ᗋᑞ Farming the Tithes

The tithes were farmed and even traded around, like the secular revenues of the crown in Valencia. This could be done at a flat rate or for a percentage. The priors of the Valencian chapter, ultimately responsible for the collecting, were expressly allowed to operate through farmers if they wished. Thus, a third-tithe was handed to a monk of Holy Crosses, Peter of Calçareyns, as a personal benefice until certain injuries done to him, and now assessed at a money value, were repaired.[153]

In 1245 King James awarded 50 solidi annually to Bernard of Cervelló, to be taken from the crown's third-tithe in the city and countryside of Valencia. He confirmed this gift again in 1260 to Bernard's daughter Silia.[154] Saltworks (not those of the Albufera) leased to royal farmers paid the church a set tithe of 100 Jaca solidi every year.[155] In 1273 Simon Guasch, the royal bailiff for the Denia and Calpe districts, incorporated the king's share of the tithe merely as another of the several crown taxes in his accounting.[156]

Sometimes the tithe was sold directly to the lord. It is not always easy to distinguish this arrangement from an arbitration-payment or even a simple infeudation of the tithe, of which it is a variant. Sometimes, by an inter-mediate form, a lord added some small compensatory money payment in his contract of infeudation. An example of a straight sale of the diocesan two-thirds is the contract given to the magnate Blaise Maza:

> We lease to you Blaise Maza knight, and yours, henceforward for ten years . . . two parts of all the fruits of the earth and trees belonging to the bishop and chapter of Valencia, in your castle and country of Villamar-chante . . . for the price of two hundred solidi every year.[157]

Another privilege, given for the lifetime of the grantee, sold the entire tithe of three regions in return for 60 solidi every Christmas:

> We, Brother Andrew, . . . with the consent of the chapter of Valencia, sell and grant only to you Furtado de Lihori knight . . . and Giles Roderick your son the whole tithe of bread, wine, trees, and all other fruits which we have . . . except the tithe on livestock, in the fortified rural areas of Sot, Villar, and Chera, which you hold.[158]

Simon of Urrea bought all the tithes of the Alcalatén area for 100 solidi yearly.

The wife of Simon Pérez of Arenós bought the third-tithe of her husband's Valencian holdings in 1263 for life at a regular payment.[159] Roderick Díaz had a similar life lease for Almonacid and Benaguacil castles from 1268; he paid 1,200 solidi a year.[160] In the Tortosa diocese in 1272 the bishop sold the tithes of Ennueyo, Ahín, and Eslida to Teresa Giles Vidaure (wife of King James) and her son; the contract was to run fifty years at an annual rent of 130 solidi.[161]

A number of other cases emerge in the realm of Valencia later in the century, such as that of the baron James of Jérica (1280). There is also con-tinuing evidence of the use of tithe farmers: for example, at Cárcer (1280), Montserrat and Montroy (1288), Cocentaina (1289), Polop and the moun-tains (1292), Luchente (1293), Biar (1294), Cárcer and Enova (1295), and Alcira (1303). Although scattered, the evidence is indicative of the system used, if not everywhere, at least not uncommonly.

A tangled case occurred in 1260. A citizen of Valencia, Peter of Pont, had bought the third-tithes of Rascaña and Algerós in the territory of Valencia city, from William of Aguiló; where the latter had acquired these tithes is not known, but the bishop was buying them back.[162] The same was done with the tithe on sea fishery. "We lease to you Raymond Jaland citizen of

Valencia, and yours, henceforth for one year, the year coming next, the whole of the tithe of the fish of the sea in the diocese."[163] He was to make payment every four months as was the custom, presumably a fixed sum.

A similar farming case, also to be paid every four months by custom, indicates that sub-farming was used:

> We sell to you Hugueto of Umanino, and yours, henceforward for the coming year, the whole tithe on the cattle tax [carnage] in the episcopate of Valencia, in the same way as it has been the custom hitherto to be sold and alienated and collected or taken, in such wise that you and whoever you wish may gather and receive the said tithe.[164]

Early in 1259 Bishop Andrew at Cocentaina farmed the revenues—probably more than the tithes alone—of Alcoy castle and territory, in return for a share of them, to his vassal Raymond of Almenara.[165] Blaise of Alagón, son of the great warrior in the Valencian crusade, transferred his share of the tithe for the township and castle of Mallo to Martin of the Lady Toda and his wife Elvira, to keep or sell or give as they chose (1289); this was done to reward them for services rendered him.[166]

William of Anglesola, when selling Culla to the Templars, included the tithes as a property value.[167] Just as King James paid debts with his third-tithe, his grandson James II was similarly to subinfeud tithes or grant them as alms to a religious house—all a form of tithe farming in effect.[168] Though circumstances in Segorbe made that diocese atypical—smallness, poverty, and a long battle for independence against the bishop of Valencia—it affords an interesting parallel of tithe farming around 1280: one-fourth of the Ademuz tithes, one-third of those of Vallanca, and so on.[169]

For transporting and merchandising the tithes, the Valencian church fortified itself with a variety of privileges, covering passage on land, sea, and fresh water. One of the most important of these was granted to the diocese in 1269.

> [You may] freely convey all the products, from your [own] revenues only, wherever you may possess them, and have them sent into the city of Valencia whenever you wish, and even transport them, tax-free, from one place to another throughout the whole realm of Valencia and market them. [You may] also export them from the realm itself, by land or by sea, and ship them to whatever place you wish, and do what you want with them. No statute, present or future, is to impede this in any way. We firmly order the bailiffs, magistrates, justiciars, and all other officials and our [individual] subjects. . . .[170]

If suspicious, an official could satisfy himself by requiring an oath to the effect that the goods in transit were indeed tithes.[171] The exporter of these products for sale was also exempt from taxes. Wine especially moved without tax, and could be brought into the city of Valencia at times when the law prohibited merchants from transporting it.[172]

Such farming of tithes was against canon law. Contemporary reformers attacked the abuse. Grosseteste called it, and aptly, "slavery" for the church.[173] The advantages were obvious, however, in passing on to an entrepreneur the risks implicit in depending upon agricultural revenue. Bishop Arnold assigned such a reason in a license of 1246 for the farming of tithes: "many dangers can threaten [farmers' incomes] both because of barrenness and because of fog, hail, and other bad weather."[174] The same idea was incorporated into the document of 1259 organizing the revenue priorates in the chapter; trouble in a given year was foreseen, from "popular discontent or on account of royal burdens, and from general loss of productivity," and provision made to recoup these deficiencies from other years or other priorates.[175]

It is not possible, unfortunately, to estimate how much the church realized from the diocesan tithes, but it must have been an impressive sum. A list of the estates of Peter Ferdinand in the realm of Valencia in 1273, for example, includes "the places on which he is obliged to pay tithe to the bishop of Valencia." His section of Cocentaina paid tithes on an income of 3,700 solidi; four of his castles had to pay tithe on castle guard to the bishop. From the document it is difficult to decide exactly how much the diocese got, but it would seem to have been a considerable sum.[176]

A much later list of a dozen small Moslem towns suggests what might be expected from such places. Either these are for properties acquired from Christians, or much more probably are the direct payment of the sums the lords here owe on their own incomes. Though dated as late as 1330, it may not be inapplicable, in a conservative agricultural situation, to an earlier time. Four of these places contributed some 500 solidi each; Guadalest, Callosa, Polop, and Castell; 366 came from Confrides, and a total of 887 from the others—Algar with Pedil, Almácera, Finestrat, Chirles (Charli), Albalat, and Tárbena.[177]

According to the contemporary Valencian historian Muntaner (born 1264 but writing at the end of the first quarter of the fourteenth century), so much tithe was collected in Valencia, Murcia, and Majorca, "that it would be difficult to say that she [the church] has as many tithes and first fruits from five other kingdoms as from these three" crusade conquests.[178] According to a Catalan census of the mid-fourteenth century, the total tithe from grain, wine, and vegetables from the Valencian area would by then have reached over 25,000 solidi a year. This is greater than the rents of the crown at that time from the cities of Murviedro (13,500) or Alcira (14,550), and almost as great as the rents of Játiva (27,328), being surpassed only by the rents of Valencia city (79,624).[179]

An index to the economic potential of the Valencian diocese in the thirteenth century is that it was to become, by the time of the Council of Constance less than two hundred years later, one of the wealthiest sees in Christendom. It would be surpassed in revenue then (1417) by only twelve dioceses. It would rank in income with Seville and Zaragoza (and with Lincoln and Norwich in England) and well above places like Paris, London, Milan, Lyons, or Utrecht.[180]

X

THE MILITARY ORDERS
AS FRONTIER INSTITUTIONS

The religious Orders present a distinct new element in the synthesis of institutions on the Valencian frontier. Each constituted an institution in itself, designed to answer some need in the Christian community. Perhaps in nothing else was King James so fortunate as in the variety and genius of the groups available in Valencia in the mid-thirteenth century. These religious establishments would continue to expand and multiply through the centuries until the kingdom of Valencia had almost two hundred and fifty of them, not counting the several Orders of chivalry and the institutions of the diocesan clergy. Convents and monasteries eventually covered a third of the superficies of the city of Valencia.[1] Since the conquered city of Valencia, like the other towns of the new kingdom, was an intricate maze of narrow streets, a number of the first religious houses had to be placed near or outside the early ring of walls to allow scope for expansion.

◊◊ FUNCTION OF THE MILITARY ORDERS ON THE FRONTIER

The great military Orders stand out clearest on the scene: the Hospital, the Temple, Calatrava, Santiago, and St. George. The Knights of Mercy (*Merced*) might be added, but they distinguished themselves rather for their hospice and ransoming work. The Order of the Holy Sepulchre was ambiguously military, consisting of a branch of canons regular under the patriarch of Jerusalem as prior, and a branch of knights under the patriarch as grand master.

The Sepulchre group had held their mother church at Calatayud now for almost a century; the church of St. Anne at Barcelona was another of their important centers. They enjoyed high esteem in the realms of Aragon. Alphonse I had even willed his kingdom in 1134 to these knights and to the Temple and Hospital—a gift of course never delivered. In 1218 the parliament of Villafranca took the Sepulchre Order under the king's special protection. After the fall of Valencia city King James gave them a large estate in Campanar, a suburb to the northwest. Despite the military flavor of their black robes with double red cross, the canons were simply a clerical group living in community under an Augustinian rule and devoting themselves to peaceful ministries. Here at Valencia city the metropolitan awarded

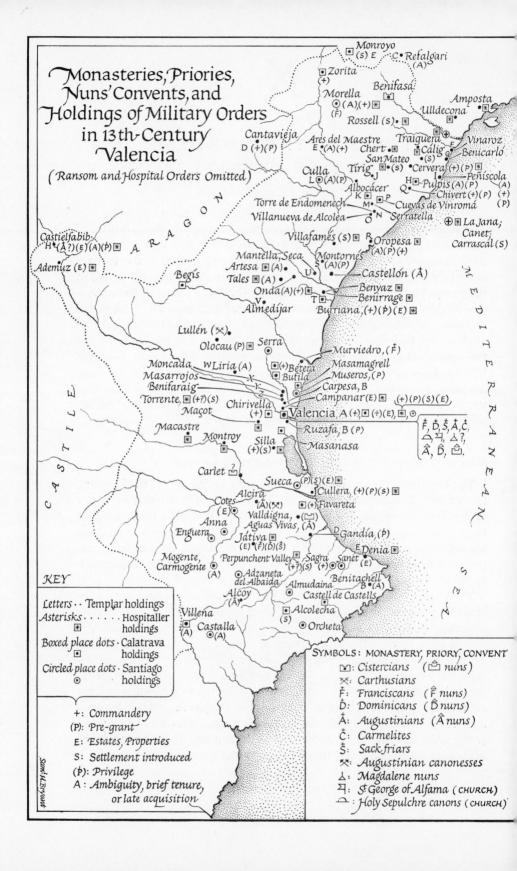

Monasteries, Priories, Nuns' Convents, and Holdings of Military Orders in 13th-Century Valencia

(Ransom and Hospital Orders Omitted)

Monroyo (S) E ·C ·Refalgari (A)
·Zorita (+)
Morella ⊙(A)(+) ⊠ Benifasa ⊠
(F)
Rossell (S) · ⊠ Amposta
Ulldecona ·⊠
Cantavieja Ares del Maestre Traiguera ⊠ ⊠
·(A)(+) E ·(A)(+) Chert ·⊠ Calig ⊠ F Vinaroz
D (+)(P) San Mateo ·(S) Cervera (+)(P)⊠ Benicarlo
Culla Tirig J ⊠·(S) H·⊠ I ·Peñiscola
L⊙(A)(P) Albocácer Q·Pulpis (A)(P) ·(A)
K·⊠ P Chivert (+)(P) (+)
Torre de Endomenech M·⊠ ·Cuevas de Vinromá (P)
Villanueva de Alcolea · N Serratella
O· ⊕⊠ La Jana;
Villafames (S) ⊠ R Canet;
Oropesa ⊠ Carrascal (S)
Mantella, Seca (A)(P)(+)
Artesa ⊠(A) Montornes
Tales ⊠(A) S·(A)(P) Castellón (Ā)
U·
Begís Onda(A)(+)⊠ Benyaz ⊠
· V T·⊠ Benirrage ⊠
Almedíjar Burriana,(+)(Þ)(E)⊠

Lullén (✕)·
Olocau (P)⊠ Serra
· Murviedro,(F̂)
Moncada W Liria (A) Masamagrell
Masarrojos ⊠(+)Bétera Museros,(P)
Benifaraig X ⊙Bufila Carpesa, B
Torrente, ⊠ (+?)(S) Y Campanar(E) ⊠
· Z· (+)(P)(S)(E),
Maçot Chirivella Valencia A (+),⊡ (+)(E),⊠,⊙,
(+) ⊙
Macastre Ruzafa, B (P) F̂, D̂, Ŝ, Ā, Ĉ,
· ⊡· Δ⋈, Δ?,
Montroy Silla Masanasa Ā, D̂, ◠,
⊠ (+)(S)·
Carlet ⌂·
Sueca (P)(S)(E)⊠
Alcira Cullera, (+)(P)(S) ⊠
Cotes ·(Ā)(✕)
(E)⊙ Valldigna, ·⌂ ⊡·+ Favareta
Anna Aguas Vivas, (Ā)
Enguera ⊙ ⊙ D Gandía, (Þ)
Játiva ⊠ E Denia ⊠
(E)·(F̂)(D̂)(Ŝ) ⊙ Sanet (E)
Mogente, Perpunchent Valley⊠ Sagra (+)⊙⊙
Carmogente (+?)(S) Almudaina
(A) Adzaneta B ·(A)
del Albaida Benitachell
Alcoy Almudaina Castell de Castells·
(Ā) ⊙ ·
Villena ⊡ Alcolecha
·⊡ (S)
Castalla ⊙Orcheta
(A) ⊙(A)

KEY

Letters ··	Templar holdings
Asterisks ····· ⊠	Hospitaller holdings
Boxed place dots · ⊡	Calatrava holdings
Circled place dots · ⊙	Santiago holdings

+: Commandery
(P): Pre-grant
E: Estates, Properties
S: Settlement introduced
(Þ): Privilege
A: Ambiguity, brief tenure,
 or late acquisition

SYMBOLS: MONASTERY, PRIORY, CONVENT

⊡: Cistercians (⌂ nuns)
✕: Carthusians
F̂: Franciscans (F̂ nuns)
D̂: Dominicans (D̂ nuns)
Ā: Augustinians (Â nuns)
Ĉ: Carmelites
Ŝ: Sack friars
⋈: Augustinian canonesses
Δ: Magdalene nuns
Δ⋈ St George of Alfama (CHURCH)
◠: Holy Sepulchre canons (CHURCH)

ARAGON

CASTILE

MEDITERRANEAN SEA

Castielfabib·
H·(Ā?)(E)(A)(P)⊠
Ademuz (E) ⊠

Sami H. Bryant

"to the Brothers of the Order of the Holy Sepulchre" the governance of the parish church of St. Bartholomew. The first bishop of Valencia promptly challenged this gift. A brief dispute concluded amicably with the bishop's reassigning St. Bartholomew's to these "canons and Brothers" (1242).[2]

"Frater Dominicus" signed a Valencian document as rector here in 1246; the same document links with him Canon Simon as superior for the Order in Aragon, Majorca, and Valencia.[3] "Raymond of Lérida, commander of the house of the Holy Sepulchre of Valencia", appears in a Valencian document of 1251. The lord of Arenós granted a field and some houses to the group.[4] William Piquer in his will desired burial in St. Bartholomew's cemetery "of the Order of the Holy Sepulchre." Bernard of Nausa in his will of 1261 left them 8 solidi; in 1276 the wife of Blaise Peter of Fuentes willed them 10.[5] These data apparently are all that remain to tell of the Order's work in Valencia.

The properly military Orders had a double function on the Valencian frontier: as religious warriors and as enterprising landowners. The latter service, with its pattern of land grants, colonization, feudal dues, and the like, was of great moment. It is in connection with landowning that most of the Valencian records of the military Orders have survived, especially the gifts and charters serving as rewards for crusade conquests and as permanent income to support their standing armies. But the Orders ought to be regarded also in the light of their religious and military influence. In this guise they have an added importance in Valencia because: they assumed spiritual obligations in some places of the new kingdom; they complicated the collection of diocesan revenues, particularly diminishing the episcopal tithal income; and they stiffened the spirit of crusade among the settlers.

Considered simply as a garrison, the diocese itself was no inconsiderable factor, the bishop with his men-at-arms being a key military figure. No less than nine bishops laid aside their swords and armor in 1238 to cosign the capitulation of besieged Valencia. At that siege the army of the bishop of Barcelona included eighty armored knights with horses, the appropriate complement of militia, and a small armed fleet.[6] The Valencian diocese could also issue an appeal to other dioceses for military assistance, as was done in 1277 during the Saracen invasion of Valencia, when the cathedral chapter wrote to the metropolitanates of Arles and Narbonne.[7] But the effect of such help was occasional and amateurish when compared with the professionalism of the force-in-being constituted by the military Orders.

Their castles and commanderies multiplied in the land during this period, and their popularity is reflected in legacies. Some of these "castles" were in reality quite small: defensive posts to protect the local farmers during raids by land or sea, or to stand briefly under a Moslem flood until help could penetrate to them. Some rather small castles and towers were keypoints in the defensive system, while some very large land grants amounted to a liability or onerous responsibility rather than a source of present revenue. Every large estate did not boast a commandery or even a staff of knights; diocesan priests served many churches under their control, and lay knights or citizens administered farms or fortresses.

Knowledge of the relative economic strength of each Valencian Order is defective, but it is possible to get a sound general view, as well as a rough appreciation of how important these Orders were to the Valencian kingdom. Though they often had agreements allowing them to keep the lion's share of what they conquered, this applied rather to expeditions undertaken on their private initiative or carried through by their individual forces operating against some special objective during a general crusade.

At the period under discussion, perhaps some of these Orders had—as the general of the Dominicans preached against the Templars—"amassed lands and castles and been defeated in their own hearts."[8] But in Valencia at least, they were now to enjoy a splendid moment, serving not only the material needs of a nascent society but their own ideals as well. For Valencia was in a state of semi-permanent crusade throughout James's reign. A Christian minority possessed of no great tact was expanding its energies, while rebellion brooded among the Moslem masses and thoughts of revenge smoldered in North Africa. King James was as afraid of massive rebellion as he was incapable of forcing his knights to assemble against it when it did come. It was no accident that the first bishop of Valencia, on his way north to a metropolitan synod, died in a Moorish ambush; that James himself died in the city of Valencia, his frontier ablaze with revolt; or that in the same year (1276) Peter of Moncada, master of the Temple, was captured with all his troop by Moslem cavalry during a "great and mighty" Christian defeat.[9]

The continued calls of the popes to support Valencia with crusading methods are reminders of this continuity of the crusade. In 1248 Innocent IV told the metropolitan at Tarragona to have his bishops and clergy give all possible aid to James against the Moor revolt. Simultaneously he exhorted the faithful to crusade there, granting indulgences; he turned the Holy Land "twentieth," then being collected in Aragon, to the needs of Valencia for three years. A similar document, directed to the archbishop of Tarragona for the next year, also urged bishops and the faithful to join the armies or subsidize them, and excommunicated all "throughout Spain and Catalonia" who aided the enemy.[10]

The military Orders constituted a set of standing armies unique for their cohesive solidarity, disinterestedness, and *esprit*. Their estates supplied a remarkable international pool of capital for warfare or frontier colonization. They possessed organization, experience, skills, and a fairly full autonomy with respect both to church and state. Above all, they combined in one vocation the two enthusiasms of that hearty age—the heroism of the monastery and the heroism of war. Grouped in local commanderies and divided into elite knights, auxiliary men-at-arms, and some chaplains, they lived their vows in their monastery barracks or died in generous numbers on some Christian frontier.

These "holy armies" meant far more to their generation than can be conveyed in a short space. Something of that meaning is caught in the historical writings of the contemporary Roderick Simon of Rada, primate of Toledo, crusader, scholar, and diplomat. He writes lyrically of the Knights of Santiago:

> They who praised God in choir [now] gird on the sword. They who prayed and sorrowed [are riding] to defend the fatherland. Meager food is their fare, the harshness of wool their covering. Unremitting monastic discipline tests them. A worshipful silence envelops them. In frequent kneeling they learn humility. Knightly vigil wastes their bodies. Devout prayer gives them wisdom. Constant effort tries them. Each guards the other's path, and brother [aids] brother in the monastic life.

They are knights "whose work is the sword of defense; the scourge of the Arabs dwells here . . . , the defender of the faith."[11]

To the newly conquered kingdom of Valencia, with its "forty or fifty"[12] formidable castles in the Moslem countryside requiring a permanent garrison, these Orders were a godsend.

⚜ KNIGHTS OF SANTIAGO

Santiago and Calatrava are thought of as Castilian Orders, yet each had a sturdy branch in Aragon. The Order of St. James (Santiago) of Compostela, named for its protective activities on the Compostela pilgrim routes, had its centers both at the city of León and at Uclés in Castile until the union of the realms under Ferdinand III. It received an Augustinian rule as early as 1171 and papal approbation in 1175. Its mild rule would eventually make it more extensive and wealthy than Alcántara and Calatrava combined.

In the opening decades of the thirteenth century, when Santiago had been achieving its definitive form under the grand prior of Uclés in Castile, its Aragonese branch was firmly establishing itself at the castle and countryside of Montalbán. Apparently the Santiago knights fought with King James's father on border raids against the Moslems.[13] They played a spirited if secondary role in the conquest of the kingdom of Valencia. Their pennon of the scarlet cross, with its curious termination in sword and pilgrim's cockleshell, was carried into battle from Burriana in the north to Orihuela in the south. At Burriana the commander of Montalbán, Roderick Buesa, led not only his knights but also the townsmen of Montalbán to the siege. At the investment of Biar these knights were among the royal forces. Near

Orihuela the experienced master of Uclés prodded the dilatory king into swifter action and took the flank of the army into battle.[14]

"Taking timely thought for the multiple labors and heavy expenses you continually bear in defending the Catholic faith and expanding the worship of God," the king gave the Order of Santiago in 1236 the castle and country-side of Museros near Moncada. This was actually a pre-grant which induced them subsequently to capture it. As early as 1241 they began to bring in settlers here, with privileges; in 1245, Pope Innocent IV formally confirmed this holding.[15] In Valencia city the king gave them (1239) some buildings on the river front, to the west of the Templars, where they soon raised a church and residence of St. James of Uclés.[16]

The Santiago knights also held, probably by military action, the castles and towns of Anna, Orcheta and Torres, of Serra and Mola, and of Engu-era.[17] By 1260 they had bought the castle of Almudaina from William of Cardona.[18] They were in possession of Culla and other castles (by exchange with William of Anglesola in 1274 for the castles of Bellpuig and Golmers or Galiners);[19] of eight jovates of land in the rural areas of Sueca and Cotes (the Sumacárcel region);[20] of Carmogente castle and territory, and of other castles;[21] of Sanet village;[22] and of Sagra, where they later had a residence.[23]

Santiago seems also to have held, or had interests in, the castles of Mogente, Castalla, and Morella; but these were brief or later holdings, and the documents preserved in connection with them offer little solid informa-tion. To the far south, beyond the properly Valencian conquest, there were buildings in Murcia, Orihuela, and Lorca (1266), and castles like Segura. The Santiago knights undoubtedly received the usual benefactions of a minor sort; but these must not have been numerous. Thus, in 1255 the knight William Ochova Alemán willed them 200 solidi for constructing a cloister for their Valencian church.[24] It is difficult to say just when Adzaneta del Albaida came into their hands—perhaps not until the fourteenth century. They were strongest south of the Júcar River, on the true frontier; but they were also well represented along the central littoral, and held by purchase a castle in the north. One result of this distribution was that their struggle over ecclesiastical revenues was with the bishop of Valencia rather than with the bishop of Tortosa.

Like most of the large military Orders, Santiago claimed exemption from episcopal jurisdiction and even to some extent from the tithe. Such claims were qualified by recent canonical restrictions and modified by practical circumstances. Privilege might be countered by contrary privilege, and by custom, rights, or need; diocesan priests would be holding beneficed chan-tries in their churches; their right of patronage over territories and parish churches could be regarded as on an equal footing with that of other knightly overlords. In any event many bishops, resentful of even legal diminution of their jurisdiction, were sure to fight exemption. During the first five years of the Christian occupation of Valencia, the Santiago knights bravely engaged the bishop and chapter, with some success.

For the churches of the lands they held, and for those of all their future acquisitions, they were allowed to keep the *ius patronatus*, half the tithes, all the first fruits, and the fees and offerings except a fourth of the death services.[25] To make victory more complete—or to adopt the pacific formula of the agreement, to assure a firmer peace—the bishop and chapter cheaply farmed their half of the tithes and revenues to the Order for a hundred years at 115 silver besants a year. Twenty-eight of these besants were for the procurations of bishop and archdeacon on the occasion of their respective visitations; the agreements cannily provided that these were to be paid even when actual visitation was omitted. All this does not necessarily mean that churches actually existed in these places, since the stream of immigration had hardly begun; but the Santiago knights were farsighted in their financial campaign.

∞ Knights of Calatrava

Like Santiago, the Knights of Calatrava had only achieved their final form during the lifetime of King James's father. In 1157 a group of lay brothers and some choir monks from the Cistercian abbey of Fitero had undertaken the defense of newly conquered Calatrava on the embattled southeast frontier of Castile. The Order (begun in 1164) and its severe rule (of 1187) were approved by Cîteaux and by Rome. It was subject to the Cistercian abbot of Morimond in Burgundy, who was also delegated its grand prior; the exact relation between knights and Cistercians was clarified and juridically solidified in the Cistercian general chapters from 1209 to 1267. By 1199 Innocent III could enumerate one hundred and eleven Calatravan forts, residences, and estates; these were especially in south-central Spain.

They bore as sign a scarlet cross *fleurdelysée* on the white Cistercian tunic. The "brother knights," grouped in commanderies with their military assistants, chanted the daily hours both in peacetime and in war. The parallel "brother clerics" under their prior took care of spiritual needs. The impressive *esprit* of the Calatravans had already led in 1246 to a request from Innocent IV for three hundred knights and a small army of support to go crusading in the Near East. In 1245 the rulers of Poland called for their help against Tartars and Prussians. Again, in 1258, Alexander IV ordered them to help repel the Tartar peril.

The first of their many estates in Aragon had been awarded as early as 1179 for their help in taking Cuenca for Aragon: the castle and countryside of Alcañiz, to the west and north of Tortosa, just above the frontier of Moslem Valencia. Here the Calatrava knights tried to center the leadership of the entire Order during the dark days after their Castilian brethren had been shattered at the battle of Alarcos in 1195; they did not resume the name Knights of Calatrava until 1216. Eventually they reached a compromise with the Castilian branch, by which the master of Alcañiz was recognized as "grand commander" for Aragon, second in dignity and power only to the grand master in Castile. King James could intervene in the election of the master of Alcañiz until he abdicated that right in 1263.[26] This may explain why the name of Simon Pérez of Tarazona, James's high steward for Aragon and royal lieutenant of Valencia, is given briefly as master of Alcañiz (at the surrender of Eslida in 1242).[27]

During the early thirteenth century, Alcañiz had been expanding its power down toward the Valencian border with an eye to conquests within that Moslem land. The strong castle of Monroyo, a hair's breadth above the northern border of Valencia, was granted to the Calatravans by Peter II in 1209, "to make of it a bulwark of Christendom and to harass the Saracens." In 1231 the brothers initiated a populating project here.[28] It is perhaps significant that King James was staying at Alcañiz when he made his final decision to conquer the kingdom of Valencia.[29]

The master of Alcañiz and sixty Calatrava knights fought by the king's side from the early days at Burriana to the closing days in Murcia. They sieged and captured Villena. At Puig, when James determined to open the attack upon Valencia city with the few troops then at his disposal, the commander of Alcañiz and his men were among these.[30] As late as 1284 they would be summoned into the field again to defend Valencia against the power of North Africa.[31]

In 1233 King James confirmed some scattered small holdings to the commanders of Calatrava, Alvar Ferrández and Roderick Pérez Pons: "the park of Hauadaiub, and the park of Arais, and the park of Abinsalmo, and the park of Algebeli which faces on the Moslem cemetery . . . a farm at the gate of Valencia . . . houses in the town of Burriana . . . with other houses, and an inn."[32] Within the city of Valencia the knights had a small church (from 1238), in a good central position. It stood in the western half of the city, where the plaza of their name was to be located. In 1271 John Pérez signed a document as commander here.[33] The walled town and castle of Bétera, together with the tower and hamlet of Bufila or Boylla, were formally signed over to them in mid-1237 by the king.[34] Early in 1238 he gave them Chilvella castle or tower (apparently modern Chirivella); later the knights sold this to the future father-in-law of the Catalan historian Muntaner.[35] In spring of 1238 the king granted them also the town of Masanasa.[36] Pulpis they had only briefly.

There were Calatrava commanderies at both Bétera and Chirivella castles before 1246.[37] Begís castle and town were theirs from before 1262 until about 1281.[38] The Order also had claims on Villena.[39] By 1245 they were conducting a settlement movement at Villanueva de Alcolea.[40] Some of their Valencian houses and lands they exchanged, before 1258, for the castle and town of Favareta where they installed a commandery.[41] Other holdings included such places as Zorita and the Christian settlement of Masamagrell.[42] Later, properties will continue to accrue—for example, the castle on the hill above Castell de Castells.[43] The abbot of Morimond in 1307 confirmed the Order's possessions in Aragon and Valencia. The Valencian holdings were not abundant, but they were well-distributed down the length of the new kingdom. They were strongest just around Valencia city itself, the other holdings being more scattered except for the area just below the Hospitaller area in the north.

The Calatrava knights' struggle with the bishop over ecclesiastical rights and revenues was brisk and intense. By 1246, however, an agreement was reached. "Finally for the sake of peace and harmony" the Order was allowed the churches and revenues of Bétera, Bufila, Chirivella, Masanasa, and all lesser and future holdings, especially for "places the said brothers with God's help shall by their efforts acquire, wrest, and deliver from the hands of the Saracens, with or without armed conflict."[44] The wording of the document seems to indicate that the four churches mentioned did not yet exist as buildings, but that they had been definitely envisioned already in the diocesan blueprint.[45]

The sum for which the episcopal and capitular share of the tithes was farmed, for a hundred years, was only slightly less than that required of the Santiago knights—indicating perhaps an equivalence of value in the possessions of the two Orders. Even in the retention of a quarter of the death fees, the bishop had to yield to the knights horses and weapons, lamps and offerings. Whenever one of their churches fell vacant, the knights could present a candidate for rector to the bishop, with the promise of support; the bishop would then confer the cure of souls. Legacies could be received entire and without obstacles, as in 1255 when the knight William Ochova Alemán left his arms and saddle to the Order of Calatrava,[46] and in 1272 when Bernard Zamora left them 50 mazmodins.[47]

The Calatrava knights reached a similar accord with the bishop of Tortosa for their holdings in the Valencian part of the Tortosa diocese. A vigorous quarrel preceded this, arbitrated finally by the archbishop of Tarragona in 1248. Here the Order kept their two-thirds of the tithe and even most of the first fruits. Cuevas de Vinromá and the towns of its countryside (Tírig, Salsadella, Albocácer, Torre de Endomenech, and Villanueva de Alcolea) were explicitly named. The Calatravans were to present candidates ("vicars or rectors, suitable secular clerics"). The Calatravans' bailiff and the episcopal bailiff together would collect the tithe, making the division later.[48] There is something odd about this block of holdings in the north; they were not properly seignorial, nor even the important properties eventually held in the diocese by Calatrava, but rather comprised a fief in the hands of the Alagón family. Perhaps either Blaise of Alagón or the crown yielded the church patronage here to Calatrava as an alms. The properties themselves were all secular until late in the century, when the crown recovered them by exchange from the Alagón family and immediately gave them away to the Templars in another exchange.

These are only glimpses of an administrative structure, not much more detailed than those we get of the knights' activity on the field of battle in the memoirs of King James. In the very bitterness of the quarreling however, and in the wide property acquisition which occasioned it one may read something of the prestige and vigor of Calatrava in Valencia.

‡‡ KNIGHTS OF ST. GEORGE

Among the Orders which answered the papal call to crusade in Valencia, and which received land grants proportionate to the contingent sent and services rendered, was a small local group named after the patron saint of Catalonia. The Knights of the Order of St. George of Alfama operated under the Augustinian rule and, until as late as 1373, with only episcopal approval. The father of King James had founded them in 1201 on the Tortosa-Valencia frontier zone; he had built a church and castle for them on a tract five leagues outside of Tortosa, toward the sea and just above the Valencian border, called Alfama. Here they guarded the coast and the mountain passes. Their habit was white with a red Cross of St. George on the breast.

John of Almenara, their first grand master, led them to the Valencian crusade, where they shared the early action in and around Burriana. In camp before the besieged town, a month before it fell, King James approved an anticipatory grant of two small country places nearby, called Carabona and Benaquite (1233).[49] Such pre-grants were valid if the holders managed to secure the property. If it went unconquered, the grant lapsed, and the successor to the original grantee had no claim. He could cause legal trouble, however, and hope for a settlement out of court.[50]

Later the St. George knights seem to have been at the siege of Valencia itself. Before its capitulation King James on August 23, 1238 deeded to their commander Gerald of Prats a farm, a park, and some buildings in the parish of St. Andrew.[51] Their small residence of St. George was established in these buildings, which stood in the southeast corner of the city. They may also have acquired properties within Murviedro, and have accumulated a few pieces of land from benefactors.[52] Some put them at the Játiva siege under the Grand Master Arnold of Castellvell.[53]

They were at first too poor to afford their own church in Valencia city. Only in 1324, some eighty-five years after their arrival in Valencia city, would they finally arrange to take over the nearby chapel of St. George. This had been one of the first churches built in the conquered city, put up before 1243 by crusaders from Barcelona to serve as a center for the confraternity of St. George, a select lay brotherhood of one hundred crossbowmen.[54]

A rector for this church appears in the lists for the crusade tithe of 1279–1280. The income for his church is equal to that of a rather poor parish church, the tithe being 60 and 36 solidi, representing a mean of 500 solidi income per annum or, if the collector is halving the assessment, 1,000 solidi. The Knights of St. George were exempted from the 1279 payment, but their commander is down in the 1280 list for a token sum of 10 solidi.[55] From their earlier activity under King Peter—in defending Alfama, in undertaking to populate Bujaraloz (1205), and in collecting alms from the public for their work (1213)—something of their activities in Valencia may be conjectured. Their merger as chaplains to the confraternity gave them only limited rights at the chapel, under the pastor of St. Andrew's.[56]

The contribution of the Knights of St. George to the spiritual fabric of the new kingdom was modest, but they did stand as a living tribute to the national patron, a symbol of the chivalrous and warlike spirit of his people. Their contiguity to the military chapel from the earliest days of the conquest argues also a spiritual sympathy and tutelage toward the brotherhood. As time went on the knights were to keep a sure hold upon the affections of the Valencians, and it was to their church that the medieval processions would first come on the yearly anniversary day of the fall of Valencia.

১৯৫ THE KNIGHTS HOSPITALLERS

The Orders of chivalry dominant in Valencia were the Hospital and the Temple. Their leaders, commissioned by Innocent III, had stood at the young king's right hand during his troubled minority. Eighty years before James's birth, Alphonse the Battler had actually willed to them and to the Sepulchre knights his entire kingdom of Aragon (1134). His colleague Raymond Berengar III of Catalonia had died with Templar vows and in the Templar habit (1131). The crown still esteemed both Orders highly; unlike their colleagues in England, Flanders, and France, the Templars and Hospitallers in the realms of Aragon had not yet achieved any great independence of the crown or of its financial support.[57]

The two Orders had a large share in instigating and financing the Valencian crusade. Their banners moved in the front ranks and at points of peril. Their respective masters could be found at the side of King James during his domestic crises, in the Majorcan and Valencian crusades, in the Murcian wars, and during the Moslem rebellions in Valencia later in the century. At the climax of the Burriana siege both their physical presence and their financial backing were especially important. The two Orders continued to be important in settling the conquered land, no less than for their service as permanent military garrison.

For almost a century prior to the fall of Valencia, valuable pre-grants had been handed to the Hospitallers and Templars for that Moslem kingdom, as an inducement to enter and conquer. They were formidable landowners and magnates; before the crusade and later in Valencia they won sweeping privileges and exemptions, such as the exemption in 1221 to all their vassals and subjects, present or future in the realms of Aragon, from the regalian and feudal dues.[58] For half of each year the masters of the Temple and Hospital took complete charge of the Valencian frontiers, each of them commanding for a four-month period a fourth of those "knights of the conquest" James had settled in the new realm.[59]

The Order of the Hospital of St. John of Jerusalem originated as a brotherhood of the late eleventh century caring for pilgrims in the Holy Land; it had taken on an ever stronger military coloring in the twelfth century. Armed escorts to protect pilgrims evolved in the Order under Raymond of Provence (1120–1160); the first mention of military service in its statutes comes as late as 1200. The Hospitaller rule was Augustinian; their badge was the white, eight-pointed cross, borne on black tunic, on shield, and on pennon. At the height of their power in the feudal kingdom of Jerusalem, they held seven great military installations there and one hundred and forty estates.

The Order was divided into "languages," subdivided into "priorates" or "bailiwicks." These in turn were separated into commanderies with their estates. The kingdom of Aragon had been under the prior of St. Giles in Provence, until the appearance of a grand master for Spain in 1171 and the founding of the castellany of Amposta in Catalonia in 1180. This last foundation made Aragon the fifth in the series of "languages." In 1319 Aragon was to be reorganized into two priorates, Amposta and Catalonia.

In the kingdom of Valencia, the encomiendas of the Hospital did not form a separate priorate but continued under the priorate of the castellan or master of Amposta. There was also a master of the Hospital for the realms of James, an Aragonese high noble named Hugh of Forcalquier. "I had made him master in my land, which I had asked of the grand master of Jerusalem," says King James; "and he was a man I loved greatly, and he me."[60] Forcalquier was Amposta castellan at least from 1224 to 1245. (The spelling of his name should not cause the confusion it has; Forcalquier was a town in the Provençal mountains east of Avignon and north of Aix.) Forcalquier had a lieutenant, or commander, at Amposta; the names of most of these commanders for the period of the Valencian crusade and settlement can be found.[61] By at least 1290, Amposta in turn had created a special lieutenant for the kingdom of Valencia.[62]

During the Valencian crusade the Hospitallers, with the Templars, were the good right arm of the king. It was in conversation with the Hospital's vice-master, according to the royal memoirs, that the king was persuaded to undertake that crusade.[63] The Hospitallers undoubtedly gave of their best during the Valencia wars, for their absence at the Majorcan conquest had "shamed" them; an unusual act of royal generosity had given them some land grants in Majorca anyway, but the memory was galling.[64] At the siege of Valencia, where the king took one of the two most critical positions, the forces of the Hospital are said to have taken the other. This distinguished service at the siege may explain the honored position accorded them later in processions, in a place and era when such honors were not lightly admitted by others; the Hospitallers marched immediately after the cathedral clergy.[65]

It has been argued recently, not without vigorous dissent, that by the thirteenth century the Hospitallers had evolved into a body of peaceful clerics, concerned with widespread land exploitation and peaceful ministries. In this view the Order was rather a socio-economic and spiritual force in Spain, centering upon their hospices, estates, and churches. Their armies would have consisted more of feudal levies with only a sprinkling of Hospitaller knights.[66] Whatever the merits of this thesis (and at least for Valencia the Order still had great military significance), it serves to intoduce their role as landholders and settlement agents.

The Order's pre-grants included the castles and townships of Oropesa (1150), Cervera along with Cullera (1157, 1177, 1208), Olocau (1180), Sueca (1210), and all the mosques and ecclesiastical revenues of the Burriana region (1210).[67] Before the fall of Valencia city James also gave the prior and prioress of Sigena ten jovates of land at Campanar, houses in Valencia city and Denia, and an estate.[68]

Their major acquisitions included: the castles and towns of Torrente (1233), Silla (1233), and Sueca;[69] the estates and houses of the Moslem Abdezalm, just outside Burriana;[70] Benirrage village (1233)[71] and Benyaz (1234), both near Burriana;[72] the castle and township of Cervera (1235);[73] rights in Castielfabib, which they had conquered and were disputing in 1236 with the bishop of Segorbe;[74] Alcudia de Silla near the closure of the Albufera lagoon, which the king gave to them in 1239 along with thirty fishing boats and their Moslem operators;[75] important towns like San Mateo and Cálig, both from sometime in the early 1230's;[76] a large part of strategic Cullera (1241); part of Sueca;[77] "good houses" and ten jovates of land at Denia (1240);[78] and an inn at Játiva (1252).[79] There were smaller holdings such as the mills received in 1235, other mills in 1253, and more mills in 1273.

Lesser acquisitions included the strongholds of Macastre and Montroy near Chiva which appear in an episcopal tithe agreement of 1243. Yet other places must be understood as comprised in the countryside of some larger holding. Thus, for example, the encomienda of Cervera included such places as San Mateo, Canet, Cálig, Ro[s]sell, La Jana with Carrascal, Xerer (Mas de Xirosa), Traiguera with San Jorge (Mas de Estellers), and Chert with Molimar and Barcella. The knights soon were negotiating over rights connected with their holding such places as the Traiguera Valley which they had received in 1235.

In exchange for their Oropesa claims, the king gave the Hospital in 1249 all his own holdings in the Burriana district, in free and frank alod, together with 8,000 solidi.[80] In 1259 the knights at Torrente bought the tower and village of Maçot.[81] Somewhat later in the century the Order was in possession of the castles and towns of Perpunchent (by 1289)[82] and Villafamés (before 1283),[83] as well as rents in Ademuz.[84] In 1280 the Hospital gave Amposta itself to the crown, receiving as partial recompense the Valencian town of Onda with its countryside, including Tales and Artesa.[85] As to their lesser holdings, it is sometimes difficult to say if a grant may have been separately acquired or lies within a large previous grant or is only being held temporarily.

A survey of the Hospitaller holdings in the new kingdom reveals how wide their extent was. The grouping, however, is odd. Below the Júcar, besides rents at Denia and Játiva, there was only the wild, almost unpopulated frontier valley of Perpunchent, itself a late acquisition. There were several well-chosen towns in the Valencia-Alcira region: especially Cullera, Silla and the Olocau castle, with a few lesser places. In the north the Onda-Burriana district was a rich prize. The northeast coastal towns and countryside in the top corner of the realm made an impressive addition to their properties in southern Catalonia; they extended south until the Calatrava claims began, and over to the Benifasá monastery's territory. But, if the north of the realm was encumbered with large religious encomiendas, it does not follow that the main Hospitaller presence was necessarily in the extreme north. The Order was also ensconced at the two richest and strategically important spots: Burriana-Onda and Valencia-Cullera.

Commanderies of the Hospitallers existed in the thirteenth century at Valencia city, Burriana, Silla, Onda, Morella, Cullera, briefly at Perpunchent, and perhaps at Torrente. Valencia city commanders whose names survive include Roslain (1242), Peter Gerald or Guerard (1245, with Gil as prior), Peter of Granyen (1248), John of Paris (1250), Bernard of Salanova (1254), Bernard of Miravalls (1280, 1282), and A. of Romaner (1298). Burriana commanders include Bernard of Valfort (1237), Peter of Alcalá (1254), Ferrer (1264), and Bernard of Bosch (1280). At Cullera there was Gaucelm (1245); at Silla William (1245); at Cervera Arnold of Bellvehí.[86]

From end to end of the Valencian kingdom these knights, who cloaked their military harness in the black robes of the monk, guarded the new dispensation and helped assure its permanence. The Hospitallers were powerful and experienced, fortified by documented privileges and by seignorial claims to rights of patronage. They did not intend to yield to the bishop more than they must. And from the first, the battle was welcomed by bishop and chapter. No solution emerged during Bishop Ferrer's reign; but in 1243 and 1244 by a variety of solemn acts—five distinct documents with their several copies remain in the cathedral archives—an agreement was worked out. The bishop of Lérida acted as arbiter. The churches specified were those of Cullera, Silla, Torrente, Montroy, and Macastre, where the Hospitallers had been taking all church revenues from 1239 to 1243. Like other documents of this kind, however, it was a general settlement for other holdings, present and future, and therefore would include many of the areas listed above.[87]

The agreement was signed under penalty of a thousand gold morabatins for violating it. The knights were to have a full half of the tithe, as also of the first fruits and other revenues of their districts. Bishop and chapter reserved a fourth of the defunctions from funerals, the visitation fees, and the right to assign to the candidate-vicars the cure of souls (with an obligation also of canonical obedience) and to set the amount of their salaries. The personal tithe on revenues taken from Moorish subjects was also insisted upon, along with payment for four years' arrears of the bishop's share in church revenues, which had been allowed to lapse during the controversy. This brought a measure of peace for those Valencian lands of the Hospitallers which fell within the diocese.

In the capital city at the heart of that diocese, however, there followed a decade of hand-wringing, as the anguished pastors of the city observed the mounting revenues of the knights' church there: pennies and candles and small offerings in a steady stream; animals and bier-coverings; old clothing and service fees. The spectacle was "multipliciter agitata" between the two parties (the previous unpleasantness had only been "diutius agitata").[88] Eventually the bitterness made arbitration a necessity. The bishop of Lérida was again chosen as umpire. A committee was organized to argue the diocesan case: the pastors of the churches of St. Catherine, St. Nicholas, and St. Martin. Though they complicated their appeal with a series of allied complaints, the pastors actually had an excellent case, based upon the agreements of 1243–1244.

The victory of the pastors, in a decision given in 1255, was incorporated into a document much more sophisticated than the previous accord. It spelled out the tedious details of possible revenue. Later the knights had a brief but intense dispute with the chapter of the cathedral, a case which was appealed to Rome in 1263.[89] Another general settlement with bishop and chapter was signed in 1264, supplementing that of two decades before.[90] But the most famous Hospitaller litigation, notable in the annals of European law, was the dispute extravagantly carried forward against the Cistercians in Valencia over Rossell.[91]

The situation in the northern part of the realm was roughly equivalent to that in the southern diocese. Here the Tortosa bishop bitterly contested the Hospitallers' privileged position. Through the mediation of the Tarragona metropolitan a compromise was reached in 1243. The holdings explicitly in question were Valencian: Cervera, Traiguera Valley, Oropesa, and Burriana, along with non-Valencian Ulldecona. These places involved their respective *termini* or countrysides, each of which in turn included smaller towns with their lesser areas of countryside. The mediation, though it concerned Valencian places, applied likewise to all holdings of the Order in the Tortosa diocese. It affords a view of the major properties of the Hospital in northern Valencia.

The agreement awarded to the knights the right of presentation to the churches of the Cervera and Oropesa districts. Revenues due to the rectors were carefully assigned along with the fees expected by bishop and archdeacon. The other churches, Burriana, and Traiguera fell completely to the diocese, the latter church going to the support of its archdeacon. In a Hospitaller patronate, wherever parish churches were as yet unbuilt, the bishop was to have the privilege of designating their locations, while the Order was to construct and endow them. The knights' share of the tithe varied: three-fourths in the Traiguera and Cervera districts, two-thirds at Ulldecona, and elsewhere half. All tithes on animals for Hospital lands anywhere in the diocese went to the bishop and chapter. The Order retained its privilege of tithe-exemption for lands worked by its own members at its own expense.[92] A separate agreement was signed that same year for Rafalguazir, and in 1259 for Cervera again.[93]

The Hospitaller church was located in the parish of St. Andrew in Valencia city. One of the first in the city to be opened to worship, it had been erected on a small plot of ground close to the gate blocked by the Hospitaller forces during the siege; this gate led to the sea, near the center of the eastern wall. Perhaps the Order had cared for soldiers wounded in the siege and had conducted the first hospital of the city.[94] But church and cemetery left little space for a permanent hospital. The residence, housing a prior with his lieutenant and four beneficed clerics (*comensales*), was perhaps already under a commander for the castle of Torrente. Non-Hospitaller priests cared for the church.[95] Though an object of jealous attention from other city churches, it seems to have been highly popular from the first, especially with the warrior class. The revenues connected with the death and burial of Hospitaller clients had alone in fifteen years mounted to over 4,000 solidi, exclusive of horses and weapons given.[96]

The public baths owned by Count Nuño Sancho of Roussillon, adjacent to the church of the Santiago knights, was given to the Hospitallers in 1241.[97] The knight William of Espailargas left to the Valencian residence in 1245 all his properties including six jovates at Campanar, given to him by the king in

1237, and houses in the city given immediately after its fall. The knights were to build an altar to the Blessed Virgin and support a priest to chant daily Mass and the office for the souls of his family and himself.[98] Another knight of the conquest, Bernard Dalmau, designated their church as his place of burial, transferring to them an estate sufficient to support an altar to St. Catherine, with a chaplaincy and perpetual lamp (1273).[99] Sometime before 1264 Simon of Luesia gave the Order a fishing ship in the Albufera lagoon.[100]

The greatest name among the Hospitaller church's clients was that of the empress of Byzantium, the Lady Constance of Swabia who fled to the protection of James I after the battle of Benevento. The daughter of Emperor Frederick II, she had been married at the age of eleven, over the opposition of Innocent IV, to the aging lecher John III, Emperor of Nicaea. Her subsequent widowhood was as unhappy as her marriage, and she had sought the protection of her brother Manfred of Sicily. After his death in 1266 her relative Prince Peter of Aragon supplied her with ample rents in the new kingdom of Valencia. She took up residence in the city of Valencia, where she lived and died (1306). Cured of "leprosy"—whatever disease may have been meant by the term—in Valencia after prayers to St. Barbara, she arranged to endow a chapel of St. Barbara in the Hospital church. She gave that church also the column of the saint, which she had carried as a relic to her new home, and a suitable tomb for herself.[101]

Few benefactions to the Hospital church are recorded, but one comes across items now and again. Thus, Peter Abrafim in 1274 left 10 solidi, with 5 more for current expenditure, and asked to be buried in a fine tomb in the cemetery of their church.[102] In 1276 the wife of Blaise Peter of Fuentes left them 10 solidi.[103] By the turn of the century a larger establishment would be needed; permission came in January 1307, and not long afterward a Gothic church was built.[104]

By the end of the century, the Knights Hospitallers had achieved an enviable reputation in the new realm not only as landlords and military establishment, but also as colonizers. The Hospitallers were experienced at bringing in settlement. In the area around Toulouse in Languedoc, for example, they founded over fifty planned villages; to the southwest of that city, in an area only 25 miles by 12, they established forty villages during the decade 1100–1110.[105] To fill up the Tortosa frontier they had accomplished "an intense" work of repopulation especially along the lower bank of the Ebro during the years of the Valencia crusade, founding new places and moving old ones.[106] Now that these holdings extended into the kingdom of Valencia, they continued that same program here.

They inaugurated populating movements in or near Cálig (1234), Cervera (1235), San Mateo and Rossell (1237), Carrascal (1239), Sueca (1244), Picaña in the estate of Torrente (1248), Silla (1238, 1243, and 1248), Cullera and eight villages near it (1244 and 1250), Cervera again (1250), and so on.[107]

In 1248 the commander at Valencia city gave a settlement charter to fifty Christians.[108] When Rome suppressed the Templars in 1312, King James II was to petition the pope to transfer their property to a proposed military Order of Montesa in Valencia rather than to the Hospitallers. The Hospital had become so powerful an element in the new kingdom of Valencia, James told the pope, that it would be prudent not to magnify their power.[109] And, indeed, just after the death of James the Conqueror in 1276, the Order in Valencia and the other realms of Aragon was able to contribute to King Peter, for his wars, 8,000 Tours solidi, 5,000 Barcelona solidi, and 2,000 Jaca solidi.[110]

Was all this only the power of richly endowed landowners? It has been suggested recently that such Hospitallers were mostly peaceful clerics with very few warrior members. But the crown of Aragon, in petitioning for the creation of a new military Order to defend Valencia and desiring the transference to it of Hospitaller holdings in Valencia, does not adduce this reason. If the Hospitallers were not of great military importance, this argument above all others would have won the pope. Whether there were armies of Hospitaller knights, however, or armies of Hospitaller vassals led by only a few knights, the Order was an important military force, a shield for the frontier kingdom.

The efforts of James II to curtail the economic power of this international brotherhood in his realms, while continuing their military work, bore fruit in 1317; the new Order of Montesa, local and Valencian, took over not only the properties of the suppressed Templars but also the Valencian encomiendas of the Hospitallers. Eighty years after their entry into the realm of Valencia, the Hospital retained only Torrente castle and the Valencia city church, with the attached local properties. Even with their forces so diminished, the Hospitallers continued to aid in defending the kingdom of Valencia.[111]

The military and economic power so freely heaped upon the knights in Valencia by King James and King Peter in the thirteenth century is a measure of their effectiveness and prestige.

It also reflects, to some extent, an aspect of their history less accessible to documentation: the influence of their churches and ministry in the new kingdom. Their physical and economic advance underlines their importance on this frontier, even as it provided them with the tools of defense: in Valencia the Knights Hospitallers were still the watchdogs of Christendom, a living example of Christian chivalry to any who might be tempted to forget their military responsibilities. They were the spirit of the Christian crusade incarnate.

෩ KNIGHTS TEMPLARS

"Lions in war, lambs in the cloister," as the contemporary bishop of Acre called them, the Knights Templars were perhaps the classic type of the cosmopolitan and purely military religious Order. Over their military harness they wore the white tunic of the monk, emblazoned with the red cross of martyrdom. Organized in the early twelfth century, they received their uncompromisingly severe rule from the great St. Bernard, founder of the Cistercians. In eleven provinces, divided into forty-two commanderies, they held influential positions and impressive properties from Ireland to the Holy Land. Matthew Paris in 1244 estimated that the Templars drew revenues from nine thousand manors in Christendom. There was a grand master at Acre, a European headquarters just outside Paris, a master over each province, and a preceptor or commander for the local residence. Their numbers were never large, but their courage was spectacular.

They were solidly established in Aragon and Catalonia by the mid-twelfth century. Monzón was their stronghold. King Peter the Catholic, the father of James, could write in 1208 of "the loyalty, dedication, and devotion with which the Knights Templars strive to defend and spread the Christian faith," and of "how valuable, how faithful, and how necessary in all things they have been to my predecessors, and how much they have been solicitous to help me too."[112] King James was to have occasion (1238) to "recall the welcome services you rendered me, and do render every day, and have rendered especially now in winning the city and realm of Valencia."[113]

When the boy king James I needed a protector and tutor, Pope Innocent III in 1214 chose the Catalan William of Monredon (or Montrodón), master of the Temple for Aragon, Catalonia, and Provence. From that early moment on, throughout the king's life, the Templars were James's faithful counselors, advisers, and companions-in-arms. Their master was at his side during the Valencian campaigns and sieges. In the great Moslem rebellion in Valencia just before James died, the master was captured while fighting in the disastrous battle of Luchente in Valencia but soon escaped from his prison at Biar.[114]

Provincial masters of the Temple for the realms of King James are: William Cadell (1231);[115] Raymond Patot (1233), at the Burriana siege;[116] Hugh of Montllor (1235–1237), in the Cullera raid;[117] Astrug of Belmonte (1238–1239), one of the five rulers of Valencia city for the king in the year after its fall;[118] William of Cardona (1244–1252), with James at the treaty of Almizra;[119] William of Montañans (1258);[120] William of Pontons (1260); Peter of Queralt, at least as representing the Temple master, in 1266;[121] Arnold of Castellnou (1267–1274);[122] and Peter of Moncada (1276), captured at Luchente.[123] Higher dignitaries occasionally appear—such as Martin Martínez, master of the three realms of Spain (1244), who was at the Almizra treaty with Cardona; or Lope Sánchez, master for the three realms of Spain and visitor in the five realms of Spain (1266).[124]

The Temple does not seem to have reached an accord with the bishop

until 1262.[125] In the intervening twenty-five years they had accumulated a
mass of privileges, properties, and possessions. They showed a marked
predilection for public ovens, even substituting an oven in the spot they had
been using as their cemetery in the city of Valencia, reflecting that an oven
would be "more advantageous and fruitful for the house" there.[126] Their
profit was to be one loaf out of every twenty baked for their neighbors.

The Templar pre-grants included the castles and townships of Oropesa
and Chivert from Alphonse in 1169.[127] The Oropesa claims clashed with
Hospitaller claims later, leading to litigation.[128] Montornés was assigned
to them in 1181;[129] but King James later gave this to a vassal and eventually
to the shrine and hospital of St. Vincent. Peter II in 1211 gave them the
village and fort of Ruzafa,[130] and Cantavieja village (1212).[131] He also conferred on them the castle and country of Culla (1213),[132] property they
actually acquired only in 1303 when they bought it for 50,000 solidi from
William of Anglesola.[133] James promised them Pulpis castle but gave it
instead to Calatrava; the Templars however did acquire it sometime before
1286.

For Templar help "to us in the conquering of Burriana" King James
handed over Chivert (1233).[134] He also granted the villages of Mantella and
Benahamet (Benejama) in the Burriana zone (June 1233);[135] a third of the
"recently acquired" city of Burriana, including six towers and defenses;[136]
the village of Seca near Burriana (1237);[137] half the shipyards of Denia
(1244);[138] the fortified villages of Moncada and Carpesa, in return for their
pre-grant of Ruzafa (1246);[139] a section of the town of Liria, with three
towers of the defensive wall and a jovate of land (1248);[140] a huge estate
near Burriana, running from the Bechí or Seco River to the mountains,
with 8,000 solidi thrown in for good measure, given in return for the castle
and town of Oropesa (1249);[141] Benitachell near Denia (at least briefly);[142]
buildings and property below the kingdom of Valencia, in Murcia (1266);[143]
and half the mintage tax paid by vassals of the Order to the crown.[144]
Escolano says they held the castle of Almedíjar near Segorbe.[145]

Peñíscola was early promised to the Templars, but the crown did not
concede it until 1294. Commanders are found here only from 1304.[146] In
exchange for their castle and town of Alventosa, in 1251 Simon Pérez of
Tarazona, the baron of Arenós, gave them his estate of Masarrojos and his
town of Benifaraig.[147] In 1294, in exchange for Tortosa, King James II was
to cede Albocácer, Ares, Benicarló, Cuevas de Vinromá, Peñíscola, Serratella, Tírig, Torre de Endomenech, Villanueva de Alcolea, and Viñaroz.[148]
Lesser or transitory properties appearing in the records indicate a number of
companion holdings. Before 1250 the Templars forcefully ousted the monks
of Benifasá from possession of Refalgari.[149] The salt monopoly at Peñíscola
was theirs.

Extensive tax exemptions were accorded to areas under Templar control.[150] In Gandía, even before its conquest, they won the privilege of a public market for the region every Tuesday.[151] In their capacity as bankers they controlled a large number of places from time to time. Against the loan of 1,000 silver marks to the king, for example, they assumed the management in 1248 of the castles and towns of Onda, Burriana, Peñíscola, Veo, Ahín, Tales, Liria, and Eslida. Ten years later, they still remained securely in control of these places plus the revenues of Tortosa and the profits of the coinage of Valencia. Similarly, in 1250 the knights held in pawn the castles of Morella and Almenara.[152] Taken as a whole, the prizes won by the Templars in the new kingdom were extensive enough but by no means extravagantly so. At Majorca where the rival Hospitallers arrived too tardily for a large share of the loot, the Templars amassed no less than one hundred and twenty-two rural townships, including almost all of one of the eight divisions of the island.

The Temple did not come out as well as the Hospital in Valencia, though it is difficult to balance total gifts and privileges satisfactorily. Omitting late acquisitions like Pulpis and abortive claims like Oropesa, and then putting aside the block of territory given only in 1294 from Ares down to Cuevas and Villanueva, the essential holdings stand out clearly. They are basically a group of towns and properties at Valencia and just north of the city, an enviable estate in and near Burriana, and the Chivert estate. The Liria rents and their many privileges enhanced this basic possession. The Templars are hardly present south of the city of Valencia; but until late in the century their northern holdings are well balanced by their central and urban properties.

At Valencia city itself the Templars received the key tower of the defenses, with a long section of wall and barbican, as well as a portion of the city in the parish of St. Stephen—including fifty buildings. This was specifically for the aid "you daily give and gave especially in the taking of the city." There were lands involved in this also, such as twenty jovates near the city wall.[153] Their residence adjoined the tower which stood on the north or river-front wall, tallest of the towers, where the flag of surrender had been raised. Here a community was established before 1246.

The Order may have delayed in organizing commanderies (or preceptories) —the Catalan commanders seem to have handled Valencia affairs—but in 1246 there was a commandery at Cantavieja or Cantavella southwest of Morella and apparently one at Valencia city.[154] Commanders from Templar communities at Burriana, Cantavieja, Chivert, and Valencia city attended a meeting in 1252. By the end of the century commanderies for Castielfabib, Cuevas de Vinromá, and Culla had probably been added.[155] The names of a number of commanders are known. Commanders, or preceptors, at Valencia city include Peter of Ager (1251), Bernard of Miravet (1255), Raymond of Bach (1263), Peter of Albanell (1270), Peter of Montpalau (1271), and Gerald Ça Corbella. At Cantavieja were Walter (1252), Raymond of

Villalba (1261), Peter of Montpalau (1270), and Galart of Josa (1271). At Chivert there were G. of Prades (1252) and Lope Sánchez of Bergua (1284). At Burriana there were Gonza (1252), and Peter Peyronet at least from 1273 to 1277. Peyronet served King James in several important capacities, as almoner, land distributor, and as crown agent in 1276 to treat with the Moslems of Eslida.[156]

Hostilities with the bishop began immediately. One mosque lay hard by the Templar tower;[157] others were probably in the villages and countryside held by them elsewhere in the realm. These they could keep, in accordance with King James's clarification of 1238, which excepted privately held mosques from his previous grant of all mosques to the diocese.[158] A number of royal grants assured the Templars control of tithes, a share of the tithes, and all the first fruits and parish revenues; these too they meant to keep. Even when trading Ruzafa for Moncada, they reserved their rights over two-thirds of the tithe there, announcing their intention to vindicate this claim (1246).[159]

It is not unreasonable to suppose that a general solution was reached concerning revenues, not differing greatly from the Hospitaller agreement— that is, half of the tithe going to the knights, along with three-fourths of the defunctions and most of the other revenues. For Borbotó and Campo de la Portella, two villages in the country of Beniferri, an agreement does exist, signed in 1262.[160] For Burriana and its area where the Temple held much land, the knights resisted an attempt by crown officials to take the Templar share of the tithe.[161] The king's bailiff in 1280 "seized the third part" of the Ademuz tithe; but the invasion of rights was promptly repulsed.[162]

Templar holdings were strong in the northern part of the kingdom. Here the knights located all but one of the early commanderies. Consequently, skirmishes broke out with the bishop of Tortosa. As early as 1243 the differences were brought to a general settlement, covering the large properties at Burriana and elsewhere. This did not settle matters. In 1260 the bishop of Tortosa advanced claims to the tithes of Chivert, an early acquisition which included villages like Alcalá de Chivert, Castelnovo, and Pulpis. Here the Templars held both secular lordship and ecclesiastical patronage. Under the arbitration of the abbot of Poblet and the archdeacon of Vich, an agreement was reached in 1263 which applied to Chivert, the Burriana holdings, Algar, and Seca. The Order came out with half the tithes of Chivert and Algar and two-thirds at Burriana.[163]

Among the important properties left to the Temple by their benefactors in the city were those of a knightly layman later judged to have been secretly heretical. The posthumous confiscation of his goods left a Temple chaplaincy without support. The affair drew from the Order loud outcries and eventually an investigation (1280), without which we should never have been aware of the gift.[164] As early as 1238 another baron, William of Çaportella.

gave the Templars the village of Borbotó which he had just received at the
siege of Valencia city.[165] Peter of Barberá, buried in the Templars' cemetery
at Valencia city in 1258, left money for his tomb there and 20 solidi for the
work on their church.[166] The wife of Blaise Peter of Fuentes left them a small
legacy in 1276.[167] Gilabert of Zanoguera, an important knight in the realm,
who died in 1296 and was buried in their church, seems to have been a
benefactor.[168] Another noble, Jazpert the viscount of Castellnou, left a
great deal of discretion to the three executors of his will in 1268—his brother
the bishop of Gerona, the count of Ampurias, and the bishop of Valencia;
he specifically favored by name as beneficiaries only the Temple.[169] Since
Jazpert left orders to sell all his castles and goods except Castellnou, and
gave the Temple such priority among the beneficiaries, one may suppose he
enriched them substantially. Several inventories of Templar movable possessions also survive, but it is not easy to draw conclusions from them.[170]

The Templars controlled and developed their Valencian lands themselves,
probably through the usual mechanism of bailiffs and estate management.
This procedure could develop and organize holdings more thoroughly, but
it involved a drain of men and capital. An occasional business document of
the Order in this region survives, such as the contract for the purchase of
wine and wheat in 1242 by the Burriana commandery.[171]

Eventually, when these properties had been transferred to the new Order
of Montesa after the Templars were suppressed, the pope in 1326 was to
allow the easier system of sub-infeudation. This applied to all their former:

> houses and possessions in the city of Valencia; those in the castle juris-
> dictions of Cervera, Peñíscola, Chivert, Pulpis, Cuevas de Vinromá, Culla,
> Ares, Onda, Villafamés, and Perpunchent; those in the places of Castiel-
> fabib, and of Ademuz; those in the towns of Burriana and of Sueca, and
> in the territories belonging to them; [all these] in the dioceses of Tortosa,
> Valencia, and Segorbe, along with the other possessions . . . in the king-
> dom of Valencia.[172]

Perpunchent, Onda, Villafamés, and Cervera of course had belonged to the
Hospitallers in the thirteenth century. The Templar places specifically
named in this late document were probably all commanderies by then. Meanwhile the movement of colonization went forward on Templar lands, but
the pace was more sluggish than on Hospitaller territory. Commissions were
awarded for settlements at or near Alcalá de Chivert (1234), Borbotó (1245),
Masarrojos (1251), Carpesa and Moncada (1252), and Pulpis (1284).[173]

Like the Hospitallers, the Templars had spread widely in the new kingdom
and had sent down deep roots. Their white tunic with its red cross could be
seen in the capital, in the countryside, and on the southern frontier. In peacetime they were a pledge of security; in time of danger they were among the
first troops to stand to arms. In their daily monastic career and ministry they

were symbol and spirit to the Christian immigrants of Valencia. In their warrior experience and in their settlement projects they represented a persistence of the original crusade spirit. In Valencia their chivalric traditions did not tarnish throughout this century. "More pure in ideals and less ambitious" than religious knights elsewhere, they owed their influence here "not to their political cunning but to the excellent military spirit of their warriors."[174]

The French project for their suppression therefore was to arouse dismay and indignation in the realms of Aragon. James II would write of the "scandal" of the French charges, and would vigorously defend the knights' "very good reputation" and way of life (1307).[175] Even after the crown weakly acquiesced in the persecution of the Temple in Aragon, the minute inquiries into their past led only to a resounding exoneration by the Council of Tarragona (1312), followed by a freeing of the prisoners.[176] One of the major actions of the reign of James II indeed was the prompt replacement of the Templars with an equivalent Order, that of Montesa, on the Valencian border. The papal bull of 1317 establishing this new Order made it clear that their principal function was to defend the frontiers of the kingdom of Valencia against the Moslems. This was the reason they received the properties of the Temple and Hospital. Nothing could illuminate better the military importance of the Temple throughout the previous period and, by implication, of the Hospital and other military Orders. Valencia had needed them, and had needed them precisely as organized religio-military frontier institutions.

XI

THE MENDICANT ORDERS

Less colorful than their military brethren, the other religious Orders on the Valencian scene nevertheless stand out by their diversity and multiplicity. Dominican, Franciscan, Mercedarian, Trinitarian, Cistercian, Carthusian, Augustinian, Antonine, Friar of the Sack, and a fair variety of nuns—each had a post, each a special work. And behind each name stands a small army of dedicated people, some of them gifted beyond the ordinary.

Theirs was by and large a life of dim routine: quietly praying in a cell or chanting the divine praises in the chilly night, tending the sick or serving the poor, arranging the ransom of captives, carrying the university culture to dull rural centers, totting up accounts for a Cistercian sheep grange, or simply being on call with the sacraments, with counsel, with moral example. But it was precisely this form of routine which helped to carry, into an environment framed by minarets, a strong accent of the homeland and a net of social services. These settlers needed this, as they demonstrated through substantial gratitude in wills.

This is not to say that these religious were faultless or uniformly edifying. Their age was a savage and litigious one; they came from the same kind of families and were fashioned by the same kinds of experience as were their fellows. There is little doubt that the visitation records of the diocese, had they survived, would betray much the same defects and even crimes as we read of in other countries. Indeed there would probably be an extra share of harrowing tales here in the warmer clime of the troubadour on a half-organized frontier. But there is enough evidence to suggest that these were in general men ennobled by their respective institutions, and in a measure ennobling their environment.

ಞ FUNCTION ON THE FRONTIER

It is only right that the Mendicants come first. Here as much as anywhere King James was well served by his institutions. Franciscans and Dominicans of the first generation, contemporaries and junior contemporaries of the great Francis and Dominic themselves, came along on the Valencian crusade. Before the city fell they had planned their establishments and secured their charters.

Probably at no time between Benedict and Loyola did a monastic or ascetic movement serve Western society during a religious crisis with such singular aptitude as did the friars. They were to leave the impact of their corporate personalities both on Christendom's heart and head: on contemporary attitudes, affections, images, and thought patterns. To them was owed the birth of the modern pulpit especially and the rise of a new form of piety and art. As a socio-political force they oriented or influenced the energies of Europe at many levels, from the intellectual and artistic to the economic and institutional.

The importance of the friars in the urban centers of the western Mediterranean needs no development here, beyond recalling that they began in the age of Albigensians and Waldensians, of an uninstructed laity who rarely heard a sermon and of a clergy not much better trained, of turmoil and economic dislocation and vague aspirations in the cities. More than any other religious group the Mendicants represented modernity and the forward trends of the thirteenth century. Their city orientation, as opposed to the feudal spirit and forms of the older monasticism, undoubtedly explains some of the attraction they had for King James.

The city and countryside of Valencia were ideally circumstanced for rapid economic advance, producing the consequent inequality of class and the teeming poor who figure in early legacies and legislation of Valencia. Notorious too was the high proportion of undesirables and troublemakers to be found with crusading troops and settlers at this time, since the penalty for a number of antisocial activities was precisely to go on crusade. Convicted murderers or church-burners could have their punishments commuted to crusading; and the rebels of Narbonne in Languedoc were sentenced to crusade at the siege of Valencia for a year, with an additional four years of fighting in the Holy Land.[1]

These and other factors of instability were operative in Valencian society. In countering them King James was shrewd enough to assess his Mendicant allies at their worth. The chronicle of San Juan de la Peña, very popular some eighty years after his death, even has him laying the cornerstones "propria manu" for each of the Franciscan and Dominican houses built in the kingdom during his reign.[2] True or not, the claim does reflect his strong sympathy for these Orders. The local clergy appraised them too, as rivals for public affection and for affection's barometer, revenues; a diocesan synod at Valencia had to admonish the local clergy to receive them with honor.

ᖆᖇ THE FRANCISCANS

Just before the Valencian crusade, two Italian Gray Friars appeared in the realms of King James, a priest and a lay brother named John of Perugia and Peter of Sassoferrato (near Ancona). After a stay at Teruel, they had descended into the kingdom of Valencia to preach to the Moslems (1228?), and to be publicly executed in the capital city for their pains.[3] Thus the Franciscan Order is closely connected with the origins of neo-Christian Valencia, since it provided its first martyrs.

The Franciscan movement was contemporary with the progress of the Valencian crusade. St. Francis of Assisi composed his celebrated Testament in the year after King James failed at the first siege of a Valencian city— Peñíscola in 1225. The companion of St. Francis, Brother Elias (†1253), headed the Order from the beginning of the crusade until well after the fall of Valencia. By 1240 the young Order was already able to divide its Spanish houses into three provinces, one being the realms of Aragon. Valencia was soon to become one of the six custodies making up this province. St. Francis himself seems to have been at Barcelona in 1214; and a Franciscan house was there before 1225, though its first church was not built until 1297. In 1226 the friars were established at Gerona, Lérida, and Balaguer; in 1239 at Valencia; in 1244 at Cervera; and in 1248 at Tarragona.[4]

Within a hundred years there would be no less than forty friaries in the realms of Aragon. But by that date there would be over fourteen hundred Franciscan residences in Europe housing thirty thousand friars. Before finis was written to the Valencian crusade, the Franciscans penetrated to the court of the Mongol khan. And just two years after King James died while putting down a Moslem revolt in Valencia, other Franciscan friars began to preach in Ethiopia and India and to establish the church in China.

While the conquered city of Valencia was undergoing its initial organization and reconstruction, academic Europe saw the work of great Franciscan thinkers like Lull, Grosseteste, Bonaventure, Alexander of Hales, and, in the last quarter of the century, Roger Bacon and Duns Scotus. The Franciscan spirit, humanizing and sympathetic, more universal and less austere than preceding devotional forms, was actively carrying to the urban poor and to others the novel emphasis on the humanity of Christ which Giotto was soon to write large upon the walls of the Assisi church.[5]

One can see how timely was the Order's arrival at Valencia during this first expansion, by comparing their progress here and in a settled country like England. Only in 1239 would they acquire a church in London, though they had arrived fifteen years earlier, and in Cambridge they did not receive a site until 1238. In England as elsewhere their popularity with bishops and people contrasted with the opposition by parochial clergy, who lost revenue and influence to them.[6] In Valencia as in all Christendom the poor men of Assisi will provide a counterweight among clergy and laity to the contemporary scandals of greed, pride, and violence.

Franciscan labors after the conquest of Valencia are (not unsurprisingly) badly documented except for property records and legacies. These, however, tell the essentials. The king established the Franciscans even while he was stationed at his forward post at Puig, before the descent on Valencia.

There were at least two Franciscans in his army, Peter of the See and Brother Illuminatus (who may have been the Illuminatus accompanying St. Francis on his journey to Syria). To these men King James gave a plot of ground, of modest proportions as befitted their ideals.[7] Escolano elaborates a fanciful tale of the converted Saʿīd summoning the Franciscans present in the king's siege camp, and donating his former palace out of repentance for having executed the martyrs of Teruel here in Valencia.

Actually their little church was situated just over the city walls, at the point of their southeast salient, on the road leading to Ruzafa. The site measured less than 500 by 300 feet. A small suburb was to form around the Franciscan nucleus.[8] There were also some houses given inside the city, in an L-shaped grouping; these the friars probably used at first for a temporary residence. By 1260 the Franciscans required a special area for a cemetery—an index of their popularity since some clients would already have been buried within the church. James gave them a very large space in front of their residence.[9] In that year too the general chapter at Narbonne reorganized the sprawling Order, making Valencia one of the seven custodies, each under its own custodian, in the province of Aragon.

Hardly a testament surviving from that era fails to advance the Franciscan work. During the very siege of Valencia the wealthy widow Toda Ladrón, sister of one of the most powerful barons of Aragon, willed 100 solidi "to the house of the Friars Minor" to be established in the city; the will was drawn in the presence of the king, who was to be an executor and who recalls here Lady Toda's "frequent and sustained services to me."[10] Maria, the wife of the porter Martin, left them ten solidi in 1241.[11] Aparisi, a porter of the queen, who had been a chaplain to the prince in 1229, left 100 solidi in 1247.[12] Peter Oller, draper of Valencia, provided another hundred in 1249, as well as a number of smaller gifts.[13]

Peter Armer, dying in 1251, began his list of legacies with the cathedral and the friars. They were to have 10 solidi, half for expenses and half for their church fund. This was as much as he left to his parish church, and more than he allowed to most charities.[14] There were two other interesting legacies from the same year. Queen Violante willed 100 solidi to each of eight Franciscan friaries in the realm, including that of Valencia. Raymond of Morella left 10 solidi.[15] The knight William Ochova Alemán in 1255 gave them his body for burial, together with the princely sum of 1,000 solidi.[16]

The Lady Jordana, wife of a knight but apparently in control of the family properties, died in 1256; she named the bishop as an executor and exhorted the king to have a care for her sons. Her major beneficiary, if one excepts a chaplaincy for her soul at the convent of St. Elizabeth and a hundred solidi for the cathedral building fund, were the Franciscans. "Brother Dominic of Tanemar of the Order of Friars Minor" (the superior perhaps) received 100 solidi and the Franciscan apostolate another hundred. There was also to be—happy custom!—a feast provided on the day of her funeral in the refectories of the Franciscan, Dominican, and St. Elizabeth communities. This thoughtful act of charity occurred in other wills too, the presence of lay paupers sometimes being specifically required.[17]

When the enormously wealthy and probably noble canon of Valencia, Bertrand of Teruel, died in 1256 he specified that his executors be guided in all their decisions by a council of friars: the Dominican prior, the Franciscan guardian, and the Dominican William of Fresney (Frexanet). He left 500 solidi to the Franciscans, 15 more to them for anniversary Masses, and a funeral-day feast.[18] The next year the wife of Bernard Olcina gave a small legacy.[19] Berengar of the Lady Rose willed them 20 solidi in 1258.[20] Peter of Barberá remembered them with 3 solidi that same year.[21] Lazarus of Vilella, who had extensive holdings in Aragon and Valencia, left them 10 solidi in 1259, as he did to four other religious houses of the city.[22] Bernard of Nausa in his will of 1261 gave 50 solidi.[23] William of Jaca, notary and citizen of Valencia, provided 100 solidi in his will of 1263.[24]

The Franciscans were the only religious houses, except for the Dominicans and the Friars of the Sack, to be remembered in the will of Barberan Oller (1271).[25] At about the same time, Berenguela Alphonse, the current mistress of the aging King James, died in Narbonne, setting aside for the Franciscans of Valencia the great sum of 1,000 morabatins. This found its way into the coffers of the king, who paid back 200 in 1273; in 1276 (the year of his death) he awarded for the remaining 700 a royal promise of payment.[26]

The cathedral canon Nicholas of Hungary remembered the Franciscans in his will (1274), giving a total of 70 solidi.[27] Peter Marqués in 1275 willed double and quadruple the amounts he left to the other eight religious Orders in the city: 20 solidi.[28] Peter Pérez, a wealthy canon of Valencia who died in 1279, chose to be buried in the cemetery of "the good Friars Minor" rather than in the cathedral, and was presumably a benefactor.[29] In the same year García Pérez of Biel left them 20 solidi.[30] A wealthy lady, Willelma, daughter of William of Soler, was far more generous to them and to the Dominicans than to any other group—leaving fifty solidi to each.[31] Similar legacies followed.[32] One assumes that the high proportion of monied ladies among the benefactors reflects their appreciation of the work done by the friars among the poor, a work much commended in those days to the ladies of noble and bourgeois households.

Read in the light of the contemporary Franciscan expansion over Europe, these fragments persuade one that the friars were performing at Valencia the welcome and vital offices which commended them elsewhere. The shoemakers, leather-workers, tailors, and potmakers held them in high regard. These four guilds, later to be disbanded with others as potential agents of urban turmoil, were to organize themselves again under the Franciscans in the early fourteenth century.[33]

Shortly after the death of King James, the guardian of the friary at Valencia appears as the confessor and intimate of his successor, King Peter, who later installed him as bishop of Segorbe. Previously the Friars Minor had entered Morella to set up a residence (1272). In 1295, answering a petition from the people of Murviedro, the guardian of the Valencia city house led three friars to found a house at Murviedro.

There had been a Franciscan presence from the first at Játiva, revealed by a document of 1248 terminating their rental of a mosque. But perhaps this abortive presence was more wish than reality. The permanent Játiva community came only after the stimulus of the Murviedro foundation. It began in 1295, after the city council had asked for a friary and set aside for it a small hospice and farm outside the walls. The Franciscans like the Dominicans, therefore, had their centers almost exclusively in the more urban and less feudalized southern part of the new kingdom. This geographical factor underlines their relevance to the frontier situation.[34]

‰ THE DOMINICANS

Like the Franciscans, the Dominicans or Black Friars were highly centralized, democratic in their electoral processes, apostolically mobile, and urban-centered. To an esteem for poverty they added an even greater esteem for learning and for the diffusion of theology. Their growth in Christendom chronologically parallels the life of King James of Aragon. Dominic had begun his work in Languedoc, around the years 1207 to 1213; King James had been born at Montpellier in 1208. Dominic had died in 1221, his Order barely founded and its constitutions just drawn for its five or perhaps eight provinces (1220–1221), as the young James was dreaming of the conquest of Valencia. Dominic would be canonized in 1234, shortly after the capture of Burriana, with the northern part of the kingdom of Valencia falling into Christian hands.

By the time Biar fell to James's crusade, the Dominicans already were conducting *studia* at the universities of Paris, Oxford, Bologna, Montpellier, Cologne, and elsewhere. In 1277, the year after the death of King James, a census of the Order shows that the Dominican houses had grown from sixty, at the time of St. Dominic's death, to four hundred and four. There were also fifty-eight convents of nuns. The number of Dominicans at this time was probably seven thousand; thirty years later this will have grown to ten thousand.

This body of clergy was well-educated, enthusiastic, and installed in key posts all over Christendom. Their numerous prelates, preachers, and scholars exercised a profound transforming influence. At the universities this was the century of Albert the Great (1206–1280), Thomas Aquinas (1225–1274), and many lesser luminaries. Just after the turn of the century Dominican penetration into Asia would be so successful that hierarchies and native clergies could be established in Persia, India, and Ethiopia.[35]

In King James's realms, the Dominicans were established at Montpellier in 1220, at Barcelona and Zaragoza in 1223, at Lérida and Majorca in 1230, at Valencia city in 1239, at Perpignan in 1243, at Tarragona about 1248, at Gerona in 1252, at Calatayud and Huesca in 1254, at Urgel at least by 1273, at Puigcerdá in 1288, at Játiva in 1291, and at Collioure in 1290. Before the first quarter of the next century was out, they were in five other places of the realms of Aragon.[36] Four of King James's confessors were Dominicans: Michael of Fabra, the great Raymond of Penyafort, Arnold of Sagarra, and Berengar of Castellbisbal.[37] An episode during the Majorcan crusade indicates how high Dominican prestige stood in James's realms. When the crusading army got out of hand and was plundering the leaders' houses, the king posted two Dominicans to guard his house and treasure, with only ten knights as a concomitant show of force.[38]

One receives the impression from legacies as well as other sources that the Dominicans were a more important element than the Franciscans in the life of newly conquered Valencia. This may be due to the nature of their apostolate, which demanded better organization and training and more elaborate equipment, and which was so wholeheartedly dedicated to public preaching, to the teaching of theology, and to the conversion of Jews and Moslems. Then, again, the Black Friars seem to have enjoyed greater favor with King James. He speaks of "the Valencian community of the Friars Preachers in our memory forever," and looks upon it as of great importance in the Christianizing of the realm.[39]

Although men of other Orders in Valencia tend to remain in group obscurity, a number of clear-cut personalities emerge from the Dominican ranks at Valencia. Arnold of Sagarra, said to have studied under Albert the Great at Paris, accompanied James on the Murcian expedition and piqued the royal sinner by refusing him absolution before going into battle.[40] Berengar of Castellbisbal, a man of noble family, was chosen to be the first bishop of Valencia but became instead the bishop of Gerona, whose tongue was partially cut out by the king. Peter of Lérida functioned as a special confessor and chaplain for the garrison at Puig; when the knights had decided to betray the king's hopes and secretly to abandon the Valencian enterprise en masse, Friar Peter informed King James and thus kept the crusade from a serious setback.[41] Later Peter, now prior of the Valencian Dominicans, signed a pact between King James and his son Alphonse in 1254.[42]

The bishop to whom the diocese owed most by way of organization was the Dominican Andrew Albalat, chancellor of the king, who annoyed James by his long campaign to recover the ecclesiastical revenues his predecessor had signed away to the crown. Michael of Fabra may have received his

Dominican habit from the hands of St. Dominic; he was the first of Dominic's men to become a professor of theology at Paris to fellow Dominicans. For a time he was confessor to King James. He played a prominent role in the Majorca siege, where he urged on the tunneling of the mines;[43] later he joined the king in the crusade against Valencia. Because he passed the first phase of the process of canonization, he bears the title "Venerable."[44] Other Dominicans also appear, like the convert-maker among the Valencian Moslems, John of Puigventós. There is even a reluctant Dominican; a citizen of Valencia named Berengar of Morena protested to the king that his son became a Dominican when not of age and then left the Order, so the Dominicans should cease threatening to discover and seize him.[45]

Five Dominicans are known to have accompanied the crusading host as it moved on Valencia; three of them were involved in an important arbitration between the king and the lord of Albarracín during the siege. To the five—Gregory, Michael of Fabra, Arnold of Barberá, Peter of Lérida, and Roderick of Lérida—James gave quarters close to the cathedral.[46] These houses were a temporary expedient; they allowed no room for the preaching mission of the friars. Besides, the bishop seems to have had an eye on the buildings; in 1241 the king gave them to him and his chapter.[47] In 1248 the king gave the Order an added site for building in the south of the kingdom, just outside the walls of Játiva. They seem to have delayed, however, in establishing themselves here.[48]

The property the friars actually built upon in the city of Valencia had been guaranteed to them by a pre-grant to Peter of Lérida on April 23, 1238. It was a sizable pleasure garden or park, outside the city at its northeast angle near the gate of the Templars. It stretched along the river front, and must have been one of the finest situations available. Its position and quality are a further indication of King James's esteem for the Order. It was prized moreover as being near the place of public execution for Moslem Valencia, and therefore hallowed by the blood of martyrs. This plot of land was confirmed in the spring of 1239.[49]

Here the Dominicans set about building a priory and tiny church. Its size may be imagined from the fact that it later served as porter's lodge for the second church.[50] About them, especially on the side facing the Templars, was their cemetery; here with the permission of Bishop Arnold and the chapter (1245) they buried many a Valencian knight.[51] Perhaps this was the first religious house in the city, and—a larger perhaps—King James himself may have laid its cornerstone. The first proposition is argued from the traditional order according to which the many religious groups marched in medieval Valencian processions; the second, quite possible in itself, is a "tradition" apparently based on a later chronicle.[52]

A larger church was needed. Aided by the indulgence of forty days granted by Innocent IV to Valencians who helped the project with alms, it was partially finished in 1252.[53] Some twenty years or more later, a protective wall brought the Dominican establishment within the city proper, though it was to keep a pleasant rural aspect down into the eighteenth century. At the same time—a hint of their popularity—they had to extend the church even further, securing more area for this purpose.

The king gave the Dominicans a privilege to prevent anyone building on the open space before their house,[54] to pay no taxes on the waters they used, to have no neighboring terraces or windows overlooking the cloistral privacy, to prohibit the noisy river men from working on their bank, to outlaw the dumping of garbage near their buildings, and to forbid the carting away of sand from their beach (their priory was always in some danger of being undermined by the river).[55] An unusual privilege came to them in 1257 when King James decreed that anyone conversing with a friar was to be immune from legal attentions or harassment for that moment.[56]

As late as 1275 the Valencian house was still not definitively assigned to one of the eight vicariates constituting the Dominican province of Spain.[57] The provincial chapter was keeping an eye on this promising area, however, and assigning good men here.[58] A second house was opened at Játiva (St. Philip's); it was formally commissioned at the chapter general in Palencia in 1291.[59] (This was a suppressed or transferred place of the Friars of the Sack.) The Valencia and Játiva houses were to quarrel seriously over their respective jurisdictions for preaching in the kingdom. An agreement finally set aside the northern half of the kingdom from Morella to the Júcar River for the Valencia house, and from the Júcar to Bañeres for the Játivans.[60]

The ideal of poverty was remarkably strong in the early Dominicans; this extended to their ownership of property even as a corporation, excepting the properties involved in their churches and areas of residence. Even the costly property they will purchase in 1291 from Raymond of Poblet, a field or farm at two thousand solidi, will be "around your monastery."[61] It is not surprising, therefore, to find that their gifts at Valencia came in the form of direct alms, as with the Franciscans. Legacies to the Franciscans here were almost always coupled with an equivalent item for the Dominicans.

Thus, Toda Ladrón willed them 300 solidi in 1238; Maria, wife of the porter Martin, left ten solidi in 1241; Aparisi left 100 solidi in 1247; and Peter Oller a total of 50 solidi in 1249. In 1251 Raymond of Morella and Peter Armer each gave 10. Dominic of Calderón, who asked to be buried in their cemetery in 1252, left 20. William Ochova Alemán gave 55 solidi in 1255. In 1256 the Lady Jordana provided enough to pay for a feast. In the same year Canon Bertrand of Teruel assigned 2,000 solidi in his will "to construct two arches in their church," 500 more to be spent "to bulwark the house against the attacks of the Guadalaviar River," 20 for annual requiems, and 200 to his friend the Dominican William of Fresney, to pay "for having a breviary made."

There were 5 solidi from the wife of Bernard Olcina in 1257; 30 solidi, and his corpse for burial, from Berengar of the Lady Rose in 1258; 2 solidi from Peter of Barberá in 1258; 10 from Lazarus of Vilella in 1259; 50 from Bernard of Nausa in 1261; a total of 150 from the notary William of Jaca in 1263; 3 from Barberan Oller in 1271; 50 from Willelma in 1272; 50 from Canon Nicholas in 1274; and 20 from Peter Marqués in 1275.[62]

García Pérez of Biel left the Dominicans 20 solidi in 1279. Crusaders like Bernard Fabra, a Montpellier man of great riches who lived in Alcira, Peter Aznar of ancient lineage, the knight Bernard Castellet, and others, left large sums to establish anniversary Masses in the chapels of their church. More ordinary citizens responded especially to the recent Dominican devotion to St. Peter Martyr; within a decade of his death, St. Peter was a favorite with Valencians.[63]

Two of the major benefactors of the Dominicans were Mark of Capracava (†1266) and William Escrivá of Ibiza. The headstone of Mark and his wife told passersby how the knight "did many favors for the friars and the house." William the son of William Escrivá senior, a jurate and justiciar of Valencia, was an unusually wealthy man. Both he and his father were benefactors of the Dominicans; he left them in one bequest 5,000 solidi. In gratitude for the gifts from Mark and William, the friars had their heraldic shields sculptured on the arches of the church.[64]

Perhaps the Játiva house was rather poor; as late as 1312 Bishop Raymond of Valencia left them 1,000 solidi in his will, "to buy rents to provide clothing for the brothers." He also gave them both *Summas* of Aquinas and a small library. Bishop Raymond left 6,000 solidi to the Dominicans of the Valencian diocese, and supported a Dominican student at the University of Paris.[65]

The Dominicans too had their confraternities to manage. Aptly enough, one of these formalized at the turn of the century a work in which they had distinguished themselves in Valencia from the beginning. "Each and every convert in the city of Valencia, regardless of social status or occupation" could, for the honor of God, the Virgin, Peter, and the house of the Dominicans in Valencia, band together under the guidance of the friars, as a social and benevolent confraternity.[66] A similar concession bound the hide dealers and belt makers to the church of the Dominicans before 1252. There was apparently a brotherhood honoring St. Peter Martyr also under Dominican care in Valencia by 1269.[67] These organizations were not simply urban, but included also the people of the surrounding countryside or hinterland.

The function of the Dominicans as teachers contributed an element to medieval civic culture which one might easily overlook, an element not readily expected on a frontier. Perhaps it was in connection with their apostolate of studies that the friars sold a small village and woods which they owned in Játiva in order to purchase an annotated Bible; the time was early 1250, before their church was yet completed, about a decade after the conquest.[68] When that latest Western institution, the Inquisition, made its way to the frontier at the turn of the century, the Dominicans were to be its instrument.[69]

Their most resounding success was the conversion of a number of Moslems. It was in connection with this apostolate that they conducted their schools of Arabic. These are an important part of the complex story of relations between the two antagonistic social groups who inhabited Valencia.[70] Dominican tactics—already successful in the heresy-ridden Languedoc area—must inevitably have had a great effect on the psychology of the Christian settlers. The beleaguered minority would need some such aggressive and expansive spirit if they were to retain their social identity and impress it upon the new land.

ᖳᖳ THE FRIARS OF THE SACK

When the Council of Lyons drastically pruned the Mendicant movement in 1274, the largest and most important of the Orders cut down was the Friars of the Sack. In less than twenty-five years of existence, it had flourished from Scotland to Palestine in seven provinces and some eighty houses. As part of their priorate or province of Spain these Brothers of Penitence of Jesus Christ had eleven houses in the realms of Aragon during the thirteenth century. The location of these Aragonese houses is significant: the main Catalan city Barcelona, the main Aragonese city Zaragoza, the university city Montpellier, the main ecclesiastical city Tarragona, the Pyrenean capital of Cerdagne Puigcerdá, in Perpignan the main city of Roussillon, in the city of Calatayud and the town of Perelada, in the main city of conquered Majorca, and in the two administrative centers of the kingdom of Valencia, Valencia and Játiva. Apparently they were determined to influence the most important centers, and they included among these the farther reaches of the frontier.[71]

Yet they had been founded as late as 1248, by a knight of Hyères in Provence. Only in 1251 did they get their Augustinian form of rule; a Franciscan note appears in their care to have poor and ordinary houses, to refuse properties except for use as alms, and to show the world "a very merry" face.[72] They dressed in the sacklike tunic of the ordinary pilgrim penitent, with a cowl and a cheap multicolored mantle. They preached, heard confessions, distributed alms, and in general helped the poor.

The great antiquarian of Valencia, Josef Teixidor, was guilty of an Homeric nod when he installed the friars in Valencia city before 1241.[73] They were here early enough, however, with an establishment running along the marketplace, at the south-central edge of the city, just outside the gate called Boatella.[74] In 1261 they received a substantial alms of ten solidi from Prince Peter.[75]

The Friars of the Sack were also at Játiva in the south some time before 1269. On that date King James I allowed them to accept a gift of land there, despite the *Furs* of Valencia which forbade transfer of real property to the church: "We approve, allow, and confirm forever to you, the prior and community of the Játiva house of the Brothers of Penitence of Jesus Christ, the gift of a section of land made to you by Raymond Dalila, a resident of Játiva."[76] A recent historian of Játiva (who erroneously dates the foundation from King James's last testament) locates it by archaeological evidence as having stood between the modern hospital and the ex-priory of the Játiva Dominicans.[77]

In the same year, the Játiva house received from the crown all the goods of a woman named Bernarda Dalila—perhaps a relative of Raymond. She had disinherited her son for becoming a Moslem, and the king transferred the inheritance to the Order. This was designated for use in building their church at Játiva.[78] The house at Valencia city was also planning expansion in 1269. King James allowed the friars here, and their superior for the province of Spain, Bartholomew of Anas, to take over a large area "in front of the entrance to the monastery"; this "extends in length from the walls of the said monastery all the way to the lower arch of some houses of Peter Stephen," and will be used as a cemetery.[79]

The Friars of the Sack were fairly popular, as is evident from the few surviving legacies for Valencia city. The testamentary documentation is only a sampling—not only because few wills remain but also because as a rule these were casually preserved by interested parties other than the suppressed friars; there is no cartulary for the Sack friars. In 1271 a man of means in Valencia, Barberan Oller, left them 2 Valencian solidi.[80] In 1272 Willelma, daughter of William of Soler and wife of Peter Gilabert, left them 20.[81] In 1275 the Valencian notary Peter Marqués left them 5.[82] A generous gift had come their way as early as 1263, when the Valencian notary William of Jaca left them 100 solidi.[83] King James in his will of 1272 left them a resounding 1,700 solidi.[84] Legacies surviving cover only the years 1263 to 1275, and are neither as frequent nor as generous as those for the Franciscans and Dominicans. Unlike the Franciscans and Dominicans, the Sack friars have left the names of no individual friars.

After 1274, as the several friars died, the Friars of the Sack diminished slowly into nonexistence. By 1275 King James was preparing for the eventual disposition of their holdings. He wrote Artal Esquerre, a member of the royal household who was collecting bits of Valencian property:

> We grant you, Artal Esquerre, that if it happens that the community of the Brothers of Penance of Jesus Christ of Valencia is reorganized, or that the brothers are sent away or vacate this house in line with the papal decree, or alienate it, you and yours are to have and to hold that open space which lies in front of the residence of the Dominicans.[85]

As the Dominican house was at the other end of the city, this grant suggests that the Dominicans had already made preparations for acquiring the property, and that some adjustment as to the expansion of their own house was being made.

The community at Valencia city lingered on, dwindling, but presumably continuing to influence their surroundings. A bull of Honorius IV in 1286 reveals that "no more than two or three of the friars are left here."[86] One wonders how many had staffed the house a quarter century before. By this papal document the Dominicans were allowed to purchase the Sack residence, either with the permission of its surviving members or else at their death. The learned Jazpert of Botonach, bishop of Valencia, was to arrange the sale to the Dominican provincial of Spain. The latter indeed had initiated this whole episode by appealing to Rome. However, the Friars of the Sack survived in Valencia city for another decade or more. As late as the summer of 1278 one Raymond Armer, son of the defunct Peter Armer, leaving all his property to his sister Mary and her husband Gerald, made legal declaration of his intent to enter the suppressed Order![87]

In 1297 Boniface VIII revoked the previous bull and donated the house to the neighboring Dominican-oriented Magdalenes.[88] These nuns may even have been behind the previous appeal of 1286. If the house was already empty, the nuns could claim it; otherwise they had to wait until the survivors were gone.[89] As for the Játiva residence—the Dominicans were allowed to purchase it, by another bull of Honorius IV (1285), because they needed a house in that city.[90] The archdeacon of Valencia city was to arrange the sale; the profits were to be sent to the Holy Land. This purchase may have been accomplished as early as 1291.[91]

A final bit of information on the Valencian Friars of the Sack comes from a document dated fifteen years after Pope Boniface's letter. The last testament of Bishop Raymond of Valencia in 1312 reveals that he had sold the Játiva house for 1,000 solidi—or more probably put up that purchase price himself as a gift for the Dominicans. The money was in the bank (*tabula*) of Bernard Planell, destined for the Holy Land. If the bishop's financial agent had recently withdrawn the money, Raymond wanted the account to be reimbursed.[92] Ironically, the last echo heard from Valencia about this Order of men so distrustful of property and money derives from this complicated financial transaction.

১৯২ THE AUGUSTINIANS

The Order of Hermits of St. Augustine organized itself just seventeen years after the fall of Valencia city. They were an amalgamation of various hermit groups brought together into one Order by Pope Alexander IV in 1256.[93] Inspired by the example of the centralized active Franciscans and Dominicans, they put aside the contemplative life of the hermit and took up the active life of preaching, teaching, and ministering to souls as Mendicants. Within a few years they had spread rapidly over Europe.

Prior to this reorganization, the Augustinian hermits had especially flourished in the countries of the Spanish peninsula. They had grouped in monasteries which in turn tended to confederate regionally. They therefore became one of the first four provinces forming the background of the new Order, and houses multiplied. A provincial for Spain ruled through his vicars. One early Augustinian historian has the hermit groups in the combined regions of Aragon uniting under a single provincial during the first quarter of the thirteenth century, and even then assuming Mendicant forms. The Italian Fabrian was provincial in 1216, the Catalan Francis Salelles in 1240, Arnold around 1257, Arnulf around 1258, William of Navarre around 1280, and William Salelles from about 1298.[94]

The Order's robes were black, or sometimes white. Various other groups followed the rule of St. Augustine, often in a semimonastic context, and might therefore be called Augustinians, but it was these new Augustinian friars who appeared on the Valencian frontier. They arrived on that frontier quite early, seeming to sense its needs and opportunities. They surely felt a special affection for the place. Long ago when the Moslems had sacked Sardinia, it was said, primitive Augustinian hermits had carried away, to a then Christian Valencia, the treasured miter and staff of St. Augustine. A comparative chronology of the Order's expansion in the thirteenth century indicates the importance of Valencia to it. In 1256, the year of formal union, the first of their houses west of the Rhone is found at Narbonne; by 1275 southern France had a strong representation, with eight priories established. Yet by 1280 the Valencian frontier alone boasted four houses, with another soon to come.[95]

The early years of these houses are lost in obscurity and conjecture. A tradition cited by Zurita in the sixteenth century has King James in conquered Valencia swearing he will raise "four columns" or Orders to support Christendom on the frontier. If the king ever said this, there is still no reason to count the Augustinians as one of the four. A late chronicler of the Order puts a friar named Francis Serelles (Salelles) with the besieging army. The friar asked the king for a priory when the city should fall, then in 1242 began a church and dormitory there. This is almost surely fantasy. The Augustinian annalist Torelli incorporates elaborate scholastic arguments from his predecessors to prove an early foundation at the city; he fails to convince.[96]

A peculiarity of the Valencian Augustinians was their taste for solitude. Despite the Mendicant activism, the spirit of the hermit seemed still to cling. This peculiarity marked their first foundation strongly. It was in the hidden valley of Aguas Vivas (Aigues Vives), considerably south of the conquered city, and somewhat southeast of Carcagente. If one accepts the traditional founding date of 1239 (and there is no strong reason to do so), this was an unconquered, dangerous hinterland. Again we must be satisfied with a tale: the king heard of hermits scattered in the Alcira mountains and gave them some land to help form a community. At any rate, there really was an Augustinian priory of Our Lady here, a member of the 1256 union, functioning by 1260 (perhaps 1267): King James spoke of the buildings at that time in extending its land holdings. Its Prior Raymond received a royal tax exemption in 1272 and free pasturage for the friars' flocks on crown lands.[97]

The Castellón Augustinians may have been founded in 1260 or 1280. Almost certainly they did not exist before 1260, though Jordán, the early historian of the Order, blandly lists the house as founded by St. William in the mid-twelfth century and moving within the walls in 1298! The Castellón house emerges clearly and noisily into prominence in 1298 when Bertrand Torrens, rector of the "Mother Church" of that town, raised great opposition to their rebuilding and especially to their efficient garnering of revenues and legacies. The dispute culminated in a truce and the sharing of monies, carefully worked out that year. (A decade later Prior James Berengar was excommunicated and St. Augustine's priory lay under interdict for declining to continue this arrangement with Bertrand's successor Francis.)[98]

St. Augustine's at Alcira was a third house, just north of Carcagente. Raymond of Canals is listed as prior (perhaps he was the founder) in 1270; this house purchased lands in 1277 and 1278. Even deeper on the frontier, a priory sprang up at Alcoy. Saurina Entenza, wife of the great admiral Roger of Lauria and close relative of James I, was foundress (1290 or 1299).[99] Sucías suggests that James placed the house in the Moslem suburb for more effective preaching to the infidel.[100] Another house has been claimed for Castielfabib, with no real evidence.[101]

A house of the friars stood in the countryside just beyond the walls of Valencia city. As with the Castellón house, it would be included within the expanding city when a new circle of walls went up in the next century. Valencia's priory was established by 1281, or perhaps a number of years previously. It does not appear, however, in the earlier wills. Among gifts received by St. Augustine's here was a service ornament from King Peter.[102] Before 1298 the priory church had become the center for such brotherhoods as the blacksmiths and silversmiths.[103]

Augustinian plans for expansion in the Valencia kingdom are recorded in a royal concession of 1273:

> We grant to the brothers-hermits of the Order of St. Augustine . . . that in some of the cities, castles or places . . . they may freely and without hindrance build for themselves monasteries, in which they ought . . . to follow their vocation, with the counsel of the deputies of the cities and

towns . . . We give them permission and full power to accept houses or other properties given them, or also to purchase these.[104]

A hint of the extent of their holdings comes from a record of debt by King Peter in 1281: "by reason of the sale you made to us of a certain estate, which the deceased Berengar . . . owned in the confines of Corbera," for 13,000 solidi of Jaca.[105] A document of December 1300 allowed the Augustinian friary "in the huerta of the city of Valencia" to purchase an additional one and a quarter cafizes of land; their holdings were freed from regalian taxes.[106] The Augustinian Order, in its first full expansion over the face of Europe during these decades, undoubtedly contributed to improving the spiritual tone of the Valencia kingdom. And, of all the Mendicants here, they were the most widely distributed.

ᙏᙏ THE CARMELITES

The White Friars or Carmelites were the last of the four great Mendicant Orders to reach the Valencian frontier. Like the Augustinians, they had resulted from the reorganization and sudden spread of a previously existing group. They had organized in Palestine in the middle of the twelfth century for a life of eremitical solitude and prayer. When Moslem pressures made their position precarious, they began to shift their forces to Europe, simultaneously undergoing a metamorphosis in favor of the active life of the Mendicant. All this occurred, as luck would have it, just after King James had conquered the northern part of Valencia and was moving to siege the capital city.

The first migration of the Order consisted of two hermits who reached Valenciennes in 1235, though perhaps a few others had come ten years earlier. Then, in about 1238, a massacre in Palestine caused the Order to approve a general transmigration. One finds them in Messina and Cyprus in 1238, in England in 1241, and in Marseilles at least from 1248. Around 1254 the greatest of their generals was elected, the Englishman Simon Stock. For twenty years he reorganized, stabilized, and defended the White Friars. From Innocent IV he secured permission thoroughly to adapt the rule to the times after the fashion of the Mendicants.

The Carmelites appeared in the cities and towns now, ever spreading. They were also at the universities: at Cambridge, Liège, and Brussels in 1249; at Oxford in 1253; at Montpellier and Cologne in 1256; at Bologna in 1260; and so on throughout the century. For the realms of Aragon, there are claims for their presence at Perelada as early as 1206, at Perpignan in 1213, and with more probability at Lérida in 1278, and at Gerona and Barcelona in 1295.[107]

In the very swirl and center of this expansive movement, the Carmelites found their way down to Valencia city, in 1281. Thus, they were on the frontier the same year in which they settled in the Rhone Valley at Lyons, and five years before they favored with a monastery such cities as Nuremberg or Ghent. The ecumenical council of Lyons had just abolished a number of new Orders but had approved the Carmelites as one of the remaining Mendicant big four (1271). When the Carmelites arrived at Valencia, they would still have been wearing their original bizarre mantle—the white and black vertical stripes which gained them the undignified name of Magpie Friars. But in 1287 a white, wool mantle replaced this dress, changing their appellation to White Friars.

In 1281 "the prior and community" received permission from the crown to acquire properties up to a total value of 3,000 solidi: "You may receive, from all places you choose outside the city walls of Valencia, buildings and lands by gift [or] purchase or any other just title, . . . to build or to construct your monastery and buildings, for the salvation of Christians."[108] By 1283 they owned properties in Roteros;[109] perhaps their temporary residence was in that suburb. The new priory was on the river bank, a short distance beyond the western wall of the city. It was completed, with church, between 1288 and 1292.[110]

From sometime before 1306, as a terminal date, the Carmelite friars directed in Valencia city a brotherhood of millers from the city and countryside.[111] Although no further documentation on their work in Valencia has survived, as the strictest of the four Mendicant Orders they would surely have had in Valencia the same invigorating and expansive effect which they were having in the other regions of Europe. And their presence, like that of the Augustinians and the Friars of the Sack, reinforced the Franciscan-Dominican influence in reshaping the new kingdom.

XII

MONKS AND NUNS ON THE VALENCIAN FRONTIER

In an earlier era the Benedictine monasteries had stood in the forefront of the crusading movement on the Spanish peninsula. Their intensive crusade propaganda and vigorous direction "flooded Spain with knights and soldiers coming from all the regions of France" to mount the mighty counteroffensive of the eleventh century.[1] Population followed these foreign monks, organized itself around their abbeys, and helped substantially to colonize the north. The monasteries formed a solid line of support, military and moral, from embattled Spain up into France. Many were under the jurisdiction of other monasteries—such as St. Mary of Lagrasse, St. Thomas, St. Victor at Marseilles, or the priory of Moissac.[2]

Their social contribution was impressive—in agriculture, industry, commerce, aid to the indigent, public works, and loans; in their architecture, music and arts; in their schools, libraries, and scriptoria; and in their liturgy and spirituality.

But the golden age had passed by the time of the Valencian crusade. The rural world was giving way to a more urbanized world, with different needs and opportunities. The monasteries tended to become somewhat isolated, less influential, bogged down in their role of landlord and litigant. Countermeasures were having some success in the realms of King James, where the monasteries formed a federation after 1215 and especially from 1233 on. They met regularly in chapters now, and took steps to sharpen religious observance.

ᗞᗞ THE CISTERCIANS: THE MONKS OF BENIFASÁ

Of the Benedictine monks, only the highly organized Cistercian Order, the White Monks who had been the new monasticism of the twelfth century, were represented on the Valencian frontier. There is something fitting in this, considering the strong tradition developed by the Cistercians as promoters of the crusades and of the crusade spirit. Less than a hundred years had passed since the time of St. Bernard (†1153) when the Cistercian tide had been sweeping over Europe. The ebb had now set in, with its gradual lessening of social influence, its decline of spiritual enthusiasm into a certain routine, its appearance of living in the past. In Spain, at about the time the crusaders of Aragon were preparing to fight their way down to Valencia, the Cistercian movement in Europe had already passed its high point. The great donations had fallen off notably, and this situation would worsen. The White Monks seemed unable to adapt themselves to an urban, centralizing, modern world, without dislocating their ideals and pattern of life. Helplessly they watched their feudal jurisdictions fall away to king and bishop and town. Tangled in debt and maladministration, they fell prey to the avarice of rural nobles whose own economic power was declining.

But if the far-flung Order was entering its season of autumn, it was a golden autumn, with a power and grandeur of its own. One example of this was the one hundred and fifty new monasteries which went up during this century, and the many eminent leaders who came from them, like the great Roderick Simon of Rada, crusader, scholar, and primate of the countries of Spain. At this very period an appreciative pope was to use a bold figure, comparing their services to Christendom to the warrior achievements of the Templars and Hospitallers.

Whatever their troubles elsewhere, the brightest spot of all the Cistercian scene on the peninsula was the advancing frontier of the king of Aragon.[3] Throughout the rest of King James's realms Cistercian monasteries were having their share of disasters and troubles. But in Majorca and Valencia the monks encountered challenges and opportunities like those of their primitive period. Important new monasteries were established, and others projected which would help change social patterns on these two frontiers.

King James loved the Order and died clothed in its robes. The statutes of the general chapter show him making requests for a foundation at Montpellier, for prayers, for a monk, for a lay brother to assist him, and so on—though a strained note can creep into the relation when money is involved.[4] The king's affection for Poblet near Tarragona was particularly strong. Here he brought his banners to be blessed for the Majorca crusade, and here he returned to give thanks. Located in the heart of the realms of Aragon, Poblet was the royal pantheon; here King James would be buried, by his own request.[5] The abbots of Poblet remained important counselors to the crown. During the first period of consolidation of the Valencian realm Peter of Albalat, the metropolitan of Tarragona and a brother of Bishop Andrew of Valencia, was a Cistercian monk; so were others of the king's bishops, like the former abbot St. Peter Calvó at Vich.

King James had planned to signalize and consecrate his first advance into the realm of Valencia by planting a Cistercian monastery on that spot. He thus added to his foundations of Escarp near Lérida, and La Real in newly conquered Majorca, the foundations of Benifasá in northern Valencia and two convents of Cistercian nuns. The king later gave the central shrine of the new kingdom, St. Vincent's, to the Cistercians of St. Victorian monastery in Aragon for a short time. In southern Valencia King James II will found Valldigna, destined to be one of the great land-owning monasteries of the realm. King James intended to establish two more Cistercian abbeys here. He also gave gifts of property and privileges in the kingdom of Valencia to the older, non-Valencian monasteries.[6]

For a moment of time, the decline of the Order was stayed. They populated towns, set their flocks grazing over the valleys of Valencia, harvested their revenues, and raised fine buildings. Again Christendom had need of them badly, to stand as monuments and reminders of the Christian way of life for the settlers trickling south. King James emphasized this liturgical-social function of the monk, when giving a vineyard and shop to the Cistercian monastery of Benifasá in the kingdom of Valencia: "mindful that religious places, built for the praise and glory of Our Lord, ought to be generously developed by kings and princes, so that the divine office may be conducted there always and continually."[7]

Of the two great Cistercian abbeys, Benifasá was the daughter and affiliate of Poblet, while Valldigna was the daughter of Holy Crosses (Santes Creus). The mount of Benifasá, whose strategic castle and surrounding, pine-dotted territory took their name from a former Moslem commander Beni Hassa, lay along the confines of Aragon, Catalonia, and Valencia, some fifteen miles from Morella. It was a bitter and windy spot, generally unsuitable for farming and not very satisfactory for flocks. "Ventus et ventus et malus conventus," punned a later abbot of Citeaux after a chilly visit here.[8] For four months of the year, snow and cold dominated this remote wilderness of mountains and hills. Even at the dawn of the nineteenth century an observer told how its few inhabitants regularly eked out their subsistence only with the aid of daily alms from the monastery.[9]

King Alphonse had pre-granted the place in 1178 to the diocese of Tortosa. But when King Peter conquered it, he gave it with Rossell as a fief to the baron William of Cervera (1208). William in time entered the Cistercians. In 1229 King James confirmed Cervera's own grant of Benifasá to the monastery of Poblet, for the erection of a Valencian monastery.[10] This soon came to include a generous and impressive sweep of country. Besides the Benifasá district, there was "the castle and valley of Malagraner, the castle of Fredes, the place and whole country of Bojar with its valleys and plains and districts, and the whole country of Rossell and Castell de Cabres, and the castle of Bel with its districts, each and every castle and place."[11] This grant the king gave to the abbot of Poblet in the year Burriana was captured. The whole seignorial estate came to be called the Tenencia or Tinença of Benifasá monastery itself.[12]

The bishop of Tortosa, opposed to the idea of a monastery here, pressed his own claims; in context these were seignorial rather than ecclesiastical. The affair was settled by arbitration in 1233, though not without the later intervention of the metropolitan and of Rome. This agreement arranged the

seignorial rights and jurisdictions, and the ecclesiastical and secular revenues.[13] Like the other baronial powers and religious Orders in this part
of Valencia, Benifasá kept a full half of the tithes as private revenue. The
bishop took the first fruits, all mills, and half the ovens. The seignorial
claims of Tortosa were further satisfied by a compensating grant from the
king. Resentment remained, however; new tithe and revenue accords had to
be negotiated with the Tortosa diocese in 1241 and 1261, with adjustments
in 1281.[14]

As for Rossell, the monastery moved into legal battle against a more
formidable foe, the Knights Hospitallers. The encounter became a classic of
its kind in European legal history. Innocent IV brought it to a halt in 1250;
but it broke out on a new front and had to run its furious course to a final
arbitration in 1268.[15]

Meanwhile the Moors were being cleared away in skirmishes of a more
material nature. In 1234 the traditional eleven monks with their abbot John
had arrived to take possession.[16] They would have carried with them from
Poblet a modest library, especially of service books, and a contingent of
auxiliary lay brothers. The first Cistercians settled in the castle, making there
a chapel to St. Scholastica, while a monastery slowly went up some distance
away. This would be no simple construction but a complex of buildings
which made the monastery a little world in itself. There would have been a
church and cloister; a dormitory, kitchen and refectory; a chapter house, a
hospice and an infirmary; a lay brothers' dormitory; and an abbot's residence. Furnishing such an establishment—from the writing materials of the
scriptorium and the agricultural implements of the fields to the equipment
of forge and shop, kitchen and library, pharmacy and choir—was itself no
easy undertaking. Still, progress continued, if haltingly.

A complaint of 1246, that "at present no more than twenty-two monks
are able to live there," shows that James had been neglecting the promises
he made over a decade ago to the God of battles.[17] The monastery should
have housed a much larger community. In a country as underdeveloped as
England in this century the average number of Benedictine monks per
monastery amounted to about fifty, though some houses held less than
twenty-five and some sixty or more. English Cistercians, however, averaged
"considerably" fewer: forty to fifty choir monks per house. Twenty-five
choir monks should be the minimum on hand; sixty were required by a
twelfth-century statute before a monastery could split to found a new
affiliate. In its early period, Rievaulx had held six hundred souls, Clairvaux
seven hundred.[18]

The bishop of Gerona came to Benifasá's aid, though involuntarily. This
prelate was the same Berengar of Castellbisbal who had been King James's
candidate for first bishop of Valencia. The king now in a fit of pique cut
away part of Berengar's tongue. The mutilation shocked the Christian

world. Matthew Paris reports how the English Cistercian John Tolet, rebuking the pope in 1247, extravagantly warned: "Spain is raging to the length of cutting out the tongues of bishops."[19] Pope Innocent reprimanded James severely: "Our mind is stunned by the enormity of the crime."[20] The outcome was a heavy penance imposed by Rome on the royal sinner. Among other items, James was ordered to expand the facilities of the Benifasá project, so as to care for twice the current number, and to add 200 silver marks (some 7,500 solidi) to help build their church.[21]

Before the decade was out, Abbot William of Almenar and forty-three monks were able to move into the edifice (1250).[22] The names of twenty-five of these monks of Benifasá are to be found on a document of 1268, including those of the abbot, prior, subprior, sacristan, cellarer major and cellarer minor, master of the works (operarius), infirmarian and sub-infirmarian, vestuarian, and porter.[23] The king saw to the completion of the monastery structure, and endowed it with an additional 1,730 morabatins (probably some 14,700 solidi) in 1259 and 1272.[24] The first stone for the ambitious church was laid in 1262 under Abbot Berengar of Concabella.[25] To push the work to a conclusion, alms were solicited throughout King James's realms with the approval of the metropolitan (1273).[26] It was finished, and gracing the conquered land, in the year James died (1276). By this time the monastic scriptorium was probably supplying copies of manuscript books on demand.[27]

This upland solitude, and the challenge presented by the poor quality of its land, were in the Cistercian tradition. By preference their area was a huge bloc of land, a single economic unit, with the monastery as a center of exploitation. At Benifasá, nearby strips of arable land were put under cultivation and granges were projected. The grange was an institution peculiar to the Cistercians; it was an outpost of the monastery, where a group of lay brothers could be installed in farm buildings under a resident master of the grange, so as to exploit the inconveniently distant fringes of monastic property.

Surprisingly, a grange was in being as early as 1244.[28] The king granted permission for others, on his own land, in 1252.[29] Still others existed before 1253 near Ballestar, near Herbés, and near Bojar.[30] These latter are mentioned in a papal document which also says: "They are so distant from the mother church that those living there cannot reach it for hearing the divine office." The nightmare travel in that district must be reckoned in terms of time consumed, rather than in geographical distance; so it is with reason that Innocent IV supplies the cause: "because of the hazards of the paths, especially in winter."

The pope therefore allowed oratories to be established here, and perhaps chapels for the people.[31] Since such places of an exempt monastery would usually be furnished with oratory and refectory, and since the papal letter deferred to the judgment of the bishop of Tortosa, permission for the "cap-pellae" may especially have concerned the laity, who attended the office even in parish churches in Valencian towns. A document of the previous year from the pope, with a similar reference to the bishop, did in fact speak of the monastery "oratorium" for monks and laity.[32] This latter circumstance must be balanced against the fact that for half a century the Cistercians had been troubled by doubts as to the legitimacy of such chapels, a scruple which was finally settled by a favorable bull of 1255, shortly after these two documents. At any rate, granges were much in evidence at Benifasá. In a document of 1261 the bishop of Tortosa referred to the granges of the Benifasá monks.[33] Any number of other granges doubtless existed but have left no trace in the fragmentary records still surviving.

King James did not altogether forget his abbey. He gave it some Tortosa properties (1234),[34] the dominion of Bojar (1235),[35] tax exemption for its flocks of sheep (1237, 1247, 1267),[36] permission to have one of the monks act as notary public (1261),[37] small bits of land such as five jovates at Beni-maclet near Valencia,[38] and license to buy salt outside the kingdom of Valencia (1261).[39] In his last testament he left the monks a thousand mora-batins to advance the construction of their church.[40]

The royal endowment had not been adequate, however, to the initial expense of sustaining the monks, and debts accrued during these early years. In 1260 King James promised 7,000 solidi of Jaca, "as a special favor, for the good of my soul."[41] This sum was not immediately available, and the creditors seem to have been pressing the monks. In 1262 the king therefore assigned 4,000 solidi of the promised sum, "to be taken from the revenue, income, fees, hospitality tax, and our other rights, including tithes, first fruits and any others" in nearby Vallibona and Herbés.[42] In 1267 he made another gift; and in 1271 he confirmed the mintage tax which he had pre-viously assigned to them in certain villages of Morella.[43] None of these piecemeal gifts met the needs of the forty monks, whose obligations were heavy; by 1272 they were barely at subsistence level. In that year James adverted to the lack of bread for the "monks and brothers." So that the monastery "can have enough bread," the king granted to it again his share in the tithe of Vallibona and Herbés (and possibly Herbesét)—this time in perpetuity.[44]

Private benefactions also helped. In 1248 a benefactor donated to the monks some buildings in Morella. Since a suit would have to be initiated to gain actual possession of these buildings, the benefactor likewise transferred his rights to recover at law.[45] A cousin of Cervera, Raymond Berengar of Ager, presented the monks in 1241 with rents of 100 solidi per annum.[46] The Knight Hospitaller castellan of Amposta granted their flocks free pasture in the country of Cervera (1245); and the Calatrava commander of Alcañiz did the same for the countries of Cuevas and Pulpis (1244). A gift came from

William of Moncada in 1249—the place called Refalgari.[47] Disturbed in this holding by the Templars, the monks provided themselves with a royal safeguard for it in 1279.[48] Refalgari (which no longer exists) had been part of the Tortosa countryside, though near the Benifasá border. Since Benifasá followed the public law of Barcelona by the terms of King Peter's 1208 donation, trouble broke out on this point between the abbot and the Tortosa bishop. By a later agreement (1306) the monastery will retain a vicar at Refalgari but the law must remain the *costums* of Tortosa.[49]

A gift came from William Bardol in 1257, his estate of Lorabar.[50] Bernard Zamora, a resident of Castellón, in his testament of 1272 left 20 solidi.[51] Tortosa citizens willed a number of gifts.[52] Evidence of other small bits of property crop up—a piece of land bought at Benifasá in 1270, another piece at Liria sold in 1260, and so on.[53] But relatively few Valencians seem to have helped the Cistercian work.

The earlier Cistercians had been against appropriations. Subsequently they had drifted toward an opposite practice, as a thirteenth-century archbishop of Canterbury complained with some feeling. "Though they be good men, if God please, still they are the hardiest neighbors that prelates or parsons could have; for where they plant their foot, they destroy towns, take away tithes, and curtail by their privileges all the power of the prelacy."[54] In consequence there were a number of brisk clashes in Valencia with their neighbors. Besides the central battles with the bishop of Tortosa, and with the Hospitallers over Rossell, there were other fights in plenty.

In 1258 the monks engaged in a boundary dispute with the knight holding Herbés.[55] In 1259 they came into conflict with the people of Morella and with its governor Peter Ferdinand of Pina over wood-gathering, grazing privileges, and other rights.[56] After skirmishing with their sister monastery of Escarp, they reached a compromise agreement in 1268 covering taxes and other problems in the countryside of Corachar, Castell de Cabres, and Bojar.[57] They met the Knights of Calatrava in a boundary dispute (1272),[58] and one Bartholomew over the estate of Pallerols in the Benifasá district (1274).[59] They battled the Templars in a "violent" controversy over Refalgari (1278),[60] with that Order again over crown rents owned by Benifasá, and with the bishop of Tortosa again over the first fruits of Ballestar where the monks maintained a grange (1278).[61] Legal clashes with both Tortosa and Peñarroya over their common borders were not settled until late in 1280. Meanwhile the Peñíscola bailiff William of Ceret had sequestered the monks' hamlet of Irca near Peñíscola; the crown investigator Peter Andrew heard both sides, had Irca returned to Benifasá, and in 1281 arranged a provisional compromise.[62]

Perhaps the litigations reflect the Cistercians' increasing financial troubles, as well as being a tribute to their large-scale, modernized system of land exploitation. In any case, the times were disjointed, and the stresses of contemporary feudal society were being felt severely within the Order's structure. The statute *de non acquirendo* had been promulgated in 1180 and repeated by the general chapters in 1190, 1191, 1205, 1206, 1229, 1230, 1239, 1240 and 1242, being discontinued thereafter as ineffective. Similarly, the monks had begun taking tithes before the thirteenth century, a practice finally approved perforce by the general chapter in 1240.

The monastery of Benifasá never became wealthy but it did achieve economic stability, if one may judge by the later ecclesiastical service tax of the fourteenth and fifteenth centuries. Though it paid less than a third of what Poblet and Holy Crosses contributed, Benifasá almost equaled the tax of St. Victorian and passed that of San Juan de la Peña.[63]

The general chapter of the Order meanwhile was rebuking the abbot of Benifasá for not attending its sessions. In 1275 the abbot petitioned to be allowed to miss one more time.[64] But by 1282 the general chapter at Citeaux was complaining that he had not shown up "for several years"; it ordered his deposition *ipso facto* if he should absent himself once more.[65] The names of at least twelve abbots in charge at Benifasá in the thirteenth century are known: John (1233), Arnold (1241), William of Almenar (1248), Peter Julia (1250), Berengar (1254), Arnold of Mantesana (1255), William Savartés (1260), Berengar of Concabella (1262), William (1283), Peter Vilarnan (1289), Raymond Bernard (1294), and Berengar of Beltall (1300).[66]

The monastic corporation constituted a secular jurisdiction, busily populating and administering its tiny province. A settlement movement was initiated at Bel (1242), at Refalgari (1242), at Benlloc and Herbés (1262), at Fredes (1267), at Malagraner (1269), at Font de la Higuera (1274), and so on.[67] Besides these organized efforts at group settlement, individual pioneers were brought in, such as the couple who received a grant in 1261.[68] By an agreement with the bishop of Tortosa—who kept a jealous eye on his share of the area—the monks took up the burden of populating the Benifasá Valley. Because they did the lion's share of the work, the bishop agreed to let them have two-thirds of the profit (1261).[69]

The Cistercians at Benifasá were also, in the tradition of their English contemporaries, a sheep-raising body. The relative frequency of documents touching upon this avocation leaves no doubt of its importance to the Benifasá economy. Castile was the dominant country of the European sheep industry at this time, but Aragon also shared in the profits. Conquered Valencia immediately became the "favorite winter grazing ground" for "most of the Aragonese and many of the Castilian transhumantes."[70] This situation had existed to some extent even when Valencia was Moslem; the Cistercians of Benifasá were well equipped to profit by its expansion now.

They were not the only sheep entrepreneurs in the region. The cattle and sheep industry, traditional here as far back as the days of Rome, grew greatly in the countryside of the Tortosa diocese all through the thirteenth

century, becoming in the next century "extraordinary." Here and in northern Valencia the brotherhood or guild of sheepmen (the *lligalo*) were an
important frontier institution; in the thirteenth century its headquarters was
at Morella.[71] It was a loose regional organization, unlike the imposing
mesta in contemporary Castile. The crown gave grazing privileges in the
kingdom of Valencia to other religious or lay groups besides the Benifasá
monks; by the early fourteenth century there will even be a special official
in charge of royal profits from alien sheep in Valencia.[72]

As early as 1237, King James gave to the projected Benifasá monastery
free pasturage on crown lands in the kingdom of Valencia and free passage
for their migratory flocks. These exemptions were confirmed from time to
time—as in 1247, just after the crown had reorganized the 1245 tolls on the
sheepwalks of the new kingdom, and in the sweeping exemptions of 1275.
The monastic flocks were defended against officious tax collectors.[73] Poblet,
the parent monastery of Benifasá, had fortified itself as early as 1225 with a
crown concession for free grazing throughout the countryside of Peñíscola,
Chivert, Pulpis, and "all other lands we shall be able to win from the Saracens." Benifasá, especially in its earlier years, must have shared in this boon.[74]

That Benifasá flocks were brought down to graze along the pleasant
coastlands can be seen from the privilege of free passage. Some of the grazing
areas are pinpointed in extant documents. Before the monks were properly
organized at Benifasá or had begun their church, for example, their flocks
were grazing the coastal country of Cuevas de Vinromá, of Pulpis, and of
Cervera (1244–1245). By 1252 the crown had given permission to the monks
to construct permanent corrals and buildings for their flocks along the empty
stretch of coastal country from Viñaroz down to Peñíscola.[75] Their flocks
were also present in Morella country.[76] Thus the monks brought their experience and skill to the less favored borderlands of the Valencian north.

Whatever its role as rural pioneer or as feudal lord in the less advanced
hinterland, Benifasá was above all a religious establishment. In the cloisters
of the central monastery of Benifasá, the choir monks continued that intense
life of prayer and asceticism and silence which they had learned so well at
Poblet. On the grange outposts, lay brothers lived out an example of prayer
and work. Of far less importance than what the monks did, was what they
were. They represented a dynamic and continuing Christian presence.
Solidly ensconced near the gateway to the conquered kingdom, they supplied in all its familiar appearances the traditional monastic backdrop to
the more vital work of the new Orders.

১০১ CISTERCIAN MONKS AT VALLDIGNA AND CARLET

Valldigna was begun by James II in 1297 under conditions similar to
those of Benifasá, but in a rich agricultural area far to the south.[77] Though

just beyond the strict chronological limits of this book, Valldigna must be included as the sister monastery of Benifasá in thirteenth-century Valencia, sharing its frontier function. The story goes that James II, returning from victories over the Moslems a year previously in Murcia, minded to found a monastery in thanksgiving, had pointed out this site to the abbot of Holy Crosses as they passed it. James remarked that this was a worthy place (*vallis digna*) for a Cistercian abbey. Three castles stood in the valley and at least four small settlements. The whole complex formed part of the general countryside or jurisdiction of prosperous Alcira. The Moslems here were numerous and well-off, as the large tax assessment by the king in 1257 proves. The name of the valley, Alfandech de Marignén, persisted even after the official change by the king to Valldigna.

The monks of Holy Crosses, not of Poblet, supplied the personnel. King James had donated to Holy Crosses, soon after the fall of Valencia, "an estate from which there will always be a substantial income for our monastery, to God's honor and yours, on the day of the Holy Cross every year."[78] This was no mean gift; the grateful Abbot Gerald gives it prominent place when, for this and other royal benefits, he plans to inscribe "your renowned name, to us sweet and precious," upon all the missals and altars of the monastery so that the monks will always remember to pray for him.[79]

James in 1263 confirmed a previously presented tax exemption for the Valencian properties of Holy Crosses, apparently dependent granges and the farms of vassals:

> Because we have made all goods of the monastery of the Holy Crosses frank and free . . . as is declared in the document . . . and especially the houses now held in the kingdom of Valencia, or in the future to be held: let no one seize or cause to be seized any appurtenances of the said houses, movable or immovable, be they in the hands of the monastery itself or in those of other persons. Indeed, they are to protect and defend, untouched and inviolate, these houses and the goods therein.[80]

At Valldigna now the monastery of St. Mary was to be founded by twelve monks and their abbot. John Bononat was the first abbot; Raymond of St. Clement, the second (from 1299). A chronicler of the Order in 1619 lists the first monks as Raymond of St. Clement, Raymond of Cambrera, Anthony Abadia, Peter Perales, Berengar Fortunoy, Bernard Valentine Carbonel, Beltran of La Cora, William Brancis (*sic*), James Tover, William of Bayanda, and James Rindadenes.[81]

A sweeping jurisdiction was conferred upon Valldigna to include the whole valley, the castles of Marignén and Alcalá, the towns here of Simat, Benifayró, Tabernes, Alfulell, Ráfol, Ombria, and Masalili—all to be held by the widest powers then possible, short of royal authority. To this the king added the unique privilege of extending this jurisdiction five miles out to sea; the monastery shield would therefore display a castle riding the ocean waves. Nearby Barig came in 1299, and later Rascaña. The crown also gave Barcheta in 1297 and Benavayren in 1298. The town and castle of Almusafes and Rugat in the Albaida Valley were purchased by the monks.[82]

The monastic jurisdiction was to last until 1814, and Valldigna was to become one of the richest and most famed of Aragon's monasteries. From the beginning, each abbot commenced his rule by going through the prescribed public ceremony of taking possession, before a notary. The valley parish, Alfandech, did not come under the Cistercians until 1335, though they acquired patronage of the church of Ráfol in 1301. When the monks will be temporarily unable to pay the agreed salary of 520 solidi in 1337, a Cistercian rector will have to be substituted for the secular holder.

Was there another monastery of Cistercians in Carlet? Several documents are encountered in the royal archives, of March 3–4, 1272, showing that one was planned. First, the king confirmed the monastery of Our Lady of Grace (Gratia Dei) in the donation a knight made them for this purpose.[83] Simultaneously James allowed them to receive of crown lands, "from purchase or gift or the generosity of the faithful, townships and other estates and properties to the sum of a thousand morabatins" or some 12,000 solidi.[84] Then, finally, he granted "a miliar of land for the monastery of Gratia Dei which is to be built in the country of Carlet."[85]

Very shortly after his conquest of Valencia, King James petitioned the general chapter at Citeaux for yet another abbey, and proffered a site in the new kingdom for their approval. This request the general chapter of 1245 processed:

> Inspection of the property, which the lord king of Aragon is assigning for the purpose of founding an abbey of monks in the kingdom of Valencia, is entrusted to the abbots of Peyrignac [in Guienne] and of Veruela [in Aragon] who are to visit the place etc., and whatever else etc., and it is to be the daughter of the monastery of Escaladieu.

The patron monastery named here was in the diocese of Toulouse, southeast of Tarbes.[86] This commission seems to have failed. At the general chapter of 1246, "the business of the abbey of monks, which the lord king of Aragon wishes to construct, is once again entrusted" to the two abbots; the abbot of Grandselve "will inform the two of this."[87] And in 1247 two abbots were told "to push the affair to its proper conclusion."[88] Nothing more however came of it.

By 1298 the Cistercians of the realm of Valencia were important enough to be spoken of, in a financial report of the Order itself, as a separate body: the monks "who are of the kingdoms of France, Navarre, Aragon, England, and Valencia."[89]

∞ The Carthusians

In the latter years of King James's reign there appeared in Valencia that strictest of all Orders of Christendom, the silent Carthusians. They led a life of extreme rigor. Little cottages centered around a cloister, and each monk lived mostly in his own residence as a hermit, in a silence nearly absolute, eating alone and only once a day, taking bread and water half the week, and burying himself in a life of prayer and union with God. The Grande Chartreuse had been functioning since 1100, but so difficult was its vocation that it counted only thirty-nine allied priories by 1300. One of these, an important establishment, the third of its Order to appear in Spain, was on the frontier of Valencia.

The Carthusians commanded the respect both of King James and of the active Dominican bishop, Andrew. Bishop Andrew, who might be thought to have imported a sufficiency of religious establishments by now into his lightly populated diocese, rather precipitately hastened to win the Carthusian services. Without thinking to ask the consent of their general chapter, he arranged to buy a property of the deceased magnate Simon Pérez of Arenós. This was a modest eminence in the quiet valley called Lullén, surrounded by pine-covered mountains. In 1272 King James, "wishing to foster by grace and favor your praiseworthy project, to the honor of Our Lord Jesus Christ and the glorious Virgin Mary," approved the bishop's plans for extensive land purchases.[90]

The valley of Lullén is in the mountain system north of Liria and south of Segorbe, a good distance to the northwest of the city of Valencia itself. Formal possession of this isolated loneliness was acknowledged by King Peter in 1277: the "place called Lullén, for building a monastery," with all its appurtenances, woods, and forests, and all kinds of lands, pastures, revenues, and rights.[91] Soon the monks were constructing their small church and nearby cells. They were allied to the great Carthusian priory of Ladder of God (Escala Dei); this was located in the hills west of Tarragona and should not be confused with the Cistercian Scala Dei, in Bigorre.[92] The first prior was Bernard Nomdedeu. The hamlet of Beniparrell near Torrente had been held by them from before 1297, but would be sold before 1313.[93] The patronage of the rich church at Liria, served by perpetual vicars, was transferred by the crown to the Carthusians here in 1273 with the approval of Pope Gregory X.[94]

A rather primitive little church now went up, with cells adjoining it. This priory of St. Mary of the Gate of Heaven (Porta Coeli) remained under the patronage of the bishop until 1301. Tithes were required in principle; but these the bishop first commuted to a token 10 solidi a year, and then waived forever. In the light of the Valencian tithe struggle even over places with feeble expectations of real settlement, Bishop Andrew's gesture reveals something of the character of the monks who could inspire it, and underlines the value of their contribution to the spirit of the frontier church.

∞ CISTERCIAN NUNS

The role of the nun on the Valencian frontier is less easy to assess than that of the cleric or male religious. Convents had an assured place in thirteenth-century society, representing the ideal of the bride of Christ. Here the medieval woman could struggle to raise her life to higher levels of devotion and selfless prayer. A host of good and sometimes very remarkable women graced these establishments; mystical writings of a high order issued from them. Such convents had become immensely popular and were multiplying on all sides.

An expansive movement like this posed serious problems of discipline. In a seizure of devotion the frivolous, the obstinate, and the haughty highborn would also be attracted to the ideal, and would remain to taint the communal purity or propriety of their respective convents. Some aristocratic parents even came to look upon convents as dumping places for their unwanted daughters, as happened so often in England.

The English, and to some extent the French, convents were more bedeviled by aristocratic dumping than were those of other lands. This may explain the lack of great English contemplatives or women of force and holiness, such as were produced in surprising number from now on in the multiplying convents of the continent. In the area today known as Belgium, however, the golden age of the convent drew to a close in the thirteenth century, as the nobility began its steady invasion.[95]

Where abuses got out of hand, a convent could decline into a club for local ladies or, worse, into truly pathological depths, with an accompanying din of hysterical slander.[96] Such convents were in the minority at this time, and usually involved within the house a minority of nuns; but incidents were frequent enough to give pause to prospective founders when selecting their Order. In Valencia this selection was wisely made. In this, as in so many other circumstances of its ecclesiastical origins, the kingdom of Valencia was singularly favored in its opportunities and in its use of them.

Of the nuns related to the monastic Orders, only the Cistercians were to be brought to the Valencian frontier. If the thirteenth century represented a twilight for the White Monk, an autumn in the history of his spiritual enthusiasm and social effectiveness, for his counterpart, the Cistercian nun, it represented a summertime of proliferation and growth. By 1228, in which year alone fifteen foundations were approved, the White Monks felt so submerged by the feminine wave that they decreed an end to further extension. Nuns might independently follow the Cistercian rule, but the general chapter henceforth refused to assume responsibility or authority over them.

It was a futile gesture. By mid-century the monks were even reduced to the expedient of securing a papal bull, safeguarding them from having new feminine communities imposed upon them by the pope. By the end of the thirteenth century the grand total of women's convents under their jurisdiction had risen to some seven hundred.

It was not until the thirteenth century that legislation for the nuns found a serious place in the general chapters of the Cistercian monks. This was then codified in 1240 and 1256. It added up to a severe Rule, involving enclosure, silence, manual labor, fasting, penance, and much prayer. The houses had to be adequately endowed; in practice, a convent was usually small and was sustained by only a few holdings. Aside from the proper work of prayer and austerity, other occupations were admitted. These included copying manuscripts, making liturgical vestments, and educating young girls of good family. Each house was an affiliate of an older established convent, and was subject to visitation by the abbess of that convent. The house was under the direction of a Cistercian monk; there might also be a chaplain appointed by him, and even a kind of detached grange nearby.

Behind the Valencian foundation was a woman of force. Though not herself a nun, she seems to have spent her declining years as doorkeeper at the convent. She is cherished in the annals of Cistercian Europe as one of their great and holy women, "the Blessed Teresa, queen." Teresa Giles of Vidaure was a noble lady possessed of beauty and character. She seems to have won completely the passionate heart of King James who gave her gifts of Valencian properties as early as 1238. Eventually, after the death of his second wife (sometime, that is, after 1251), he took her in clandestine marriage.[97] The bride was soon endowed with estates like Jérica castle west of Segorbe and a particularly handsome holding in Valencia city (both in 1255). This latter was the alcazar or fortified palace of the Moslem rulers of Valencia, the same property which the Moslem king of Valencia had once offered to convert into a royal residence for King James as part of a qualified surrender involving tributary status.[98]

In 1260 it seemed more practical to exchange this alcazar for the fine Zaidia or Lady's Palace, close to the city but across the river, to the north; this estate likewise included an alcazar.[99] The Zaidia, together with the nearby buildings along the city wall and a farm, had previously been held by the archbishop of Narbonne for his signal services at the siege of Valencia. Not long after these nuptial property transactions, however, the royal ardors cooled—or at least, under fresher winds, they burned in new directions. Twenty years of suffering lay ahead for the Lady Teresa.

It was at this time that the spurned wife turned her energies to the founding of a convent in her palace. The records of the general chapter at Citeaux for the year 1263 introduce the project. Teresa's offer was provisionally accepted in that year: "Item: Inspection of the place, in which the noble lady

Teresa Giles proposes to found an abbey of nuns, is entrusted to the abbots of Benifasá and Escarp. The abbot of Benifasá will inform the latter of this."[100] The monastery of Our Lady of Grace—Gratia Dei or, simply, La Zaidia—was inaugurated by Teresa early in 1265.

Teresa was not the only relative of the king guiding a convent. His sister Constance—widow of the viscount of Béarn who was killed on the Majorca crusade—recruited for and administered a convent in the Lérida diocese, first as a laywoman and then as superior; she founded another convent on Majorca. The Lady Sancha of Aragon (†1254) was a nun in the Lérida house. The king's daughter Mary (†1307) became superior of a convent in the Perpignan diocese.

In November of 1265 the crown exempted Teresa's convent from all legal restrictions on purchasing or inheriting properties. Episcopal permission for the establishment was belatedly sought and granted early in 1266. Citeaux had not as yet committed itself to acceptance. But the abbots of Benifasá and Escarp were formally involved, and the Cistercian convent of Vallbona had undertaken the actual organization, in the persons of the nuns Beatrice of Anglesola (who was to remain as abbess throughout Teresa's life),[101] Catalana of Montblanch, and Willelma.[102]

The wandering eye of the crusader king had by now definitively alighted upon the person of Lady Berenguela Alphonse. In an ill-advised moment James even had the impertinence to ask his admirer, Pope Clement IV, for an annulment of his marriage with Teresa (1266). Few kings can have been so cuttingly tongue-lashed by a pope as was the old warrior. Clement "marveled greatly" at the "irresponsible" request, so "antagonistic to God, abominable to the angels, and monstrous to men," by which the pope would be made to "share in the pollution of [your] illicit union." The papal letter concluded: "whom God has joined together, how shall the vicar of God put apart? Far from us be this crime!" And in mid-year, when congratulating his majesty on the brilliant conquest over the Moslems of Murcia, the pope thrust deeply into the wound. "Conqueror of armies, you are conquered by your own body, so badly that you have forgotten the fear of God and gravely offend the eyes of the divine majesty . . . , carrying about with you an adulteress, as a bad example to many."[103] On the perilous battlefield of Murcia, the king's confessor had refused him absolution.[104]

King James refused to take back his wife. Teresa now seems to have plunged more deeply into her monastic project. By 1268 the Cistercian chapter was finally prepared to admit her group. "The incorporation of the convent of nuns of the Grace of God in great Valencia is committed to the abbots of Escarp and Benifasá, and it is to be a daughter of Citeaux."[105] In February of that year the abbot of Benifasá, the bishop, and other dignitaries solemnly refounded the Zaidia convent. As an endowment the entire site was given, plus rentals from three separate places at the capital amounting to almost 250 mazmodins yearly. Teresa was to be patroness for life, with a veto right over postulants female or male—this last suggesting the attached cell or grange alluded to above.[106]

A later document affords a glimpse of the administrative officers. The abbess was the same Beatrice of Anglesola already spoken of; Catalana of Montblanch was prioress, with Suriana as cellaress and Elissenda of Tornamira as sacristan; the nun Margaret also appears. Other unnamed nuns are mentioned, of whom "counsel" has been taken.[107] Three noble ladies who became nuns in the convent in this century were Ursula Omedes, Beatrice of Agreda, and Violante of Cardona.[108]

The convent is mentioned in the royal registers half a dozen times. There was a privilege to the abbess and community in 1268 to "buy freely, in any place at all, properties up to the amount of a thousand morabatins," a total of 12,000 solidi.[109] At about the same time the king awarded them all the goods of the deceased Peter Maciot, confiscated by the crown because he had willed them to "unworthy persons who ought not to inherit the aforesaid goods."[110] The residence was then in process of reconstruction, to adapt it to the needs of religious life, and the confiscated properties were to be used "according to the counsel of the director of works there."[111] Shortly after this gift, the king transferred "our part, and all our rights which we receive and hold and ought to receive, from the mills in the confines of Campanar, in which we receive and should receive the third part."[112] Three years later he allowed them to build and operate a public oven (1271),[113] and to buy a piece of land "for a vineyard."[114] James also transferred to them his third-tithe of the Ruzafa suburb at Valencia city.[115]

The Zaidia nuns were remembered in a number of wills still extant. The citizen of Valencia William of Barcelona left to his niece Elissenda, who was a nun here, his rents "from certain mills located in the district of Patraix," a suburb southwest of Valencia city.[116] These were to continue in the possession of the convent after her death, and may possibly have been meant as a dowry. In 1272 the Lady Willelma left them ten solidi, through the abbess, and twelve pence for each nun.[117] A layman's will of 1275 left them 10 solidi.[118] Other considerable gifts accrued: 600 solidi in 1271 from the Játiva estates of Hugh of Baux; 100 solidi from Louis of Procida; and from Arnold Escrivá some Campanar lands and Ruzafa estates.[119]

Teresa seems to have remained at the convent, but to have traveled to her Jérica estates upon occasion for business purposes.[120] By 1274 the old king, infatuated with his latest mistress, had managed to wangle a divorce from the complaisant bishop of Valencia, a circumstance not calculated to increase admiration for local ecclesiastical policy.[121] The king pleaded that Teresa had been stricken with leprosy. Such a charge was irrelevant, and probably untrue; but it does indicate an illness of Teresa serious enough to suggest the fabrication. The saintly pope known to posterity as Blessed

Gregory X struck back immediately. In a letter of July 1275, he underlined the double adultery of which James and Berenguela were guilty. Later, ten months before James died, Pope Gregory ordered a change in the king's life within a week, instructing the archbishop of Tarragona to excommunicate the royal sinner in case of noncompliance and to put all Aragon under interdict.

Teresa survived her unfaithful husband only two years. She seems to have died in the spring of 1278.[122] In her will she left the convent 1,000 gold morabatins (some 12,000 solidi) with which to buy properties, another thousand morabatins for the construction or upkeep of the chapel, and a foundation to support four chaplains.[123] A series of Valencian towns and castles in her possession (some had already passed to her sons) were left to relatives, with provision for their reverting to the convent should the legatees die without issue. The towns of Altura and Castellmontán were given to the nuns. A clue to Teresa's enthusiasms and spirit is that the only preference she displays in her last testament, besides the Cistercian Order, is for the vital new Mendicant groups.

Buried by her own request at the convent and in the habit of a Cistercian nun, the "holy queen's" body remained incorrupt in the tomb. She had obviously been the soul and support of her establishment. It was to continue now for many centuries without her. But in her own turbulent time, so parlous for the spirit of religion and dedication, it owed much to her generosity, to her choice of rule, to her forceful role as patroness, and to the example she gave as portress in the convent.

ɷɕ Franciscan Nuns

The Franciscan movement for women was still in its vigorous, sturdy youth during the progress of the crusade against Valencia. The friend and intimate of St. Francis, St. Clare of Assisi, had founded the Order under his guidance; she continued to direct it until her death in 1253. (It was only at that late year too, that her rule finally was approved by Rome.) In 1241, three years after the fall of Valencia city, occurred the famous scene in which Clare bravely confronted the Saracen troops of Frederick II in the convent garden. Less than a decade after that event, and about fifteen years before the great woman's death, a convent of Franciscan nuns had been organized in Valencia city. Nuns of the Order had come to Barcelona in 1234, and to Balaguer and Valencia soon after; just after mid-century they were at Tarragona and Majorca; in 1267 they reached Tortosa, and by the end of the century Montblanch.[124]

These Poor Clares, or Poor Ladies of San Damiano, followed a rigorously severe life characterized by enclosure, perpetual silence, fasts, mortifications, and strict poverty. The practical lawyer-pope Innocent IV had just arranged

(1247) for communal ownership of properties, so that the convents might be decently supported. St. Clare had fought back with the fervor of the idealist, wishing to subsist on alms alone. One must not expect, then, to find any considerable holdings of the convent in this century. There would be need for financing the construction and the outfitting of the establishment at Valencia, for the soliciting of alms, and for the founding of chapels and chaplaincies. Beyond this, it is difficult to decide whether the Valencian convent had yielded to the practicalities and actually owned other supporting properties.

The nuns had been in Valencia city perhaps since 1239, but in more informal quarters than they subsequently occupied.[125] In the late 1240's the baron Simon Pérez, lord of Arenós and lieutenant general for the kingdom of Valencia, granted to the nuns his buildings just outside the city walls at their southwest angle; his condition was that the convent be placed here rather than somewhere in the Valencian countryside. The property bordered along the Moslem quarter, just beyond a suburb called Roteros. It was flanked by a major highway, and conveniently included a small mosque.[126] Wherever the convent may previously have been housed, it was already in juridical existence. The abbess at this time was Tarina, and the prioress was Catherine (though the two names involve problems).[127]

Another substantial gift came in 1249, from the noble Roderick and his wife, 60 solidi annually in rent from properties lying somewhat to the west of the city in the Mislata suburb.[128] The convent itself was named after a recently deceased and canonized in-law of King James, St. Elizabeth or Isabel of Hungary (1204–1231), wife of Ludwig IV of Thuringia, a Poor Clare tertiary and mystic known for her labors among the poor. The nuns had a public chapel and many loyal clients.

They appear quite often in the wills. The king, though he left 100 morabatins to each of four convents of Poor Clares in his realms, left 200 to that of Valencia city.[129] A quarter century earlier, in 1251, Queen Violante assigned to them the same amount, together with some valuable cloaks— presumably to be sewn into vestments.[130] That same year Raymond of Morella left them 5 solidi. In 1252 Dominic Calderón gave twelve pence. In 1255 the knight William Ochova Alemán provided 200 solidi for their church.

Canon Bertrand of Teruel in 1256 put aside 100 solidi for them, and the Lady Jordana settled a benefice worth 150 solidi a year on their church— where she also assigned her body to be buried. In 1258 Peter of Barberá remembered them with two solidi. In 1259 Lazarus of Vilella gave 10 solidi, and in 1261 Bernard of Nausa gave five. In 1262 the son of the Moslem ex-king of Valencia, a Christian convert named Ferdinand, willed them 200 solidi. In 1271 Barberan Oller left two solidi. Next year the king's concubine Berenguela Alphonse founded a chaplaincy at the convent (providing one

Simon of Ort as chaplain). In 1275 Peter Marqués gave 10 solidi; and in 1272 Willelma left 10, as well as twelve pence for every nun.[131]

By early 1252 the Abbess Tarina possessed sufficient capital to purchase from Peter Ferrer, a draper in the city, a farm in nearby Roteros suburb. Looking toward further purchases and gifts, she secured a license for this purpose from the king, up to the amount required for building her monastery.[132] The nun Raymunda here must have been a close friend or relative of Catalina, the wife of William of Montagut, for Catalina left her 30 mazmodins in her will of 1288, and gave 10 more to the convent.[133]

∞ DOMINICAN NUNS

The Dominican friars also had their counterpart in Valencia, an Order of cloistered nuns likewise in its vigorous formative years. St. Dominic was a senior contemporary of King James; in fact, it was partly owing to Dominic's presence and inspiration that James's father had lost the critical battle of Muret and with it his life. Dominic's first foundation, and the center from which his work was to develop and spread, was the convent for nuns at Prouille near Toulouse in 1205. The Dominicans were reluctant, however, to make a regular policy of governing convents of women. This struggle within the Order was still going strenuously at mid-century.

Meanwhile, a rule of life for nuns was being progressively worked out; this assumed its final form by 1259. Each convent was to be properly endowed, and was to hold property as a corporate community. An elected prioress would be superior. Each house was independent but subject to a hierarchy consisting of the provincial prior, the master of the Order, and the Dominican general chapter. The life was to be a mixture of prayer, penance, choir, and manual work.

The Dominican convent of St. Mary Magdalene stood just beyond the southern wall of Valencia city, close to the residence of the Knights of Mercy.[134] It must have been projected even before the capture of the city, for a small building had been donated toward its support and perhaps to serve as a temporary residence, in the 1239 division of city properties.[135] Immediately after the fall of the city, during those hectic days when the metropolitan was multiplying acts of jurisdiction to establish his claims, he reconciled "some mosque" as the chapel of St. Mary Magdalene; perhaps this was the temporary convent for the nuns who meant to come to Valencia.[136] Further gifts from king and benefactors followed. By 1246 work was going forward on a large convent. Even before that year Pope Innocent IV had already offered indulgences to all who would contribute to the building, and to such necessary furnishings as books, lamps, and clothing. Bishop Andrew of Valencia offered a similar indulgence in 1246, as did the prelates of Tarragona, Lérida, Zaragoza, Tortosa, and Majorca.[137]

In view of the contemporary opposition of the Dominicans to accepting new convents, the Valencian house seems to have remained juridically a local Augustinian foundation, under the special direction of the Valencian Dominicans and with Dominican admixtures in their rule. They were fully incorporated as Dominicans only by the bull of Honorius IV in 1286, and by the letters of the Dominican master in the following year. A Valencian Dominican of noble family, Bernard Riusech, was named their prior.[138]

King James speaks of their church in a grant of mid-1271: "we grant to you, Alanda of Romaní . . . and to all the ladies of that monastery . . . forever as much space, from the property where the market is held in the city of Valencia, next to your houses and church, as is required for the entrance way to the door of your church."[139] Alanda or Adelaide de Romaní was possibly a relative of Arnold of Romaní, a man with wide holdings in Valencia who figures many times in James's registers for this period, once as bailiff of Valencia. In 1268, James had granted this prioress 10 Josephine mazmodins annually (40 solidi), to be collected from the rents of certain mills.[140] And, when an estate of over two hundred jovates came onto the market in 1271, after the death of its owner Bononat Gía, a crown functionary, King James allowed Prioress Alanda to buy it.[141]

The Dominican nuns were remembered in many wills. The queen's porter Aparisi left them 10 solidi in 1247; the draper Peter Oller 10 in 1249; in 1251 Peter Armer and Raymond of Morella each willed them 5 solidi. Dominic Calderón provided twelve pence in 1252; William Ochova Alemán 100 solidi in 1255; Canon Bertrand of Teruel 50 solidi in 1256; Peter of Barberá twelve pence in 1258; Lazarus of Vilella 10 solidi in 1259; and Bernard of Nausa 5 solidi in 1261. Ferdinand Pérez, the son of the Moslem ex-king of Valencia, left 50 solidi in 1262; Barberan Oller willed 2 in 1271. Willelma gave 10 solidi for the prioress in 1272 and twelve pence for each nun. Peter Marqués left 10 solidi in 1275. Catalina the wife of William of Montagut willed them another 10 in 1288.[142] Other properties were acquired later; for example, James II will give them his third-tithe for the town and region of Foyos near Valencia.[143]

A letter of 1282 from King Peter to the prioress of the house at Valencia city, herself of a very wealthy family, requested her "to accept as a sister and nun of the said monastery, at our request, Agnes the sister of William of Sala, scribe of the venerable bishop of Valencia."[144]

∞ OTHER NUNS: MAGDALENES, AUGUSTINIANS, AUGUSTINIAN CANONESSES

There was yet another group, settled perhaps close to those Augustinian nuns who became Dominicans. They even bear the same name, St. Mary Magdalene. These were the Magdalenes or White Ladies. Their chronological origins are obscure, but their convents emerge into the light of frequent documentation in the thirteenth century; perhaps this century could even be accounted their time of origin. They appear in Germany in the early thirteenth century, in France only from 1272, and in Valencia perhaps from 1239.

The vocation was an unusual one, since it sought recruits among wayward women—by which term one may understand anything from former prostitutes or incorrigible sinners to simple unfortunates. The name Magdalene thus had a literal and very Christian meaning. But in fact many innocent women were drawn to this life of penance and humility, so that some houses were completely composed of them. Such a convent was often at once a striking work of social rehabilitation and a monument to the basic teachings of Christianity. As the century progressed, numbers of these convents were to affiliate with the strict new Mendicant Orders.

Was this vocation represented on the Valencian frontier? There are provocative bits of evidence which hint at this; but it is only in deference to the authority of the great antiquarian Teixidor that one can give them much weight.[145] Detailed contemporary wills inexplicably seem to overlook this single convent. Besides, the appellation "Sisters of Penance" was a common one for many penitential convents of quite different origins; and many groups precisely so named were then under Dominican direction. More seriously, the term appears in the documentation of the previous Augustinian-Dominican house at Valencia. Still, it is just possible that there existed a sort of dependent ministry, a species of third Order attached to and supported by the main convent of St. Mary Magdalene. Such a suggestion may find support, though it is unlikely, in the somewhat tautological reference of 1265 to "the church or monastery of Blessed Mary Magdalene, and the community [*conventus*] of nuns [*dominarum*] who are to dwell there for reason of penance."[146]

This conclusion may also appease the lovers of legend, who feel an attachment for the tale told by the fourteenth-century James Roig. The poet tells how an outraged husband, one of the high nobles on the Valencian crusade, founded such a convent to confine his unchaste and wandering wife:

> la pecadora
> qui gran senyora
> fon, e contesa.

Quite apart from the dangers of using creative poetry as a source of narrative history, the legend may have some relevance to the other convent or possibly to its ministries.

Returning again to solid ground, an establishment of Augustinian nuns, the Ladies of St. Julian, may be noted. They were situated beyond the city walls to the north, on the road to Murviedro (Sagunto). Their name derives from the small sub-church of St. Julian which was a dependency of the city parish of Holy Savior from about the year 1250.[147] These nuns seem to have appeared only in the last decades of the century. They turn up occasionally in the testaments of the day. For instance, the will of the widow of Bernard William of Mompalau left them three solidi in 1298.[148] They were the feminine counterpart of the Mendicant Augustinian friars, but they had no part in the 1256 union nor were they a confederation. Their houses were autonomous, often with some sympathetic bond or affiliation with the friars. Their life was an open and active one, the activity varying from place to place.

Another type of Augustinian nun—counterpart to the older Augustinian canons who were halfway between the monastic and diocesan clerical states—was the convent founded by the king at Alcira. The documentation for endowing the convent, which James "in pious gesture built and endowed"[149] for them there in 1273, is useful for rounding out one's knowledge of what was required to found such an establishment. In that year the king handed over to the Lady Timbors, prioress of the Augustinian canonesses of St. Mary Magdalene at Montpellier, a complicated series of rents to be used in founding and supporting a house of the Order at Alcira.[150]

The rents came especially from mills operating on the Albaida River and from such public properties as ovens and meat-stalls; Játiva rents were prominent. This ultimately represented an endowment of over 1,300 solidi per annum. King James laid down certain conditions: the community was to consist of thirteen nuns, each to be replaced on death; the income must be spent on this house, none of it going to the governing house at Montpellier. The manner of electing the local prioress was also spelled out. The document names three of the nuns coming to found the convent under Lady Timbors: Willelma, Bonafos, and Auda.

In a companion document the king listed the holdings given: fifteen groups of mills, of which they are to have the king's rent (here, usually half of the profits); a plot of land; rents totaling 380 solidi; 60 more solidi; 60 morabatins; and from ovens at Játiva rents of 30, 22, 20, and 40 solidi.[151] In 1275, King James gave: "permission . . . to buy for your purposes, a farm . . . which fronts on your aforesaid monastery, and to buy in the country around Alcira a hundred pedonates of crown land to make into vineyards."[152] In 1279 King Peter confirmed his father's gifts to the convent, and renewed their privilege for buying Alcira crown lands; he added the boon of his royal protection over the establishment.[153] These nuns contributed generously to the crusade tax, apparently rejecting the privileged status granted to most other religious Orders in Valencia. In 1279 they gave 306 solidi; in 1280 they gave three separate contributions, totaling 625 solidi, one of the largest sums taken that year.[154]

Some years after the turn of the century, a terrible flood wrecked their building. The bishop of Valencia, moreover, had appropriated and alienated much of their endowment for his own purposes.[155] As a consequence, the nuns thought it wise to remove to Játiva. They changed their affiliation as well, becoming Cistercians under the direction of Valldigna (1316).[156]

As for hermitages for women, and the associations of Mendicant tertiaries so prominent and effective at this period in Europe, there is no information for Valencia in its frontier period. In the hospitals like St. Vincent's or St. Lazarus, pious laywomen of the towns of Valencia undoubtedly added their services to those of the staffs, as was done in the rest of Christendom.

The period of the Valencian crusade, with the previous generation or two, saw a release of women's energies into service outside the home. If it was hardly the Female Era (tempus muliebre) hailed by the feminist abbess St. Hildegard of Bingen (†1179), in which the public efforts of women were destined to restore a Christendom shattered by male ineptitude, it did offer many women some public role in the community. The strong tide of feminine monasticism was reflected here in Valencia. Along with the monks, who continued to be an important element in the Reconquista settlement now as in centuries past, the nuns too found a place on the frontier for their devotion, example, and talents.

XIII

THE HOSPITALS OF THE
KINGDOM OF VALENCIA

Of special importance in the social fabric of the new kingdom was the hospital, an institution possessed of its own juridical personality.[1] By the middle of the thirteenth century, the hospital movement was in full flower over Christendom. Of the thirty medieval hospitals in Rome, for example, four were founded in the eleventh century, six in the twelfth, ten in the thirteenth, five in the fourteenth, and five in the fifteenth. The Italian communes were foremost in the possession of municipal hospitals; by the fourteenth century the city of Florence had thirty such institutions. Some of the hospitals were quite large, but most were fairly small—from seven to twenty-five beds.

England could boast one hundred and fifty-five hospitals at the beginning of the thirteenth century and four hundred and fifteen by its end; the number rose to over six hundred during the next fifty years. In 1250 Toulouse in Languedoc had twelve hospitals plus seven small leprosaries, five hospices, and six refuges—thirty institutions, "all but five of which had been founded after 1180."[2] The realms of Aragon shared in the hospital movement. Barcelona in the thirteenth century had nine hospitals and hospices; one of them also cared for abandoned children. At least eleven hospitals appear haphazardly in the thirteenth-century documents for Zaragoza; there were probably more. Tortosa city had at least half a dozen. Tarragona must have preferred parish hospitals, as did Zaragoza, since only two big central hospitals appear in the thirteenth-century records.[3] Castile too was rich in hospitals, leprosaries, hospitality houses, and reception centers for redeemed captives.[4] In the realms of King James the parliament of 1225 at Tortosa placed all hospitals and their holdings under crown protection.[5]

Such hospitals admitted Christian, Jew, or Moslem. The rector could be a layman, but religious groups usually staffed them. It was a pious custom for ladies and townsmen to visit and cheer the sick. The hospitals supplied a desperately needed service to the community. And they were an expression of concern about the poor, as well as a reminder and stimulus for such concern. Thus, the hospitals were a social service for the poor and ill, a civilizing factor benefiting their total environment, and a contribution toward a resolution of tensions inherent in the presence of extensive poverty.

The hospitals combined care of the sick and care of the poor. The well-off could afford to have doctor and nurses at home. The documents therefore

237

speak, as a rule, only about care for the "poor."[6] But by indirection, in an aside or a legacy, it is shown that these poor were sick people and not just guests. Even as great a scholar as Teixidor was led astray by the references to the "needy"; he came deliberately to the conclusion that hospitality, not care of the ill, was the purpose of a great hospital like St. Vincent's at Valencia.[7] Actually St. Vincent's had two establishments for the sick: one building for men and one for women. Care of the sick was neither absent in them nor a minor duty.[8] In the hospitals of Valencia for which there is good documentation, this identity of "poor" and "sick" is assumed.[9]

One sees this also in the thirteenth-century novel *Blanquerna*, written by the Majorcan Raymond Lull who was familiar with the Valencian and the analogous Majorcan frontiers. He describes the founding of a hospital for the "poor and destitute," where all is done "in the service of the poor"; only in a later chapter does one find that the workers daily "tended the sick" here and "healed many sick folk in the hospital."[10] Lull describes the establishment in detail, including the many servitors and even the beds for the sick; the poorest bed had to be contrived from vine-branches, straw, and a coverlet.[11] Maternity wards were common enough in larger hospitals; orphans or abandoned children might be received.[12] Physicians were not resident, but contributed their services as in a clinic.[13]

There were also other, less formal, ways of caring for sick people who were poor or of small means. The trade confraternities cared for their own; the Cistercian monasteries like Benifasá and Valldigna in the Valencia kingdom had both hospice and infirmary; and a portion of the first fruits in each parish was set aside for its poor. But the hospitals were the cornerstone and major institution for this social service. Care of the sick was here elevated to the status of "a genuine religious observance," on a sustained and dedicated level by a religious congregation, often with lay help.[14]

☙ HOSPITALS AND HOSPICES AT VALENCIA CITY

A well-established hospital comprised a group of buildings, including chapel or church, hospital for ill women and one for ill men, house of hospitality for the poor, some housing for domestics and lay staff, a monastery or religious residence, and lesser buildings connected with administration, kitchen, farming and the like.[15] At the other end of the scale, there could also be simple hospices and convalescent houses. The elaborate hospital of St. Vincent, just outside Valencia city, was a national shrine as well; for this reason it will be treated at length in Chapter XV.

"At the head of the bridge of the city of Valencia" and in the parish of Holy Savior stood the Trinitarian hospital for the sick, St. William's.[16] Though readily accessible by the bridge, it enjoyed the solitude of fairly open country and the amenity of a flowing river, circumstances prized as hygienic by the medieval man. The Order of the Most Holy Trinity for the Ransom of Captives conducted the hospital.

This Order was a fairly new creation; its founder, the Provençal St. John of Matha, had died only recently in 1213. The mother house was at Cerfroy near Chateau-Thierry; but their active headquarters, where the grand minister resided, was St. Maturin's at Paris (whence their alternate name "Maturins"). Contemporaries sometimes confused these Trinitarians with the Mendicant Orders. Like the Mendicants they were still in their first vigor. The members were commonly called the "Donkey Brothers," because of their predilection for that humble form of transport in an age of pomp and circumstance. Their costume was a white tunic emblazoned with a distinctive cross: the upright bar was red, the crossbar blue.

Innocent III allowed the Trinitarians to be organized in 1198, just a decade before King James was born. James's father King Peter had welcomed them to Lérida, in Catalonia. In France James's great contemporary St. Louis IX especially favored them, choosing Trinitarians as chaplains, taking them on his crusades, and installing them in the chateau of Fontainebleau. In the thirteenth century over a hundred houses were founded from Canterbury to Bethlehem, Valencia being among the first fifty. Elsewhere in James's realms the Order worked at Daroca (1206), Tortosa (1211), Montpellier (1216), Urgel, Lérida, Teruel, Palma de Mallorca, and Barcelona.

The contemporary bishop of Acre described them at length, with appropriate reflections on their being a lesson to one and all. The head of the Order resided at Marseilles, he wrote; the brothers ate meat only on Sundays or feast days, used no linen for themselves, cared for the sick personally, and divided all revenues into three parts in honor of the Trinity: a part for the sick in their hospitals, one for ransoming captives, and one for the support of the Order.

The Trinitarians had been invited down from Toulouse less to ransom captives than to conduct a hospital. Only a third of their income went into ransoming, and in Spain their ransom efforts were much inferior to those of their colleagues in Valencia, the Mercedarians or Knights of Mercy. Still, ransoming was their major work, so that their hospitals sometimes were ephemeral.[17] In Valencia their hospital establishment fortunately proved to be solid and lasting.

William Escrivá founded the Valencia hospital in 1242. The city had only recently been conquered, so actual organization of the hospital seems to have been slow. Besides, William soon died, leaving his project in the hands of his father, also named William. In 1256 the elder William writes:

> Let all know that . . . William Escrivá, the guardian of the children and heirs of his son the former William Escrivá deceased, founded (according to the last wishes of the same William Escrivá, deceased) a xenodox or hospital at the head of the bridge of the city of Valencia, and put in charge of it the minister and Order of the Holy Trinity.[18]

This elder William was a knight, a royal counselor who received both the secretariat of the conquered city and the fief of Patraix. He was a man of great wealth and prominent in local affairs, serving as justiciar of Valencia and twice as jurate. He and his family were particular patrons of the Valencia Dominicans.

It is not easy to untangle the immediate family spoken of in this document. The elder William died perhaps in 1260; his son William died sometime before 1256; his other son Arnold flourished (he was bailiff of Valencia city and procurator general of the realm of Valencia) through the next reign. The younger William had children, and Arnold had at least one son, William; this latter may be the William Escrivá of Ibiza who was to increase the family fortunes and die in 1303.[19] The senior William also founded a chaplaincy in the St. William's hospital church, endowed with two hundred mazmodins from his Valencian rents. The titular patron of the monastery and probably of the benefactors was William the duke of Aquitaine; the duke had become a solitary (†1156), was canonized in 1202, and was currently enjoying a vogue.[20]

St. William's appears only infrequently in Valencian wills. The earliest legacy for the hospital dates from 1251. In 1258 Peter of Barberá left 12 pence. In 1272, the Lady Willelma left 10 solidi. The Lady Raynes, apparently under treatment at the hospital, or else an oblate or volunteer worker there, willed them a vineyard sometime before 1276:

> At the request of the venerable Brother A., abbot of Fontfroide [southwest of Narbonne], we grant you, Brother Peter of Sigena, minister of the hospital of St. William, a Valencian establishment of the Order of the Most Holy Trinity, that you may purchase or keep, for the work of your institution or aforesaid hospital, a certain vineyard which Lady Raynes, a woman of the hospital, left you in her will. However, [this is to be] on condition that the said vineyard be always crown land subject to feudal service to you and to us as are other crown estates.[21]

If the continued receipt of legacies is an index to popularity, however, it does not follow that their relative absence always betokens little esteem. The Escrivá clan were wealthy enough to arrange all by themselves a competent endowment for St. William's. The scale on which the hospital was operating by mid-1256 suggests that they had done so. In that year, Brother Ferrer and his Trinitarian community petitioned the bishop for approval of their plans to raise an "oratory" or "church" for their clients. A reference in this petition to the "establishing" of a hospital already in operation seems strange. In fact, it indicates that the Order, firmly rooted and with a clientele, was in a position to request formal approbation by the bishop, including elevation of the church, already actually constructed with its ambient cemetery, to a more favorable canonical status.

The Trinitarians were obviously regarded by diocesan authorities as potential rivals of the city parishes. The answer to their petition fenced them in with restrictions. Parishioners were not to be regularly admitted. The street entrance to the church was to be closed on feast days until the parish Mass was over. (This closing of church doors was a stipulation found elsewhere; it was similarly imposed, for example, on two contemporary hospitals in England.) Half of the free-will offerings at St. William's were to go to the parish. Only the personnel and resident paupers could be buried in the cemetery without special ecclesiastical permission. Confessions and communions of all except the religious community were to be taken care of by the pastor of Holy Savior's, unless he was unable to come. Full tithes and first fruits were to be paid on all their lands, except for a single garden farm.[22] All this may indicate a desire to inhibit potential growth of the hospital as a spiritual power. St. William's position in this respect contrasted strongly with the power of a hospital like St. Vincent's.

Disparate bits of data tell a little more about St. William's hospital. The pastor of St. William's church of the Holy Trinity, who was perhaps a diocesan priest, contributed 44 solidi to the crusade tax of 1279, and 41 solidi to that of 1280.[23] The confraternity of calkers seems to have been under the care of the hospital's Trinitarians.[24] The rents supporting St. William's attracted the greedy fingers of James Pérez, the son of King Peter. In 1285 the king had to order the justiciar and the municipal authorities to resist such exploitation.[25] Another document of that year reveals that the hospital had been receiving twelve morabatins rent from the commercial taxes of the capital.[26]

The Hospitallers of St. Mary of Roncesvalles were also established at the capital city. They were noted at this time for their care of the sick and of poor pilgrims in the hospital of the "Blessed Mary of Roncesvalles, at the gateway into Spain."[27] They had organized in the last century as a local group of canons regular to care for sick and weary Compostela pilgrims passing through the diocese of Pamplona. They dressed like the canons of Pamplona cathedral. They also had three establishments in France.[28] A contemporary cardinal eulogizes them, along with another hospital at Rome and one at Constantinople, as outstanding in Christendom for their "warm charity, deep piety, uprightness of life, and severity of discipline."[29]

These hospitallers of Roncesvalles may well have attended the siege of Valencia, helping the wounded. But perhaps the king invited them here shortly after the city's surrender. King James offered them a third of the township of Puzol in 1243, which he had bought (possibly from William of Entenza), plus some Murviedro vineyards and rural houses.[30] They installed themselves in the suburban parish church of Holy Cross, in Roteros suburb, just beyond the city's western wall. Their commander Lope was pastor here in 1245. They acquired some lands in Roteros. And "all the churches of Roteros" had been committed to their care as early as 1242. In 1272 Prince Peter gave the Roncesvalles commander a letter of safeguard in the kingdom of Valencia.[31]

No unpleasantness arose between them and the bishop. A settlement of revenues and jurisdiction came swiftly, in an amicable document glowing with welcome for these "canons and brothers," whose reputation for charity and work among the poor "obliges" the Valencian church to encourage them.[32] The brothers were to have their parishes, all the usual revenues, plus a third of the tithe in the area of Puzol and Roteros—the latter including Castellón, Raytor, Rafalaxat, Vinocabo, and Ort. The vicar could be a diocesan priest or one of their own, though the bishop required canonical obedience and reserved the granting of the cure of souls.

Contemporary Valencian wills rarely mention the Roncesvalles hospitallers, a circumstance which suggests that their hospital was quite small. Perhaps their strong identification with one locality, Pamplona, made them at once less cosmopolitan and more foreign than the other Orders, and thus affected their fortunes. The knight William Ochova Alemán left them a generous 50 solidi in 1255.[33] Bishop Jazpert of Valencia gave their hospital twenty solidi in his will, later in the century.[34] Their land holdings were important enough nevertheless to win them inclusion in a roll call of the important Valencian lords obliged to send a military contingent in the 1277 troubles.[35]

The hospital of St. Lazarus at Valencia city specialized in incurable and contagious diseases. Was it conducted by the Order of St. Lazarus of Jerusalem? This is by no means certain, though the early appearance of the house in Valencia suggests initiative by some organization. The Order, at its most expansive and active then, also became at the time of the Valencian crusade a military Order fielding troops in the East. Its insignia was a green cross. The houses were each autonomous; there were over eight hundred of them in thirteenth-century France alone. Support derived largely from properties contributed by the incurables themselves. They lived together with the religious in a close, permanent, almost familial relation under an Augustinian rule. In some houses the superior had to be himself a leper; it has been said that the Grand Master had to be both a knight in the Order and a leper.[36]

At the city of Valencia the Lazarus hospital was just outside the city, on the road to Murviedro.[37] Testaments contain such items as: "I leave two solidi for the sick people at St. Lazarus" in 1251; 12 pence "to the leper house of Valencia" in 1258; 50 solidi in 1263 "to the lepers of St. Lazarus"; an item of 5 solidi in 1275; one of 12 pence in 1274; one of 10 solidi in 1277; and in 1279 one of 12 pence for "the sick of St. Lazarus." The wife of Blaise Peter of Fuentes in 1276 willed the hospital her bed.[38] St. Lazarus seems to have had its confraternity also.[39] In the crusade tax lists of 1279 and 1280, the hospital chaplain returned a contribution of respectively 39 and 36 solidi.[40] There were similar "leper" houses in James's realms at mid-century at Vich, at Montpellier, and elsewhere.[41] By the end of the century leprosy itself, though still a problem, will be on the wane.

The brotherhood of St. James, the benevolent fraternity of clergy and laymen described in Chapter VII, conducted a small hospital or hospice of their own. This is discovered quite by chance, fully functioning, in a late document of 1316.[42] It does not seem to be identified with any of the other hospitals.[43] At the turn of the century, in 1301 or 1302, the queen in her testament was to found the municipal hospital of St. Lucy.[44] The municipal hospital of St. Mary, even better endowed, will be given by a citizen in 1311.[45] The Knights Hospitallers hospital in the city is discussed below. A number of other hospitals followed in the next century.

১৯ঃ HOSPITALS ELSEWHERE IN THE KINGDOM OF VALENCIA

Near the end of King James's life, a landowner in Villarreal received the king's permission to endow a hospital there:

> We give and concede to you Peter Daher, settler of Villarreal, permission to construct and build in that town a hospital for sheltering the poor, and to transfer and assign to the same hospital buildings and estates which we granted you in that town.[46]

This institution prospered, receiving Peter's remaining estate at his death. In 1290 the procurator of this hospital, a Bernard of Nomdedeu, received some land from Bernard Gostanc and his wife Elisenda on which to plant a vineyard to provide wine for the poor.[47] This was a municipal hospital, and so the gift was accepted "in the presence, and into the possession, of the city fathers." It was a separate juridical person at this time, with tutelage by the city council.[48]

A similar city hospital was planned in Segorbe, as can be seen from a record of land exchange in the royal register. Since García Anadón had previously had his land confiscated, so that the city council might construct a hospital on it, in 1271 he was receiving in recompense "another plot of ground."[49] The hospital may well have been founded some years before this act of restitution. It was located beside the Teruel gate.

While King James was besieging Murcia in 1266, he granted Peter of Soler, perhaps a relative of the cathedral dignitary, "a hospice in Játiva, with its appurtenances and with all present and future improvements, for the maintenance of the hospital and for the hospital there constructed and built."[50] This "hospital of the poor at Játiva"[51] is mentioned in the *Book of Land Division* as receiving three jovates partly planted in vines. The king also gave it three hundred solidi from local revenues, to support a chaplaincy.[52] When the Franciscans came in 1295 to establish themselves at Játiva by invitation of the city council, they occupied some buildings outside the walls which had been used as a hospice for poor transients.[53] This may have been yet another Játiva hospital. The claim for a Trinitarian hospital at Játiva by 1259 has little probability. The Order does seem to have had one at Murviedro by 1275.[54]

In Algar, a town not far from Segorbe, another hospital operated. Its owner transferred it in 1251 to the Knights of Mercy.[55] These Mercedarians may also have had a small hospital at Puig, an important shrine; the patronal family there richly endowed, and perhaps even refounded, this hospital early in the fourteenth century.[56] There was a Mercedarian hospital at Denia[57] and another at Borriol.[58] But these Mercedarian establishments in general were probably refuges connected with their ransom work, or hospices.

A hospitaller Order almost unnoticed in the history of Valencia is the Antonines—the Brothers Hospitallers of St. Anthony. They had been founded around 1095 by Gaston of Dauphiné, next to the church of St. Anthony at St. Didier de la Mothe, and had spread through France, Spain, and Italy. Eventually the sick in the medieval papal household were to come under their care. The epidemic disease of St. Anthony's Fire had been their specialty. They dressed in a black habit, marked with a blue "T" or cross of St. Anthony. Previously laymen, they had just been reorganized with monastic vows in 1218. From 1297 on, their canonical status was to be that of canons regular under the rule of St. Augustine; in 1777 they would merge with the Knights of Malta.

A single document, copied in 1811 from the archives of Valldigna monastery, tells much of what can be known about them in the kingdom of Valencia. They established themselves here before 1276. Their commander for the dioceses of Valencia and Tortosa was one Geoffrey (Jaufrid) of Casca. They had their regional center at Fortaleny in Valencia. In July of 1276, William Rocafull by means of this document formally consigned to Geoffrey in person and to the Order, "the chapel which I caused to be constructed from the buildings I own in the village of Fortaleny." Properties were assigned as endowment. A special condition was that the commander had to reside here for a longer time each year than he spent elsewhere in the realm of Valencia.[59] It is reasonable to suppose, therefore, that this residence involved a small hospital. The sense of the document is that the Order managed other houses in the kingdom of Valencia, presumably including hospitals.

In 1290 the commander of the Order there, Garino of Romaní, received permission from King Alphonse at Valencia to buy "lands and houses and the like" owned by the crown, anywhere in the kingdom of Valencia.[60] There is no information on the use actually made of this document, but a similar privilege of 1330 was used to buy lands in 1333 at Orriols near Valencia city and to build a hospital.[61]

A hospital at Burriana appears in the *Book of Land Division*, under the care perhaps of a Knight Hospitaller.[62] The hospitals of the knights have left only rare traces, though this had once been among the primary works of their institute. Respect for the poor, whom they cared for in hospices and hospitals, was so strong among the knights, according to a contemporary, that it was their habit to "call the poor 'Sirs.'" An obstacle to interpretation in Hospitaller documents, of course, is the ambiguity inherent in the word "hospital" then, as well as the fact that legacies and other documents do not feel it necessary to single out and express this aspect of the Order's work.[63]

In the case of Valencia city, a document drawn during the siege allowed them houses for a convent, a hospital, and a cemetery for those who should die in the hospital.[64] There is another hint in a patronage contract concerning the parish of Cullera in 1256, where the pastor agreed to give 60 solidi annually not only to the Order but also to the poor of their hospital.[65] Elsewhere in Christendom their hospital work had seriously declined, as their military aspect became predominant.[66] But care of the sick may still have been an important vocation for the Knights Hospitallers in the kingdom of Valencia.

Since all these hospitals and hospices were uncovered in stray documents, some of them quite indirectly, it is logical to suppose that others existed as well, of which no records survive. Nor should it be forgotten that the indigent sick at this period often received care in their homes from visiting confraternity members or from tertiaries.[67] Moreover, parish hospitals were apparently common in Aragon; thirteenth-century Zaragoza had one in every parish.[68]

The parochial establishments probably were hospices. The traditional situation for both city and parish churches is described in a late decree (1343) from the Tortosa diocese. The description would probably apply also to the Valencian diocese in the southern part of the kingdom. In this decree the bishop indignantly reprimanded the "very many rectors and vicars" who provided no hospitality "in the domiciles, hospices, or buildings" of their churches. "Very many" who had hospices displayed only a few beds, or beds "of little value, broken, in disrepair, worn out"—all this "to the horror of the viewer rather than to the honor of the rector." The poorest churches were expected to maintain at least four decent beds complete with bedclothes.[69]

৯৭ REGARD FOR THE POOR

Even when the hospital was municipally owned, the religious wellsprings for its existence and for the sacrifices involved in endowing and maintaining
10—I

it were clearly expressed. "It is a religious thing and great charity to support the poor of Christ, who are in need and suffer want," as the Valencian Bernard Gostanc wrote in helping the Villarreal hospital.[70] The same spirit was written into the *Furs* of Valencia. The courts were commanded to hear both poor and rich, and to assign a lawyer free to the poor, because "we ought to maintain in their rights orphans, widows, people elderly and weak, and those whom one should pity as being borne down by poverty and enfeebled by misfortune."[71]

Mendicancy was allowed, since public aid fell short of solving the problem of poverty. But authorities legally controlled such begging, and they prosecuted frauds. Housing was supplied to poor folk, not only at hospitals and religious establishments but even in the division of the conquered city's buildings; one house went to "the poor old woman Loba," another to "two poor people," a "very small house" to a poor man, others to a poor woman and to "some poor knight."[72]

The ban in Valencian law against clerics exercising the profession of civil law incorporated a proviso that they might offer their services in court for the "wretched," a technical term applying to the widow, orphan, ill, old, blind, mutilated, or generally handicapped.[73] Because a Christian should not afflict the poor, but mercifully help them, a law of 1255 obliged the city jailer to let his prisoners go, when legally freed, without demanding a further stay from those too poor to pay rent for the lodging so far provided.[74] The dowering of poor maidens was a favorite medieval philanthropy, often found in thirteenth-century Valencian wills; it meant the difference between being able to find a husband or remaining a burden on one's poor relatives.

An intriguing aspect of the medieval character is the manner in which the mystical entered into even the most prosaic material, so that from high piety issued the lowly and pragmatic. A clear example of this was the passion for building bridges, in the name of Christian brotherhood, for the convenience of travelers, pilgrims, and merchants. It was one of the common items remembered in Valencian wills. Direct organization was resorted to also; King James licensed one Peter Mariner to solicit alms for constructing in wood a rural bridge in the Denia district.[75] The diocesan almshouse or *almoyna*, founded around the end of the century, is perhaps indicative of the previous drift of interests; here, under the direction of two priests, the hungry would be fed and alms distributed.[76]

Valencians were generous to the poor, judging from their wills; many singled out the "ashamed" poor who concealed from the general public the fall in their fortunes. Peter Oller, the draper who made his will in 1249, left 300 solidi to the poor, 200 more for clothing them, and 100 solidi in alms to be distributed by St. Vincent's and by the Dominicans; the remainder of his fortune, after other legacies had been taken care of, was to be given "to widows, orphans, and the ashamed poor." The notary of Valencia, William of Jaca, in his will of 1263 provided for orphans, for feeding the poor, and for dowering poor maidens. García Chicot in 1279 provided for the ashamed poor, for orphans, and for dowries. A final example is the testament of Peter Marqués in 1275, where 50 solidi were left to the poor, but 100 to the ashamed poor at 10 solidi each.[77]

All this reflects the character of those settling in the kingdom. From King James down, almsgiving was a serious obligation for the well-off. A junior contemporary, the historian Muntaner, even claims this consideration for the poor and lowly as a distinguishing mark of the rulers of Aragon, who "show themselves to their people, and if a poor man or woman calls to them, they draw rein and listen to them, and at once relieve their poverty." A complacent local patriotism is not absent from this judgment; similar concern for the poor by the wealthy and the rulers may be found elsewhere in Christendom.[78]

Such incidents ought not to be used as an excuse for taking a cheery view of life in frontier Valencia. But enough of this spirit was here to found these hospitals, promote these laws, give alms in legacies and in the philanthropic work of the guilds, and in general to make a savage age somewhat less savage, more civilized. It was an element in the refashioning of the kingdom which—though it should not be exaggerated—should not be disregarded.

๛ THE KNIGHTS OF MERCY, RANSOMERS

In a crusading world anyone might be carried away into slavery by Moslem raiders, or lose his freedom in a sudden revolt. Ransoming these Christian captives could no longer be adequately done on a small and private scale. Even the efforts of the crown, especially through a coordinating officer called the *exea*, was by itself relatively ineffective. Here again the church was the only force capable of developing the necessary institutions on a large scale. As a practice of Christian charity, she did so. From the beginning of the thirteenth century, the great work of the ransom Orders grew to impressive proportions. This need would continue to be felt in Valencia. Even after the conquest and a decade or so of settlement, for example, when the Moslems of Valencia rebelled, "many Christians" of Valencia were "thrown into chains" and led away captive.[79]

One of the most important of the ransomer groups was the Order of Our Lady of Mercy (Mercedarians), or of St. Eulalia of Mercy. Probably a military Order (until 1317), they "exercised their religious vocation of redeeming captives," and were "daily prospering and growing."[80] It seems more proper to consider this Order here, though technically they might have been discussed with the military Orders. Conversely, even so military an Order as Santiago had an hospitaller function and operated hospices on the

Compostela route, while the Calatravans and the Trinitarians similarly exercised a ransoming function.[81]

Like the Mendicants, the Mercedarian knights had appeared at just the right time, when the need for them was deeply felt, scarcely a decade before the fall of Valencia. At the core of the Order's structure was a special vow, of a steely and chilling heroism which won the hearts of contemporaries: when funds were depleted, the knights would trade their own lives away lest weaker captives should despair. They conducted refuge houses for captives just returned and did a bit of hospital work.

The Mercedarians spread rapidly in Europe. They had been founded by the friend of King James, St. Peter Nolasco (1182?–1256?).[82] Nolasco's story is clouded by a multitude of forged documents, designed to promote his canonization (1628), and by involved controversies between Mercedarian and Dominican scholars. Born at Barcelona or possibly in Languedoc, of merchant or improbably of knightly family, Nolasco either evolved his Order from an already existing lay confraternity for ransoming or else, with King James and Raymond of Penyafort, directly co-founded it (in 1218 or 1223 or 1228 or better 1234). At any rate, the Order came into being just as the southward thrust of Aragon into Valencia was beginning.

Nolasco was commander general, an office to which William of Bas from Montpellier succeeded before mid-century. Nolasco himself supposedly rescued fourteen hundred slaves.[83] He was also ransomer, the Order's official who made the dangerous contacts within Moslem lands and haggled for prisoners. His friend St. Raymond Nonnatus, a Catalan noble, succeeded him in the latter function, in the exercise of which he suffered cruel imprisonment, was narrowly saved from being impaled, and had his lips pierced with a hot iron and padlocked. Nonnatus had returned to Aragon, and had been named a cardinal, at the time Valencia city fell.

Though the Mercedarian mother-house was in Barcelona, it was rather the Valencian frontier which had demanded them. Long before the crusaders rode south, St. Peter Nolasco may have been active in the Moslem city of Valencia, pouring out his inheritance money for captives in five trips there. It is said that the Order ransomed its first slaves in Moslem Valencia and that the only other major theater of ransoms for the Order in those early years was Algiers.[84]

King James spoke of himself as "the patron and founder of this Order."[85] He was to present to William of Bas as the Mercedarian "habit or sign" forever "the royal shield, to wit, of our battle insignia, and a white cross placed upon it."[86] Nolasco may have been among those who encouraged James in his crusade against Majorca; "it happened as you had told me," said the king when writing him from the field to ask for prayers, "that God was on our side."[87]

By the end of the century the Mercedarians had three hundred men in over fifty houses, half of these houses with an attached church. Eight or more were in Catalonia, perhaps eleven in Aragon. In Valencia seven houses formed a separate entity, to which were assimilated the two Murcian houses. The Valencian establishments were at Valencia, Puig, Játiva, Arguines, Denia, Burriana, and Segorbe; the last three may have become moribund in time, since they do not appear in the 1317 general chapter.[88] By 1319 there were provinces of Aragon and of Castile-Portugal.

These Knights of Mercy seem to have come on the Valencian crusade. During the siege, King James gave them (1238) a mosque and some houses hard by the city of Valencia, just beyond the south wall at the head of the public market and near the Boatella gate. Here the Mercedarians established their little church and their hospice. They first named the church St. Eulalia's, but soon changed the title to honor St. Dominic, the great abbot of Silos who rescued captives. The mosque-as-church was flourishing at least by 1245 as St. Dominic's.[89] In 1238 too the king gave them a small estate at Andarella,[90] and in 1242 some more properties in the area,[91] to support the establishment.

Arnold of Carcassonne was their central figure in the capital. Bernard headed the Valencia house in 1241, apparently between two incumbencies of Arnold; he was probably the Bernard of San Román who is in charge for a while shortly after mid-century. Raymond is listed in a document of 1248 as prior of both Valencia city and Denia. A chapter of the Mercedarian Order held at Valencia in 1257 has William of Isona as prior of both Valencia city and of Puig hill (though William of Castellfollit is pastor of the Puig church), and Bernard of San Román as Játiva commander. A fairly complete roster can be compiled of the early Mercedarians.[92]

Before the siege, Nolasco is said to have chanced upon an ancient painting of the Virgin, hidden long before by Mozarab Christians; it was under a bell in the hill castle at Puig which defended the northern approaches to the city (September 1237).[93] This was the same place where St. George was to rush up angelic reinforcements during a critical battle. The name of the hill was promptly altered from Puig de Cebolla (Onion Hill) to Puig de Santa María (Hill of St. Mary).[94] It was the first important shrine established by the king in honor of the Virgin as patroness of the realm he was conquering.

Such religious objects were commonly buried in Spanish countries by Christians fleeing during times of persecution or war, and were later "miraculously" discovered. An image of the Virgin was also found at Carcagente in Valencia in 1250. In fact, in Catalonia, of a hundred and seventy-one celebrated images of the Virgin, "no less then forty-eight were disinterred from their long-forgotten hiding places in caves or beneath the soil by oxen or bulls" in marvelous fashion—a coincidence which may be of interest to the student of religious folklore.[95]

Over half a century before, King Alphonse had envisioned a Cistercian monastery for this eminence of Puig, to have "a hundred priests." Alphonse and James's father had each planned to be buried in such a monastery here, "if I can conquer Valencia and build the monastery."[96] It was here, before the altar of the Virgin and surrounded by his knights, that James made his vow never to return north until Valencia was conquered.[97]

In summer of 1240 the king handed this hill to the Mercedarians for a church and shrine, including in the gift a liberal sum of money and eventually a portion of the royal share of tithes.[98] A wide ecclesiastical jurisdiction here, designated as a parish in a tax document of 1247, was under Mercedarian control.[99] The castle and town belonged to the Entenza family until 1343, when both came to the crown; the patronage of the monastery also pertained to them.[100] The bishop and chapter, apparently without the usual tug-of-war, immediately arbitrated the question of presentation of candidates and of ecclesiastical revenues; Pope Innocent IV approved the arbitration.

The amicable prelude to this document reflects Mercedarian popularity and influence at this time (1240):

> Be it known to all that we Ferrer, by the divine mercy bishop-elect of Valencia and provost [dean] of the diocese of Tarragona, wishing and desiring to become partaker of the almsgiving and the other works of mercy of the Order of the Brothers of Mercy, on behalf of ourselves and our successors give and forever concede, for the salvation of our soul, to the aforesaid brothers the church called the Hill of St. Mary.[101]

They could keep half the tithes, three-fourths of the first fruits, and most of the other revenues. They had the cure of souls "of the people dwelling there,"[102] and were under the obedience of the bishop. There may have been some misunderstandings nevertheless, because in 1244 a longer and fulsomely amicable document specified the accord in more detail.[103] Puig became one of the few large Mercedarian houses; by 1317, when other houses averaged less than five members, Puig had the largest community in the whole Order, nineteen.

The shrine would always hold a place in the affections of the Valencians. The relatively modest buildings first erected fell into some disrepair during the next century. They were replaced and expanded at great cost around the year 1340 by Lady Margaret of Lauria, the last of the patronal family.[104] There were legacies for the shrine too in the wills of the Valencians. In 1241 Maria left it twelve pence. In 1251 Peter Armer left two solidi, and in 1258 Peter of Barberá gave three. Lazarus of Vilella willed five solidi, in 1272 the Lady Willelma left another five, and in 1274 Peter Abrafim left twelve. In 1279 García Chicot gave twelve pence. During King James's reign, William Bruny had provided a legacy from the revenues of Rahalaceyt and the Segó Valley; King Peter in 1281 ordered the city fathers of Murviedro to respect this.[105]

The Valencian house was also remembered. In 1241 Maria left "to the house of the captives of Valencia" five solidi. And in 1252 Dominic Calderón gave "to the house of Merced of captives of Valencia twelve pence." Other small gifts for the shrine appear, including five shops and a group of adjoining buildings, all in the parish of Holy Savior in the southern part of the city of Valencia (1266); and houses in the parish of St. John near the Mercedarian church (1273 and 1278). King James left sixty gold pieces to the shrine near the end of his life, and remembered it again in the codicil to his last testament.[106]

In 1255 the great shrine of the realm at St. Vincent's was given briefly into Mercedarian care.[107] Their services were also sought elsewhere. Carroz, admiral of Catalonia and lord of Rebollet, gave them a building site and lands in 1241 and 1242, to attract the Order into his territory.[108] In Denia the king presented them with eight jovates of land, four fanecates more, and a hospice (1245); these were to support a "hospital in the town of Denia for the honor of God and the service of destitute captives"—a receiving station for those rescued.[109] The knights had a residence halfway between Cocentaina and Muro, at the foot of Mt. Castillo, as well as valuable lands (1248); its commander appears in a document of 1262.[110] There were holdings in Gandía, and a fort at Ondara.[111] There were also "certain houses in Segorbe, next to the houses of the castellan Dominic, with a farm";[112] and an ever-increasing supply of estates from donnés and benefactors.

King James gave the Mercedarians the village of Canet de Berenguer, which they soon sold to a knight of Segorbe.[113] Raymond of Morella handed over to them his estate of Arguines to be a house of the Order, in a valley to the west of the Segorbe-Torres road (1244).[114] Here they built a church of St. Mary and a residence, both functioning in 1251.[115] The nearby township of Algar was joined to this estate by Raymond's last will, and a hospital or refuge house as well (1251).[116] At Játiva the king granted them a park in 1248.[117] The knights set up a residence and a chapel of St. Michael just beyond the Játiva city walls. They were active here from before 1253, on which date their establishment received a legacy of 300 solidi.[118] Earlier, in 1251, the diocesan chapter turned over to this church a valuable property.

In 1297 the bishop, though denying the Mercedarians a cemetery or parochial rights, elevated the Játiva chapel to the status of a public church, to facilitate their work.[119] But even as late as 1317 the Játiva house remained fairly poor.[120] This house had its own commander at first; later in the century it seems to have passed more directly under the Valencia house.[121]

Gifts came to the Mercedarians from Dominic of Teruel in 1254;[122] and from the baron Simon Pérez of Arenós in the Murviedro area in 1255, including Borriol castle.[123] Bernard of Peñafiel in 1281 willed them his castellanship of the important castle of Rebollet, a gift its overlord-owner then confirmed.[124] Dominic Carnicer in a will of 1292 gave the Játiva house his Benixira estate, over the protests of his daughter.[125]

A number of people joined the Mercedarians in Valencia as oblates or demi-conversi of one kind or other. Such people had no religious profession in an Order, but commonly made some promise of obedience or loyalty. Arnold of Béarn and his wife became oblates in 1245, surrendering all their properties.[126] Boniface and his wife Maria did the same in 1253,[127] as did Raymond of Talavera in 1268, with his holdings at Lérida, Valencia, and elsewhere.[128] In 1256 at Játiva Bartholomew Cucufat brought himself and his goods to the Order.[129] And other cases are recorded.

To help the expanding Order, the king in 1255 drew up a sweeping permission: "that all men and women of our entire land or realm, noble or base, soldiers or citizens, may exchange, give or leave to you any estates, properties, and buildings—crown property or otherwise—wheresoever they may be."[130] This was confirmed and extended in 1275.[131] There were still more gifts: art objects from King James, his decree that a free space ten palms wide must be respected by persons building next to their Valencia house, a township of Beniabdulmel (which one finds the Order leasing out in 1293), a vineyard and 1,000 solidi from donnés, and so on. Business records show the Mercedarians buying a Játiva estate in 1298 for 3,200 solidi, renting Cocentaina lands in 1262 at 100 solidi yearly, renting their Denia buildings in 1248 to two brothers, and in general improving their situation.[132]

At the end of the century (1291), some fifty years after the fall of the capital, Pope Nicholas IV took the Mercedarian lands and houses in the Valencia kingdom under his protection. He made specific reference to Puig, to the "houses, lands, and vines you have in the city and diocese of Valencia," to those in Denia, to their church of St. Dominic in Valencia city, to their holdings in the dioceses of Murcia and Cartagena in the south, to all the properties in such places as "Burriana, Játiva, Algar, Rafelinardha, Rafelatrer, Gandía, Cocentaina, Segorbe, Murla, Artana, Almazora, and Biar" and other "towns and castles."[133]

Like vague footprints left by a traveler, these property records suggest something of the size, strength, and personality of the Valencia Mercedarians, and the esteem in which contemporaries held them. These Knights of Mercy had combined in one institute the ideals of crusade, corporal works of mercy, and prayer. The vigorous new Order in turn gives a clue to the mentality of the population which supported and approved it.

XIV

THE SHADOW OF CASTILE:
WARDING OFF THE STRANGER

Valencia was the king's bright hope and counterweight in his unceasing struggle to elevate the power of the crown, throughout his dominions, from half-effective suzerainty to some form of real sovereignty. And, in this ill-populated frontier kingdom of Valencia, the most important of all the king's instruments for consolidation was the church. King James would go to any length to preserve the freedom of that church from foreign manipulation. Consequently, long before he moved his forces to the siege of Valencia, the king had devoted attention to the problem of the metropolitan under whose jurisdiction the bishop of Valencia would fall.

In pursuit of his aims, he did not hesitate to slander the primate of Toledo, during the lawsuit about to be examined,[1] as he had not hesitated to hang at Játiva a relative and emissary of the bishop of Cuenca on account of his pro-Castilian activities.[2] This antagonism between Aragonese and Castilian political interests was to dominate the trial scenes. In the intimate fusion of church and state which characterized the times, it had to be the political body of King James which would fuse with the church of Valencia. To fail would be to put a stranger in his councils, a potential enemy in his castle.

ꙮ TOLEDO VERSUS TARRAGONA

The rapid conquests of the later twelfth and early thirteenth century were creating a new ecclesiastical geography for the peninsula. In theory and in law each ancient diocese should have fallen, upon reconquest, under the metropolitan who had held it during Visigothic days, although squabbles had to be expected because of the long interval of time, lost documents, and the like. Thus, history and law should have awarded the diocese of Valencia to the metropolitan at Toledo in Castile. Circumstances, however, rendered this conclusion an absurdity. Spain was no longer the Visigothic unity which could tolerate the old Roman axes of authority, running east and west. It was a collection of rival and proudly independent kingdoms, whose jealously guarded autonomy ran in lines from north to south.

Within such a kingdom a bishop was an important lay figure, a vassal with extensive revenues, estates, and castles, enjoying a measure of political, military, personal, and economic power. Conversely, the king was immersed in ecclesiastical affairs, and looked to the influence of his spiritual powers for support in his projects. The very origins of Catalonia as a territorial entity had largely depended upon this interplay of civil and ecclesiastical politics.[3] In the thirteenth century the metropolitan had important rights within his subject dioceses, and no little influence in affairs of state. If the church of Aragon had been uneasy under the mild yoke of a relatively weak metropolitan at Narbonne, the church of Valencia would have been much more unhappy under the intrusive and aggressive influence of Castile.

Even the fairly innocuous supremacy of Toledo as primate was repugnant to the bishops of King James's realms. By this office, the metropolitan of Toledo claimed in the Spanish peninsula certain jurisdictional privileges such as convoking national councils and hearing appeals from bishops. These privileges had evolved during the ancient days of national unity which were now an anachronism. Urban II had chosen Toledo, on the occasion of that city's recapture from Islam in 1085, to be the modern bearer of the primatial status. But peninsular unity was long past. Besides, the centralizing activities of the medieval papacy alone would soon have rendered the primatial institution obsolete. At the fourth ecumenical council of the Lateran in 1215, the most important parliament ever held in medieval Christendom, the prelates of Aragon repudiated these Castilian claims to primacy. Rising to address the august assemblage, "the bishop of Vich answered [the claims] in place of the absent archbishop of Tarragona, on behalf of all the [Tarragona] suffragans, many of whom were present, [saying] that the Toledo archbishop was not their primate, nor were they bound to obey him in anything."[4]

At the time of the Valencian crusade, the metropolitan of Toledo was waging a hard battle to retain his prerogatives as primate over the peninsula. Braga claimed the primacy, as having been the first to achieve independence from the Moslems. Compostela claimed it as the heir of Braga. Narbonne claimed it as the successor, after the Arab invasion, to the rights of Tarragona. In the coming struggle for the metropolitan jurisdiction over Valencia, the forces of Tarragona were to yield so far as to concede that Toledo could intervene in Valencia as primate though not as metropolitan.[5] Ironically, in this question of the metropolitanate, Toledo had the clear claim over Valencia; and its archbishop felt impelled to defend that claim. But Toledo was acting in a vacuum, insensible to the forces of what may be called Aragonese nationalism.

This proto-nationalist trend is discernible in King James's realms in the thirteenth century. In conformity with it, a tendency developed to identify dioceses, and even the personnel and administration of religious Orders, with "national" or rather dynastic units.[6] The rulers of Aragon were concerned that their clerics be not subject to bishops, monasteries, or superiors of a foreign land. This was partly a capture and exploitation of the church for

dynastic or regional purposes, deliberate and progressively ever more successful; it was also the negative defense mechanism accompanying a nascent
nationalism. Ironically, the primate of Castile himself had fought the metropolitan of Tarragona over the control of the diocese of Burgos, for similarly
nationalist reasons.[7] In the same spirit the contemporary historian Muntaner (b. 1265), when relating the reception of the Castilian sovereigns on
their way to the ecumenical council of Lyons in 1276, was proudly to remind
his readers that "the archbishop of Tarragona with ten bishops of his province . . . are all ruled by the lord king of Aragon."[8] The situation could not
have been phrased more neatly.

Later in the century James II would not even tolerate Castilian Dominicans in his Murcian lands south of Valencia (1297); he took up the topic
with some petulance on the eve of the Dominican provincial chapter to be
held at Valencia city. Nor did he want the Castilian Cistercians at Piedra
(1299). In 1284, as a reprisal for ejection of Aragonese subjects from France,
King Peter would not allow the visitation of Roda monastery by French
monks. When the diocese of Cartagena was erected south of Valencia,
James II protested strongly against it, and in terms explicitly nationalist
rather than ecclesiastical.[9] In the next century the crown of Aragon would
blatantly continue to pursue such policies.[10]

King James I had a lively sense of the political issues involved in the allo-
cation and "ordination" of suffragan dioceses. He had made determined
efforts to incorporate his military conquest of Majorca into his ecclesiastical
system as well. Majorca in ancient times fell under the metropolitan of
Sardinia; now, after long wrangling between Toledo and Tarragona, Rome
lost patience and declared Majorca an "exempt" diocese, directly under the
pope (1232).[11] In 1245 James I complained to Rome about the activities of
the Narbonne metropolitan in the suffragan diocese of Elne (Perpignan),
because the diocese was in the realms of Aragon; Innocent IV therefore
ordered Narbonne to make express mention of this political fact when
drawing commissions for agents to Elne.[12] In the quarrel over the Valencia
province, the lawyers of King James ringingly restated the principle behind
the royal policy: the diocese of Valencia must go to the metropolitan of
Tarragona because the kingdom of Valencia belonged to the crown of
Aragon.[13]

In language, character, and institutions the realms of King James differed
acutely from those of Castile. Nor was any love lost between the two lands,
as one can easily see in reading the memoirs of King James. Thus, the precise
legal issues at stake in the lawsuit between Tarragona and Toledo over
Valencia were in effect superficial. The real point at issue was whether a
bishop of an important diocese in one strong kingdom could be compelled
to accept the permanent rule of a metropolitan belonging to an alien and not
always friendly kingdom. Neither side adverted openly to this situation as a

factor in the dispute—except in an occasional indiscretion—and the court-room struggle soon degenerated into a series of near-farcical maneuvers on the part of the Aragonese to evade the legal issue.

What was the general ecclesiastical structure into which Valencia was coming? After the wave of Islamic conquest had destroyed the old ecclesi-astical province of Tarragona, the churches of Navarre and of Aragon pro-per came to be under the metropolitan of Auch. The Catalan dioceses—Barcelona, Urgel, Vich, Gerona, and Roda—fell to Narbonne. The struggle to be independent of Narbonne, and under a metropolitan more traditionally native to the region, succeeded in 1089. It was still necessary, however, to reclaim the metropolitan city of Tarragona from the Moors (1117), and to name its bishop (1118). The suffragan bishops of this new metropolitanate were the Catalan dioceses of Barcelona, Gerona, Vich, Lérida, Tortosa, and Urgel; the Aragonese dioceses of Huesca, Zaragoza, and Tarazona; the Castilian diocese of Calahorra; and the Navarrese diocese of Pamplona. This was still the situation a hundred years later when King James I began his career of conquest. The dioceses in areas he conquered all became objects of dispute: Majorca, Segorbe, Valencia, and Cartagena in Murcia (exempted and put directly under the pope in 1250).

Only in 1318 would another metropolitanate be added to the peninsular holdings of the king of Aragon; this was at Zaragoza, and for the Aragonese, who themselves resented the dominance of a Catalan metropolitanate. Moreover, bishoprics in the lands of the king of Aragon north of the Pyrenees had yet a different organization.[14] Taking the Spanish peninsula as a whole, at the time of the Valencia crusade, there were four Spanish metropolitans, in the four rival states of the peninsula—Santiago (from 1120) for León; Braga (1090) for Portugal; Tarragona (1089); and Toledo (1088). Seville became the fifth metropolitanate in 1248, Zaragoza the sixth in 1318.

The problem of metropolitan jurisdiction over Valencia had been foreseen long before the crusade. There was a background of ancient supporting claims on the side of Toledo and of Tarragona. At the trial, the Aragonese were to adduce a celebrated grant by the Moslem king of Denia—a copy of which has been preserved under the significant date of 1230. As early as 1228, before the Valencian crusade had been undertaken, King James had used this grant to settle the metropolitanate in favor of Tarragona; he did so by addicting to the suffragan Barcelona any future conquests from the Balearics down to the Denia-Orihuela region. At the parliament of Monzón in 1236, as the king prepared his move from Burriana against the capital of the kingdom of Valencia, he formally proclaimed that the diocese of Valencia belonged to the metropolitan of Tarragona because of the latter's many services to the crown. This was a piece of audacity, since the king had no right at this time, in law or in custom, directly to appoint even a bishop, much less to intrude in questions of ecclesiastical organization. As for the claims emanating from the king of Denia, the Toledo party would simply retort: "a Saracen cannot confer churches."[15]

The metropolitan of Tarragona did not hesitate to exercise his new authority in the captured capital, intending this as a deliberate preparation for the legal battle which he knew would follow. Traveling with the crusaders, he had ostentatiously performed the many functions proper to the office of metropolitan, even to organizing personally in detail the fallen city's parishes. He was not alone. The agent for Toledo matched his colleague of Tarragona function for function. Representatives of Castile were few enough, but they sufficed to foil the Aragonese plot to claim the diocese by default when the legal battle began. Still, the transfer of churches made by the king in October 1238 was effected through the metropolitan of Tarragona.[16] And at no point in diocesan reconstruction did King James ask advice of, or pay any official attention to, Toledo.

Peter of Albalat, the forceful Catalan crusader and prelate, was metropolitan of Tarragona during the dispute.[17] His brother was to be installed as bishop of Valencia about five years after the final settlement of the quarrel.[18] On the side of Toledo, what manner of adversary faced Archbishop Peter and King James? Roderick Simon of Rada was a man of far greater stature than Peter. As crusader, as statesman, as papal representative and apostolic legate, and as historian (he wrote the *De rebus Hispaniae*) he is a celebrated figure in Spanish history.

Roderick served as the main chancellor to the crown of Castile. At the decisive battle of Las Navas de Tolosa, the turning point in the Spanish crusade still celebrated by Spaniards today, his primatial cross had been a rallying point, and his fierce spirit a spur. On a less sanguinary plane he battled heartily to preserve the primatial privileges of his see. He had extended his metropolitan jurisdiction quite widely as well, especially by the use of two principles: that rescued sees were to return to their old jurisdiction; and that he was to have those sees and territories whose own metropolitan still lay under the Moslem yoke.[19]

Archbishop Roderick traveled to Rome to table in person his plea for control of Valencia, probably late in 1238 just after the fall of Valencia city. We lack a precise date for his going and coming, but there is no trace of him in Castile from autumn of 1238 to spring of 1239. A papal document of February 23, 1239 indicates that he had explained his case at least before that date. And bulls of April 22–24 show that he made his explanation in person. He returned to Spain perhaps in May.[20] Archbishop Roderick based his appeal on a double claim: the new diocese belonged to Toledo *de iure communi*, inasmuch as it fell within the historic boundaries of that province; it belonged *de iure speciali*, inasmuch as Pope Alexander III had specifically bestowed upon Toledo in 1166 "the dioceses of those cities which lost their own metropolitans at the Saracen invasion."[21] Urban II had also supplied Toledo with a similar permission for recovered bishoprics; the pope had been looking to a unified crusade of peninsular forces under Castile, in an earlier period when political circumstances justified this program.

Agents for the archbishop of Tarragona undoubtedly resisted these pleas with their own counterclaims. Pope Gregory IX therefore decided, "with the consent of the representatives of both sides," that the case was sufficiently tangled to merit investigation by a legal commission.[22] His bull of April 22, 1239 ordered hearings to be held for two months. One catches a hint in this document of economic threats by the crown of Aragon. King James's slowness to endow the Valencia diocese, here touched on, may well be related to the dispute over metropolitan jurisdiction.[23] One even wonders whether the initial harsh attitude of the *Furs* toward property acquisition by the Valencian church might not owe at least something to these uncertainties over ecclesiastical ownership?

Three judges were named to sift evidence: the canon of Toledo John Pérez of Arroniz (probably Aranjuez), the Official of the see of Tarragona William Vidal, and Bishop John of Oloron in Languedoc.[24] They were instructed to decide the case; if it could not be resolved, they were to appoint a man of their choice to be bishop. Alternatively, an appeal could be carried to Rome. The claims of Berengar of Castellbisbal, who had been put forward by Tarragona already as candidate for the new diocese, would have been canceled by this document, if they were not already formally voided. Consequently, no bishop or procurator for Valencia was at the provincial council of May 1239.

Through their delegates, the abbot and prior of the Cistercian monastery of Fitero in Navarre, these judges cited the agents of the two archbishops to appear, inviting also the agents for the respective metropolitan episcopal chapters (November 3, 1239).[25] Prior William delivered his citation to Archbishop Peter at Barbastro in Aragon. The sessions were to be held at Tudela, then the capital of Navarre. This was neutral territory, though ecclesiastically suffragan to Tarragona, and readily accessible to both factions. Its ruler Theobald was away with his vassals on crusade in the East. Pamplona, the only diocese for Navarre, lacked a bishop at this time; the vacancy lasted from 1238 to January 1242.[26] When the citations were issued the judges were already sitting in Tudela, at the beautiful new Gothic church of St. Mary (1194–1234) with its twelfth-century Romanesque cloisters. Only five months had been allowed for gathering of documents and drawing of arguments, but this was quite adequate, since both sides had been long prepared.

To underline the importance of the case, both metropolitans took care to be present in person at Tudela when the preliminary sitting went forward on Friday, December 1, 1239. They remained to guide and watch the proceedings for many days; Archbishop Roderick apparently was present for the larger portion of the trial.[27] Toledo named as its procurator the canon Gutiérrez Ferdinand; Tarragona named Raymond of Barberá.[28] In the opening arguments, Raymond made a formal counterclaim to the position assumed by Toledo. Gutiérrez made no answer for the present. Both parties were ordered to prepare their evidence for the morrow.

Fortunately a transcript of this trial has survived. It affords valuable glimpses into the organizing of the Valencian frontier and into the mentality of the organizers. The trial was a full-scale display of legal talent, costing the Tarragona metropolitan alone 2,300 marks of silver or almost 87,500 solidi.[29] This expense may help explain why, fifteen years later, the Valencia diocese remained deeply in debt.[30]

☙ A MEDIEVAL TRIAL

A certain gusto and engagement of feeling might be expected to characterize so provocative a situation as this politico-ecclesiastical struggle for control of the Valencia diocese. Bishops and metropolitans must act as watchdogs for the privileges belonging to their respective churches. Moreover, any considerable enlargement of one's province or diocese brought in its train a corresponding augmentation of prestige. And the revenues alone were a not inconsiderable prize. National rivalries, the previous angry scenes between representatives of the two metropolitans during the crusade, and similar elements—each contributed its measure of feeling and conspired to stir the blood of the participants.

Beyond all this, the participants were afloat on the full tide of the legal renaissance. The medieval lawyer, like the later humanist and the scientist, was a dedicated man. His enthusiasms shook and rattled Christendom with a disconcerting ferocity, even while they were contributing to its growth. The realms of Aragon shared enthusiastically in these juridical excitements. And in the kingdom of Valencia, new as it was, lawsuits threatened to be the ruin of the citizenry, so that "the malice" of the lawyers had to be curbed by law.[31] A similar phenomenon was visible in the church throughout Europe. Gregory IX in 1234 had to deplore excessive clerical litigation as a plague threatening to "exile harmony beyond the world's frontiers"; his *Decretals*, a landmark in legal history, were meant to serve as a remedy.[32] Pierre Dubois (ca. 1250–1320), the celebrated French legist, viewed the litigation in both civil and ecclesiastical courts as one of the major abuses crying out for reform in Christendom—"the greatest common evil."[33]

From the mid-twelfth century, ecclesiastical lawsuits had increased considerably. The prelates of Spain enjoyed a bewildering series of actions and appeals, some extending over a century or two, others engaging the attention of successive teams of litigants. An empire-building instinct for garnering suffragans occasioned some of the best of these. For example, the suit of the dioceses of Huesca and Roda concerning Barbastro began under Gregory VII in the eleventh century, and ended under Innocent III in the thirteenth. The diocese of Zamora, from its restoration in 1123 until 1228, was fought over by the bishops of Toledo and Braga, of Braga and Santiago, and finally of Toledo and Santiago; the latter emerged victor.

When the legal dust of these more Olympian strivings had settled down at last and the mettlesome metropolitans had abandoned the field, the score would be as follows: Toledo would be holding eight suffragans in place of its Visigothic twenty-one; Seville two for its former ten; Santiago eleven and Braga eight (about the same as in Visigothic times); and Tarragona twelve for a former fourteen. Five would be directly under Rome, four remained unconquered, and a few like Alcalá and Oreto never reappeared.[34] Against this background of *furor legalis*, the metropolitan of Toledo now faced the metropolitan of Tarragona.

On December 2, both parties having been sworn in, the Toledans presented their documents in evidence. These included provincial councils of 610 and 675 when the bishop of Valencia had signed as a subject of Toledo; St. Isidore's descriptions of the Spanish church (which Tarragona was to reject as "fictions");[35] auxiliary witnesses like Pliny, the emperor Constantine, and Innocent III;[36] the important privilege of Pope Alexander III (1166); and one unfortunate document referring to another Valencia. Especially in evidence was the celebrated ecclesiastical division of the Visigothic king Wamba (672–680), supposedly drawn up at a Toledo council in order to make fairer distribution of church jurisdiction. There is some dispute as to whether the document is a forgery by Bishop Pelayo of Oviedo (1119–1143), using older documents, or else an authentic document preserved in a corrupt text. The Tarragona party scoffed at its use in this trial; but the bishop of Valencia did not hesitate to use it himself less than a decade later, to claim and seize the churches of the diocese of Segorbe.[37]

Since the trial was intended to be a careful examination of the documentation and traditional claims to Valencia, much more than of any recent facts which affected those claims, the lawyers of Tarragona had perforce to offer some kind of argumentation against the writings. Each metropolitan now proffered a statement under oath, that Valencia had belonged to his province alone. Then the procurator of Tarragona presented his rejoinders: the documents cited could only refer to Toledo's privileges as primate, not as metropolitan; the rescript of 1166 was irrelevant, being at most a property grant; the evidence involving Isidore, Pliny, Constantine, and Wamba was inadmissible because its form in the Toledan evidence was only a translation from the Arabic. One may imagine the indignation of the Toledan party at this lawyer's-mixture of bold denial and delaying tactics.

The next session opened with a presentation of Tarragona's own positive claims: actual possession of Valencia, privileges of crusade, "and other reasons." The archbishop of Toledo then took the floor "in propria persona," denouncing each of the Tarragonan responses of the previous day as "irrelevant." The question of translation, he admitted, applied to some of the copies, but only to some.[38] One of the prelate's points was particularly well taken; it touches the heart of the whole case. The Tarragona spokesman had openly urged the question of national unity: "the kingdom of Valencia is part of the province called Aragon."[39] The archbishop of Toledo retorted that the kingdom of Aragon possessed Valencia, but was not itself a province of the church. The argument was solid; there never had been an ecclesiastical province called Aragon, nor was this "kingdom of Valencia" conterminous with the diocese of Valencia. Thus the Tarragonan argument is clearly exposed and challenged: that a national division should dictate an important ecclesiastical partitioning.

Toledo then presented an impressive array of documents gathered from various archives, each of them an official copy witnessed and sealed, giving concrete form to the points previously made as generalities. The documents came from Abbot John at St. Emilian (San Millán de la Cogolla), a Benedictine abbey west of Calahorra and in that diocese; from Abbot Michael at St. Iñigo of Oña, a famous Benedictine abbey in Burgos diocese; from the distinguished Abbot William at the very influential Sts. Facundus and Primitivus near Sahagún in the diocese of León; Prior Nicholas, whose monastery of St. Peter of Cardeña near Burgos was closely connected with the Cid and was his burial place; Guy the chamberlain of St. Zoil at Carrión de los Condes in the Palencia diocese, one of the most important Cluniac priories in Spain; Abbot Martin of St. Isidore in León; the abbot-elect of St. Dominic of Silos, a well-known Benedictine abbey in Burgos diocese; and the bishop of Oviedo.

There being no ready answer to this wealth of parchment, the Tarragona procurator took the offensive. Ignoring the uncomfortable fact that Valencia *should* belong to Toledo, he asserted that it *did actually* belong at the present moment to Tarragona, because the king so willed it and prescription confirmed it. He advanced this position in an elaborate charge of over twenty-five separate items. In sum: the metropolitan "had taken possession of the mosques of Valencia by the authority of the illustrious king of Aragon, who actually held the city and kingdom."[40] This right of conquest was a paralegal argument but was perhaps the strongest of all those put forward by Tarragona. Toledo itself, in happer circumstances, had urged this same claim for the churches of Sabiote, Garciez, and Xodar, against the diocese of Baeza.[41]

Aragon was not without its own documents. "The king of Aragon was able to give and grant churches in the diocese of Valencia, which had been established for the archbishop of Tarragona, by reason of a privilege the lord pope had conceded to the king of Aragon."[42] This documentary claim the Tarragonans buttressed with practical arguments. All James's predecessors had done everything in their power to liberate the church of Valencia from the pagans. James himself and his bishops had finally succeeded. The Tarragona metropolitanate had always intended to have Valencia as its own, nor had Toledo made objections. That Valencia belongs in fact to Tarragona in our own day is "fama publica" among the people. The metropolitan had in fact exercised his rights in this diocese: chose its bishop and canons, erected altars and established parishes, displayed the pallium and consecrated the bishop of Lérida here, received the obedience of all the clergy, consecrated a cemetery, absolved, excommunicated, and so on.

As a damaging negative argument, the Tarragonese assumed the position that the Toledo documents were unauthentic anyway. They alleged them to have been improperly drawn. Making these well-known documents "public" now would be easy enough but would consume much time, which was precisely what Tarragona wanted.[43]

In reviewing his own case later for the appeals court, the procurator of Tarragona emphasized some interesting arguments which are only touched upon briefly by the official transcript. One is that possession is nine-tenths of the law, and that the presumption of law is in favor of the possessor.[44] This is a good argument; it was hardly applicable to cases of recent theft, however, which was the point at issue. As for the legal precedents, ostentatiously performed by the agent of Toledo during the crusade, Tarragona contended that one does not actually possess what one is physically unable to keep—and that it was the army of Aragon which kept Valencia while Toledo was establishing its own claims. Tarragona also threw in a large doubt that the bishop of Albarracín-Segorbe, the agent of Toledo, could prove that he represented Toledo or had carried documents to that effect.[45] Besides, the bishop of Tortosa, who was a suffragan of Tarragona, had exercised ministries like confirmation among the Valencian Mozarabs forty years ago during a daring raid by Alphonse of Aragon, without protest at all from Toledo.

The most shameful of all the sophistries marshaled by Tarragona was the charge of neglect of Valencia by Toledo. In this argument, the "diligence" displayed by Tarragona in the conquest of Valencia fulfilled a church canon which allowed one's fellow bishops to absorb a place belonging to one's own diocese, if that place had been willfully allowed to remain in pagan hands.[46] An analogy was appended from civil law, that the man who neglects to redeem a captive slave loses title to him. To appreciate the unfairness of this charge, one should recall that the incumbent of Toledo was by far the most prominent and untiring crusader among the prelates of the peninsula; indeed, he was one of the great warrior bishops of the Middle Ages.[47] Besides, even before the conquest of Valencia had become feasible, its capture had been reserved by treaty to the troops of Aragon! The archbishop of Toledo, however, was modest in his reply: "he had done much to harm the Saracens," at least insofar as it had been in his power.[48]

The Toledans opened the session on Tuesday by contending that the claims of Tarragona added up to usurpation and robbery.[49] They protested that Tarragona had reversed the roles of plaintiff and defendant by assuming the offensive. The resultant argument consumed much time. The judges finally decided, over Toledo's formal protest, to let Tarragona pursue its positive arguments, as long as this was not understood to commit the judges to the position of acquiescing in the reversal of roles. This was a practical victory for Tarragona even though it involved a suspension of judgment as to its implications in law.

Tarragona now hurried in a parade of witnesses of its own, over continuing protests from Toledo. There were the bishops of Huesca and Tarazona, clerical dignitaries from the realms of King James, and three knights. Several sets of documents were also brought in. These included the charters by which King James had given the church of Valencia to Tarragona and had endowed it, and the bulls of Anastasius IV and Urban II. Toledo would reject the Anastasius privilege as inapplicable, since in law the general principle is assumed even when such a special exception is granted. The bull of Urban would be accepted without a challenge, though it was a forgery; but Toledo would point out that it applied only to patronage of churches within a diocese, not to the larger question of the diocese itself.[50] A final document from the Tarragona party was a history of the martyr St. Vincent, which contained a phrase useful to their cause but probably interpolated.[51]

All of this rather deliberately extended the trial—with speeches, copying, authenticating, resuming, minutely describing, and so forth. Toledo doggedly ignored this positive attack and continued to introduce its own documentation, gathered from as far away as Cluny in Burgundy and St. Denis near Paris. These in turn were ignored by the Tarragona party; they blandly refused to answer the evidence produced by Toledo, on the grounds that Toledo must yield and answer the positive claims of Tarragona first.

❦ INTERVIEWING WITNESSES

Further to confuse the issue, Tarragona now demanded that agents be dispatched by the court to collect evidence and documents as a preliminary to the introduction of further witnesses. Toledo reluctantly agreed, as long as the same would be done for their side. The judges therefore adjourned the court until the day after Epiphany—January 7, 1240. To conduct the search for evidence, the court swore in one Peter Roland, a cathedral functionary of Toledo, and Master John of Guardia, notary to the bishop of Tarragona. (Master John was to turn up in 1264 as agent, along with two canons, for the metropolitan of Tarragona in building a galley for a campaign of James I against the Moslems of Granada.)[52]

A phrase included in the agents' instructions suggests that the judges were becoming weary: "taking care that you do not interview an unreasonable number of witnesses, as forbidden by canon law." They were to question crusaders and others as to the acts of jurisdiction exercised by the archbishop of Tarragona, and his clergy, during the crusade and later in the capital. Questionnaires were provided. Did the Tarragona metropolitan "take possession of the greater mosque by the king's will?" "Did he order three altars made?" Did he receive the keys to the mosque, post guards, consecrate the altars, and so on?[53]

While these two officials were applying their questionnaire in Catalonia and Aragon, another team was to travel over Aragon also and Castile, interviewing witnesses on the claims advanced by Toledo, especially as to authenticity of documents and as to public opinion on the rights to Valencia. This group was headed by Stephen Giles, a cleric from the diocese of Zaragoza who belonged to the party of Tarragona, and by the notary Master Peter, a canon of Toledo. (Stephen appears later in the lists for the crusade collections for Zaragoza in 1279, paying nothing, and again in 1280, paying only eight solidi.)[54] Both teams were in fact delegate judges, with letters patent allowing them to subpoena witnesses.

Two delaying tactics were introduced by Tarragona, in the form of objections to the wording of the instructions. The judges refused to sustain or to overrule these points, however, simply suspending consideration of them, "lest it happen that while such points are being argued, the progress of the trial be retarded." To this implied rebuke the judges added that they did not wish to disregard the rights of either party, "insofar as these rights ought to be maintained by the law."[55] This was a tactical defeat for the Tarragona party, whose objections were generally designed to confine the Toledan case largely to proving—against much badgering—that Valencia had belonged to them in ancient times now long past.

It was the obvious intention of the archbishop of Tarragona to adopt, irregularly, the pose of plaintiff. His strategy was to insist always upon the present *de facto* possession; upon his prescriptive rights in the actual exercise of current jurisdiction; on the role of equity as attaching to the right of conquest and to unremitting crusading; and upon the confusion in the popular mind, especially at Valencia, as to who really was metropolitan. Above all, occasional hints must keep alive, in the consciousness of the Toledans, the power situation of a king determined to use any device for keeping his prize. At worst such a situation would end at Rome, where diplomacy might effect something or where perhaps the pattern of Majorcan exemption could be repeated. As for sound legal arguments on Tarragona's side, they were almost nonexistent despite the solemn oaths. On the other hand, Toledo's impeccable legal position was, in the changed modern circumstances, unrealistic. Meanwhile, the organization and staffing of the Valencian diocese could go merrily ahead.

The interviews by the traveling investigators are full of human interest. Descending upon St. Emilian monastery with their staff, the delegates secured the documents there, compiled a minute description of the external qualities of each,[56] and harried the prior. Were the books authentic? The prior replied that he was sure of it. Why? Because they were in the monastery, and he saw them there constantly. Did he himself think them authentic? Yes. Why? Because he saw many councils recorded, and many other good documents, and because the monks here—or most of them—held that these were authentic. How did he know the monks thought so? Because he saw them consulting the books on matters of doubt. What had he heard from the elderly monks? He had heard one say that the script was Toledan and therefore ancient; and the old men read them.[57] Did he know such older monks? Yes. When? From as early as forty years ago. Had they ever said that the books were authentic? Yes. What did authentic mean? What the church approves!

One witness, the priest Brother Peter, nettled by the questions, retorted crossly that he didn't *know* they were authentic because he hadn't watched them being made. Pressed for his opinion by the unrelenting inquisitors, he allowed that they were considered authentic by the old monks whom he had known here fifty-one years previously. Asked what authentic meant, he answered: the Gospels, the Epistles, and whatever has the approval of the church and is considered as authentic. The elderly priest Brother Roderick, who had been in the monastery sixty years, offered a good definition of authentic: matching the original.

More cautious, the prior at the monastery of Oña said that "he didn't know whether they were authentic or not because he did not have the required training." Under pressure, he refused to say more, except that he believed them to be good and true because of the script. Another priest here, Brother John, a member of the community for fifty-two years, reasoned that the documents were authentic because good clerics had drawn proofs from them before in legal suits.

As for public opinion concerning the metropolitanate, Toledo had a clear case. The married layman Peter Michael, a citizen of Sahagún and a veteran of the epic battle at Las Navas de Tolosa, had never heard otherwise from old or young, whenever the subject came up. Where, for example? In Toledo, in the crusading army at Las Navas, at Sahagún, and in Pamplona. Personally, he preferred Toledo anyway. The priest Peter Sancho had heard that Toledo was the metropolitan over Valencia, especially from the folks of Medinaceli, but he had no other evidence for his belief. He remembered, in a rambling kind of way, that, "after the capture of the city of Valencia, he

heard that there was controversy . . . on this point, and except for this hear-
say he did not know what was the general opinion, but some said . . . the
Toledans and others the Tarragonans, but more said the Toledans."
Gutiérrez, the archpriest of Hita, had heard Toledo commonly claimed as
metropolitan in Valencia by many places of the Toledo and Burgos regions,
for "ten years now, give or take a bit of time."

The priest Sancho was sure of it, for he had been at the siege of Valencia
and had received his ministerial faculties there from the head chaplain of the
prince of Portugal; this head chaplain served as a vicar in those parts for the
archbishop of Toledo. Sancho had also heard clerics talk of going "to
Valencia in the province of Toledo." The layman Peter Felix of Sahagún
told of an incident in the bishop's house at Pamplona some sixteen years
ago, when a gathering of ten or more good clerics had voiced belief in the
metropolitan claims of Toledo. A certain Martin Peter opined that "many"
people were on either side of the question; when pressed, he admitted that he
knew only four or so.

Similar interviews were held in the realms of King James. The archpriest
of Molina remembered hearing of Toledo as metropolitan, for instance, ever
since he had attained the age of reason, twenty-one years ago. Suspicious of
lawyers, he added: "but who they were, he does not remember, and if he
could remember, he wouldn't tell." This compromising position was soon
amended to an equally unhelpful: "if he could remember, he would tell."
The priest Paschase had heard Toledo backed commonly by the majority of
the people of Molina. The priest López had heard Toledo given often, both
before and after the fall of Valencia. The priest Martin John had heard the
same, as long ago as ten years before the conquest of Valencia. The priest of
Casteller, Martin, had also heard it, "before the king of Aragon came to
besiege Valencia and afterwards" at Teruel, Daroca, Albarracín, Cuenca,
and elsewhere.[58]

The knight Gonsalvo Ferdinand named five towns in which he had heard
it. Dominic Abbot, a deacon and rector of a church near Calatayud in the
diocese of Tarazona (who later appears in the crusade-tax lists), reported
that the metropolitan jurisdiction of Toledo had been common talk here,
"ever since Valencia was put to siege"; this was true especially in the conversation of the knights and squires of Peter Ferdinand of Azagra, the lord
of Albarracín.[59] The layman López Sancho attested that it was said "that
Valencia fell within the area of conquest of the king or Aragon, and that its
church should be subordinate to the church of Toledo." An important
Catalan baron was reported as having asserted (his name was withheld by
the witness) "that when Valencia would be taken, it would be a suffragan of
Toledo."[60]

The deacon García had heard about the claims of Toledo more than
twenty-five years ago from the bishop of Albarracín. This was also com-

monly talked of by the people (perhaps sixty of them) in Albarracín. Roderick, archdeacon of Alpuente in the Segorbe diocese, testified in favor of the claims of Toledo for the past twenty-five or thirty years. One of his colleagues was willing to push the time back forty or fifty years; and he did not hesitate to testify that he had heard such comment also recently after the fall of Burriana at least a hundred times in homes, in clerical gatherings, and from veterans returning from the Valencian crusade. Canon Benedict had been with the army besieging Burriana; he remembered the question as disputed then, though only "some" held for Tarragona. Diego, the sacristan of Segorbe, also testified for Toledo. These clerics of course belonged to the party of Segorbe-Albarracín, and were not without their prejudices against the claims of King James.

A series of crusaders deposed that the bishop of Albarracín, representing Toledo, was exercising acts of jurisdiction in the army of siege before the Tarragona archbishop reached the scene. At Valencia after the surrender, the inquiry showed, few had seemed disposed to question openly the claims of Tarragona, who was in possession. Still, "some obeyed and some didn't, and it was said in the city by important barons that Valencia belonged to the archbishop of Toledo, and by others that it belonged to the archbishop of Tarragona."[61] Naturally enough, the opinion of the majority in the army itself favored Tarragona, who held actual power under King James despite the busy show of defiance by Toledo's agent, the bishop of Albarracín.[62]

Quondam crusaders in Teruel told much the same tale. Ferdinand Peter felt that Tarragona enjoyed actual possession; but he had "heard often, and from many people, that Valencia was the suffragan of the archbishop of Toledo; and they even complained, during the time they were serving in the war of Valencia, because the archbishop of Toledo was not present in the army."[63] Others swore that most men had presumed Tarragona owned Valencia, until the bishop of Albarracín had arrived to cause trouble.

৩৫ THE SECOND PHASE OF THE TRIAL

When the sessions reopened at Tudela, early in January 1240, a library of the original documents in the most authentic copies available had been gathered; each manuscript book had been requisitioned under pain of excommunication. The covering letters by owners sometimes show trepidation, begging their prompt return, "since of all the church treasures, we hold ancient books the greatest."[64] Poring over this evidence painstakingly, the judges inspected titles and *incipits*, miniatures and coloring, the rubrics, dates, script, seals, marginalia, and externals, concluding each examination with a measured opinion as to the antiquity and authenticity of the volume in question.[65]

The care and shrewdness of their report on these heads, it has been remarked, might surprise a modern paleographer or sigillographer. In one manuscript Valencia was spelled both with "v" and "b"; the prior of St. Emilian and the sacristan of San Juan de la Peña, present in the capacity of experts, were consulted as to this Toledan peculiarity.[66] Where the seal has disappeared on another document, the judges note: "on the upper part there remains a bit of wax" with the bare impression of a cross. A Jew and an Arab—there were four books in Arabic—were also sworn ("by their own laws") as experts. The Tarragonan member of the judges' bench proved reluctant to offer an opinion, apparently caught between fear of perjury and fear for his later career in Aragon: "although he was present, he didn't want to say anything as to his impressions of the book, despite our insistence."

Faced with this embarrassing wealth of evidence, the Tarragona faction blandly requested that a full copy of every single book be made for their perusal. Again the agile judges side-stepped the obstacle. Tarragona could choose pertinent passages for official copying. The request for complete copies was not denied, but deferred indefinitely. The ingenuity of lawyers, however, is not to be foiled. A geographic scruple now affected the Tarragona camp. It seems there was another city, in Castile, called Valencia. Could the documents perhaps refer to this place? The judges countered this nonsense by requesting a sworn statement as to whether the Castilian "Valencia" was, or ever had been, a city.

"After some small delay" the bishop's procurator asserted "that he believed it to be a good-sized town, and at one time to have been a city." This brought the Toledans to their feet: "it had never been a city but a mere village," called "Coianca," which had been renamed in a modern settlement program. Coyanza, today called Valencia de Don Juan, is on the right bank of the Esla, southeast of Oviedo and southwest of Santander. Though at the time geographically within the diocese of León, it really belonged *iure diocesano* to the diocese of Oviedo. This diversionary movement had to be shelved while the attestations gathered by the two teams were presented— along with some belated books, introduced over the protests of Tarragona that this phase of the trial had passed.[67]

The question of a second Valencia was agitated in the next day's session. It came up again later, during the diligent[68] collation of the various manuscripts, whose authenticity had previously been examined. It continued to crop up as a serious issue. This absurd question was even gone into, to the extent of seeking out witnesses as to the change of name. One of these said he knew, as surely as he knew there was a God,[69] that the town had always been Coyanza until twenty years ago. A peppery old soldier, who had fought on the walls of Coyanza, asserted warmly that "he himself had not been present at the founding of the said town" but he had served there for five years before the king had changed the name to Valencia; he also knew from witnesses—three of them, a hundred of them—how the king had imposed fines on those using the old name. A knight had heard of the name change from fifty or sixty good witnesses over León, Castile, and Navarre.

Many of the key Tarragona documents failed to impress the judges. Of several they conclude: "however, we judges have not seen this privilege nor do we know if it has been properly copied, because we have not seen a version stamped with seals; nor do we know or believe this version was properly drawn by the officials, nor do we know if it was taken from a legal document." Even the treaty of Cazorla was introduced, by which Valencia had been conceded to Aragon in the mutual division of future conquests; this affected the metropolitanate only indirectly as bearing on the question of neglecting to crusade.

"The work of collating manuscripts" managed to inch forward through these and other excursions, and the hour of judgment was nearing. Again the Tarragona lawyer threw in the question of the second Valencia, which by now he believed "had been a city and an episcopal see, and a bishop had been there, and he believed that from the beginning it had been called Valencia." This led to a protracted wrangle on a point of order, which dragged on until terminated by the lateness of the hour.

The next day two judges decreed that Toledo might introduce more witnesses without having to delay first on the question of the second Valencia. The Tarragona judge had abstained from this decision. The Tarragona party appealed from it to a future court. And Toledo promptly appealed from whatever decision the Tarragona judge might be contemplating, though the latter had said nothing on the point. When the court began to consider the Toledan evidence, the Tarragona judge stalked out of the court, despite the pleas of his two colleagues. He was followed by his bishop, the procurator, and the whole Tarragona party in procession. Irate, the other judges sent after the group to command their presence at the session. If this demand were not received, the messenger was to stand with witnesses "before the door of the inn" to deliver it, then he was to register the proceedings before a notary public.

The maneuver of the Tarragonans had been only a feint, a bit of stage thunder devised by the Bologna professionals. All were on hand for the next court, cheerfully waiving the previous difficulty and presenting (over Toledo's violent objections) a full day of new evidence for their side. This included a lengthy letter from the bishop of Barcelona and another from the bishop of Gerona, predictably recording in detail the practical exercise of jurisdiction by their metropolitan after the fall of Valencia.

The Tarragona party also questioned in outspoken terms the competence of the Visigothic king Wamba, a man they dismissed as "exceedingly presumptuous and tyrannical with regard to his churches." They insisted again that "there were formerly a number of Valencias," at least *three* of these having their own bishops. Anyway, the manuscripts produced had not been authentic, they charged; they were willing to accept them, however, in order to turn them to the confusion of the Toledans. A restatement of the previously cited documents ensued though these had not gained relevance merely by the passing of days.[70]

∞ Sentence and Appeal

Even court trials have an end. The argumentation had been tedious and spun out far beyond the measure of its syncopated transcript, itself the size of a small book. Phrases crop up such as: "and when the presentation had gone on rather lengthily," or "and the same day the factions made lengthy allegation."[71] Court was in session by December 2, 1239, and, after an interim, had reconvened on January 7 of the new year. This allows just over a month for the entire trial, including the process of gathering new testimony in the field, unless there is question here of a calendar confusion.

Finally the great day arrived. On Tuesday, the vigil of the Conversion of St. Paul, the judges gathered in the chapel of the Holy Spirit at St. Mary's to debate as to the sentence. Unanimity was impossible because of the Tarragona member of the bench. The considerations concluded, the court reconvened in the cloister (crowded with interested spectators), anxious to finish off the business as soon as possible. The date was January 24, 1240.

Before the apostolic rescript could be read, the procurator of Tarragona rose to effect a desperate last-minute maneuver. It was directed against John Pérez of Aranjuez, the canon of Toledo appointed by Rome to be one of the three judges. The procurator denounced him as in fact excommunicate, "on account of the many churches he holds." This had come to his attention only recently, the procurator alleged, and precluded the outlaw judge's further participation in the trial.

Should the excommunicated canon's judgment be taken, however, then "we appeal to the Holy See." Moreover, warned the procurator, Tarragona had proved its case; so, if Valencia were awarded to any but to them, they served notice now of their appeal to Rome. John Pérez was not disconcerted; he had anticipated the trickery. On the spot he presented to the court a privilege from Pope Gregory IX lauding his learning, noble birth, and good life, for which he had been rewarded with plural benefices—a document "bullatum, non abolitum, non cancellatum, non viciatum in aliqua parte sui."[72]

The Tarragonans protested that this privilege could not help him. The judges heard the document out and concluded that Canon John was not excommunicated, that in any case he did not hold "several" churches, and that the procurator had neither proved his point nor could be expected to add to it in the reasonable future. The whole incident was more complicated and protracted than this brief summary might indicate. In the transcript of the trial one senses the tension of the Aragonese as they play these final cards of their game.

"The hour for delivering sentence was pressing." While the Tarragona judge sat glumly listening, with both metropolitans personally present, the decision of the court was proclaimed. The bishop of Oloron, the neutral member of the trio of judges, began the reading. Then the warrior archbishop of Toledo and his lawyer began to shout to their own judge, Master John: "read with him, read with him!" "Both of them reading together, they thus pronounced sentence." The decision included a summary account of the proceedings and arguments, with the fateful conclusion: "sentencing with the advice of good lawyers, we award the control of the Valencian church to the archbishop of Toledo." A copy, signed by only two judges, was dispatched to King James of Aragon on January 31, 1240. This was prefaced by anxious references to the king's love of justice, and urged that he quell any popular resentment in his realms—"far be it!"—over the decision.[73]

There was an epilogue. The sentence having been read, the Tarragonan member of the board of judges produced a long document of his own which he begged to read to the court. Before he could begin, however, the Toledo procurator was on his feet, repudiating in advance whatever contribution the judge had in mind, and rejecting his views as void even as he simultaneously appealed from them, whatever they were. The archbishop of Toledo supported his man. The Tarragona procurator nevertheless proceeded to unburden himself of a "long recitation of fact and of law," awarding Valencia to Tarragona and imposing silence on the archbishop of Toledo. He concluded with an appeal of his own to the Holy See against the sentence of his fellow judges. The latter had stalked out when this hubbub began, ignoring the demands to stay which their colleague shouted after them. The cloisters were left in Tarragonan hands. A formal document was now drawn up here by the Tarragona dignitaries.

The following morning, Tuesday, this troop of worthies marched on the "house of St. Christina" where the bishop of Oloron had his quarters. Here the Tarragona procurator began to read out their protestation in the presence of Oloron. No one was in a peaceable mood, and the bishop of Oloron "had words" (as the record discreetly puts it) with a Tarragona champion, Bishop Vidal of Huesca. The upshot of it all was that the bishop of Oloron, finding the battle of stout lungs going against him and wishing to avoid the possible complications in law which might arise from having heard the document through, got up from where he sat and fled with his followers to his own room.

The whole crowd tumbled along after him. Stopped by the locked door of Oloron's chambers, the procurator of Tarragona shouted his message "at the door of the room." Not to be thus easily outwitted, "some of those who were inside, within the room, made a noisy outcry in order to keep the voice of Raymond from being heard." While heads were ringing from this clamor, Procurator Raymond cleverly slipped the paper into the bishop's room through some crevice or opening in the door.

The Tarragonese returned to the attack next morning. But by now all parties had been alerted; and the bishop of Oloron had had time to gather a few shreds of his scattered dignity. All three judges were on hand. They listened stoically to the appeal by Tarragona. There was a brief tussle as the latter tried to force a copy into the hands of the bishop of Oloron. All then sat through a counterprotest read by the procurator of Toledo. The Tarragona procurator demanded a copy of this last document and, when refused, scoffed at its worth.[74]

Perhaps on the principle that there cannot be too much of a good thing, the Tarragonans presented themselves again next day at Oloron's habitation, to assail his weary ear with a fresh appeal to Rome, based on newly researched quibbles. Later the judge from Tarragona devoted much care to composing his own special account of the whole trial.

The case went immediately to Rome where in February 1240 the cardinal priest Sinibald, of St. Lawrence in Lucina, began hearing both litigants at his palace near the church of St. Martin in the Hills.[75]

At this juncture a cloud of unknowing envelopes the modern researcher, from which only a few facts emerge. We know that both sides claimed victory and court expenses; in Tarragona's claim these latter were 2,000 gold pieces, in Toledo's claim 1,000 silver marks (38,000 solidi). The latter sum is much less than half the total cost of some 87,500 solidi eventually expended by Tarragona; it is evident that the hearings in Rome were more elaborate and costly even than those at Tudela. The old arguments were windily reviewed at Rome, and some fresh dust was thrown up. Fifteen days were devoted merely to Tarragonan objections to the Toledan petition.

There was of course the question of the excommunicate judge; the sharp-eyed lawyers of Tarragona had, in the interim, discerned yet a second "excommunication" weighing upon the culprit. Tarragona also attempted to twist the sentence of the Tudela court into being a personal opinion of the judge who had delivered it, with both colleagues in disagreement; or else with a neutral member of the bench neglecting to state his own views; or finally with the neutral member refusing to let those views be known, even locking himself in his room in conspiracy with the judge from Toledo. The agents for Toledo pleaded the fact that two judges had actually agreed upon a sentence. The Tarragonans prescinded from the fact and sought to confine the court's attention to the faint ambiguity of the written acts on this point. Tarragona also tended to center its case on the quasi-possession of Valencia.[76]

The outcome of Cardinal Sinibald's hearing was a decision rejecting

Tarragona's claims to have already voided the Tudela sentence by means of their previous appeal to Rome. He also declared null the independent sentence of the Tarragona judge. The main point of the trial, however, was cannily deferred. And the wording of the sentence suggests fresh legal battles to come. Subsequently, a document of mid-July 1241 arranged for a further stage of the appeal. Almost two years later, in 1243, a similar document was entered in the papal registers. After that there is only silence; apparently the scene shifted from the courtroom to the discreet chambers of the diplomats.

ɷ THE FRONTIER CHURCH IN NATIVE HANDS

To stop at this point would be to abandon the historian's task. Historians have generally been aware that this sudden ending to the trial is both unsatisfactory and disconcerting. They have tried to soften its abruptness by postulating a decision favorable to Tarragona, preferably in October 1240. Escolano, Teixidor, Villanueva, and some others give the date as October 3, 1239; one may graciously allow a calendar confusion (nativity vs. incarnation) and substitute the year 1240.[77] The argument is based on a document certainly misunderstood, and now apparently nonexistent.[78] Chabás has suggested that the final sentence is missing in the transcript of the trial, "por ser contra Toledo."[79] This is improbable; nor does it explain why no trace exists anywhere else of the decision in so important a case.

Sanchís Sivera believed that he had discovered the date by a comparison of a series of letters in which the "bishop-elect" of Valencia turned into the "bishop." This is founded on a misconception as will be seen below; besides, it does not take into consideration the renewal of the trial at Rome in 1243. Gorosterratzu reasons that the Toledo archbishop finally dropped the case out of despair of ever seeing it solved.[80] But this trial was young, as medieval lawsuits go; and Archbishop Roderick was a tenacious man in the courtroom. That the case merely withered and died is, for those litigious days, the least satisfactory solution of all.

The Valencian archives have been searched in vain, during the preparation for this book, for further documentation on the problem. The Vatican manuscripts, after a year of work among the materials pertaining to Spain, likewise yielded nothing on this vital point. Assume, then, that the pieces of the puzzle lie before us. They need to be placed against their proper background before they can reveal anything. Both the Roman and peninsular political scenes during these precise years must be examined.

When the appeal reached Rome the reigning pope was stouthearted old Gregory IX, admirer and friend of the crusading king of Aragon. To him, James was one of the few rays of light on a military scene beleaguered by emperor, heretics, Tartars, and Islam.[81] Much might be hoped from Gregory, at the very least in the form of an exempt diocese as in the case of Majorca. In due time the appeal very nearly arrived before Pope Gregory in person. But there was one great enemy—time. Gregory was nearly a hundred years old.

Things began well. The auditor chosen by Gregory to care for the Valencian case, as was seen above, was the brilliant cardinal Sinibald of Fieschi. Sinibald held the offices of papal vice-chancellor and governor of a critical principality, the Ancona March. As a contemporary poem puts it, he was "the pope's second hand." Only thirty-five years old, of a temperament courtly and firm, he enjoyed a growing legal reputation in academic Christendom. Sometime professor of law at Bologna University, he was to win a permanent place in the history of legal thought under the proud title *pater iuris*.[82]

The metropolitan of Tarragona had appointed his procurator for the Roman appeal on February 22, 1240; this was the canon of Lérida, Master William of Soler.[83] The metropolitan of Toledo had appointed as his procurator the archdeacon of Calatrava, Master Bernard. It may have been during these hearings of 1240 that Archbishop Roderick of Toledo journeyed across the Spanish countries to take personal part in the fight at Rome. On the way, he had his primatial cross carried before him, somewhere in lands subject to the metropolitan of Tarragona. Tempers were running high, and the incident raised a storm of indignant feeling in Aragonese breasts. The episode may have pertinence for the Roman trial.

The incident of the cross occurred in April or May of 1240. Its locale was possibly Segorbe, which was then claimed by the diocese of Valencia and was equally an object of strife between the metropolitans of Tarragona and Toledo. It might have happened somewhere in Navarre, Pamplona being a suffragan of Tarragona. We are not even sure whether Roderick was going or coming at the time of the incident.[84] The provincial council of bishops under the metropolitan of Tarragona, assembled in the city of Valencia on May 8 of that year, actually put the primate under excommunication in the event that he should repeat such an act. They also placed under interdict all places where he should happen to stay, for the duration of his passage, while attempting such acts of jurisdiction.[85] In this episode the resented primatial rights are apparently to the fore, but the metropolitan claims to Valencia seem also to be present at least peripherally. This may be because the primate went out of his way to cross Valencian territory (if he did), or because he spoke too freely and indiscreetly on this subject during the passage (as well he might), or simply because of the psychological advantage gained by an authoritative primatial gesture at this critical moment. The papal rebuke seems to allow for this ambiguity.[86]

The Roman document also went out of its way to stress the locale of the protesting council and its metropolitan frame-of-reference: "at Valencia, which he asserts belongs to his province." Gorosterratzu suggests that Rada had secured his series of bulls of mid-1239, in support of his primatial claims, precisely for use in the Valencia trial over metropolitan jurisdiction. It is interesting and perhaps significant to note that not until 1245 would the metropolitan of Tarragona receive from Rome the privilege of having his cross carried before him within his own province. The primate of Toledo was to be excommunicated by the metropolitans of the realms of Aragon yet again in 1320, for having his cross carried before him here.[87]

Before the year was out, Sinibald had reached the preliminary decision already mentioned. He could not form a more definitive opinion without in effect initiating a new trial; his own hearing seems to have centered upon a review of procedure. Pope Gregory IX had meanwhile been waging his interminable wars with Emperor Frederick II, a struggle which reached its crisis in 1240 and the following years. He now called the princes and bishops of Christendom to meet at Rome, in Easter week of 1241, for an ecumenical council. By this means he sought wider support against his opponent who was "more cruel than Herod and more impious than Nero."[88] The fleets of the emperor foiled this plan. In May 1241, Frederick could boast of having "over a hundred" prelates and ambassadors, from many countries, in his prisons.[89] The council was never held.

Under such circumstances, with papal finances and administration in confusion, it is not surprising that the Valencian case made little progress during the first six months of 1241. Sinibald himself had been called away from his residence into Rome in December 1240 just after the hearings had ended. In April 1241 the pope had to advert again to the Valencian situation; he delivered a stinging rebuke to the church of Tarragona for the childish conduct of its prelates during the cross-bearing incident.[90] In the month of July, when the emperor and his army had advanced as far as Rieti and were preparing to move directly on Rome, the pope did manage to reactivate the Valencian case.

"Since it had not been possible to decide the case on its merits" in the first review, the pope now assigned three judges to renew the trial.[91] These were Master Pérez of Bayonne, a canon of Toledo; Peter Albert, a jurist and canon of Barcelona; and the Dominican Peter Guarner of Bordeaux. Both factions were instructed to summon witnesses before the judges. The points at issue were to be those chosen by Sinibald for more intensive investigation. Four months were allowed for the taking of evidence; and the materials were to be turned over to the pope for a personal decision.[92]

The case could be expected to have reached a conclusion by the end of 1241. It might have dragged on for years, as had many another case, but the pope seems to have hurried it along. The legal issues were not complicated as they were, for example, in the Segorbe case. Tarragona had gained its desired procrastination. There were several diplomatic pieces on the chessboard now—especially the possibility of help from Aragon against Frederick

II, and King James's almost successful project of joining Provence to Toulouse so as to contain the French advance southward. But the game ended abruptly. Gregory had been ailing for some time; on August 22, 1241 he died.

Rome was immediately plunged into turmoil. The Valencian trial must have ground to a halt a little more than a month after its inception, as savagery and self-interest combined to effect the notorious "conclave of terror." The emperor had just laid waste the Campagna, and had brought his armies within sight of Rome. Senator Matthew Orsini, who held almost tyrannical power in the city, tried to force a rapid election. He had the ten cardinals thrust rudely and forcibly into conclave before the emperor could bring influence to bear upon them. They were held prisoner in a half-ruined building, under appalling conditions. The leaky roof of their chamber was mockingly used as a latrine by the soldiery. The impact of brutality, ugly threats, and the August heat of Rome brought all the cardinals down sick. The English cardinal, Robert of Somercote, died miserably while the soldiers jeered; two others were to succumb later from the effects of their treatment. Sinibald himself was brought to death's door.

When a new pope was finally chosen on October 25, he lasted only seventeen days, dying on Sunday, November 10. The cardinals immediately fled the nightmare atmosphere of Rome. There would be no pope for over a year and a half. During this long interregnum Christendom had only thirteen cardinals; ten of them were in Italy—four held at Rome, four in refuge at Anagni, and two prisoners of the emperor. The administrative machinery of the church was badly crippled by war and deprived of leadership. There would have been small prospect at this time for progress on the Valencia case. At mid-year, and again in 1243, the emperor attempted to capture Rome. His military failures coupled with an indignant public opinion made it wise for him to allow a free election.

The new pope (June 25) proved to be none other than Sinibald of Fieschi, count of Lavagna, the very cardinal who had been auditor for the first appeal in the Valencian case. One of his first acts as Innocent IV, even before he went down to Rome, was to order a fresh trial between the partisans of Tarragona and Toledo over Valencia (July 14, 1243). Four months were again allowed. Witnesses were to be "called and diligently examined."[93] The judges were the same—in fact, the whole process was to be a repetition of the 1241 decree. But nothing seems to have come of the move. This was to be a year of trouble and woe.

The imperial program of Frederick II involved a slavery of church to state such as could not be tolerated even by a well-disposed pontiff. Alternatively, the canonists' pretensions to papal dominance in the unitary Christian society, which Innocent IV held in an even more flagrant form than had his predecessor, were equally impossible of acceptance by an emperor. Half-hearted gestures of diplomacy were attempted, but there was no middle ground. The cudgels were taken up again, and the fight was to go on to a finish. In mid-1244, Innocent had to flee in disguise from Italy. By early December he had set up his court in the fortresslike monastery of St. Just at Lyons, where he began to prepare the ecumenical council of 1245. All the resources of propaganda were marshaled by papal and imperial partisans; each of the antagonists called on the princes of Christendom to rally to his just cause. Despite the uproar Innocent IV managed to bring to a solution any number of less pressing problems. But he seems never again to have taken up the Valencian case. It is not impossible that the case had become a dead issue by this time.

A clue to the final solution of the quarrel may perhaps be found in peninsular affairs of late 1243. It was becoming obvious that nothing would be settled by the pope for a year or two, and that he was so encompassed by problems, both in and out of Christendom, as to be amenable to para-legal reliefs. Aragon and Castile had come very near to war at just this time. Castile had feared that King James would not stop his conquest at the agreed southern border of Valencia. Conversely, Castile coveted Játiva and Alcira, deep within the Valencian area she had assured to Aragon. The Moslem ruler of Murcia, adjacent to Valencia on the south, had given homage for his region to Castile in 1243, and most of it was now safely in Castilian possession. Alphonse the Learned (not yet king but prince) seized Enguera; King James seized Villena. On the brink of war, Castile requested a conference. It proved to be stormy but ultimately successful, resulting in the treaty of Almizra (March 26, 1244). This was a general settlement of outstanding differences, an amicable agreement on a Valencia-Murcia boundary, and an alliance. The atmosphere at the signing was one of friendship and concession on the part of Castile.

It seems probable that during these conferences a secret understanding was reached concerning the diocese of Valencia. As part of the *quid pro quo* interchange, Castile may have agreed to withdraw her support of Bishop Roderick's suit at the papal court, and even to intimate to the pope—himself a resourceful diplomat—her satisfaction with the situation at Valencia as it stood. This could hardly have been openly stated because theoretically neither country had a say in such a strictly ecclesiastical affair. Any documentation, however slight, of collusion would have embarrassed both kings; Bishop Roderick would then have been able to reopen his case from a strong moral as well as legal position. Yet this diplomatic procedure would have been the sensible solution, at this time, to what had become in fact a political problem. Nothing more could be gained by either king in the courtroom. Exemption was the likeliest outlook, as had happened to the Aragonese conquest at Majorca in 1232, and as would happen soon in Murcia to the Castilian conquest in 1250. An exempt diocese would be a diminished victory for

James—and there was always the chance that he might lose anyway. The civil authorities of Castile by now could hardly have hoped for a victory; exemption would be a loss for them in any case, and King James's claims were politically reasonable.

The problem was not like that of Segorbe, where the prize was less important, where there still remained much to be said by the lawyers on the Castilian side, and where at that precise moment, as a consequence of definite papal decisions, both the legal and the psychological advantages lay on the side of Castile. The renewed activity of the Segorbe bishop just after the treaty of Almizra, however, suggests that events there had been waiting on a solution of the Valencia dispute, and that such a solution had at last been reached. Significantly, the bishop of Valencia himself was present at the conferences of Almizra, though he was not an active politician like his successor Bishop Andrew, nor notably a crusader.[94] His presence might be explained to the curious on the grounds that the southern borders of his diocese would be affected by the treaty. His signature at the treaty-making is not proof positive of the signatory's presence, but it is very persuasive evidence; as a methodological principle, therefore, the two are normally equated. A final query: would Innocent IV have permitted himself to intrude thus into local politics or lend himself to such solutions? The pope who mixed himself into the politics of France, England, Italy, Portugal, Germany, and Bohemia, who deposed and confirmed kings and interfered in the English civil strife, would not have hesitated.

Archbishop Roderick could not be expected to retreat, despite the diplomatic situation. But his chances of success would have been diminished almost to the vanishing point. After the ecumenical council he again journeyed to visit Innocent IV, who was still at Lyons. We do not know the reasons for this trip, though a combination of the primacy question and the Valencian injustice seems a reasonable conjecture. He died there, however, perhaps by shipwreck in the Rhone River (June 1247).[95] With this strong and prestigious fighter removed from the scene, any hope of reopening such a case died.

During all the incident and maneuver, what was the status of the bishop of Valencia? Berengar of Castellbisbal seems quietly to have been shunted aside. We do not know whether the metropolitan had consecrated him. It does not seem probable, since no evidence of his action as bishop appears anywhere, even in the records of the trial at Tudela. As late as April 1239 Rome urged that the king endow Valencia for its "future" bishop. Chabás contends that Castellbisbal was previously proposed but not elected. Escolano has him performing some functions as episcopal nominee, but Escolano's authority is dubious. (And the bishop-elect of July 7, 1239 proposed by Olmos y Canalda, Chabás, Teixidor, Raynaldus and others actually belongs to the diocese of Valence in France).

Ferrer of Pallarés appears suddenly as bishop-elect in documents of May and June 1240. He is traditionally regarded as the first bishop of Valencia; the cathedral constitutions assign June 22 as the date of his consecration. The modern historian Fita has him consecrated on April 5, 1240 and has him offer formal obedience to the Tarragona metropolitan on October 21.[96] As for actual evidence, much of the argumentation turns upon the precise time at which Ferrer ceased to designate himself "elect" and began to employ the term "bishop." Analysis here can occasionally be confounded by the difference between nativity and incarnational chronology, which renders suspect the dates between late December and the subsequent late March.

Sanchís Sivera believes Ferrer to have been consecrated on October 21, 1240 because on that date he signed one document "elect"[97] and another document "bishop."[98] But Ferrer had confusingly done the same thing earlier,[99] so the signature as such proves nothing. What is more to the point, and vitiates this line of reasoning, is the circumstance that neither "elect" nor "bishop" was a stable term. Thus, the Toledo metropolitan Roderick Simon of Rada, when previously bishop of Osma, had designated himself usually "elect" but sometimes "bishop."[100] It was the custom in medieval León and Castile for the bishop-elect to allow himself the title bishop.[101] On the other hand, even when an actively ruling bishop regularly signed himself as such, "it meant only that he governed his see with full authority, but not that he had been consecrated";[102] at Osma, for example, Roderick had been only in deacon's orders.

Nor had any conclusion been reached at Rome as to the Valencian case then, to clear the way for an early consecration. There seems to be some question as to whether Ferrer ever was confirmed by Rome. Affairs there had fallen into chaos, and remained thus during the year and a half of papal interregnum which parallels much of Bishop Ferrer's reign; Ferrer was dead, and his successor elected, before Innocent IV could be chosen. Any concession from Rome concerning the Valencia episcopate, which would fit current theories on Ferrer's consecration, would have had to come during or at the end of Sinibald's inconclusive first hearing. Even the final endowing of the diocese in 1241 by King James offers no clue; it was apparently prepared during the conclave of terror at Rome, and published only a week after the election of the fifteen-day interim pope, Celestine IV. The Tarragona metropolitan called Ferrer bishop in 1242, and in May 1243 the provincial council did the same. The term is as ambiguous here as in the earlier documents. Innocent IV referred back to him in 1245 as the bishop, and the cathedral necrology placed him as the first bishop.[103] In the absence of any definitive evidence, all one can say is that Ferrer was elected in 1239 or early in 1240, and probably consecrated by the metropolitan—either immediately, or after a few months' delay to see in which direction the appeal at Rome was drifting, or just after the tumultuous interregnum had begun at Rome.

Since there was no pope to judge or confirm the situation, Ferrer's moral and legal status in the latter case would have been somewhat superior to that of his predecessor Castellbisbal. The confirmation of his successor would also have to be postponed, while Innocent IV reopened the old trial. But then chaos would take over again; finally, the settlement of Almizra (1244) cleared the way for definitive abandonment of the appeal on the part of the Toledo church, and a consequent quiet confirmation for Bishop Arnold. If these conclusions are not altogether satisfactory, they seem at least to represent the furthest penetration of the problem which is possible on the present evidence.

The legal virtuosos who fought for Tarragona doubtless prospered in their subsequent shifty careers. Raymond of Barberá turns up in 1244 as "chamberlain of Tarragona," delegated by the metropolitan to arbitrate a tithe dispute between the bishop of Tortosa and the monastery of San Cugat. William Vidal, who held the dignity of Official for the see of Tarragona and who served as judge at the Tudela trial, was to be one of the nine candidates —luminaries such as abbots and archdeacons—proposed in 1248 for election to the see of Valencia. William Soler, the Lérida canon who handled the first appeal at Rome for Tarragona, emerges in a 1252 document as part of the legal machinery in an action involving the king; in a 1257 document he and a Dominican have just concluded a successful flushing of heretics from the Lérida diocese.[104]

It comes as no surprise to learn that King James of Aragon eventually carried the day. The breach in the walls of his national church had been stoutly defended, and the entire legal campaign had been conducted and finished, before the Valencian southlands were conquered or the reorganization of the conquered areas had been carried to maturity.

The scene of these conflicts in law lay far from the land of Valencia. But they had all formed a definite part of the reorganization of that realm. They had been meticulously prepared, before and during the crusade, with as much care as was devoted to the construction of catapults or the provisioning of troops. No expense had been spared, no legal pebble left unturned. In caution and sure-footedness, in bold planning, and in fierce tenacity of purpose, the project bears the characteristics found in all the conquest and reorganization of Valencia by James of Aragon, the Conqueror.

King James was no mere warrior on horseback, surrounded by stout arms and empty heads. He was the central and dominant figure of a smoothly functioning organization, staffed by clever bureaucrats and lawyers. Perhaps our concept of the crusades is a shade too romantic. These were hardheaded, well trained, clear-visioned men who knew just what must be done to achieve their purposes. The banners and the flashing steel and the brave show on battlefields were not unimportant. But the patiently moving pens of scribe and notary—recording the plans, forestalling the opportunities, clarifying, dissembling, pettifogging, pleading, commanding, denouncing, reckoning, and rewarding—were mightier than the swords.

XV

ST. VINCENT'S: CROWN OF THE
IDEOLOGICAL RECONSTRUCTION

King James had circled his new city with religious houses. He had dotted its interior with small churches. To each religious Order, each type of ministry, he had assigned a post. Proud of these foundations, he kept a patriarchal eye upon their affairs through the years. But the jewel and crown of all, with a special claim to kingly patronage, was the royal foundation of St. Vincent of Valencia.

⚜ FOUNDATION: SHRINE, MONASTERY, HOSPICE, AND HOSPITAL

To King James, St. Vincent had done as much in conquering the kingdom as had any company of knights. The king proposed to tender a proper thanks. There was to be a monastery and hospital near the shrine "where blessed Vincent had been buried."[1] "Our conviction is that the Lord Jesus Christ subjected to us the city and whole kingdom of Valencia, and wrested it from the power and hands of the pagans, because of the special prayers of St. Vincent."[2] James's son King Peter was similarly to acknowledge the crown's obligation to Vincent's shrine. Yet oddly enough the origins and early evolution of St. Vincent's in this century seem never to have been investigated in detail.[3]

The religious feelings of a medieval group could be focused effectively around a local shrine. There were Marian shrines in Valencia; Our Lady of Puig, for example, was the patronal establishment for the new kingdom. But something in the way of a resident saint was desirable. James's dominions in general were well populated by the bones of spiritual heroes. His subjects entertained no doubts but that there had even been a remarkable emigration of characters from the New Testament to the lands of the *langue d'oc*. The capital of James's newest kingdom unfortunately could boast no Lazarus nor Magdalene, much less those distinguished figures of Catalan folklore Salome's ghost and Adam. But it did have an authentic saint to rival the best. This was Vincent, deacon at the church of Roman Zaragoza, who had "been crowned with martyrdom hard by the city of Valencia."[4]

To Vincent's memory Emperor Constantine the Great had caused a church to be erected here at Valencia. Vincent's bones were apparently later spirited away by the Christians during the Moslem persecution of the eighth century, either to Castres in France or to Cabo de San Vicente in Portugal. But his place of burial remained as a tangible relic to be cherished by native Christians through the dark night of Moslem rule.[5] St. Vincent's church became the focus of devotion for the ever-diminishing Mozarabic community at Valencia.

Nor was it forgotten by the Christian north. As the Reconquest gathered strength in the twelfth century, Alphonse VIII of Castile made a demonstration of solidarity with the Christians in remote Moslem Valencia. He presented an elaborate grant of Fuentidueña and other properties to the church of St. Vincent in Valencia and "to all the brothers serving the church of the same martyr."[6] In 1172 a raid in depth by Alphonse II of Aragon forced the Moslem ruler of Valencia to adopt a tributary policy; among his concessions to Aragon the Moslem yielded the church of St. Vincent with all its rights. Alphonse in turn, out of gratitude for material help in his adventure, handed these claims over to his monastery of San Juan de la Peña (1177). James's father, Peter the Catholic, confirmed this transfer in 1212.[7] But James himself in a 1232 pre-grant assured the place and church of St. Vincent's "at Valencia that admirable city" to the powerful St. Victorian monastery in the diocese of Huesca.[8]

Neither place retained ownership. When James was concentrating his hosts at Puig for the final drive on Valencia city he had a charter drawn granting the church and place to the Languedocian monastery of St. Mary at Lagrasse—situated halfway between, but to the south of, Narbonne and Carcassonne (1237). King James was a patron of Lagrasse, which had holdings and rights elsewhere in his realms. Its total holdings everywhere included five monasteries, two priories, one hundred and two parish churches, ninety-four castles and towns, and other properties, scattered in eight dioceses. James proposed to have Lagrasse establish a monastery at St. Vincent's, as soon as was feasible.[9]

Early the following year Lagrasse received papal confirmation for the lands involved in this grant, thirty jovates "around" the church or perhaps "near" it; but in the document nothing appears concerning St. Vincent's itself. This vigorous charter, so important to the early history of the place, is transcribed below in a note.[10] The claim seems soon to have lapsed, or to have been waived in return for other properties. King James later, as patron and proprietor, several times confirmed the Lagrasse holdings in his realms, but St. Vincent's was no longer part of them. In practice, oddly enough, the monastery of St. Victorian seems to have taken charge here from the very beginning. This was apparently because of the scandals which rocked Lagrasse at precisely this time.

Benedictine monasticism in Languedoc was at a low ebb, and Lagrasse was particularly bad. An investigation of the monastery, ordered by the papal legate in 1236, found affairs "depraved." A papal commission in

1248 discovered even worse conditions; they removed twenty-eight monks to other monasteries as a punitive measure. Abbot Bernard, too often accused of unchastity, finally resigned in 1255. It is not hard to see why King James in 1238 preferred to honor, not his ill-advised pre-grant of 1237 to Lagrasse, but his pre-grant of 1232 to St. Victorian.[11]

The church of St. Vincent stood just outside Valencia city. The eighteenth-century author Finestres loosely locates it as two arquebus-shots distant from the city walls, out on the royal road to Játiva. More precisely it was some 4,000 feet to the southwest of the city in the Rayosa suburb. A few Mozarab houses may have clustered at its skirts; more probably this Christian group had entirely disappeared. St. Vincent's may have been doing service as a mosque by 1238; according to the record of the trial between Toledo and Tarragona, the Tarragona archbishop felt it necessary to purify and consecrate it before offering Mass there.[12]

Even while it lay dangerously within the enemy zone, it had welcomed the crusaders. A small force had pushed up to the church to offer services.[13] By his *ius patronatus* as crusader King James now assumed special responsibility for it. Before the city surrendered, he took care to petition Pope Gregory IX for its patronage specifically; Gregory's reply reveals that James already intended to have a hospital as well as a monastery here.[14] As soon as Valencia fell, St. Vincent's was carefully fortified for protection against Moslem raiders.[15] The special protection and proprietorship of the Holy See was sought and given; dues of one silver mark, to be sent annually to Rome, sealed the compact (January 1239).[16] By this action St. Vincent's and its grounds became in effect exempt from diocesan control, much like the Templar or Dominican religious Orders. The king's prerogatives as patron were to be in no way impeded. A compromise was later worked out with the Valencia parishes and the metropolitan of Tarragona, as to fees, burial rights, and the like received at the shrine.[17]

The royal standard, which had been raised on the walls of the city to proclaim its surrender to the Christians, was to be kept at St. Vincent's.[18] Later, on the recurring centenaries of Valencia's conquest, the Valencians would stage a formal procession to St. Vincent's to offer thanks for winning the kingdom.[19] And in the first years after the conquest the townsmen are said to have paved part of the street where the martyr had walked, lest human feet defile the hallowed ground.[20] St. Vincent's and "the public road leading" there became landmarks in assigning post-crusade properties.[21] In 1274, when King James received the king and queen of Castile in royal state at Valencia, the visiting party would first go to "the church of St. Vincent where they dismounted to pay their respects, as they approached" the city.[22]

By mid-1240 the prior Bernard had broadcast an appeal for funds. He noted progress on the fortifications and on the refurbishing of the church, and begged alms for the proposed hospital, "where the poor may find refuge, the thirsty be satisfied, the sick be most excellently cared for, and other works of mercy be exercised."[23] Pope Gregory IX, surely due to another request from King James, took St. Vincent's again under the special protection of the Holy See in 1242, exempting it from local excommunication and the like. Rome confirmed and spelled out the privileges again in 1245 and 1246.[24]

As the symbol and center of Valencian spiritual life, St. Vincent's was planned on an elaborate scale even before Valencia fell. It was to be an ambitious complex of buildings housing three units: "a secular church,"[25] a hospital, and a monastery. The king began a new church; apparently the monastery assumed from this early period the Gothic aspect it was to bear, though at least one great door was Byzantine.[26] In this establishment the corporal and spiritual works of mercy were to be joined to the splendor of the liturgy. The buildings were all constructed and functioning within little more than a decade, though the establishment's considerable revenues became sadly disjointed in the process.[27] They were all one unit: "domus seu hospitalis" or "hospitalis sive monasterium" or "prior seu ecclesia." The income was for all elements of the complex but "especially for the support and use of the hospital."[28]

ᔛ BENEFICIARIES, STAFF, PENSIONERS

The hospital included separate infirmaries for men and women patients, a handsomely endowed chapel, quarters for the domestics, and hostel for the poor. There may possibly have been provision for orphans.[29] Contemporary documents speak of the ill here, of the separate infirmaries, and of medical supplies. The "house" of St. Vincent, as distinct from "its hospital," had a threefold personnel: clergy, pensioners, and staff. There is no information as to who conducted the daily operations of the hospital, or how; probably neither clerics nor pensioners were involved but rather a hired or beneficed sub-staff.[30]

Historical documentation survives in odd patterns; it may leave in obscurity whole areas of a subject, yet throw light into other hidden corners. From St. Vincent's records we are fortunate to have a series of charters illustrating a bizarre social phenomenon of the thirteenth century: the crown pensioners. As patron of a monastery, the king could lodge his retired functionaries there for life, with a corody of food and clothing. Though not properly a right, nor connected with the hospitality owed to a patron, the burdensome charge on monastic revenues could not effectively be refused. In fact, by this period it had come to be a natural form of taxation upon the monastic corporation in Christendom.

In contemporary England, for example, "this was among the services most often required in the second half of the century by the king" from monasteries.[31] A monastery thus became as well a retirement home for aging couples or civil servants, or an old soldiers' home. The institution assumed many ingenious forms. Laymen and women even purchased corodies outright at high prices; this was a popular version of annuity in the thirteenth century. Vicars of nearby parishes, or monastic employees, sometimes received such room-and-board pensions in lieu of salary.

A large number of dependents drew this primitive form of social security at St. Vincent's. All were crown appointees. "We and our successors," King James reminds the Mercedarians supplanting the monks as administrators here in 1255, "can establish and leave there corodians, [taken] according to our pleasure from our household and familiars, due regard being had for the capacities of the said place."[32] When reorganizing St. Vincent's in 1265–1266 and putting it on a more stable financial course, King James reaffirmed the crown's privilege of naming corodians; but he limited their number to twenty.[33] The twenty were to include both men and women, who had the choice of living within the wider monastic or religious family or else completely outside the house.[34] James's constitution of 1266 makes it clear that these people are not to be confused with the ordinary guests in the hospital; the poor sick were to be cared for at St. Vincent's just as "has been the custom heretofore."[35]

Who were these pensioners? In 1267 a Peter Martin received his corody; he had been attached to the royal chancellor, the bishop of Valencia.[36] In 1277 King Peter assigned a pension to Andrew Almerich, "bearing in mind the many services you rendered the lord James of renowned memory, the king of Aragon my father, as a member of his household."[37] Almerich or Aymerich was falconer to James the Conqueror; in 1271 the king had given him a farm and tower at Valencia.[38]

In 1262 King James conferred a pension on a family group, Michael of Spain and his wife Simone.[39] This, like some other corodian documents, was a confirmation of a previous gift already bestowed "with a charter." The yearly measures of grain and wine were specified. A similar confirmation, noting the more formal charter held by the grantee, went to Peter of Amaldán in 1268. As illustrative of a common formula, it is worth reading at length:

> We and our successors give and grant you, Peter of Amaldán, for all the days of your life, food and clothing in the house or hospital of St. Vincent of Valencia, ordering the rector or procurator of the said house or said hospital, incumbent or to be appointed, that from now on they are to consider you a stipendiary of the said house or said hospital, and are to care for you in food and clothing as they are obliged to do for the other stipendiaries of the said house or said hospital, and that they are not to alter this for any reason.[40]

In 1277 the crown granted, "as a personal benefice, to you Peter of Fores by reason of the service you have long given us, food and dress for life in the house of St. Vincent of Valencia."[41] Possibly this was King Peter's cross-bowman of that name. Sometimes the pension came as a straight money-payment; in 1255 William of Narbonne made out a receipt for the sixty solidi he received for the year "as my pension."[42] William seems to be the Murcian citizen (1274) who had farmed several kinds of taxes from the crown (in 1262, 1263, 1271, and 1272, for example), and who was bailiff for the realm of Valencia beyond the Júcar in 1264.

A servitor of low estate might hope for a pension. In 1282 the crown "assigned a certain portion to Solarmunda, a woman of the household, both because of the service she gave as guardian and wet nurse for some time to our brother Peter, and also because she is poor and in need."[43] In 1268 King James gave Bernard of Calatayud "food and clothing in the hospital of St. Vincent's of Valencia all the days of your life"; the formula of the gift was that of "the other beneficiaries of the same hospital."[44] In 1277 Raymond of Torroella acquired a crown pension.[45] A document of 1279 spells out its details: a yearly four cafizes of wheat, 100 solidi for wine and food, and 50 solidi for clothing.[46]

A special case is the maiden Floreta. King James apparently gave Floreta's father, Dominic of Montearagón, a small estate at Navarrés; he is probably the Dominic Gómez of Montearagón appearing in the *Book of Land Division*. James granted a corody to the daughter in 1268, to become effective when Floreta reached the age of fifteen. It was apparently a sub-stitute or compensation for the Navarrés estate, because later King Peter extended her stay at St. Vincent's until she was satisfied in connection with the Navarrés affair.[47]

Besides Michael of Spain there were other family groups. Frederick of Alessandria, from Lombardy, with his wife, Sybil, and daughter Blanche, received a pension from James. This included a yearly allowance of grain, 60 "quarterios" of wine, and 80 solidi paid out in pennies.[48] Later, when Blanche married and was no longer a charge on the hospital's revenues, the king reduced this grant by a third (in 1278). At the same time, however, the money allowance was increased 200 solidi for clothing. This pension was confirmed by King Peter and again by King Alphonse.[49] A certain Martin and his wife, apparently connected with King James but now fallen on poor times, got a corody at St. Vincent's from King Peter; Alphonse confirmed this again in 1283.[50] William Oller and his wife were awarded in 1263 their gift of board and lodging for life "just as the other beneficiaries of the said monastery."[51]

Among the clergy serving St. Vincent's it is not always easy to distinguish a proper foundation or benefice from a corody upon the general revenues. In the original establishment of St. Vincent's, as reflected in a 1255 document transferring its administration, King James required the liturgical services of "five priests continually and five other clerics [divided] between deacons and subdeacons." These five were Mercedarians; presumably they replaced the Benedictines previously at worship here; they seem to have been supported from the general funds but without the intervention of corodies.[52] When the hospital returned under the administration of St. Victorian in 1259, however, secular clergy were appointed and corodies granted.

One of these appeared in 1258, perhaps because the Mercedarians were already preparing to withdraw, or perhaps as part of a long-range plan which would have gone into operation anyway. "William of Aymeric, cleric" received his grant of "board and keep in the house of St. Vincent" in 1258.[53] In 1259 a similar grant went to "Peter Gros, priest, for a personal benefice."[54] King James awarded another in 1259 to Bernard of Caldes or Calvó, who owned houses in Murcia and who had been one of the group granted a settlement charter in the city of Valencia in 1239. The formula is a common one: "We grant you Bernard Caldes, priest, food and clothing in the monastery of St. Vincent of Valencia, all the days of your life, so that from now on you are to receive in the said monastery food and clothing as the other canons of the same place."[55] In 1264 James gave "to you Ferdinand of Vilella, cleric, all the days of your life, a daily portion in the monastery" with the perquisites of a canon.[56]

Then, in 1266, the crown had to reorganize St. Vincent's thoroughly. King James published a constitution regulating its internal structure. He allowed six chaplaincies plus three minor clerics, all of them to praise God in worship by day and by night.[57] In 1269 he broadened this, substituting for the minor clerics two deacons, two subdeacons, and a scholar. Each priest was to receive 70 solidi (soon raised to 80) and his clothing, a deacon 60, a subdeacon 50, and a scholar 50.[58] The king included in the constitution a rule for clerical decorum: the clergy of St. Vincent's might walk into the city only by pairs and only in clerical dress.

Meanwhile the priest William of Apiera received his "canonry of the monastery of St. Vincent's" on corodian terms.[59] (He acquired the crown chaplaincy of the cathedral five years later also, with an annual income of forty-four morabatins.)[60] William may have belonged to an influential family of the kingdom of Valencia.[61] The roll call of canons at St. Vincent's in 1269 appears in a document of that year. They were Dominic, John, William, Aymeric, Bernard, and another Bernard. James and Bonanatus were the subdeacons, William Bernard the scholar.[62] As late as 1283 there were still only six canons at St. Vincent's.[63] And in that year William Bernard, the scholar of 1269 now became a priest, received one of the canons' corodies.[64]

When the crown surrendered the administration of St. Vincent's to the care of Poblet in 1286, it agreed to waive the royal right to name pensioners.

But the king retained a patron's corrective control. Thus, in 1290 King Alphonse noted that pensioners had been added at St. Vincent's in such numbers as to strain its finances; he ordered the number in the 1263 constitution of James I to be respected.[65]

While the monastery itself was under the charge consecutively of St. Victorian's and Merced, there was presumably a body of religious resident in that part of the St. Vincent's complex. Besides, there were the domestics and staff as well as the transient poor and the ill. Together with the body of pensioners and corodian secular clergy, this amounted to a heavy charge on the revenues of St. Vincent's. In all, with building and furnishing the place, St. Vincent's required of the Conqueror a formidable output, and at a time when he was heavily involved in other ecclesiastical and civil projects. But the expense was minimal for the effect achieved; St. Vincent's did more to make Valencia a Christian kingdom than James could have done with a similar outlay in any secular project.

∞ GIFTS AND LEGACIES

King James generously endowed his central shrine at Valencia city. The appeal to the public in 1240 probably brought sufficient contributions to begin the rebuilding. Then, in 1244 James handed over the castle and village of Cuart de Poblet, a little over two miles west of Valencia city, along with the hamlet of Aldaya just south of Cuart.[66] These places seem to have come to St. Vincent's fully, without an intervening feudatory. (Raymond of San Ramón nominally held Aldaya, and in 1245 acquired the fief of the third-tithe; but the king had actually recovered title before that date.)

The inhabitants here remained mostly Moslem for many years afterward; they paid St. Vincent's a third of all their produce, one penny annually for every animal, and two lesser services. Only in 1303 would the crown yield criminal jurisdiction over these Moslems to the monastery, and even then cases involving death or loss of a member were retained. And only in 1334 would St. Vincent's issue a settlement charter for Cuart, though James the Conqueror acquired and populated lands in this area. When the Aldaya country was being settled by Christians in 1279 King Peter ordered all farmers taking up irrigated lands to pay St. Vincent's as rent a fifth of their produce.[67]

King James also turned over to St. Vincent's in 1244 a most valuable source of revenue: a tenth of the king's tenth on the Albufera, the great fresh-water lagoon near Valencia city, and his tenth on the nearby saltworks. This had nothing to do with the diocesan tithe but was simply a tenth of all the rents and profits from this important crown property, especially the fishing and salt industries. The money was to be paid promptly each year, even before the king received his own nine-tenths. This gift James reconfirmed in 1255 when the Knights of Mercy briefly took possession of St. Vincent's.[68] And, in 1253, when turning over the Albufera revenues to his son Prince Alphonse, the king carefully reserved "the tenth of the church of St. Vincent."[69]

The hospital-monastery had begun the year 1244 with a solid endowment. That fall the king added another valuable property: "the town and castle of Castellón de Burriana" with its countryside and villages.[70] There is something strange here. Less than a month before, James had given this place to his relative the Prince of Portugal in fief; the prince had promised, in the event of his dying without issue, to restore this completely to the crown. Prince Peter still retained lordship in 1249 and 1250. One hesitates to seek refuge in the theory of a scribal misdating; perhaps the case is analogous to that of Montornés, with the monastery as Prince Peter's overlord for this one place or else as holding castellan rights under the prince. Certainly the king retained residual rights; their exercise led to a quarrel between king and prince, issuing in favor of the crown in 1251.[71]

King James promptly moved the town down onto the Castellón plain, incorporated some local settlement into it, and started it on its way to being a major town. If St. Vincent's had not owned it before, or at least had not held for the full civil seignory and revenues, it received them now. St. Vincent's was in control at least by 1255, when Castellón was included among the holdings of St. Vincent's being transferred to a new administration. And, in November 1260, the Moslem subjects of St. Vincent's successfully concluded an appeal against the monastery concerning rents.[72]

King James considerably amplified the revenues of St. Vincent's in 1245–1246, as part of his penance for cutting off the tongue of Bishop Castellbisbal. The king gave enough in properties to guarantee annually an extra 600 marks of silver, or 23,000 solidi. He also founded an extra chaplaincy.[73] In 1259 he yielded title to 600 solidi annual income from the hamlet of Benimargo in the Castellón countryside.[74] The Benimargo money and the full control of Castellón might have been part of James's penitential obligation, or they may be wholly separate.

Despite these considerable holdings, financial difficulties multiplied for the monks of St. Vincent's, possibly due to an injudicious building program. For a single "signum crucis" the monastery had paid out 1,000 solidi. St. Vincent's was "burdened with debts, [its] revenues diminished." King James reorganized the finances and added further grants. The most important of the new estates came in 1268. James made over to the monks "the whole feudal jurisdiction and lordship and power" of Montornés castle and village.[75] Its lord, Peter Simon of Arenós, continued to hold the place well into the next reign, but only as a fief of St. Vincent's; all the crown seignory and revenues went to St. Vincent's, which held them until 1295 when they were resold to James II.[76] Montornés was located "before Castellón de Burriana" and should not be confused with the castle and fief of the same name near Montblanch.[77]

The next sizable gift came eight years later, in the form of Almonacid, Sollana, and Benizaron (1276).[78] Almonacid was a valley north of Segorbe, boasting a castle and town and prosperous Moslem settlements. The bishop of Barcelona received it in 1238 for his crusading services; the diocese of Barcelona was still trying to vindicate his claim as late as 1272. King James had given it in fief to William Montclús (1241) and then to Peter Martin of Luna from at least 1259 to 1276; after 1280 Peter Cornel held it. Thus St. Vincent's had overlord rights here without direct jurisdiction, much as at Montornés. Perhaps the monastery possessed this only briefly. Sollana and Benizaron were strongholds with small settlements annexed. The first is probably Sollana near the west coast of the Albufera; the second name is susceptible of several interpretations, from the castle of Benasal to Benasa below Denia.

The last of the major acquisitions appeared shortly after the death of James. This was the castle and town of Chirello, and at about the same time the castle and town of Cortes or Cotes.[79] Only the revenues were included, not the seignory; and at a change of administration in St. Vincent's in 1282 these two places would be specifically excepted from doing homage. Chirello was more important, appearing a number of times in the documents of King Peter. It is not easy to identify these two places. There was a castle at Chirivella near Valencia city, for example, held for a time by Calatrava, while both Cotes and Cortes can be suggested for the second castle. At any rate the castellan of Chirello in 1278 was Arnold of Gloria, who drew from St. Vincent's his yearly expenses plus 3,000 solidi salary.

The crown gave other holdings and privileges, smaller in scope but nonetheless valuable. Thus, in 1273 King James transferred one of the important irrigation canals of the Valencian huerta, along with the rent owed by its users.[80] He allowed to "the procurator of the hospital or monastery" and his successors "annually a fair in the town of Castellón"; it was to last ten days (1269). The most important fair of that area, it meant extra profit for St. Vincent's as secular lord.[81] This privilege he protected when granting subsequent fairs in the region.[82] In 1279 King Peter ordered the highway from Valencia toward Requena to be rerouted through the town because travelers were "damaging" the hospital's lands at Cuart.[83]

In 1261 James conferred a charter protecting their property from violence and rendering the hospital immune from official harassment in connection with debts.[84] James also transferred to St. Vincent's his hospitality tax of 400 solidi a year owed by the citizens of Castellón (1271).[85] Similarly he freed the establishment from a number of taxes. In 1269 he allowed St. Vincent's to share with Benifasá the privilege of selling produce in Valencia city at times when such sales were restricted.[86] In 1244 he decreed that "all the flocks of St. Vincent's can pasture throughout the whole dominion of the king free, without payment of carnage or herbage."[87] For one of the pensions at the hospital the crown in 1278 assigned 200 solidi, to be drawn from the municipal tax for weighing at Valencia city.[88] In 1263 James consigned to St. Vincent's all the furnishings of his own chapel, including crosses, chalices, pictures, tabernacles, relics, and ornaments; this, which seems to be the chapel he carried along on his interminable wanderings, was given to the hospital on his death.[89]

Other small possessions are indicated. Some are at Alcira and Játiva.[90] A farm in the Valencian huerta brought a yearly rent of 90 fanecates of wheat.[91] A property in the Patraix countryside turns up in a dispute between St. Vincent's and Raymond of Berga; an arbitration in 1272 awarded it to Raymond but with a rental to St. Vincent's.[92] In 1262 a settler in the Cuart area promised to pay a yearly rent of four pounds of wax. And in 1282 the hospital leased a vineyard to the pastor of St. John's of Valencia city, in return for a share of the yield.[93] Finally, in 1280 the crown confirmed all these accumulated properties and privileges.[94]

Lay people added their bit to swell the income of St. Vincent's. To facilitate this further, King James in 1260 chartered the monastery with a privilege by which it could acquire or inherit Valencian lands, houses, and rents up to a total of 2,000 morabatins—some 17,000 solidi.[95] In 1241 a small contribution of 12 pence came all the way from Tarragona, at the village of Santa Coloma de Queralt, from one who had crusaded to Valencia.[96]

Maria, the wife of the porter Martin, asked to be buried here in 1241, leaving 5 solidi to its "hospital of the poor" and 25 solidi more.[97] In 1242 Martin of Sicily the holder of Argensola castle, and his wife Madonna, with mills and other property established chaplaincies for "two secular priests."[98] An annual gift of grain came in 1243 for the poor, from Peregrin of Atrosillo, one of the most important barons of Aragon and a member of King James's entourage.[99] In 1244 William of Espailargas contributed a plot of land at Campanar to finance a perpetual lamp at the altar of St. Vincent.[100] In 1247 the official of the queen, Aparisi, arranging to be buried at St. Vincent's, established a chaplaincy with a vineyard on the Melilla road; his brother John was to retain and pass on the patronage of this post.[101] In 1249 the draper of Valencia Peter Oller left an impressive 3,000 solidi to the monastery. He added 50 more for his "honorific" burial there, "if I die in the kingdom of Valencia," and 100 solidi for the chapel, with another 550 for Masses, 100 for alms here, and 140 for his tomb. The Masses were for himself, his mother, sister, three brothers, uncle, and relatives.[102]

Queen Violante in 1251 willed two silk cloaks, or perhaps coverlets, which had belonged to the lord king, "as she had promised."[103] In the same year Raymond of Morella, who left 1,600 solidi to his parish of St. Bartholomew, willed a modest 10 solidi to St. Vincent's.[104] In 1254 Arnold Cardona gave the hospital his bed.[105] William Ochova Alemán in 1255 left 200 solidi to St. Vincent's, as contrasted with 100 to his parish of St. Lawrence.[106] Peter of Barberá in 1258 gave 2 solidi for work on the buildings.[107] A parishioner of St. Mary's died at St. Vincent's hospital and was buried there in 1262, leaving benefactions.[108] In 1263 the notary and citizen of Valencia, William of Jaca, left "properties, rents, possessions," establishing a chaplaincy with his Fortaleny land and his rents, naming to the post a priest of his choice, and bequeathing a sizable alms for inmates and staff here.[109]

In 1262 a noble in the south, Arnold of Puig Monzón, left all his honors and possessions in and around Játiva, except a single piece of land, to establish a chaplaincy at the hospital. The prior was to have in his gift the patronage of the altar.[110] Like a number of such property donations, it was buttressed with a confirmatory charter from the crown.[111] In 1267 Bernard Zamora of Castellón, asking burial at St. Vincent's, made two bequests. The first was 300 solidi; there was a temporary charge on this fund, however, the care of his son Bernard "until he has grown up." The second bequest was a full chaplaincy to support a priest at St. Vincent's; for this he provided buildings in Castellón, a half-interest in a mill, and some vineyards and farm lands.[112]

A lady of high family in 1272 willed two beds with their furnishings, one for the men's infirmary and one for the women's.[113] At this period women not uncommonly willed beds to hospitals as men willed armor or saddles to military Orders. In 1276 the wife of Blaise Peter of Fuentes left St. Vincent's 10 solidi.[114] The wealthy Berengar of Conques and others loaned, to their subsequent fiscal regret, funds for advancing the work on the church, and for its current expenses, in 1278.[115] García Chicot, a "resident and inhabitant of the parish of St. Bartholomew of Valencia," left 12 pence for the hospital in 1279.[116] Among continuing gifts was the grant of May 1282 by King Peter of a town named Araunost, near La Ainsa, northwest of Barbastro in Aragon. It was given in frankalmoin from piety; all the surrounding countryside was frank and free, though the crown retained certain taxes and jurisdiction *mero imperio*.[117]

Bit by bit, a box full of deeds and charters accumulated, witnessing to the esteem of the settlers, until their value required that the procurator James Sarroca seal and deposit them in the strongroom of the Valencia Templars.[118] This action reminds us of another social service the religious houses provided in their communities in that century. People used them as strongboxes. Examples come to light only incidentally, as in this Valencian document where the crown is ordering the surrender of such a "box" of St. Vincent's papers. All legacies—presumably money, small movables, and papers—in the diocese of Valencia were to be deposited "in a religious building" by the lawyers or executors, by a law of 1262, to safeguard them until the testament of the deceased could be processed.[119] Similarly, the crusade tithes collected at Valencia and elsewhere in the realms of Aragon were partially deposited in 1280 with the Hospitaller castellan of Amposta. Temptation in this case overcame the good religious; he "converted the money to the payment of debts, out of urgent necessity," and tried to flee the country under pretext of business in the Holy Land.[120] In 1240 the Dominican house at Valencia city was used as depository for a particularly valuable document; the friars were ordered to guard it, allowing neither king nor Templars to repossess it until the Templars paid the crown a 48,000-solidi debt.[121]

Similar examples can be cited, though from elsewhere in James's realms. King James kept the original of the Majorca record of land division at the local commandery of the Templars. He filed the most important state documents for his kingdoms in the convent of the Hospitaller nuns at Sigena.[122] And he recounts how the magnates of Montpellier, facing public wrath, "carried possessions from their houses at night, and put them in religious houses and in other places of the town," and ran away.[123]

What was the total worth of St. Vincent's holdings? It is not easy to declare the value, but some general idea can be formed. A tax farmer paid 10,000 solidi in 1279 for the privilege of farming the revenues for one year; this undoubtedly represented a far lower figure than he eventually collected. In 1284 the Cuart revenues were assessed at 3,000 a year. And, when the crown bought back Castellón and Montornés late in the century, the price was 170,000 solidi outright plus a steady 6,500 solidi annually from Valencia city revenues.[124]

∞ The Throne and the Shrine

Because of its central importance St. Vincent's was exempted from episcopal control and placed directly under the protection of the Holy See. The bishop did not always remember this. In 1278 the king had to warn him to "desist" from his attentions; the bishop apparently was interfering in matters of dress at St. Vincent's and had "intruded himself into the governance of the said house."[125] Again, in 1282 the bishop acted badly, "seizing clerics of that house and inflicting a number of other injuries." Letters were therefore sent by the authorities to the justiciar of Valencia and to the Official of the diocese.[126]

King James himself chose the monastic group who administered the shrine. Dissatisfied with them after a decade or so, he unceremoniously ejected them, with a certain amount of spirited recrimination all around (1255). To replace the St. Victorian monks, he brought in a favorite Order ("of which I am patron and founder"), the Mercedarians.[127] The motive for this "reform" seems to have been maladministration, probably resulting in financial loss; in context of the circumstances, there seems to be no need to conjecture a spiritually lax community here as do Sanchís Sivera, Teixidor, and others.[128]

The monks threw themselves into a lawsuit to recover ownership. There were high words; some slanders by the monks stung King James to reply. He sent an account of the quarrel to each of the bishops of his kingdom (1257). "Led by a spirit of malice they slander the Mercedarian master and brothers throughout provinces and places," he protested resentfully; "they do not leave our person immune from this slander, publicly saying and firmly asserting that the aforesaid [Mercedarians] got the monastery by purchasing it from us."[129] To terminate the unseemly tussle, King James appointed Gonzalvo Pérez, archdeacon of Valencia, to pass final judgment. The victory went to St. Victorian (1259). The vindictive monks then sought further judgment, in connection with debts incurred on the property and furnishings carried off by the retreating Mercedarians. But the king cleared the latter of any obligation.[130]

A scant five years later King James again had to interfere at St. Vincent's. The establishment was tottering toward financial ruin in 1265 because of "senseless, useless, and extravagant spending."[131] His was the hand which steadied it. But the monks were a litigious lot. They drew up an appeal against the king, had it notarized by "the notary public Peter of Paul," and dispatched it to Rome. Somehow James felt the notary at least should have requested "my permission"; he had acted "to the prejudice of my jurisdiction." The breach was healed, nevertheless, the king supplying a document absolving the hapless notary from any legal consequences of the action.[132]

Still, the crown seems not to have been satisfied with the St. Victorian monks. Two decades later, another transfer of jurisdiction occurred. The process began on James's deathbed, when the king became a Cistercian monk as an act of piety. In recompense for properties promised to the Cistercians but never delivered, the dying king willed the castle and town of Piera to Poblet, the premier Cistercian abbey of his realms. This castle, however, the only real stronghold between Barcelona and Cervera, was strategically too valuable to alienate. King Peter hung on to it. On his own deathbed Peter, perhaps in a fit of conscience, ordered his successor to surrender Piera to Poblet,[133] so that finally in 1286 the castle was tardily and reluctantly delivered. Almost immediately James's grandson Alphonse III took steps to recover it. He could offer in exchange an irresistible plum, the prestigious and well-endowed complex of St. Vincent's "in the suburbs of Valencia." The transfer, arranged in December 1287, carried with it title to Castellón, Cuart, Aldaya, Montornés, and other holdings.[134] The folk of Castellón now offered their homage, formal and fully documented, to the new masters of St. Vincent's.[135]

The monks of St. Victorian sued. They adduced the 1232 grant, the 1280 confirmation, and undoubtedly the legal dossier of the fight during the fifties against the Mercedarians. A compromise solution was worked out in March 1288 and recorded in a further document of May 1289.[136] It fully confirmed Poblet in possession of St. Vincent's, while amply compensating St. Victorian's with valuable properties outside the kingdom of Valencia. From now on, the Cistercians administered St. Vincent's. In 1297 Pope Boniface VIII would approve and confirm this conveyance.[137] As early as 1301, however, the crown found it necessary to reproach Poblet for its neglect of the poor at St. Vincent's. This is in itself a commentary on the problems of monastic administration in a nonfeudal world, and on the close surveillance the crown gave its shrine.[138]

The esteem James the Conqueror felt for St. Vincent's is mirrored especially in two actions. First, he saw to it that the place enjoyed the right of asylum in Valencian law, applying this generously to monastery, hospital, church, odd buildings, and adjacent land.[139] This is a remarkable privilege, allowed by the king sparingly only to the "major church" of each geographical unit. At Valencia city St. Vincent's shared the distinction only with the cathedral. The concession naturally attracted malefactors—too many of them eventually, so that St. Vincent's renounced it in 1329.[140]

King James thought of St. Vincent's especially as his own end approached. One of his last actions was to insert a codicil into his will, providing for an elaborate expansion of facilities. Five new buildings were to be added to the existing one, each to be the equal of the latter. These were to face one another and be connected by covered bridges. An endowed altar was to be situated on each bridge, "in such wise that the sick people who lie in the hospital can watch" the daily celebration of Mass. A cloister was to be erected beside the church, and a refectory, and a "fairly long" dormitory. There were to be four additional walls, besides the walls now guarding the hospital grounds, to insure privacy. The codicil also provided for two crosses and some vestments for the church, and gave to the hospital the king's clothes and his own bed with its furnishings. The document containing all this testifies to the king's attachment for St. Vincent's; other important business he covers summarily, but the hospital he discusses at length and with enthusiasm.[141]

The crown had a great deal to do with the officers conducting the affairs of the monastery. There were two principal officers, a prior or general director and a procurator or treasurer. It is not always easy to distinguish the two functions, and in fact a prior could act for a time as his own procurator. The first prior or rector was Bernard. Little is known about him except that he was not the Lagrasse abbot suggested by Sanchís Sivera. Nor is there any reason for thinking that he was the abbot of St. Victorian insisted upon by Teixidor; very definitely he was not the Bernard whom Teixidor had in mind. He appears as fund-raiser for the building program in 1240 and again in official documents of 1243 and early 1244.[142]

Prior Ferrer replaced him very soon, his appointment being confirmed by the pope in November 1247. Ferrer was involved in a rental in 1248, was rewarded with a life pension from St. Vincent's revenues in 1259, and appeared in another rental in 1253.[143] He may have been supplanted by a Mercedarian during the brief take-over and reform by that Order (1255–1258). The St. Victorian monks resumed control in 1259, but King James had already appointed his own prior. This was the king's chaplain Berengar of Prats or of Prades. His appointment came in July 1258 when he was given full power over "all affairs" of the establishment. He is prior in a series of documents in 1259, 1260, 1262, and 1263, and then in a will of 1267.[144]

The next appointee is a figure of mystery. Named Peter of the King, he was installed for life in 1269. An inscription from the old cathedral of Lérida used to mark the burial place of "Peter of the King, canon and sacristan of this see, who was the son of the illustrious lord king Peter of Aragon." Acting upon this evidence, which included a burial date of 1254, the historian Prosper de Bofarull made him a brother of James I. Miret y Sans accepted this and even incorporated it into his genealogical chart of the royal family; later he wavered in his belief sufficiently to suspect that the epitaph was miscopied.[145] Others have doubted any royal connection. The name de Rege alone of course cannot advance the argumentation.

Fortunately, other evidence is at hand. In a document of 1248 Peter described himself: "I, Peter, brother of the lord king of Aragon and sacristan of Lérida."[146] The pope characterized him in a 1274 document as King James's "nepos," a nephew or vaguely a relative.[147] In 1269 he was prior at St. Vincent's. In 1276 "Peter of the King, sacristan of Lérida" was with the mortally ill King James at Alcira, according to the king's will as read by Tourtoulon and Miret y Sans from a later transcription; Soldevila corrects their "de Rege" to "de Roca" (brother of James Sarroca and royal clerk in documents of 1264–1269). Far from solving the problem, this change raises the wider question of confusion by copyists, medieval and modern, in the other records.[148] When the crusade tithe was collected in the diocese of Lérida in 1279 and 1280, the chief collector was "Peter of the King, sacristan of Lérida."[149] Peter of the King turns up two decades later as bishop of Lérida (1299–1308); his episcopate was an important one for that diocese. Possibly there were two men of the same rather uncommon name successively occupying the honorific post of sacristan at Lérida; if the first died in 1254, the two could be father and son. If he is one man, however, and the son of King Peter the Catholic (he could hardly be the son of Peter the Great), then he enjoyed an unusually long and vigorous life, some ninety-five years of it.

Whatever way the mystery is resolved, this royal relative did receive in 1269 "the priorate of the house or hospital of St. Vincent's," with control over "the regimen and administration of that house or hospital as well as its priorate for your whole life." Subsequently he was prior in documents of 1274, 1276, 1281, and indeed up to 1286.[150] The new prior was open to easy attack by those who might covet his job. He was a pluralist, already holding positions as sacristan in the cathedral chapter of Lérida and as prior of another secular church in Lérida. The fact that St. Vincent's carried no obligation for the parochial cure of souls, however, must have made it easier to secure a dispensation now from Rome. Pope Gregory allowed Peter to remain as prior by a special privilege in 1272. Criticism apparently continued, for shortly afterward Peter fortified himself with a second such approbation from Gregory.[151]

Bernard of Biela, elected abbot of St. Victorian in 1276, seems to have decided to take more direct control sometime around 1280, for in that year he fortified himself with a royal confirmation of the monastic ownership.[152] And from 1281 he appears as prior, though acting at times through a vicar Peter Marqués.[153] This Peter March, not to be confused with the secretary of James II, was a notary of Barcelona often called upon to draw important state documents. He seems to have been a kind of assistant to Prince Peter (for example, in documenting claims to Navarre in 1274). He held a minor office in Valencia city (1280), owned lands in Pego and Villarreal in the new realm, acted here as agent in crown affairs sometimes, and is described at least once as a crown secretary.

But Peter of the King refused to be supplanted in his life-office. Forcibly removed by King Peter, he took his case to law. Soon King Alphonse committed the problem to the procurator of the realm of Valencia; the procurator's decision early in 1285 favored the ex-prior against the crown. The judgment involved restoration of priorate and of holdings except for Castellón; Alphonse soon restored Castellón as well. As a result, Peter of the King appears as prior once again in 1285–1286. He was involved in the negotiations to transfer St. Vincent's from the Benedictines of St. Victorian to the Cistercians of Poblet (1286–1287). A month later he quietly sold his revenues and rights here to the new administrators, in return for a large biannual pension.[154]

The procurators resembled tax farmers. Men high in official circles could buy the office at a flat sum, retaining all surplus profit as salary. The procurator himself probably acted through a staff of bailiffs and *ad hoc* tax farmers. Perhaps the device of a single such farmer or procurator over all the revenues was resorted to only occasionally. There was none at St. Vincent's until 1258 when Berengar of Prats became prior under the designation of "special and general procurator" over all business.[155] In 1268 James Sarroca (or de Roca), one of the king's most important counselors and soon to be bishop of Huesca (1273–1277), was procurator. He may be the first true procurator, distinct from the prior; he may also be part of James's financial reform at St. Vincent's, which was specifically directed against the mismanagement of the priors.[156] Peter of the King succeeded him but, like Berengar of Prats, he was primarily prior.

For almost a decade Berengar of Conques was closely involved in the hospital's finances.[157] He was a trusted crown agent and sometime bailiff of Valencia. Berengar of Conques did not always act as procurator, but he held that office at least from late 1279 to 1283. In October 1279 he paid 10,000 solidi as the price for the procuratorship for one year.[158] In November 1280 he extended this for two years more. King James licenced him in the contract to provide for the hospital ill and for the clerics, beneficiaries, and servitors.[159]

During the closing months of his second tenure, Berengar of Conques resisted the efforts of Abbot Bernard of St. Victorian to control the finances. In April 1282 King Peter notified Berengar that when his term was up he must relinquish his office to the abbot. As late as December 1282 the king had to command him to restore the procuratorship to St. Victorian.[160] The king commissioned the procurator of Valencia, Raymond of Sanllei, to enforce the removal order, and the lawyer Raymond of Sales to settle the quarrel between procurator and abbot. Perhaps Berengar felt he had not realized a sufficient profit from his investment, and suggested a compromise. A royal functionary took over the office briefly in 1282 or 1283; this was Peter of St. Clement, secretary to Peter both as prince and king.[161] The last of the procurators took office for a year in 1284; his name significantly was Nadal of Conques.[162]

Even as a scheme of patronage to reward the meritorious, the king's control of St. Vincent's was not without economic advantage. Not only would the procurators and priors reap their comfortable profit, however; the crown itself took some of the revenues. Prior Peter of the King exemplifies this, a member of the family being provided for. King Peter also helped his uncle Ferdinand study at Paris with revenues in large part from St. Vincent's. (Of the 10,000 solidi demanded from the hospital, only 2,000 seem to have been needed for the education itself.)[163] Again, as an institution exempt from episcopal control even in its properties and revenues, St. Vincent's collected its own tithes and turned a full half over to King James and King Peter.[164]

Property and administrative documents have survived where the deeper story of St. Vincent's has gone unrecorded. These elements, while telling something of St. Vincent's, are subordinate to the less complicated but overriding function of St. Vincent's as a symbol of local antiquities shared by the newly arrived settlers, of suffering to be borne, and of ultimate triumph. The king in his piety had poured money into the institution. He had constructed for it an admirable setting, and had seen that it was properly staffed. But its core he had been lucky enough to find, ready and at hand.

Once again, we see the institution serving James the Conqueror. Deep in an alien land, he had at hand a genuine tradition and a hallowed relic, to intensify and draw together the region's religio-patriotic feelings, and to create a local *esprit*, a sense of age-old community among the Christian minority. The land was theirs; it had only been abandoned for a bit and now reclaimed. They were neither an occupying army nor brash colonizers. They had come home.

In a land where arabesqued mosques for a time had to serve as churches, and where the Moslem tongue and ways were oppressively ubiquitous, it was most important to cultivate this spirit of identification, of being the dominant culture, the true heirs. This spirit of identification would be fostered to some degree by every religious establishment or institution in the new kingdom of Valencia, but especially by the shrine of St. Vincent.

XVI

CONCLUSION

The phenomenon of a frontier movement—sudden, violent, and brief—captures the imagination. Dramatic surges in history are all too few, and where they exist are largely undocumented. Here in Valencia it has been possible to assemble a mosaic out of small data, revealing something of such a movement. Even putting aside most of its important elements—the government agencies, the land distribution, the evolution of the cities and their institutions—in order to concentrate upon the church alone, one gains some feeling of that movement's scope.

Accustomed to consider as modern any social enterprise on a great and highly organized scale, we are surprised at the sophistication of the activity here in Valencia, the sureness of purpose, the attention to detail, the paper work, and the legal safeguards. Considered in its financial aspects alone, the ecclesiastical reorganization of Valencia was a business of some complexity. Taken from the institutional side, it was remarkably prolific and swift. Wherever we look—from parish to hospital to tithe-network to school to military Order—there is activity, intense, purposeful, and widespread. It is the energy of an elemental wave, impersonal and formidable.

A peculiarity of this activity stands out. It is not monolithic and hierarchic. In its over-all pattern it is organic. A whole little world of independent energy sources is at work, a plurality of separate thrusts, combining with apparent fortuity to the same end. Each source labors toward its own goal, fights for its own privileges, brings up from afar its own prepared reserves, attracts the support of its own kind, fends off the encroachments of companion sources. In short, each represents a kind of private enterprise.

Each saw the new kingdom as open territory for its own purposes. There was a Franciscan map of Valencia, a Templar map, a parish map, and a tithe map. These had little enough to do with the map of the feudal countryside or of the free communes, the diverse map of legal codes, or the map of royal government agencies. But they surpassed in importance such secular divisions, and they did more toward creating the Christian community in the realm.

Activity was not only pluralistic, it was dynamic. One would not have thought the medieval religious world to have had such energies to throw away upon the frontier. Yet the effort was prodigal, and it continued long after this chronological period ended. For example, it was precisely to the frontier that so many Orders sent a representation; even before the rhythm of settlement had begun, Orders were setting up their centers. Without much prospect of settlement the cathedral early planned its grand expansion, and the parishes proliferated.

None of this is a necessary note of Christianity. Its proper energies theoretically might have embodied themselves in any number of different forms. It might have drifted quietly over the frontier, assuming shapes more sympathetic to the native culture. But the activist Western culture of the thirteenth century comprised a very definite body to the Christian spirit it held. The Valencian church stands, for this reason, as a mirror of the times. The Mediterranean European community was still open, still offering opportunities and growth; it was only just beginning to congeal into an urban class structure and a new-model nobility. Law was its science and its passion, building its hobby, corporative forms its natural expression. Already it had advanced beyond its non-European Mediterranean neighbors in technology and in administrative technique.

All this can be seen on the frontier. The university movement was reflected, along with the wider movement in elementary and secondary education. The mendicant phenomenon shook the Valencian kingdom much as it did the settled parts of Europe. The hospital and eleemosynary enthusiasms were as strong here as anywhere. The crusade motif, the ransomer and military Orders, the new parish, the emphasis on proto-nationalism within the church, the new centralization, the conscious definition of self in opposition to Islam—all were part of the Valencian frontier. The problems were here too: the tithe struggle, the capture of benefices by revenue-seeking upper classes, the clerical laxness, the legalism, and the malignant rivalries.

Both the problems and the movements, however, assumed different forms. Valencia was not the settled homeland. There was an urgency here, a thinness of resources, a sense of the Moslem danger sullenly abroad. Tithe quarrels abounded elsewhere, but in Valencia the elements in the quarrel were unique. Universities were going up throughout Europe but none with quite the background of the Valencian experiment. Cathedral chapters existed in the settled countries, as did the new parishes; but again the Valencian flavor was different, the pressures and orientations were different.

The very concurrence of so many diverse peoples to settle this one region would have lent distinction to its institutions, even without political novelties or Moslem milieu. And on a frontier of opportunity there is always the nuance of freedom: of being mobile, of being needed, of demanding and receiving support, of being bound to no unalterable ancient tradition. The Valencian frontier was not only an embodiment of the medieval energies, and a mirror of its great movements; it was also a specific laboratory for examining these in an unusual local adaptation.

As this book progressed, the Moslem inhabitants of the kingdom seem to have dropped from sight. This oddity is a reflection of the documents themselves; churchmen refer to Moslems only in passing and where necessary. The conquered Moslem, without voice or presence, is submerged in a rush of parish-making, boundary-drawing, and the like. He becomes irrelevant, the servile tiller in the countryside, or the alien native on the periphery of a better world. The reader must actually make an effort to remember that there were very few Christians at all in the Valencia kingdom for about half of this period, almost for its first quarter-century. Even after the waves of immigrants which came toward the end of King James's reign, Moslem households still outnumbered Christian by four or five to one. The Christian towns displayed Moorish street plans and tastes in building. The general language in the realm remained Arabic. The most common political and social forms were Moslem. In terms of sheer numbers, the dominant religion was overwhelmingly Islam.

Yet the conquering minority did manage to prescind from this massive fact. They created all around themselves the illusion of a single presence, which slowly took on a bizarre reality. They achieved this in the traditional way of colonials: by creating an urban and landlord superstructure, endowing their immediate surroundings with every quality they could borrow from the homeland, and treating the native population as a lesser caste to be tolerated in ghettos apart. They did this spontaneously, naturally, and without conscious arrogance.

This process is never easy for a small minority to contrive in a land where the native levels of competence and sophistication are embarrassingly close to those of the conquerors. The secret of doing so does not lie only in military power. Nor is it merely a matter of transplanting institutions and habits. To be effective the process must derive from an underlying dynamism. And this usually arises from some special self-image. In the thirteenth century, where the Valencian case involved two cultures rooted in two antagonistic religions, that image owed much to the church and in many ways was kept alive by the church.

All the forms by which a society assumes and maintains its identity—legal, educational, social, charitable, political, and moral—were fused with the theological principles and the ecclesiastical forms. The society was penetrated with clerical and monastic ideals, and to a surprising extent staffed by clerics. The medieval Mediterranean man, materialistic and anarchic at bottom, functioned fairly effectively in a society so organized. The common religious motive was the easiest way to rally him when there was need of caring for the sick, building bridges, manning unpleasant outposts, policing violence, or providing schools.

Thus, even had the motives of property acquisition and primitive imperialism sufficed for the colonial adventure in Valencia, the church would inevitably have had a role in building the frontier. As it was, with an alien religious ideology to displace, her role was paramount. It was from an instinctive knowledge of this importance that the Christians made Valencia city, to borrow a phrase from Fuster, a fortress of Christian spirituality; even in the thirteenth century the city was well on its way toward becoming "an enormous ecclesiastical concentration."[1] Entrenched wherever she could dig in, up and down the length of the frontier kingdom, the church expanded her presence to the limits of her capacity.

The word "church" here is imprecise. It had too many levels of meaning for such casual use as it is given. But take it even at its most external and least profound level: all the institutions, services, and centers, all the inspirations, applied values, familiar customs, disciplines, and consolations. This congeries contributed mightily to the psychology behind frontier reconstruction in Valencia, and provided springs of action for the pioneer. This aspect of the church represented to the pioneer a continuity with his past, identity with his group, essential and significant framework in which he moved and had his being. At this level too the church most reflects the limitations of its century and locale, incarnating the common assumptions, creative and intellectual directions, and inherited culture patterns, as well as the human needs, stupidities, hopes, and worries.

The waves of friars, contemplatives, military monks, canons, parish clerics, and nuns, transported like a numerous garrison into this borderland, gave tangible shape to the Christian self-image, making it a living thing. What is more, these people in city and countryside represented to the Moslem majority, by implication in this unitary Christian society, the directive super-power, the conquerors. The theme might be carried beyond the purely ecclesiastical into the less direct agencies of transformation—the Christian calendar, the Christian money, the Christian law codes, and so on, each elaborated with the conscious intention of dissipating the Moslem atmosphere. Even in the limited field of ecclesiastical institutions, however, the note of confident dynamism in Valencia sounded clearly. These men were building their special world. They were serenely sure that the Moslem world would dim before it and mysteriously recede. And they were right.

The great social philosopher Ibn Khaldûn was to speak wisely in the following century of the remarkable power and capacity which result when "religious feeling" combines with "group feeling" in an expanding society; and, conversely, how the people whom such a society subjects will lose hope, lose the energy generated by hope, and lose the creative, civilizing and commercial results of the energy. Disintegration in such circumstances "is in human nature" and inevitable for the conquered society.[2]

This extreme afflicted Moslem Valencia. Moslem forms and society persisted. A certain stir of life continued within the segregated Moslem community. Rebellious outbreaks had always to be guarded against. But the dominant society was the minority Christian group. The religious institutions so carefully erected in the frontier Christian kingdom functioned as a main instrument in subduing and transforming Moslem Valencia.